THE
COMPLETE
GOSPEL
PARALLELS

THE
COMPLETE
GOSPEL
PARALLELS

Arthur J. Dewey

Robert J. Miller

POLEBRIDGE PRESS
Salem, Oregon

Copyright © 2012 by Polebridge Press

Cover and interior design by Robaire Ream

Library of Congress Cataloging-in-Publication Data
Bible. N.T. Gospels. English. Scholars. 2012.
  The complete Gospel parallels / [compiled by] Arthur J. Dewey, Robert J. Miller.
    p. cm.
  Includes indexes.
  ISBN 978-1-59815-035-3 (alk. paper)
  1. Bible. N.T. Gospels--Harmonies, English. I. Dewey, Arthur J. II. Miller,
Robert J. (Robert Joseph), 1954- III. Title.
  BS2560.F84 2012
  226'.1--dc23
                                                                2011044542

Table of Contents

Acknowledgments

~

A work of such complexity requires vision, artistry and precision. Larry Alexander, from the outset seeing the need for a gospel parallels that went beyond the standard fare, provided sustained encouragement and welcome prodding. Ever the artist, Robaire Ream ably created an intricate design that caught and resolved the complexity of the project. Char Matejovsky brought her experienced eye to the page and steadfastly steered this work to completion. Jim Kasper and Lucy Hansen, having generously supported the production of previous Polebridge publications, have done so once again. The authors gratefully acknowledge the invaluable contributions of all those who assisted in this project.

Sigla

Column headings in **bold print** indicate primary parallels (parallels with a high degree of verbal similarity).

Column headings in regular print indicate secondary parallels (parallels with a moderate degree of verbal similarity).

References within columns to verses in that column (see #8) indicate parallel verses out of their narrative order.

References within columns to texts not in that column indicate related verses (passages with some verbal similarity).

Italicized references within columns to texts not in that column indicate related verses or passages with a similar narrative function but with little verbal similarity.

\# Section number

* † ‡ Asterisks , daggers, and double daggers refer to texts listed below a section. These are verses or passages with comparable themes that have their own parallels.

Ⓓ A doublet: a duplicate version of a story or saying within the same gospel.

ᵃᵇ Superscript letters refer to text-critical notes below the section.

References at the bottom of a column indicate the location of the section containing the next passage in that gospel when that section does not immediately follow. (These references are given only in the synoptic gospels part of the book, #1–275).

Sigla in the Translation

⟨ ⟩ Pointed brackets indicate a subject, object, or other element implied by the original language and supplied by the translation.

[ ] Square brackets indicate words that have been restored from a lacuna or emended from a scribal error.

( ) Parentheses are used in the usual sense, to indicate parenthetical remarks and narrative asides in the original text.

Special Sigla for the Q Gospel

Verses in *italics* indicate passages attested only in Luke or Matthew.

?? Verse numbers enclosed by question marks indicate passages about which there is a very low degree of certainty as to whether the text belongs to Q.

. . . Three dots mean that there must have been some text in Q, but it cannot be reconstructed at all.

Q^{Mt} Chapter and verse numbers for verses attested only in Matthew.

How to use this book

Primary parallels

Secondary parallel

Related verse with little verbal similarity

Verses with comparable themes

Secondary parallel

Primary parallel

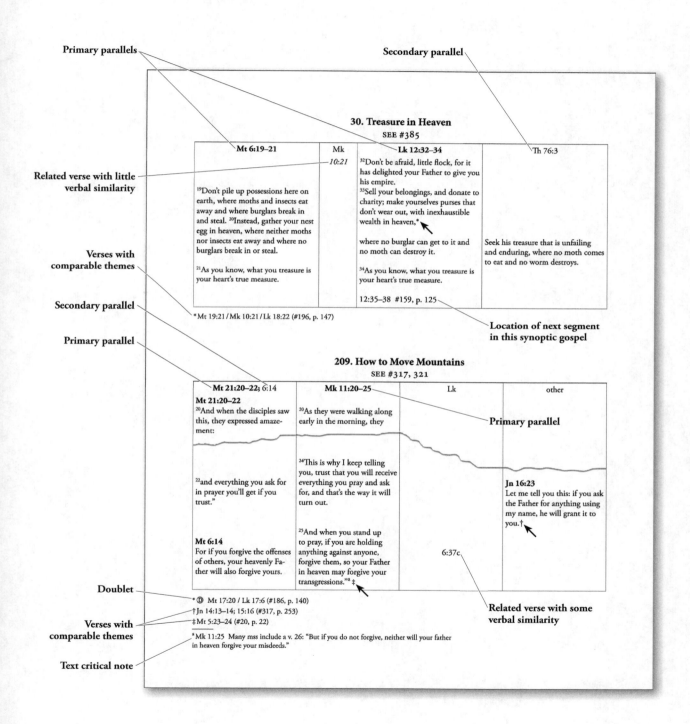

30. Treasure in Heaven
SEE #385

Mt 6:19–21	Mk	Lk 12:32–34	Th 76:3
	10:21		
[19]Don't pile up possessions here on earth, where moths and insects eat away and where burglars break in and steal. [20]Instead, gather your nest egg in heaven, where neither moths nor insects eat away and where no burglars break in or steal.		[32]Don't be afraid, little flock, for it has delighted your Father to give you his empire. [33]Sell your belongings, and donate to charity; make yourselves purses that don't wear out, with inexhaustible wealth in heaven,*	
		where no burglar can get to it and no moth can destroy it.	Seek his treasure that is unfailing and enduring, where no moth comes to eat and no worm destroys.
[21]As you know, what you treasure is your heart's true measure.		[34]As you know, what you treasure is your heart's true measure.	
		12:35–38 #159, p. 125	

* Mt 19:21 / Mk 10:21 / Lk 18:22 (#196, p. 147)

Location of next segment in this synoptic gospel

209. How to Move Mountains
SEE #317, 321

Mt 21:20–22; 6:14	Mk 11:20–25	Lk	other
Mt 21:20–22 [20]And when the disciples saw this, they expressed amazement:	[20]As they were walking along early in the morning, they		
	[24]This is why I keep telling you, trust that you will receive everything you pray and ask for, and that's the way it will turn out.		**Primary parallel**
[22]and everything you ask for in prayer you'll get if you trust."			**Jn 16:23** Let me tell you this: if you ask the Father for anything using my name, he will grant it to you.†
Mt 6:14 For if you forgive the offenses of others, your heavenly Father will also forgive yours.	[25]And when you stand up to pray, if you are holding anything against anyone, forgive them, so your Father in heaven may forgive your transgressions."ª ‡	6:37c	

Primary parallel

Doublet

Verses with comparable themes

Text critical note

Related verse with some verbal similarity

* ① Mt 17:20 / Lk 17:6 (#186, p. 140)
† Jn 14:13–14; 15:16 (#317, p. 253)
‡ Mt 5:23–24 (#20, p. 22)

ª Mk 11:25 Many mss include a v. 26: "But if you do not forgive, neither will your father in heaven forgive your misdeeds."

Introduction

The Complete Gospel Parallels is an essential resource for readers and students of the gospels. This book goes beyond the standard gospel parallels. Rather than offering a comparative reading of just the canonical gospels, it gives those who study the gospels in English a one-volume compendium of synopses to the Gospels of Matthew, Mark, Luke, John, Thomas, Peter, and a few smaller gospel fragments, as well as a synopsis for the reconstructed Sayings Gospel (Q). Indeed, this volume highlights the Q Gospel as a text in its own right, enabling the reader to discern, through the relevant parallels, how the text of Q can be derived. Likewise, *The Complete Gospel Parallels* takes the non-canonical Gospel of Thomas, the Gospel of Peter, and the other fragmentary gospels seriously as part of the ancient data base. Moreover, the parallels from the Gospel of John will present surprising and suggestive lines of research and investigation to the discerning reader.

The Complete Gospel Parallels is designed to enable readers to study the similarities and differences between and among these ancient texts. Its broad range of material will enhance and deepen the reader's questions and appreciation of early Christian tradition and literature. Once a reader sees that material in the Gospel of Thomas or Peter, or a fragment from Oxyrhynchus, parallels a saying or story in a well-known canonical gospel, the investigation into early Christian origins moves to an entirely different level.

A New Translation
(The Scholars Version)

This book features the fresh and vibrant translation of the Scholars Version (SV), which was thoroughly revised in 2010 for the fourth edition of *The Complete Gospels*. The primary aim of the SV is to recreate for the contemporary reader the experience of the original audiences of the gospels. In striving to achieve this ideal, the translators of SV have been guided by three convictions about the original language of the gospels: that it was the language of everyday life, that it was intended to be read aloud, and that it often used ordinary words to express religious

meanings. Much of SV's distinctiveness is the result of its translators' determination that those qualities of the ancient language should shine through in SV's contemporary English. (For a fuller introduction to the Scholars Version, see pp. 9–15 of *The Complete Gospels*.)

A specific aim of the 2010 SV is to use consistent English for the same Greek and different English where the original varies, whenever that practice is compatible with SV's primary aim of producing English that is fluent, accurate, and familiar. Thus, the translation of every gospel passage was checked against its parallel passages and adjusted so that the similarities and differences in the Greek would, when feasible, be reflected in the English. This fine tuning of SV is intended to facilitate the careful comparison of passages. The wording of SV in *The Complete Gospel Parallels* has been occasionally modified from the original in order to meet this goal more precisely.

Eleven Gospels

Although all the ancient gospels obviously merit study each in their own right, the gospel texts in this volume are presented for the purpose of comparative study. Because the comparative study of the gospels has always focused most intensely on the synoptic gospels, this book presents Matthew, Mark, and Luke in their entirety, including even those passages that are unique to a single gospel. (The only exceptions are the infancy narratives in Matthew 1–2 and Luke 1–2. Since none of the stories in those chapters have any parallels in the gospels in this volume, it would serve no purpose to print this singly-attested material.)

Although the outlines of the three synoptic gospels are similar, each has its own distinct narrative sequence. Because all three synoptic gospels are presented together in the same part of this book, it is not possible for each individual gospel to appear in its own sequence. To help the reader follow the order of a given synoptic gospel, there are references at the bottom of columns that indicate where the next passage can be found; the absence of such a reference means that the next passage follows immediately. In addition, three longer discourses (the Sermon on the Mount/Plain, the mission discourse, and Jesus' denunciation of the Pharisees and scholars) for which the order of verses differs significantly in a different gospel are presented twice so that each version can be studied in its own literary integrity.

The Gospels of John, Thomas, Peter, and the other gospel fragments do not appear in their entirety. This volume presents every passage in those gospels that has parallels, even if those parallels are not quoted (see, for example, the prologue to John, #276). However, material in the non-synoptic gospels that is unique and unparalleled does not appear here, as the editors see no purpose in adding dozens of additional pages to an already long volume simply to display singly-attested passages. Readers can infer which passages are unique to John, Thomas, Peter, and the others simply by noting which passages have been skipped over.

The non-canonical gospels included in this book were selected because of their importance for the study of the development of the synoptic tradition. Although the nature of the evidence puts such matters beyond clear proof, there are strong scholarly arguments that the Gospels of Thomas and Peter, the Egerton Gospel, the Gospels of the Nazoreans and the Hebrews, and Gospel Oxyrynchus 1224 afford independent access to some of the sayings of Jesus and the stories about him that were committed to writing by Mark, Matthew, and Luke. Whether or not one is persuaded by such arguments, the case for or against the independence of these non-canonical traditions must be made on the basis of careful comparison of the parallel texts presented in this book.

The Gospel of Thomas is composed entirely of sayings attributed to Jesus, without any stories or narrative framework. Recent scholarship has argued that a number of the sayings may actually go back to the historical Jesus. Over one-half of the sayings in Thomas have parallels in the canonical gospels.

The Gospel of Peter, in the partial form in which we have it, is an early passion gospel with important differences from the other passion narratives. It may contain, in an embedded source document, the primary material for the passion and resurrection stories in the canonical gospels.

The Egerton Gospel and the Oxyrhychus Gospel 1224 are fragmentary remnants of early and otherwise unknown gospels that display parallels to the canonical gospels. The fragments of the Gospels of the Hebrews and the Nazoreans, representing distinctive ways in which Jewish Christians interpreted the Jesus tradition, also offer parallels to the canonical material.

The synopses of the various gospels display the primary and secondary parallel passages, and references to other related passages, in a format that facilitates their comparative study. Cross references to related passages are noted either in the columns or by asterisks and daggers that refer to information below the sections (see the explanation of the sigla for the specifics). Text-critical notes have been kept to a minimum; we note only those variants that materially affect the comparison of parallel texts. In sections comparing sayings and parables, extraneous introductory formulas (such as, "He said to them") or linking conjunctions or prepositions (such as, "and" or "for") are sometimes omitted in order to focus on the sayings themselves.

The Q Gospel

The Q Gospel is believed to be the source for those teachings of Jesus recorded in the Gospels of Matthew and Luke but not found in the Gospel of Mark. Because no text of this gospel has ever been discovered, it has had to be reconstructed through painstaking comparisons of parallel material found in Matthew and Luke.

The Complete Gospel Parallels presents the synopsis of the Q Gospel in a distinct format that accommodates the unique character of this hypothetical text. The reconstructed text of Q appears in the center of the synopsis, flanked by the texts of Matthew and Luke. Parallels to Q in Mark and the other gospels are noted, but not quoted, in the outer columns. This arrangement makes for a less crowded page and thus facilitates the precise analysis of how Q was adopted and adapted by Matthew and Luke.

The text of Q presented in this book is taken from the reconstruction in *The Complete Gospels*, which, with a few exceptions, is translated from the Greek text reconstructed by the International Q Project. The few places where SV Q differs from the IQP text are duly noted.

The reconstruction of a lost text like the Q Gospel inescapably involves varying degrees of certainty in different passages. For example, in some places there is so little agreement between Matthew and Luke that the wording of Q cannot be recovered with any acceptable probability. In a few other cases there are good reasons to think that a passage that occurs only in Matthew or Luke nevertheless comes from Q. Such passages can be counted as Q texts, but with caution. Accordingly, *The*

Complete Gospel Parallels employs different sigla to identify the more problematic passages in the reconstruction of Q (see Sigla). In keeping with scholarly custom, references to Q adopt the chapter and verse numbers of Luke. Those few verses attested only in Matthew are identified by their chapter and verse in that gospel, preceded by "QMt."

The Synoptic Gospels

1. Opening

SEE #276, P. 226

Mt 1:1	Mk 1:1	Lk 1:1–4	Jn
This is the Book of Genesis of Jesus the Anointed, son of David, son of Abraham.	The good news of Jesus the Anointed[a] begins . . .	[1]Since so many have undertaken to compile an orderly narrative of the events that have run their course among us, [2]just as the original eyewitnesses and ministers of the word transmitted them to us, [3]it seemed good that I too, after thoroughly researching everything from the beginning, should set them systematically in writing for you, Theophilus, [4]so that Your Excellency may realize the reliability of the teachings in which you have been instructed.	*1:1–18*
	1:1–6 #3, p. 10		

[a] Mk 1:1 Many mss add "son of God" after *Anointed.*

2. Jesus' Genealogy (according to Matthew)

Mt 1:1–17	Mk	Lk 3:23–38 *(names only—in reverse order)* [see #7]
[1]This is the Book of Genesis of Jesus the Anointed, son of David, son of Abraham.		
		[38]God, Adam, Seth, Enos, [37]Kenan, Mahalel, Jared, Enoch, Methuselah, [36]Lamech, Noah, Shem, Arphachshad, Kenan, [35]Shelah, Ever, Peleg, Reu, Serug, [34]Nahor, Terah,
[2]Abraham was the father of Isaac, Isaac of Jacob, Jacob of Judah and his brothers, [3]and Judah and Tamar were the parents of Perez and Zerah. Perez was the father of Hezron, Hezron of Aram,		Abraham, Isaac, Jacob, [33]Judah, Perez, Hezron, Arni, Admin,
[4]Aram of Amminadab, Amminadab of Nahshon, Nahshon of Salmon, [5]and Salmon and Rahab were the parents of Boaz. Boaz and Ruth were the parents of Obed. Obed was the father of Jesse, [6]and Jesse of David the king.		Amminadab, [32]Nahshon, Sala, Boaz, Obed, Jesse, [31]David,
David and Uriah's wife were the parents of Solomon. [7]Solomon was the father of Rehoboam, Rehoboam of Abijah, Abijah of Asaph, [8]Asaph of Jehoshaphat, Jehoshaphat of Joram, Joram of Uzziah, [9]Uzziah of Jotham, Jotham of Ahaz, Ahaz of Hezekiah, [10]Hezekiah of Manasseh, Manasseh of Amos, Amos of Josiah, [11]and Josiah was the father of Jeconiah and his brothers at the time of the exile to Babylon.		Nathan,
		Mattatha, Menna, Melea, [30]Eliakim, Jonam, Joseph, Judah, Simeon, [29]Levi, Maththat, Jorim, Eliezer, Jesus, [28]Er, Elmadam, Kosam, Addi, Melchi, [27]Neri,
[12]After the Babylonian exile, Jeconiah was the father of Shealtiel, Shealtiel of Zerubbabel, [13]Zerubbabel of Abiud, Abiud of Eliakim, Eliakim of Azor, [14]Azor of Zadok, Zadok of Achim, Achim of Eliud, [15]Eliud of Eleazar, Eleazar of Matthan, Matthan of Jacob.		Shealtiel, Zerubbabel,
		Rhesa, Johanan, [26]Joda, Josech, Semein, Mattathiah, Maath, [25]Naggai, Hesli, Nahum, Amos, Mattathiah, [24]Joseph, Jannai, Melchi, Levi, Maththat,
[16]And Jacob was the father of Joseph, the husband of Mary, who was the mother of Jesus. Jesus is known as the Anointed. [17]In sum, the generations from Abraham to David come to fourteen, those from David to the Babylonian Exile come to fourteen, and those from the Babylonian Exile to the Anointed also come to fourteen.		[23]Eli, Joseph (supposedly), Jesus.

NOTE: Except for the two genealogies of Jesus, the infancy narratives in Matthew and Luke (Matthew 1–2 and Luke 1–2) have no passages that are paralleled in any gospel included in this synopsis. Since all of the material in Matthew 1–2 and Luke 1–2 (except for the genealogies) is unique to either Matthew or Luke, it is not printed in this book.

3. Introduction of John the Baptizer
SEE #277, 349, PP. 227, 286

Mt 3:1–6	Mk 1:1–6	Lk 3:1–6
	[1]The good news of Jesus the Anointed[a] begins	[1]In the fifteenth year of the rule of Tiberius Caesar, when Pontius Pilate was governor of Judea, Herod tetrarch of Galilee, his brother Philip tetrarch of the district of Iturea and Trachonitis, and Lysanias tetrarch of Abilene, [2]while Annas and Caiaphas were chief priests, the word of God came to John, son of Zechariah, in the desert. [3]And he went into the whole region around the Jordan, calling for baptism and a change of heart that lead to forgiveness of sins.
[1]In due course John the Baptizer appears in the Judean desert, [2]calling out, "change your ways because the empire of Heaven is arriving." [3]No doubt this is the person described by Isaiah the prophet:	v. 4	
	[2]with something Isaiah the prophet wrote: "Here is my messenger, whom I send on ahead of you to prepare your way!* [3]A voice of someone shouting in the desert, 'Make ready the way of the Lord, make his paths straight.'"†	[4]As is written in the book of the sayings of Isaiah the prophet:
"A voice of someone shouting in the desert, 'Make ready the way of the Lord; make his paths straight.'"†		"The voice of someone shouting in the desert: 'Make ready the way of the Lord, make his paths straight.' † [5]Every valley will be filled, and every mountain and hill leveled. What is crooked will be made straight, and the rough ways smooth. [6]Then the whole human race will see the salvation of God."
	[4]So, John the Baptizer appeared in the desert calling for baptism and a change of heart that lead to forgiveness of sins. [5]And everyone from the Judean countryside and all the residents of Jerusalem streamed out to him and got baptized by him in the Jordan River, admitting their sins. [6]And John wore a mantle made of camel hair and had a leather belt around his waist and lived on grasshoppers and wild honey.	v. 3
[4]Now this same John wore clothes made of camel hair and had a leather belt around his waist; he lived on grasshoppers and wild honey. [5]Then Jerusalem, and all Judea, and all the region around the Jordan streamed out to him, [6]and got baptized in the Jordan River by him, admitting their sins.	1:7–8 #5, p. 12	

* Mt 11:10 / Lk 7:27 (#55, p. 45)

† Jn 1:23 John replied, "I am 'the voice of someone shouting in the desert, "Make the way of the Lord straight"—that's how Isaiah the prophet put it.'" (#277, p. 227)

[a] Mk 1:1 Many mss add "son of God" after *Anointed.*

4. The Preaching of John the Baptizer

SEE #350, P. 286

Mt 3:7–10	Mk	Lk 3:7–14
7When he saw that many of the Pharisees and Sadducees were coming for baptism, John said to them, "You spawn of Satan! Who warned you to flee from the impending doom? 8Well then, start producing fruit suitable for a change of heart, 9and don't even think of saying to yourselves, 'We have Abraham for our father.' Let me tell you, God can raise up children for Abraham right out of these rocks! 10Even now the axe is aimed at the root of the trees. So every tree not producing choice fruit gets cut down and tossed into the fire."		7So John would say to the crowds that came out to get baptized by him, "You spawn of Satan! Who warned you to flee from the impending doom? 8Well then, start producing fruits suitable for a change of heart, and don't even start saying to yourselves, 'We have Abraham for our father.' Let me tell you, God can raise up children for Abraham right out of these rocks! 9Even now the axe is aimed at the root of the trees. So every tree not producing choice fruit gets cut down and tossed into the fire." 10The crowds would ask him, "So what should we do?" 11And he would answer them, "Whoever has two shirts should share with someone who has none; whoever has food should do the same." 12Toll collectors also came to get baptized, and they would ask him, "Teacher, what should we do?" 13He told them, "Charge nothing above the official rates." 14Soldiers also asked him, "And what about us?" And he said to them, "No more shakedowns! No more frame-ups either! And be satisfied with your pay."

5. Someone More Powerful than John

SEE #278, 351, PP. 228, 287

Mt 3:11–12	Mk 1:7–8	Lk 3:15–18	Jn 1:26–27
		[15]The people were filled with expectation and everyone was trying to figure out whether John might be the Anointed One.	
	[7]And he began his proclamation by saying,	[16]John's answer was the same to everyone:	[26]John answered them,
[11]"I baptize you with water for a change of heart, but someone more powerful than I will succeed me. I'm not fit to take off his sandals.	"Someone more powerful than I will succeed me, whose sandal straps I am not fit to bend down and untie. [8]I've been baptizing you with water, but	"I baptize you with water; but someone more powerful than I is coming. I'm not fit to untie his sandal straps.	"I baptize, yes, but only with water. Right there with you is someone you don't yet recognize; [27]he's the one who is coming after me. I don't even deserve to untie his sandal straps."
He'll baptize you with holy spirit and fire. [12]His pitchfork is in his hand, and he'll make a clean sweep of his threshing floor, and gather the wheat into his granary, but the chaff he'll burn in a fire that can't be put out."	he'll baptize you with holy spirit."	He'll baptize you with holy spirit and fire. [17]His pitchfork is in his hand, to make a clean sweep of his threshing floor and to gather the wheat into his granary, but the chaff he'll burn in a fire that can't be put out." [18]And so, with many other exhortations he preached to the people.	

6. Jesus is baptized
SEE #280, 352, PP. 229, 287

Mt 3:13–17 14:3–4	Mk 1:9–11 6:17–18	Lk 3:19–22	other
		[19]But Herod the tetrarch, who had been denounced by John over the matter of Herodias, his brother's wife, [20]topped off all his other crimes by shutting John up in prison.	
[13]Then Jesus comes from Galilee to John at the Jordan to get baptized by him. [14]And John tried to stop him with these words: "I'm the one who needs to get baptized by you, yet you come to me?" [15]In response, Jesus said to him, "Let it go for now. This is the right thing for us to do." Then John gave into to him.	[9]During that same period Jesus came from Nazareth, Galilee, and was baptized in the Jordan by John.	[21]And it came to pass when all the people were baptized,	**GHeb 2:1–2** [1]The mother of the Lord and his brothers said to him, "John the Baptizer baptized for the forgiveness of sins. Let's go and get baptized by him." [2]But he said to them, "How have I sinned? So why should I go and get baptized by him? Only if I don't what I'm talking about."
[16]Right after Jesus had been baptized, he got up out of the water, and—amazingly—the skies opened up and he saw God's spirit coming down on him like a dove, perching on him,	[10]And right away as he got up out of the water, he saw the skies torn open and the spirit coming down toward him like a dove.	and after Jesus had been baptized and while he was praying, that the sky opened up, [22]and the holy spirit came down on him in bodily form like a dove,	**Jn 1:32** John continued his testimony: "I have seen the spirit coming down like a dove out of the sky, and it hovered over him." **GHeb 3:2–4** [2]And it happened that when the Lord came up out of the water, the whole fountain of the holy spirit came down on him and rested on him. [3]It said to him,
[17]and—listen!—there was a voice from the skies, which said, "This is my son, the one I love—I fully approve of him."*	[11]There was also a voice from the skies: "You are my son, the one I love—I fully approve of you."*	and a voice came from the sky, "You are my son; today I have fathered you."*[a]	"My son, I was waiting for you in all the prophets, waiting for you to come so I could rest in you. [4]For you are my rest; you are my first-begotten son who rules forever."
4:1–11 #8, p. 15	1:12–13 #8, p. 15		

* Ⓓ Mt 17:5 / Mk 9:7 / Lk 9:35 (#122, p. 103)

[a] Lk 3:22 Most mss read "You are my son, the one I love—I fully approve of you" (as in Mark 1:11).

7. Jesus' Genealogy (according to Luke)

Mt 1:2–16 *(names only—in reverse order)* [see #2]	Mk	Lk 3:23–38
[16]Jesus, Joseph (husband of Mary), Jacob,		[23]Jesus was about thirty years old when he began his work. He was (supposedly) the son of Joseph, son of Eli, [24]son of Maththat, son of Levi, son of Melchi, son of Jannai, son of Joseph, [25]son of Mattathiah, son of Amos, son of Nahum, son of Hesli, son of Naggai, [26]son of Maath, son of Mattathiah, son of Semein, son of Josech, son of Joda, [27]son of Johanan, son of Rhesa,
[15]Matthan, Eleazar, Eliud, [14]Achim, Zadok, Azor, [13]Eliakim, Abiud, Zerubbabel, [12]Shealtiel,		son of Zerubbabel, son of Shealtiel, son of Neri, [28]son of Melchi, son of Addi, son of Kosam, son of Elmadam, son of Er, [29]son of Jesus, son of Eliezer, son of Jorim, son of Maththat, son of Levi, [30]son of Simeon, son of Judah, son of Joseph, son of Jonam, son of Eliakim, [31]son of Melea, son of Menna, son of Mattatha, son of Nathan,
Jeconiah (*and his brothers*), [11]Josiah, [10]Amos, Manasseh, Hezekiah, [9]Ahaz, Jotham, Uzziah, [8]Joram, Jehoshaphat, Asaph, [7]Abijah, Rehoboam, Solomon, [6]David & Uriah's wife, Jesse, [5]Obed, Boaz & Ruth, Salmon & Rahab, [4]Nahshon, Amminadab, Aram, [3]Hezron, Perez (*and Zerah*), Judah (*and his brothers*) & Tamar, [2]Jacob, Isaac, Abraham		son of David, [32]son of Jesse, son of Obed, son of Boaz, son of Sala, son of Nahshon, [33]son of Amminadab, son of Admin, son of Arni, son of Hezron, son of Perez, son of Judah, [34]son of Jacob, son of Isaac, son of Abraham, son of Terah, son of Nahor, [35]son of Serug, son of Reu, son of Peleg, son of Eber, son of Shelah, [36]son of Kenan, son of Arphachshad, son of Shem, son of Noah, son of Lamech, [37]son of Methuselah, son of Enoch, son of Jared, son of Mahalalel, son of Kenan, [38]son of Enos, son of Seth, son of Adam, son of God.

8. Jesus is tempted
SEE #353, P. 288

Mt 4:1–11	Mk 1:12–13	Lk 4:1–13
[1]Then Jesus was guided into the desert by the spirit* to be put to the test by the devil. [2]And after he had fasted forty days and forty nights, he was famished. [3]And the tester confronted him and said, "To prove you're God's son, order these stones to turn into bread." [4]He responded, "It is written, 'Human beings shall not live on bread alone, but on every word that comes from God's mouth.'" [5]Then the devil conducts him to the holy city, sets him on the high point of the temple, [6]and says to him, "To prove you're God's son, jump off; remember, it is written, 'To his heavenly messengers he will give orders about you," and 'With their hands they will catch you, so you won't even stub your toe on a stone.'" [7]Jesus said to him, "Elsewhere it is written, 'You shall not put the Lord your God to the test.'" [8]Again the devil takes him to a very high mountain and shows him all the empires of the world and their splendor,* [9]and says to him, "I'll give you all these, if you will kneel down and pay homage to me." [10]Finally Jesus says to him, "Get out of here, Satan! Remember, it is written, 'You shall pay homage to the Lord your God, and him alone shall you revere.'" vv. 5–7	[12]And right away the spirit drives him out into the desert.* [13]And he was in the desert for forty days, being put to the test by Satan. And he was among the wild animals,	[1]Jesus departed from the Jordan full of holy spirit and was guided by the spirit into the desert,* [2]where he was put to the test by the devil for forty days. He ate nothing that whole time; and when it was all over, he was famished. [3]The devil said to him, "To prove you're God's son, order this stone to turn into bread." [4]Jesus responded to him, "It is written, 'Human beings shall not live on bread alone.'" vv. 9–12 [5]Then he took Jesus up, and in an instant of time showed him all the empires of the civilized world.* [6]The devil said to him, "I'll give you authority over all this and the glory that comes with it; it has been turned over to me, and I can give it to anyone I want. [7]So, if you will pay homage to me, it will all be yours." [8]Jesus responded, "It is written, 'You shall pay homage to the Lord your God, and him alone shall you revere.'" [9]Then he took him to Jerusalem, set him on the high point of the temple, and said to him, "To prove you're God's son, jump off from here; [10]remember, it is written, 'To his heavenly messengers he will give orders about you, to protect you,' [11]and 'With their hands they will catch you, so you won't even stub your toe on a stone.'" [12]And in response Jesus said to him, "It is said, 'You shall not put the Lord your God to the test.'"

Mt 4:1–11	Mk 1:12–13	Lk 4:1–13
[11]Then the devil leaves him, and heavenly messengers arrive out of nowhere and look after him.	and the heavenly messengers looked after him.	[13]So when the devil had tried every kind of test, he let him alone, for the time being.

*GHeb 4a Just now my mother, the holy spirit, took me by one of my hairs and brought me to Tabor, the great mountain. (#516, p. 392)

9. Jesus' First Preaching

Mt 4:12–17	Mk 1:14–15	Lk 4:14–15
[12]When Jesus heard that John had been locked up, he headed for Galilee. [13]He took leave of Nazareth to go and settle down in Capernaum-by-the-sea, in the territory of Zebulun and Naphtali,	[14]After John was turned in, Jesus came to Galilee proclaiming God's good news.	[14]Then Jesus returned in the power of the spirit to Galilee.
		News about him spread throughout all the surrounding area. [15]He used to teach in their meeting places and was acclaimed by everyone.
[14]in order to fulfill the prediction spoken through Isaiah the prophet: "[15]Land of Zebulun and of Naphtali, the way to the sea, across the Jordan, Galilee of the pagans. [16]The people who languished in darkness have seen a great light, those who have wasted away in the shadow of death, for them a light has risen. [17]From that time on Jesus began to proclaim: "Change your ways because[a] the empire of Heaven is arriving."	[15]His message went: "The time is up: the empire of God is arriving! Change your ways, and put your trust in the good news."	4:16–30 #95, p. 75

[a] Mt 4:17 A few mss omit *Change your ways because.*

10. Recruiting the First Disciples

Mt 4:18–22	Mk 1:16–20	Lk *5:1–11*	Jn *1:35–42*
[18]As he was walking by the Sea of Galilee, he spotted two brothers, Simon, also known as Peter, and Andrew his brother, throwing their net in the sea, since they were fishermen. [19]And Jesus says to them, "Follow me and I'll have you fishing for people!"* [20]So right then and there they abandoned their nets and followed him. [21]When he had gone on a little farther, he caught sight of two other brothers, James, son of Zebedee, and his brother John, in the boat with Zebedee their father, mending their nets, and he also called out to them. [22] Right then and there they abandoned their boat and their father and followed him. 4:23–25 #15, p. 19	[16]As he was walking along by the Sea of Galilee, he spotted Simon and Andrew, Simon's brother, casting ⟨their nets⟩ into the sea—since they were fishermen—[17]and Jesus said to them, "Follow me and I'll have you fishing for people!"* [18]And right then and there they abandoned their nets and followed him. [19]When he had gone a little farther, he caught sight of James, son of Zebedee, and his brother John mending their nets in the boat. [20]And right away he called out to them as well, and they left their father Zebedee behind in the boat with the hired hands and accompanied him.		

*Lk 5:10b Jesus said to Simon, "Don't be afraid; from now on you'll be catching people."
(#50, p. 40)

11. Exorcism at Capernaum

Mt	Mk 1:21–28	Lk 4:31–37
7:28–29	[21]Then they come to Capernaum, and right away on the Sabbath he went to the meeting place and started teaching. [22]They were astonished at his teaching, since he would teach them on his own authority, unlike the scholars. [23]Now right then and there in their meeting place was a person possessed by an unclean spirit, which shouted, [24]"Jesus! What do you want with us, you Nazarene? Have you come to destroy us? I know who you are: God's holy man!" [25]But Jesus yelled at it, "Shut up and get out of him!" [26]Then the unclean spirit threw the man into convulsions, and it came out of him with a loud shriek. [27]And they were all so amazed that they asked themselves, "What's this? A new kind of teaching backed by authority! He gives orders even to unclean spirits and they obey him!" [28]And right away his reputation spread everywhere throughout the whole area of Galilee.	[31]He went down to Capernaum, a town in Galilee, and he would teach them on the Sabbath. [32]They were astonished at his teaching because his message carried authority. [33]Now in the meeting place there was a man who was possessed by the spirit of an unclean demon, which screamed at the top of its voice, [34]"Hey Jesus! What do you want with us, you Nazarene? Have you come to destroy us? I know who you are: God's holy man." [35]But Jesus yelled at it, "Shut up and get out of him!" Then the demon threw the man down in full view of everyone and came out of him without doing him any harm. [36]And so amazement came over them all and they were saying to one another, "What kind of message is this? With authority and power he gives orders to unclean spirits, and they leave." [37]So rumors about him began to spread to every corner of the surrounding region.

12. Simon's mother-in-law is healed

Mt 8:14–15	Mk 1:29–31	Lk 4:38–39
[14]And when Jesus came to Peter's house, he noticed his mother-in-law lying sick with a fever. [15]He touched her hand and the fever disappeared. Then she got up and started looking after him.	[29]And right away they left the meeting place and entered the house of Simon and Andrew along with James and John. [30]Simon's mother-in-law was in bed with a fever, and they told him about her right away. [31]He went up to her, took hold of her hand, raised her up, and the fever disappeared. Then she started looking after them.	[38]He got up from the meeting place and entered the house of Simon. Simon's mother-in-law was suffering from a high fever, and they made an appeal to him on her behalf. [39]He stood over her, rebuked the fever, and it disappeared. She immediately got up and started looking after them.

13. Evening Healings

Mt 8:16–18	Mk 1:32–34	Lk 4:40–41
[16]In the evening, they brought him many who were demon possessed. He drove out the spirits with a command, and all those who were ill he cured, [17]in order to fulfill the prediction spoken through Isaiah the prophet: "He took away our illnesses and carried off our diseases." [18]When Jesus saw the crowds around him, he gave orders to cross over to the other side. 8:19–22 #137, p. 112	[32]In the evening, at sundown, they would bring all the sick and demon possessed to him. [33]And the whole town would crowd around the door. [34]On such occasions he cured many people afflicted with various diseases and drove out many demons. He would never let the demons speak, because they realized who he was. 4:35	[40]As the sun was setting, all those who had people sick with various diseases brought them to him. He would lay his hands on each one of them and cure them. [41]Demons would also come out of many of them screaming, and saying, "You son of God, you!" But he would rebuke them and not allow them to speak, because they knew that he was the Anointed One.

14. Jesus leaves Capernaum

Mt	Mk 1:35–38	Lk 4:42–43
	[35]And rising early, while it was still very dark, he went outside and stole away to an isolated place, where he started praying. [36]Then Simon and those with him hunted him down. [37]When they had found him they say to him, "They're all looking for you." [38]But he replies, "Let's go somewhere else, to the neighboring villages, so I can speak there too, since that's what I came for."	[42]The next morning he went outside and withdrew to an isolated place. Then the crowds came looking for him, and when they got to him they tried to keep him from leaving them. [43]He said to them, "I have to tell the good news of the empire of God to the other towns as well; after all, that's why I was sent."

15. Preaching in Galilee

Mt 4:23–25	Mk 1:39	Lk 4:44
[23]And he toured all over Galilee, teaching in their meeting places, proclaiming the good news of the empire ⟨of Heaven⟩, and healing every disease and every ailment the people had. [24]And his reputation spread through the whole of Syria. They brought him everyone who was ill, who suffered from any kind of disease or was in intense pain, who was possessed, who was epileptic, or paralyzed, and he cured them. [25]And huge crowds followed him from Galilee and the Ten Cities and Jerusalem and Judea and from across the Jordan.	[39]So he went all around Galilee speaking in their meeting places and driving out demons. 3:7–12 1:40–45 #51, p. 41	[44]And he continued to preach in the meeting places of Judea. 6:17–19 5:1–11 #50, p. 40

16. The Setting of the Sermon on the Mount

Mt 4:24–5:2	Mk 3:7–8	Lk 6:17b–18, 12, 17a, 20a
[24]And his reputation spread through the whole of Syria. They brought him everyone who was ill, who suffered from any kind of disease or was in intense pain, who was possessed, who was epileptic, or paralyzed, and he cured them. [25]And huge crowds followed him from Galilee and the Ten Cities and Jerusalem and Judea and from across the Jordan. 5 [1]Seeing the crowds, he climbed up the mountain, and when he had sat down, his disciples came to him. [2]He then began to speak, and this is what he would teach them:	[7]Then Jesus withdrew with his disciples to the sea, and a huge crowd from Galilee followed. When they heard what he was doing, a huge crowd from Judea, [8]and from Jerusalem and Idumea and across the Jordan, and from around Tyre and Sidon, collected around him. *3:13* 3:7–12 #66, p. 54	[17b]There was a huge crowd of his disciples and a great throng of people from all Judea and Jerusalem and the coast of Tyre and Sidon. [18]They came to hear him and to be healed of their diseases. Those who were tormented by unclean spirits were cured. [12]During that time it came to pass that he went out to the mountain to pray, and spent the night in prayer to God . . . [17a]On the way down with them, Jesus stopped at a level place . . . [20a]Then he would look squarely at his disciples and say:

17. Congratulations (and Curses)

SEE #44, 354, PP. 35, 289

Mt 5:3–12	Mk	Lk 6:20b–26	Th 54; 69:2; 69:1; 68:1–2

[3]Congratulations to the poor in spirit!
   The empire of Heaven belongs to them.
		[20]Congratulations, you poor!
		
		   God's empire belongs to you.
			Th 54
			Congratulations to the poor,
			
			   for the empire of Heaven belongs to you.

[4]Congratulations to those who grieve!
   They will be consoled.
		[21b]Congratulations, you who weep now!
		   You will laugh.	

[5]Congratulations to the gentle! They will inherit the earth.			

[6]Congratulations to those who hunger and thirst for justice!
 	
   They will have a feast.
		[21a]Congratulations, you hungry!
		
		   You will have a feast.
			Th 69:2
			Congratulations to those who go hungry,
			   so the stomach of the needy may be filled.

[7]Congratulations to the merciful! They will receive mercy.			
[8]Congratulations to those whose motives are pure! They will see God.			
[9]Congratulations to those who work for peace! They will be called God's children.			
[10]Congratulations to those who have suffered persecution for the sake of justice! The empire of Heaven belongs to them.			**Th 69:1** [1]Congratulations to those who've been persecuted in their hearts: they are the ones who have truly come to know the Father. **Th 68:1–2**
[11]Congratulations to you when they denounce you and persecute you and spread malicious gossip[a] about you because of me. [12]Rejoice and be glad! Your reward is great in heaven. Remember, that is how they persecuted the prophets who preceded you.		[22]Congratulations to you when people hate you, and when they ostracize you and spread malicious gossip about you and scorn your name as evil, because of the Human One! [23]Rejoice on that day and jump for joy! Because look: your reward is great in heaven. Bear in mind that their ancestors treated the prophets the same way. [24]Damn you rich! You already have your consolation. [25]Damn you who are well-fed now! You will know hunger. Damn you who laugh now! You will learn to weep and grieve.	[1]Congratulations to you when you are hated and persecuted; [2]and no place will be found, wherever you've been persecuted.

| | | [26]Damn you when everybody speaks well of you! Bear in mind that their ancestors treated the phony prophets the same way.

6:27–36 #45, p. 36 | |

[a] Mt 5:11 A few mss add "and tell lies" to the triad of *denounce and persecute and spread malicious gossip.*

18. Salt and Light
SEE #400, 376, PP. 321, 307

Mt 5:13–16	Mk 9:49–50; 4:21	Lk 14:34–35; 11:33	other
[13]You are the salt of the earth. But if salt loses its zing, how will it be made salty? It's then good for nothing, except to be thrown out and stomped on.	**Mk 9:49–50** [49]You see, everyone will be salted with fire. [50]Salt is good, but if salt becomes tasteless, how will you renew it? Maintain "salt" among yourselves and be at peace with one another.	**Lk 14:34–35** [34]Salt is good, but if it loses its zing, how will it be renewed? [35]It's no good for either earth or manure. It just gets thrown away. Anyone here with two good ears, use 'em!*	
[14]You are the light of the world. A city sitting on top of a mountain can't be concealed.			**Jn 8:12** I am the light of the world.† **Th 32** A city fortified and built on a high hill cannot fall, nor can it be hidden.
[15]Nor do people light a lamp and put it under a bushel basket, but instead on a lampstand, where it sheds light for everyone in the house. [16]That's how your light should shine in public, so others can see your good deeds and praise your Father in the heavens.	**Mk 4:21** Since when is the lamp brought in to be put under the bushel basket or under the bed? It's put on the lampstand, isn't it?	**Lk 11:33** No one lights a lamp and then puts it in a cellar or under a bushel basket, but instead on a lampstand so that those who come in can see the light.‡	**Th 33:2–3** [2]After all, no one lights a lamp and puts it under a basket, nor does one put it in a hidden place. [3]Rather, one puts it on a lampstand so that all who come and go will see its light.

* Mt 11:15; 13:9; 13:43b; Mk 4:9; 4:23; Lk 8:8b; Th 8:4; 21:10; 24:2; 63:4; 65:8; 96:3
† Ⓓ Jn 9:5 (#301, p. 242)
‡ Ⓓ Lk 8:16 (#79, p. 64)

19. Law and Prophets

SEE #402, P. 321

Mt 5:17–20	Mk	Lk 16:17
[17]Don't imagine that I have come to annul the Law or the Prophets. I have come not to annul but to fulfill. [18]Let me tell you, before earth and sky pass away, not one iota, not one serif, will disappear from the Law, until it all happens. * [19]Whoever ignores one of the least ⟨important⟩ of these commandments, and teaches others to do so, will be called least ⟨important⟩ in the empire of Heaven. But whoever acts on ⟨these commandments⟩ and teaches ⟨others to do so⟩ will be called great in the empire of Heaven. [20]Let me tell you, unless you live your religion more fully than the scholars and Pharisees, you won't set foot in the empire of Heaven.	*13:31*	It's easier for earth and sky to pass away than for one serif of the Law to drop out.*
		16:18 #22, p. 23

* Th 11:1 This heaven will pass away and the one above it will pass away. (#422, p. 335)

20. On Murder and Anger

SEE #390, P. 316

Mt 5:21–26	Mk 11:25	Lk 12:58–59
[21]As you know, our ancestors were told, "You shall not kill" and "Whoever kills will be subject to judgment." [22]But I tell you, those who are angry with a companion will be brought before a tribunal. And those who say to a companion,[a] "You moron," will be subject to the sentence of the court. And whoever says, "You idiot," deserves the fires of Gehenna. [23]So, even if you happen to be offering your gift at the altar and recall that your friend has some claim against you, [24]leave your gift there at the altar. First go and be reconciled with your friend, and only then return and offer your gift. [25]You should settle quickly with your accuser while you are both on the way ⟨to court⟩, or else your accuser will turn you over to the judge, and the judge to the bailiff, and you are thrown in jail. [26]Let me tell you, you'll never get out of there until you've paid the last dime.	And when you stand up to pray, if you are holding anything against anyone, forgive them, so your Father in heaven may forgive your transgressions.*	[58]When you're about to appear with your accuser before the magistrate, do your best to settle with him on the way, or else he might drag you up before the judge, and the judge turn you over to the jailer, and the jailer throw you in prison. [59]I'm telling you, you'll never get out of there until you've paid every last cent.
	11:20–25 #209, p. 159	13:1–5 #165, p. 128

* Mt 6:14 (#290, p. 236)

---

[a] Mt 5:22 Some mss add "without cause" after *a companion*.

21. On Adultery and Lust

Mt 5:27–30	Mk 9:47–48, 43–45	Lk
[27]As you know, we once were told, "You shall not commit adultery." [28]But I tell you, those who leer at a woman with lust have already committed adultery with her in their minds. [29]And if your right eye gets you into trouble, rip it out and throw it away! You'd be better off losing a part of your body, than having your whole body thrown into Gehenna. [30]And if your right hand gets you into trouble, cut it off and throw it away! You'd be better off losing a part of your body, than having your whole body wind up in Gehenna.*	[47]And if your eye gets you into trouble, rip it out! It's better for you to enter God's empire one-eyed than to be thrown into Gehenna with both eyes, [48]where the worm never dies and the fire never goes out! [43]And if your hand gets you into trouble, cut it off! It's better for you to enter life maimed than to wind up in Gehenna, in the unquenchable fire, with both hands! [45]And if your foot gets you into trouble, cut it off! It's better for you to enter life lame than to be thrown into Gehenna with both feet! 9:49–50 #18, p. 21	

* Ⓓ Mt 18:8–9 (#131, p. 109)

22. On Divorce and Adultery*

SEE #403, P. 322

Mt 5:31–32	Mt 19:9	Mk 10:11–12	Lk 16:18
[31]We once were told, "Whoever divorces his wife must give her a certificate of divorce." [32]But I tell you, anyone who divorces his wife (except in the case of immorality) forces her into adultery; and whoever marries a divorced woman commits adultery.	[9]Whoever divorces his wife, except for immorality, and marries another commits adultery. 19:1–9 #193, p. 145	[11]Whoever divorces his wife and marries another commits adultery against her; [12]and if she divorces her husband and marries another, she commits adultery. 10:13–16 #195, p. 146	[18]Everyone who divorces his wife and marries another commits adultery; and the one who marries a woman divorced from her husband commits adultery. 16:19–31 #184, p. 139

* 1 Cor 7:10–11 [10]To the married my instruction (not mine, but the lord's) is that a wife should not divorce her husband—[11]but if she is already divorced, she should remain unmarried or be reconciled with her husband—and that a husband should not leave his wife. (#525, p. 398)

23. On Oaths

Mt 5:33–37	Mk	Lk
[33]Again, as you know, our ancestors were told, "You shall not break an oath," and "Oaths sworn in the name of God shall be kept." [34]But I tell you, don't swear at all. Don't invoke heaven, because it is the throne of God, [35]and don't invoke earth, because it is God's footstool, and don't invoke Jerusalem, because it is the city of the great king.* [36]You shouldn't swear by your head either, since you aren't able to turn a single hair either white or black. [37]Rather, your responses should be simply "Yes" and "No." Anything beyond that is inspired by the evil one.		

* Mt 23:16–22 (#219, p. 169)

24. On Revenge

SEE #355, P. 290

Mt 5:38–42	Mk	Lk 6:29–30	Th 95:1–2
[38]As you know, we once were told, "An eye for an eye" and "A tooth for a tooth." [39]But I tell you, don't react violently against the one who is evil; when someone slaps you on the right cheek, turn the other as well. [40]If someone is determined to sue you for your shirt, let him have your coat along with it. [41]Further, when anyone conscripts you for one mile, go along an extra mile. [42]Give to those who beg from you; and don't turn away those who want to borrow from you.		[29]When someone strikes you on the cheek, offer the other as well. If someone takes away your coat, don't prevent him from taking your shirt along with it. [30]Give to everyone who begs from you; and when someone takes your things, don't ask for them back. 6:27–36 #45, p. 36	[1]If you have money, don't lend it at interest. [2]Instead, give [it] to someone from whom you won't get it back.

25. Love your Enemies (according to Matthew)

SEE #45, 355–356, PP. 36, 290–91

Mt 5:43–48	Mk	Lk 6:27–28, 32–36	GOxy 1224 6:1
[43]As you know, we once were told, "You shall love your neighbor" and "You shall hate your enemy." [44]But I tell you, love your enemies and pray for your persecutors.		[27]But to you who listen I say: love your enemies, do good to those who hate you, [28]bless those who curse you, pray for your abusers.	P[r]ay for your [ene]mies. For whoever is not [against y]ou is on your side.
[45]You'll then become children of your Father in the heavens, for God makes the sun rise on both the bad and the good, and sends rain on both the just and the unjust. [46]Tell me, if you love those who love you, why should you be rewarded for that? Even the toll collectors do as much, don't they? [47]And if you greet only your friends, what have you done that is exceptional? Even the pagans[a] do as much, don't they?		v. 35b	
		[32]If you love those who love you, what merit is there in that? After all, even sinners love those who love them. [33]And if you do good to those who do good to you, what merit is there in that? After all, even sinners do as much. [34]If you lend to those from whom you hope to gain, what merit is there in that? Even sinners lend to sinners, in order to get as much in return. [35]But love your enemies, and do good, and lend, expecting nothing in return. Your reward will be great, and you'll be children of the Most High. As you know, the Most High is generous to the ungrateful and the evil.	
v. 45			
[48]To sum up, you shall be perfect, in the same way your heavenly Father is perfect.		[36]Be as compassionate as your Father is.	
		6:37–42 #46, p. 37	

[a] Mt 5:47 Many mss read "toll collectors" instead of *pagans*.

26. Giving to Charity

Mt 6:1–4	Mk	Lk	Th 62:2
¹Take care that you don't flaunt your religion in public to be noticed by others. Otherwise, you'll have no reward from your Father in the heavens. ²For example, when you give to charity, don't bother to toot your own horn as some phonies do in synagogues and on the street.* They are seeking human recognition. Let me tell you, they've already received their reward. ³Instead, when you give to charity, don't let your left hand in on what your right hand is up to, ⁴so your acts of charity will stay secret. And your Father, who sees what happens in secret, will reward you.			Don't let your left hand know what your right hand is doing.

*Th 14:3 If you give to charity, you'll harm your spirits. (#424, p. 336)

27. On Prayer

Mt 6:5–8	Mk	Lk
⁵And when you pray, don't act like phonies. They love to stand up and pray in synagogues and on street corners, so they can show off in public. Let me tell you, they've already received their reward. ⁶When you pray, go into a room by yourself and shut the door behind you. Then pray to your Father, the hidden one. And your Father, who sees what happens in secret, will reward you. ⁷And when you pray, you should not babble on as the pagans do.* They imagine that the more they say, the more attention they get. ⁸So don't imitate them. After all, your Father knows what you need before you ask.†		

*Th 14:2 If you pray, you'll be condemned. (#424, p. 336)
† Mt 6:32 / Lk 12:30 (#33, p. 29)

28. The Lord's Prayer
SEE #371, P. 303

Mt 6:9–15	Mk	Lk 11:1–4	GNaz 3
[9]You should pray like this: Our Father in the heavens, your name be revered. [10]Your empire be established, your will be done on earth as it is in heaven. [11]Provide us with the bread we need for the day. [12]Forgive our debts to the extent that we have forgiven[a] those in debt to us. [13]And don't make us face the test, but rescue us from the evil one.[b] [14]For if you forgive the offenses of others, your heavenly Father will also forgive yours, [15]and if you don't forgive others, neither will your heavenly Father forgive your offenses.*	*11:25* 11:5–8 #147, p. 118	[1]And it came to pass when he was praying somewhere that, when he had finished, one of his disciples said to him, "Master, teach us how to pray, just as John taught his disciples." [2]He said to them, "When you pray, you should say: Father, your name be revered. Your empire be established. [3]Provide us with the bread we need day by day. [4]Forgive our sins, since we too forgive everyone in debt to us. And don't make us face the test.	Provide us today with the bread we need for tomorrow.

* Mt 18:35 (#135, p. 111)

[a] Mt 6:12 Many mss read "we forgive" instead of *we have forgiven*.
[b] Mt 6:13 At the end of the verse, many mss insert "for yours is the kingdom, the power, and the glory. Amen."

29. On Fasting

Mt 6:16–18	Mk	Lk
[16]When you fast, don't make a spectacle of your remorse as the phonies do. As you know, they make their faces unrecognizable so their fasting may be publicly recognized. Let me tell you, they've already received their reward.* [17]When you fast, brush your hair and wash your face, [18]so your fasting will not be noticed by others, but by your Father, the hidden one, and your Father, who sees what happens in secret, will reward you.		

* Th 14:1 If you fast, you'll bring sin upon yourselves. (#424, p. 336)

30. Treasure in Heaven
SEE #385, P. 313

Mt 6:19–21	Mk	Lk 12:32–34	Th 76:3
	10:21		
¹⁹Don't pile up possessions here on earth, where moths and insects eat away and where burglars break in and steal. ²⁰Instead, gather your nest egg in heaven, where neither moths nor insects eat away and where no burglars break in or steal.		³²Don't be afraid, little flock, for it has delighted your Father to give you his empire. ³³Sell your belongings, and donate to charity; make yourselves purses that don't wear out, with inexhaustible wealth in heaven,* where no burglar can get to it and no moth can destroy it.	Seek his treasure that is unfailing and enduring, where no moth comes to eat and no worm destroys.
²¹As you know, what you treasure is your heart's true measure.		³⁴As you know, what you treasure is your heart's true measure. 12:35–38 #159, p. 125	

* Mt 19:21 / Mk 10:21 / Lk 18:22 (#196, p. 147)

31. The Light Within
SEE #377, P. 307

Mt 6:22–23	Mk	Lk 11:34–36
²²The eye is the body's lamp. It follows that if your eye is clear, your whole body will be flooded with light. ²³If your eye is clouded, your whole body will be shrouded in darkness.* If, then, the light within you is darkness, how dark that can be!		³⁴Your eye is the body's lamp. When your eye is clear, your whole body is flooded with light. When your eye is clouded, your body is shrouded in darkness.* ³⁵Take care, then, that the light within you is not darkness. ³⁶So if your whole body is flooded with light, and no corner of it is darkness, it will be completely illuminated as when a lamp's rays engulf you. 11:37–54 #153, p. 121

* Th 24:3 There is light within a person of light, and it shines on the whole world. If it does not shine, it is dark. (#433, p. 339)

32. Two Masters
SEE #401, P. 321

Mt 6:24	Mk	Lk 16:13	Th 47:2
No one can be a slave to two masters. That slave will either hate one and love the other, or be devoted to one and disdain the other. You can't be enslaved to both God and Mammon.		No servant can be a slave to two masters. That slave will either hate one and love the other, or be devoted to one and disdain the other. You can't be enslaved to both God and mammon. 16:14–15 #182, p. 138	And a slave cannot serve two masters, otherwise that slave will honor the one and offend the other.

33. Don't fret about life

SEE #384, P. 312

Mt 6:25–34	Mk	Lk 12:22–31	Th 36
25That's why I'm telling you, don't fret about your life, what you're going to eat and drink—or about your body—what you're going to wear. There's more to living than food and clothing, isn't there? 26Take a look at the birds of the sky: they don't plant or harvest or gather into barns. Yet your heavenly Father feeds them. You're worth more than they, aren't you?* 27Can any of you add one hour to life by fretting about it? 28Why worry about clothes? Notice how the wild lilies grow: they don't toil and they never spin. 29But let me tell you, even Solomon at the height of his glory was never decked out like one of them. 30If God dresses up the grass in the field, which is here today and is thrown into an oven tomorrow, won't ⟨God care for⟩ you even more, you with your meager trust? 31So don't fret. Don't say, "What are we going to eat?" or "What are we going to drink?" or "What are we going to wear?" 32These are all things pagans seek. After all, your heavenly Father is aware that you need them all.† 33Seek God's empire and his justice first, and all these things will come to you as a bonus. 34So don't fret about tomorrow. Let tomorrow fret about itself. The troubles that the day brings are enough.		22That's why I'm telling you: don't fret about life, what you're going to eat—or about your body, what you're going to wear. 23Remember, there is more to living than food and clothing. 24Think about the crows: they don't plant or harvest, they don't have storerooms or barns. Yet God feeds them. You're worth a lot more than the birds!* 25Can any of you add an hour to life by fretting about it? 26So if you can't do a little thing like that, why worry about the rest? 27Think about how the lilies grow: they don't toil and they never spin. But let me tell you, even Solomon at the height of his glory was never decked out like one of them. 28If God dresses up the grass in the field, which is here today and is tossed into the oven tomorrow, how much more will ⟨God take care of⟩ you, you with your meager trust? 29And don't be constantly on the lookout for what you're going to eat and what you're going to drink. Don't give it a thought. 30These are all things the world's pagans seek, and your Father is aware that you need them.† 31Instead, seek his empire and these things will come to you as a bonus.	Don't fret, from morning to evening and from evening to morning, about what you're going to wear.[a]
		12:32–34 #30, p. 28	

* Ⓓ Mt 10:31 / Lk 12:7 (#155, p. 123)
† Mt 6:7–8 (#27, p. 26)

---

[a] Th 36 The Greek version of this saying is longer. After the second *morning* it adds: "[about] your [food], what [you're going to] eat, or about [your clothing], . . ." At the end of the saying it adds: 2"[You're much] better than the lilies, which don't card and never [spin]. 3As for you, when you have no garment, what [are you going to put] on? 4Who could add to your life span? That same one will give you your garment."

34. On Passing Judgment (according to Matthew)
SEE #46, 357, 358, pp. 37, 392, 393

Mt 7:1–5	Mk 4:24	Lk 6:37–38, 41–42	Th 26:1–2
Don't pass judgment, so you won't be judged. [2]Don't forget, the judgment you hand out will be the judgment you get back.		[37]Don't pass judgment, and you won't be judged; don't condemn, and you won't be condemned; forgive, and you'll be forgiven. [38]Give, and it'll be given to you: they'll put in your lap a full measure, packed down, sifted, and overflowing. For the standard you apply will be the standard applied to you.	
And the standard you apply will be the standard applied to you. [3]Why do you notice the sliver in your friend's eye, but overlook the timber in your own? [4]How can you say to your friend, "Let me get the sliver out of your eye," when there is that timber in your own?	Pay attention to what you hear! The standard you apply will be the standard applied to you, and then some.	[41]Why do you notice the sliver in your friend's eye, but overlook the timber in your own? [42]How can you say to your friend, "Friend, let me get the sliver in your eye," when you don't notice the timber in your own?	[1]You see the sliver in your friend's eye, but you don't see the timber in your own eye.
[5]You phony, first take the timber out of your own eye and then you'll see well enough to remove the sliver from your friend's eye.		You phony, first take the timber out of your own eye, and then you'll see well enough to remove the sliver in your friend's eye.	[2]When you take the timber out of your own eye, then you will see well enough to remove the sliver from your friend's eye.
	4:24–25 #80, p. 65	6:43–45 #47, p. 38	

35. Profaning the Holy

Mt 7:6	Mk	Lk	Th 93:1–2
Don't offer to dogs what is sacred, and don't throw your pearls to pigs, or they'll trample them underfoot and turn and tear you to shreds.			[1]Don't give what is sacred to dogs, or else they might throw them on the manure pile. [2]Don't throw pearls [to] pigs, or they might . . . it [. . .].[a]

[a] Th 93:2 The text is deficient here. Among proposals for its restoration are the following: "bring it [to naught]" and "grind it [to bits]."

36. Ask, Seek, Knock
SEE #318, 372, PP. 254, 303

Mt 7:7–11	Mk	Lk 11:9–13	Th 92:1; 2:1; 94:1–2
[7]Ask—it'll be given to you; seek—you'll find; knock—it'll be opened for you.*		[9]And I'm telling you, ask—it'll be given to you; seek—you'll find; knock—it'll be opened for you.*	**Th 92:1** Seek and you will find. **Th 2:1** Those who seek should not stop seeking until they find.†
[8]For everyone who asks receives; everyone who seeks finds; and for the one who knocks it is opened.		[10]For everyone who asks receives; everyone who seeks finds; and for the one who knocks it is opened.	**Th 94:1–2** [1]The one who seeks will find, [2]and for [one who knocks] it will be opened.
[9]Who among you would hand a son a stone when he's asking for bread? [10]Again, who would hand him a snake when he's asking for fish? Of course no one would! [11]So if you, worthless as you are, know how to give your children good gifts, isn't it much more likely that your Father in the heavens will give good things to those who ask him?		[11]Which of you fathers would hand his son a snake[a] instead of a fish when he's asking for fish? [12]Or a scorpion when he's asking for an egg? [13]So if you, worthless as you are, know how to give your children good gifts, isn't it much more likely that the heavenly Father will give holy spirit to those who ask him? 11:14–15 #69, p. 56	

*Jn 15:5–8; 16:23–24 (#209, 318, 321, pp. 159, 254, 256)
†GHeb 6b (#517, p. 392)

---

[a] Lk 11:11 Some mss insert "stone, if he asks for bread, or give him a" before *snake*.

37. The Golden Rule
SEE #356, P. 291

Mt 7:12	Mk	Lk 6:31
Always treat people the way you want them to treat you. This sums up the Law and the Prophets.		Treat people the same way you want them to treat you. 6:27–36 #45, p. 36

38. The Narrow Gate
SEE #393, P. 317

Mt 7:13–14	Mk	Lk 13:24
[13]Get in through the narrow gate. Wide and smooth is the road that leads to destruction. Many are taking that route. [14]Narrow and rough is the road that leads to life. Only a few discover it.*		Struggle to get in through the narrow door; I'm telling you, many will try to get in, but won't be able.* 13:22–27 #168, p. 129

*Th 75 There are many standing at the door, but those who are solitary will enter the wedding hall. (#468, p. 354)

39. By their Fruits (according to Matthew)
SEE #47, 359, PP. 38, 293

Mt 7:15–20	Mk	Lk 6:44, 43	Th 45:1
[15]Be on the lookout for phony prophets, who make their pitch disguised as sheep; inside they are really voracious wolves. [16]You'll know who they are by what they produce. Since when do people pick grapes from thorns or figs from thistles? [17]Every healthy tree produces choice fruit, but the rotten tree produces spoiled fruit. [18]A healthy tree cannot produce spoiled fruit, any more than a rotten tree can produce choice fruit. [19]Every tree that does not produce choice fruit gets cut down and tossed on the fire.* [20]Remember, you'll know who they are by what they produce.†		[44]for each tree is known by its fruit. Figs are not gathered from thorns, nor are grapes picked from brambles. [43]A choice tree does not produce rotten fruit, any more than a rotten tree produces choice fruit. 6:43–45 #47, p. 38	Grapes are not harvested from thorn trees, nor are figs gathered from thistles, for they yield no fruit.

* Ⓓ Mt 3:10 / Lk 3:9 (#4, p. 11)
† Mt 12:33 (#47, p. 38)

40. Futile Flattery
SEE #360, 393, PP. 294, 317

Mt 7:21–23	Mk	Lk 6:46; 13:25–27	EgerG 3:5
[21]Not everyone who addresses me as "Master, master," will get into the empire of Heaven—only those who carry out the will of my Father in heaven. [22]On that day many will say to me, "Master, master, didn't we use your name when we prophesied? Didn't we use your name when we exorcised demons? Didn't we use your name when we performed all those miracles?" [23]Then I will tell them honestly, "I never knew you; get away from me, you subverters of the Law!"†		**Lk 6:46** Why do you call me "Master, master," and not do what I tell you? **Lk 13:25–27** [25]Once the master of the house gets up and bars the door, you'll be left standing outside and knocking at the door: "Master, open up for us." But he'll answer you, "I don't know where you come from."* [26]Then you'll start saying, "We ate and drank with you, and you taught in our streets." [27]But he'll reply, "I don't know where you come from; get away from me, all you evildoers!"† 13:28–29 #169, p. 130	Why do you pay me lip service as a teacher but not [do] what I say?

* Mt 25:10–12 (#232, p. 178)
† Mt 25:41 (#233, p. 179)

41. House Built on Rock

SEE #360, P. 294

Mt 7:24–27	Mk	Lk 6:47–49
[24]Everyone who listens to these words of mine and acts on them will be like a prudent man who built a house on bedrock. [25]Later the rain fell, and the torrents came, and the winds blew and pounded that house, yet it did not collapse, since its foundation rested on bedrock. [26]Everyone who listens to these words of mine and doesn't act on them will be like a stupid man, who built a house on sand. [27]When the rain fell, and the torrents came, and the winds blew and pounded that house, it collapsed —it totally collapsed.		[47]Everyone who comes to me and pays attention to my words and acts on them—I'll show you what such a person is like: [48]That one is like a person building a house, who dug deep and laid the foundation on bedrock; when a flood came, the torrent slammed against that house, but could not shake it, because it was well built. [49]But the one who listens ⟨to my words⟩ and doesn't act ⟨on them⟩ is like a person who built a house on the ground without a foundation; when the torrent slammed against it, it immediately collapsed. And so the ruin of that house was total.

42. Conclusion to the Sermon

Mt 7:28–29	Mk	Lk 7:1
[28]And so it happened that, when Jesus had finished this discourse, the crowds were astonished at his teaching,* [29]since he had been teaching them on his own authority, unlike their own scholars. 8:1–4 #51, p. 41	*1:21–22*	After he had completed all he had to say to his audience, he went into Capernaum. *4:32* 7:1–10 #52, p. 42

* Mt 22:33 (#214, p. 165)

43. The Setting of the Sermon on the Plain

Mt 4:25, 24; 5:1–2	Mk 3:7–8, 10	Lk 6:17–20a
		[12]During that time it came to pass that he went out to the mountain to pray, and spent the night in prayer to God.
[25]And huge crowds followed him from Galilee and the Ten Cities and Jerusalem and Judea and from across the Jordan. [24]And his reputation spread through the whole of Syria.	[7]Then Jesus withdrew with his disciples to the sea, and a huge crowd from Galilee followed. When they heard what he was doing, a huge crowd from Judea, [8]and from Jerusalem and Idumea and across the Jordan, and from around Tyre and Sidon, collected around him.	[17]On the way down with them, Jesus stopped at a level place. There was a huge crowd of his disciples and a great throng of people from all Judea and Jerusalem and the coast of Tyre and Sidon.
They brought him everyone who was ill, who suffered from any kind of disease or was in intense pain, who was possessed, who was epileptic, or paralyzed, and he cured them.	([10]You see, he had healed so many that all who had diseases were pushing forward to touch him.)*	[18]They came to hear him and to be healed of their diseases. Those who were tormented by unclean spirits were cured. [19]And everyone in the crowd tried to touch him, since power would flow out from him and heal them all.*
5 Seeing the crowds, he climbed up the mountain, and when he had sat down, his disciples came to him. [2]He then began to speak, and this is what he would teach them:		[20a]Then he would look squarely at his disciples and say:
	3:7–12 #66, p. 54	

* Mt 14:36 / Mk 6:56 (#109, p. 90)

44. Congratulations and Curses
SEE #17, 354, PP. 20, 289

Mt 5:3–12	Mk	Lk 6:20b–26	Th 54; 69:2; 69:1; 68:1–2

[3]Congratulations to the poor in spirit!
  The empire of Heaven belongs to them.
[5]Congratulations to the gentle!
  They will inherit the earth.
[6]Congratulations to those who hunger and thirst for justice!
  They will have a feast.
[4]Congratulations to those who grieve!
  They will be consoled.
[7]Congratulations to the merciful!
  They will receive mercy.
[8]Congratulations to those whose motives are pure!
  They will see God.
[9]Congratulations to those who work for peace!
  They will be called God's children.
[10]Congratulations to those who have suffered persecution for the sake of justice!
  The empire of Heaven belongs to them.
[11]Congratulations to you when they denounce you and persecute you and spread malicious gossip[a] about you because of me.
 	
[12]Rejoice and be glad! Your reward is great in heaven. Remember, that is how they persecuted the prophets who preceded you.
		Congratulations, you poor!
		
		  God's empire belongs to you.
		
		[21]Congratulations, you hungry!
		
		  You will have a feast.
		Congratulations, you who weep now!
		  You will laugh.
		
		[22]Congratulations to you when people hate you, and when they ostracize you and spread malicious gossip about you and scorn your name as evil, because of the Human One!
		[23]Rejoice on that day and jump for joy! Because look: your reward is great in heaven. Bear in mind that their ancestors treated the prophets the same way.
		[24]Damn you rich!
		You already have your consolation.
		[25]Damn you who are well-fed now!
		You will know hunger.
		Damn you who laugh now!
		You will learn to weep and grieve.
		[26]Damn you when everybody speaks well of you! Bear in mind that their ancestors treated the phony prophets the same way.
			Th 54
			Congratulations to the poor,
			
			for the empire of Heaven belongs to you.
			
			Th 69:2
			Congratulations to those who go hungry, so the stomach of the needy may be filled.
			
			Th 69:1
			Congratulations to those who've been persecuted in their hearts: they are the ones who have truly come to know the Father.
			Th 68:1–2
			[1]Congratulations to you when you are hated and persecuted; [2]and no place will be found, wherever you've been persecuted.

5:13–16 #18, p. 21

[a] Mt 5:11 A few mss add "tell lies" to the triad of *denounce and persecute and spread malicious gossip*.

45. Love your enemies (according to Luke)

SEE #25, 355, 356, PP. 25, 290, 291

Mt 5:43–44, 38–42; 7:12; 5:46–47, 45, 48	Lk 6:27–36	other
Mt 5:43–44 [43]As you know, we once were told, "You shall love your neighbor" and "You shall hate your enemy." [44]But I tell you, love your enemies and pray for your persecutors.		
	[27]But to you who listen I say: love your enemies, do good to those who hate you, [28]bless those who curse you, pray for your abusers.	**GOxy 1224 6:1** P[r]ay for your [ene]mies. For whoever is not [against y]ou is on your side.
Mt 5:38–42 [38]As you know, we once were told, "An eye for an eye" and "A tooth for a tooth." [39]But I tell you, don't react violently against the one who is evil; when someone slaps you on the right cheek, turn the other as well. [40]If someone is determined to sue you for your shirt, let him have your coat along with it. [41]Further, when anyone conscripts you for one mile, go along an extra mile.	[29]When someone strikes you on the cheek, offer the other as well. If someone takes away your coat, don't prevent him from taking your shirt along with it.	
[42]Give to those who beg from you; and don't turn away those who want to borrow from you.	[30]Give to everyone who begs from you; and when someone takes your things, don't ask for them back.	
Mt 7:12 Always treat people the way you want them to treat you. This sums up the Law and the Prophets.	[31]Treat people the same way you want them to treat you.	
Mt 5:46–47, 45, 48 [46]Tell me, if you love those who love you, why should you be rewarded for that? Even the toll collectors do as much, don't they? [47]And if you greet only your friends, what have you done that is exceptional? Even the pagans[a] do as much, don't they?	[32]If you love those who love you, what merit is there in that? After all, even sinners love those who love them. [33]And if you do good to those who do good to you, what merit is there in that? After all, even sinners do as much.	
	[34]If you lend to those from whom you hope to gain, what merit is there in that? Even sinners lend to sinners, in order to get as much in return. [35]But love your enemies, and do good, and lend, expecting nothing in return. Your reward will be great, and you'll be children of the Most High. As you know, the Most High is generous to the ungrateful and the evil.	**Th 95:1–2** [1]If you have money, don't lend it at interest. [2]Instead, give [it] to someone from whom you won't get it back.
[45]You'll then become children of your Father in the heavens, for God makes the sun rise on both the bad and the good, and sends rain on both the just and the unjust. [48]To sum up, you shall be perfect, in the same way your heavenly Father is perfect.	[36]Be as compassionate as your Father is.	

[a] Mt 5:47 Many mss read "toll collectors" instead of *pagans*.

46. On Passing Judgment (according to Luke)
SEE #34, 357, 358, PP. 30, 292, 293

Mt 7:1–2; 15:14; 10:24–25; 7:3–5	Mk 4:24	Lk 6:37–42	other
Mt 7:1–2 ¹Don't pass judgment, so you won't be judged. ²Don't forget, the judgment you hand out will be the judgment you get back.		³⁷Don't pass judgment, and you won't be judged; don't condemn, and you won't be condemned; forgive, and you'll be forgiven. ³⁸Give, and it'll be given to you: they'll put in your lap a full measure, packed down, sifted, and overflowing.	
And the standard you apply will be the standard applied to you.	The standard you apply will be the standard applied to you, and then some.	For the standard you apply will be the standard applied to you.	
Mt 15:14 They are blind guides of blind people! If one blind person guides another, both will end up in some ditch.		³⁹And he posed a riddle for them: Can one blind person guide another? Won't they both end up in some ditch?	**Th 34** If a blind person leads a blind person, both of them will fall into a hole.
Mt 10:24–25a ²⁴Students are not above their teachers, nor slaves above their masters.		⁴⁰Students are not above their teachers.	**Jn 13:16a** Slaves are never better than their masters.*
²⁵ᵃIt's enough for students to become like their teachers and slaves to be like their masters.		But those who are fully taught will be like their teachers.	
Mt 7:3–5 ³Why do you notice the sliver in your friend's eye, but overlook the timber in your own? ⁴How can you say to your friend, "Let me get the sliver out of your eye," when there is that timber in your own? ⁵You phony, first take the timber out of your own eye and then you'll see well enough to remove the sliver from your friend's eye.		⁴¹Why do you notice the sliver in your friend's eye, but overlook the timber in your own? ⁴²How can you say to your friend, "Friend, let me get the sliver in your eye," when you don't notice the timber in your own? You phony, first take the timber out of your own eye, and then you'll see well enough to remove the sliver in your friend's eye.	**Th 26:1–2** ¹You see the sliver in your friend's eye, but you don't see the timber in your own eye. ²When you take the timber out of your own eye, then you will see well enough to remove the sliver from your friend's eye.
	4:24–25 #80, p. 65		

* Ⓓ Jn 15:20 (#319, p. 255)

47. By their Fruits (according to Luke)

SEE #39, 359, PP. 32, 293

Mt 7:18; 12:33; 7:16; 12:35, 34	Mk	Lk 6:43–45	Th 45:1–3
Mt 7:18 A healthy tree cannot produce spoiled fruit, any more than a rotten tree can produce choice fruit.		[43]A choice tree does not produce rotten fruit, any more than a rotten tree produces choice fruit;	
Mt 12:33 If you make the tree choice, its fruit will be choice; if you make the tree rotten, its fruit will be rotten. After all, the tree is known by its fruit.		[44]for each tree is known by its fruit.	
Mt 7:16 You'll know who they are by what they produce. Since when do people pick grapes from thorns or figs from thistles?		Figs are not gathered from thorns, nor are grapes picked from brambles.	[1]Grapes are not harvested from thorn trees, nor are figs gathered from thistles, for they yield no fruit.
Mt 12:35, 34 [35]The good person produces good things out of a fund of good; and the evil person produces evil things out of a fund of evil.		[45]The good person produces good from the fund of good in the heart, and the evil person produces evil from the evil within.	[2]Good persons produce good from what they've stored up; [3]bad persons produce evil from the wickedness they've stored up in their hearts, and say evil things. For from the overflow of the heart comes evil.
[34]You spawn of Satan, how can your speech be good when you are evil? As you know, the mouth gives voice to what the heart is full of.		As you know, the mouth gives voice to what the heart is full of.	

48. Empty Praise
SEE #360, P. 294

Mt 7:21	Mk	Lk 6:46	EgerG 3:5
Not everyone who addresses me as "Master, master," will get into the empire of Heaven—only those who carry out the will of my Father in heaven.		Why do you call me "Master, master," and not do what I tell you?	Why do you pay me lip service as a teacher, but not [do] what I say?
7:21–23 #40, p. 32			

49. House Built on Rock
SEE #360, P. 294

Mt 7:24–27	Mk	Lk 6:47–49
[24]Everyone who listens to these words of mine and acts on them will be like a prudent man who built a house on bedrock. [25]Later the rain fell, and the torrents came, and the winds blew and pounded that house, yet it did not collapse, since its foundation rested on bedrock. [26]Everyone who listens to these words of mine and doesn't act on them will be like a stupid man, who built a house on sand. [27]When the rain fell, and the torrents came, and the winds blew and pounded that house, it collapsed— it totally collapsed.		[47]Everyone who comes to me and pays attention to my words and acts on them—I'll show you what such a person is like: [48]That one is like a person building a house, who dug deep and laid the foundation on bedrock; when a flood came, the torrent slammed against that house, but could not shake it, because it was well built. [49]But the one who listens ⟨to my words⟩ and doesn't act ⟨on them⟩ is like a person who built a house on the ground without a foundation; when the torrent slammed against it, it immediately collapsed. And so the ruin of that house was total.
7:28–29 #42, p. 33		7:1 #42, p. 33

50. A Miraculous Catch of Fish

SEE #347, P. 282

Mt	Mk	Lk 5:1–11	Jn 21:1–11
13:1–3	4:1–2	It came to pass, when the crowd pressed him to hear the word of God, that he was standing by Lake Gennesaret. [2]He noticed two boats moored there at the shore; the fishermen had left them and were washing their nets. [3]He got into one of the boats, the one belonging to Simon, and asked him to put out a little from the shore. Then he sat down and began to teach the crowds from the boat. [4]When he had finished speaking, he said to Simon, "Put out into deep water and lower your nets for a catch." [5]But Simon replied, "Master, we've been hard at it all night and haven't caught a thing. But if you insist, I'll lower the nets." [6]So they did and netted such a huge number of fish that their nets began to tear apart. [7]They signaled to their partners in the other boat to come and lend a hand. They came and loaded both boats until they nearly sank.	Some time after these events, Jesus again appeared to his disciples by the Sea of Tiberias. This is how he did it. [2]When Simon Peter and Thomas, the one known as "the Twin," were together, along with Nathanael from Cana, Galilee, the sons of Zebedee, and two other disciples, [3]Simon Peter says to them, "I'm going fishing." "We're coming with you," they reply. They went down and got into the boat, but that night they didn't catch a thing. [4]It was already getting light when Jesus appeared on the shore, but his disciples didn't recognize that it was Jesus. [5]"You boys haven't caught any fish, have you?" Jesus asks them. "No," they replied. [6]He told them, "Cast your net on the right side of the boat and you'll have better luck." So they cast the net, but then couldn't haul it in because of the huge number of fish. [7]That disciple whom Jesus loved exclaims to Peter, "It's the Master!"
4:18–22	1:16–20	[8]At the sight of this, Simon Peter fell to his knees in front of Jesus and said, "Get away from me, Master; I'm a sinful man." [9](You see, he and his companions were stunned at the catch of fish they had taken, [10]as were James and John, sons of Zebedee and partners of Simon.) Jesus said to Simon, "Don't be afraid; from now on you'll be catching people." [11]They then brought their boats to shore, abandoned everything, and followed him.	When Simon Peter heard, "It's the Master," he tied his cloak around himself, since he was stripped for work, and threw himself into the water. [8]The rest of the disciples came by boat, dragging the net full of fish. (Actually, they were not far from land, only about a hundred yards.) [9]When they got to shore, they see a charcoal fire burning, with fish cooking on it, and some bread. [10]Jesus says to them, "Bring some of the fish you've just caught." [11]Then Simon Peter went aboard and ⟨helped⟩ haul in the net full of large fish ashore—one hundred fifty-three of them. Even though there were so many of them, the net still didn't tear.

51. A leper is healed

Mt 8:1–4	Mk 1:40–45	Lk 5:12–16	EgerG 2:1–4
[1]When he came down from the mountain, huge crowds followed him. [2]Just then a leper appeared, bowed down to him, and said,	[40]Then a leper comes up to him, pleads with him, falls down on his knees, and says to him,	[12]And it came to pass, while he was in one of the towns, that there was this man covered with leprosy. Seeing Jesus, he knelt with his face to the ground and begged him,	[1]Just then a leper comes up to him and says, "Teacher Jesus, in wandering around with lepers and eating with them in the inn, I became a leper myself. [2]If you want to, I'll be made clean."
"Master, if you want to, you can make me clean."	"If you want to, you can make me clean." [41]Although Jesus was indignant,[a]	"Master, if you want to, you can make me clean."	
[3]And he stretched out his hand, touched him, and says,	he stretched out his hand, touched him, and says to him,	[13]Jesus stretched out his hand, touched him, saying,	[3]The Master said to him,
"Okay—you're clean!" And right away his leprosy was cleansed.	"Okay—you're clean!" [42]And right away the leprosy disappeared, and he was made clean. [43]And Jesus snapped at him, and right away threw him out [44]with this warning:	"Okay—you're clean!" And right away the leprosy disappeared.	"Okay—you're clean!" And right away his leprosy disappeared from him.
[4]Then Jesus warns him, "Don't tell anyone, but go, have a priest examine you. Then offer the gift that Moses commanded, as evidence ⟨of your cure⟩."	"Don't tell anyone anything, but go, have a priest examine you. Then offer for your cleansing what Moses commanded, as evidence ⟨of your cure⟩."	[14]He ordered him to tell no one. "But go, have a priest examine you. Then make an offering, as Moses commanded, for your cleansing, as evidence ⟨of your cure⟩."	[4]Jesus says to him, "Go and have the priests examine ⟨your skin⟩. Then offer for your purification what Moses commanded —and no more sinning."
	[45]But after he left, he started telling everyone and spreading the story, so that Jesus could no longer enter a town openly, but had to stay out in isolated places. Yet they continued to come to him from everywhere.	[15]Yet the story about him spread around all the more. Great crowds would gather to hear him and to be healed of their diseases. [16]But he would withdraw to isolated places and pray.	
	2:1–12 #59, p. 48	5:17–26 #59, p. 48	

[a] Mk 1:41 Most mss read "And Jesus was moved" in place of *Although Jesus was indignant.*

52. An official's boy is healed

SEE #288, 361, PP. 234, 295

Mt 8:5–13	Mk	Lk 7:1–10	Jn 4:46b–54
7:28		¹After he had completed all he had to say to his audience, he went into Capernaum.	
⁵When he had entered Capernaum, a Roman officer approached him and pleaded with him, ⁶"Sir, my servant boy was struck down with paralysis and is in terrible pain."		²A Roman officer had a slave he was very fond of but who was sick and about to die. ³So when he heard about Jesus, the officer sent some elders of the Jewish community to him, and asked him to come and cure his slave. ⁴When they came to Jesus, they pleaded with him urgently, saying, "He deserves to have you do this for him ⁵because he loves our people, and even built a meeting place for us."	⁴⁶ᵇIn Capernaum there was a government official whose son was sick. ⁴⁷When he heard that Jesus had returned to Galilee from Judea, he approached him and pleaded with him to come down and cure his son, who was about to die.
			⁴⁸Jesus said to him, "You people refuse to believe unless you see signs and omens."
			⁴⁹The official responds, "Sir, please come down before my child dies."
			⁵⁰Jesus says, "Go home, your son will live."
⁷And he said to him, "I'll come and cure him."		⁶So Jesus went with them. When he got close to the house, the officer dispatched friends to say to him, "Don't trouble yourself, sir, for I don't deserve to have you in my house;	
⁸And the officer replied, "Sir, I don't deserve to have you in my house,		⁷that's why I didn't presume to come to you in person. Just say the word, and let my boy be cured.	
but only say the word and my boy will be cured. ⁹After all, I myself am under orders, and I have soldiers under me. I order one to go, and he goes; I order another to come, and he comes; and I order my slave to do something, and he does it."		⁸After all, I myself am under orders and I have soldiers under me. I order one to go, and he goes; I order another to come, and he comes; and I order my slave to do something, and he does it."	
¹⁰As Jesus listened he was amazed and said to those who followed, "Let me tell you, I have not found such trust in a single Israelite! ¹¹I predict that many will come from east and west and dine with Abraham and Isaac and Jacob in the empire of Heaven, ¹²but those who		⁹As Jesus listened to this he was amazed at him. He turned and said to the crowd that followed, "I'm telling you, not even in Israel have I found such trust."	
		13:28–29	

think the empire of Heaven belongs to them will be thrown out into the utter darkness. There'll be weeping and grinding of teeth out there."

[13]And Jesus said to the Roman officer, "Be on your way. Let it happen for you according to your trust." And the boy was cured at that precise moment.[a]

[10]And when the emissaries returned to the house, they found the slave in good health.

The man believed what Jesus told him and went home. [51]While he was still on his way home, his slaves met him and told him that his boy was alive. [52]So he asked them when he had begun to recover, and they told him, "The fever broke yesterday at one o'clock."

[53]Then the father realized that one o'clock was precisely the time Jesus had said to him, "Your son will live." And he believed, as did his whole household. [54]Jesus performed this second sign after he had returned from Judea to Galilee.

8:14–15 #12, p. 18

[a] Mt 8:13 Several mss add: "The Roman official returned to his house and found at that very moment that the boy was in good health."

53. Jesus raises a widow's son

Mt	Mk	Lk 7:11–17
		[11]And it came to pass soon afterward that he went to a town called Nain, accompanied by his disciples and a large crowd. [12]As he neared the town gate, just then a dead man was being carried out, the only son of his mother, who was herself a widow. And a considerable crowd from the town was with her. [13]When the Master saw her, his heart went out to her and he said to her, "Don't cry." [14]And he went up and touched the bier. The bearers paused, and he said, "Young man—I'm talking to you—get up." [15]And the dead man sat up and began to speak; then Jesus gave him back to his mother. [16]Fear gripped them all and they praised God, saying, "A great prophet has been raised up among us!" and "God has visited his people!" [17]And this story about him spread throughout Judea and all the surrounding area.

54. Messengers from John the Baptizer

SEE #362, P. 296

Mt 11:2–6	Mk	Lk 7:18–23
[2]While John was in prison he heard about what the Anointed One had been doing and he sent his disciples [3]to ask, "Are you the one who is to come or do we have to wait for another?" [4]And so Jesus answered them, "Go report to John what you have heard and seen: [5]The blind see again and the lame walk; lepers are cleansed and the deaf hear; the dead are raised, and the poor have the good news preached to them. [6]Congratulations to those who don't take offense at me."		[18]John's disciples reported all these things to him. [19]John summoned a couple of his disciples and sent them to the Master to ask, "Are you the one who is to come, or do we have to wait for someone else?" [20]And when the men came to Jesus, they said, "John the Baptizer sent us to you to ask: 'Are you the one who is to come, or do we have to wait for someone else?'" [21]Jesus had just cured many of their diseases and plagues and evil spirits, and restored sight to many who were blind. [22]And so he answered them, "Go report to John what you have seen and heard: the blind see again, the lame walk, lepers are cleansed, the deaf hear, the dead are raised, and the poor have the good news preached to them. [23]Congratulations to those who don't take offense at me."

55. More than a Prophet

SEE #363, P. 297

Mt 11:7–11	Mk	Lk 7:24–30	Th 78:1–3; 46:1–2
[7]After ⟨John's disciples⟩ had departed, Jesus began to talk to the crowds about John. "What did you go out to the desert to gawk at? A reed shaking in the wind? [8]What did you really go out to see? A man dressed in fancy clothes? But wait! Those who wear fancy clothes are found in royal houses. [9]Come on, what did you go out to see? A prophet? Yes, that's what you went out to see, and even more than a prophet. [10]This is the one about whom it was written: 'Here is my messenger, whom I send on ahead of you to prepare your way before you.' [11]"Let me tell you, among those born of women no one has arisen who is greater than John the Baptizer;	1:2	[24]After John's messengers had left, Jesus began to talk to the crowds about John. "What did you go out to the desert to gawk at? A reed shaking in the wind? [25]What did you really go out to see? A man dressed in fancy clothes? But wait! Those who dress fashionably and live in luxury are found in palaces. [26]Come on, what did you go out to see? A prophet? Yes, that's what you went out to see, and even more than a prophet. [27]This is the one about whom it was written: 'Here is my messenger, whom I send on ahead of you to prepare your way before you.' [28]I'm telling you, among those born of women none is greater than John;	**Th 78:1–3** [1]Why have you come out to the countryside? To see a reed shaken by the wind? [2]And to see a person dressed in soft clothes, [like your] rulers and your powerful ones? [3]They are dressed in soft clothes and they cannot understand truth.
yet the least ⟨important⟩ in the empire of Heaven is greater than he is.		yet the least ⟨important⟩ in God's empire is greater than he is."	**Th 46:1–2** [1]From Adam to John the Baptizer, among those born of women, no one is so much greater than John the Baptizer, so his eyes should not be downcast. [2]But I have said that whoever among you becomes a child will recognize the ⟨Father's⟩ empire and will become greater than John.
		([29]All the people, even the toll collectors, who were listening and had been baptized by John, vindicated God's plan; [30]but the Pharisees and the legal experts, who had not been baptized by him, subverted God's plan for themselves.)	
21:32			
11:12–13 #183, p. 138			

56. Like Children in the Marketplace

SEE #364, P. 298

Mt 11:16–19	Mk	Lk 7:31–35
[16]What does this generation remind me of? It is like children sitting in marketplaces who call out to others, [17]"We played the flute for you, but you wouldn't dance; we sang a dirge but you wouldn't mourn." [18]Just remember, John appeared on the scene neither eating nor drinking, and they say, 'He's possessed.' [19]The Human One appeared on the scene both eating and drinking, and they say, 'There's a glutton and a drunk, a crony of toll collectors and sinners!' Indeed, Wisdom is vindicated by her deeds. 11:20–24 #139, p. 114		[31]What do the people of this generation remind me of? What are they like? [32]They are like children sitting in the marketplace and calling out to one another, "We played the flute for you, but you wouldn't dance; we sang a dirge, but you wouldn't weep." [33]Just remember, John the Baptizer appeared on the scene, eating no bread and drinking no wine, and you say, 'He's possessed.' [34]The Human One appeared on the scene both eating and drinking, and you say, 'There's a glutton and a drunk, a crony of toll collectors and sinners!' [35]Indeed, Wisdom is vindicated by all her children.

57. The Woman Who Loved Much

Mt	Mk	Lk 7:36–50	Jn
26:6–9	14:3–5	[36]One of the Pharisees invited him to dinner; he entered the Pharisee's house, and reclined ⟨for the meal⟩. [37]A local woman, who was a sinner, found out that he was having dinner at the Pharisee's house. She suddenly showed up with an alabaster jar of aromatic ointment, [38]and stood there behind him weeping at his feet. Her tears wet his feet, and she wiped them dry with her hair; she kissed his feet, and anointed them with the ointment. [39]The Pharisee who had invited him saw this and said to himself, "If this man were a prophet, he would know who this is and what kind of woman is touching him, since she is a sinner." [40]And Jesus answered him, "Simon, I have something to tell you." "Teacher," he said, "speak up." [41]"This moneylender had two debtors; one owed five hundred denarii, and the other fifty. [42]Since neither one of them could pay, he wrote off both debts. Now which of them will love him more?" [43]Simon answered, "I would imagine, the one for whom he wrote off the larger debt." And he said to him, "You're right." [44]Then turning to the woman, he said to Simon, "Do you see this woman? I walked into your house and you didn't offer me water for my feet; yet she has washed my feet with her tears and dried them with her hair. [45]You didn't offer me a kiss, but she hasn't stopped kissing my feet since I arrived. [46]You didn't anoint my head with oil, but she has anointed my feet with ointment. [47]For this reason, I'm telling you, her many sins have been forgiven, as this outpouring of her love shows. But the one who is forgiven little shows little love." [48]And he said to her, "Your sins have been forgiven." [49]Then those having dinner with him began to mutter to themselves, "Who is this who even forgives sins?" [50]And he said to the woman, "Your trust has saved you; go in peace."	12:1–5

58. The Women Who Supported Jesus

Mt	Mk	Lk 8:1–3
9:35	6:6b	[1]And it came to pass soon afterward that he traveled through towns and villages, preaching and announcing the good news of the empire of God. The Twelve were with him, [2]and also some women whom he had cured of evil spirits and diseases: Mary, the one from Magdala, from whom seven demons had departed, [3]and Joanna, the wife of Chuza, Herod's steward, and Susanna, and many other women, who provided for them out of their resources. 8:4–8 #76, p. 61

59. The Healing of the Paralytic
SEE #289, P. 235

Mt 9:1–8	Mk 2:1–12	Lk 5:17–26
[1]After he got on board the boat, he crossed over and came to his own town.	[1]Some days later he went back to Capernaum and was rumored to be at home. [2]And many people crowded around so there was no longer any room, even outside the door. Then he started speaking to them.	[17]And it came to pass one day, as he was teaching, that the Lord's healing power was with him. Now Pharisees and teachers of the Law, who had come from every village of Galilee and Judea and from Jerusalem, were sitting around.
[2]The next thing you know, some people were bringing him a paralytic lying on a bed.	[3]Some people then show up with a paralytic being carried by four of them. [4]And when they couldn't get near him because of the crowd, they removed the roof above him. After digging it out, they lowered the mat on which the paralytic was lying.	[18]The next thing you know, some men showed up, carrying a paralyzed man on a bed. They attempted to bring him in and lay him in front of Jesus. [19]But finding no way to get him in because of the crowd, they went up onto the roof and lowered him on his pallet through the tiles into the middle of the crowd in front of Jesus.
When Jesus noticed their trust, he said to the paralytic, "Be brave, child, your sins are forgiven."	[5]When Jesus noticed their trust, he says to the paralytic, "Child, your sins are forgiven."	[20]When Jesus noticed their trust, he said, "Mister, your sins have been forgiven."
[3]At that some of the scholars said to themselves, "This guy is blaspheming!"	[6]Some of the scholars were sitting there and silently objecting: [7]"Why does this guy talk like this? He's blaspheming! Who can forgive sins except the one God?"	[21]And the scholars and the Pharisees began to object: "Who is this guy who utters blasphemies? Who can forgive sins except God alone?"
[4]Because he understood the way they thought, Jesus said,	[8]And right away, because Jesus could sense that they were objecting to what he had said, he says to them:	[22]Because Jesus was aware of their objections, he responded to them,
"Why do you harbor evil thoughts? [5]Which is easier: to say, 'Your sins are forgiven,' or to say, 'Get up and walk'? [6]But just so you realize that on earth the Human One has authority to forgive sins"—he then says to the paralytic—	"Why are you objecting to all this? [9]Which is easier: to say to the paralytic, 'Your sins are forgiven,' or to say, 'Get up, pick up your mat and walk'? [10]But just so you realize that on earth the Human One has authority to forgive sins"—he says to the paralytic—	"Why are you objecting? [23]Which is easier: to say, 'Your sins have been forgiven,' or to say, 'Get up and walk'?" [24]But just so you realize that on earth the Human One has authority to forgive sins"—he said to the paralyzed man—
"Get up, pick up your bed and go home." [7]And he got up and went home.*	[11]"You there, get up, pick up your mat and go home!" [12]And he got up, picked his mat right up, and walked out as everyone looked on.*	"You there, get up, pick up your pallet and go home." [25]And immediately he stood up in front of them, picked up what he had been lying on, and went home praising God.*
[8]When the crowds saw this, they became fearful, and praised God for giving such authority to humans.	So they all became ecstatic, extolled God, and exclaimed, "We've never seen the likes of this!"	[26]They all became ecstatic, and they began to praise God, but they were also filled with fear and exclaimed, "We saw some incredible things today!"

* Jn 5:8–9 [8]"Get up, pick up your mat, and walk around," Jesus tells him. [9]And at once the man recovered; he picked up his mat and started walking. (#289, p. 235)

60. The Recruitment of Levi

Mt 9:9–13	Mk 2:13–17	Lk 5:27–32	GOxy 1224 5:1–2
	[13]Again he went out by the sea. And, with a huge crowd gathered around him, he started teaching.		
[9]As Jesus was walking along there, he caught sight of a man sitting at the toll booth, one named Matthew, and he says to him, "Follow me!" And he got up and followed him.	[14]As he was walking along, he caught sight of Levi, the son of Alphaeus, sitting at the toll booth, and he says to him, "Follow me." And Levi got up and followed him.	[27]After these events he went out and observed a toll collector named Levi sitting at the toll booth. He said to him, "Follow me." [28]Leaving everything behind, he got up, and followed him.	
[10]And it so happened, while he was dining in his house, that many toll collectors and sinners showed up just then and dined with Jesus and his disciples.	[15]It so happened that Jesus was reclining ⟨for dinner⟩ in his house, along with many toll collectors and sinners and Jesus' disciples. (You see, there were many of these people and they were all following him.)	[29]And Levi gave him a great banquet in his house, and a large group of toll collectors and others were dining with them.	
[11]And whenever the Pharisees saw this, they would question his disciples, "Why does your teacher eat with toll collectors and sinners?"	[16]And whenever the Pharisees' scholars saw him eating with sinners and toll collectors, they would question his disciples, "What's he doing eating with toll collectors and sinners?"	[30]The Pharisees and their scholars would complain to his disciples, "Why do you people eat and drink with toll collectors and sinners?"	[1]When the scholars an[d Pharise]es and priests observ[ed hi]m, they were indignant [because he reclined ⟨at table⟩ in the com]pany of sin[ners].
[12]When Jesus overheard, he said, "Since when do the able-bodied need a doctor? It's the sick who do. [13]Go and learn what this means, 'It's mercy I desire instead of sacrifice.' After all, I did not come to enlist the upright but sinners!"	[17]When Jesus overhears, he says to them, "Since when do the able-bodied need a doctor? It's the sick who do. I did not come to enlist the upright but sinners!"	[31]In response Jesus said to them: "Since when do the healthy need a doctor? It's the sick who do. [32]I have not come to enlist the upright to change their hearts, but sinners."	[2]But Jesus overheard [them and said,] "Those who are he[althy don't need a doctor."]

61. A Controversy over Fasting

Mt 9:14–17	Mk 2:18–22	Lk 5:33–39	Th 104:1–3; 47:5, 4, 3
[14]Then the disciples of John come up to him, and ask, "Why do we fast, and the Pharisees fast, but not your disciples?"	[18]John's disciples and the Pharisees had the custom of fasting, and they come and ask him, "Why do the disciples of John fast, and the disciples of the Pharisees, but your disciples don't?"	[33]They said to him, "The disciples of John are always fasting and offering prayers, and so are those of the Pharisees, but yours just eat and drink."	**Th 104:1–3** [1]They said to Jesus, "Come on, let's pray today, and let's fast." [2]Jesus said, "What sin have I committed, or how have I been undone?
[15]And Jesus said to them, "The groom's friends can't mourn as long as the groom is around, can they?	[19]And Jesus said to them, "The groom's friends can't fast while the groom is around, can they? So long as the groom is around, you can't expect them to fast.	[34]And Jesus said to them, "You can't make the groom's friends fast as long as the groom is around, can you?	
But the days will come when the groom is taken away from them, and then they will fast.	[20]But the days will come when the groom is taken away from them, and then they will fast, on that day.	[35]But the days will come when the groom is taken away from them, and then they will fast, in those days."	[3]When the groom leaves the wedding hall, then let people fast and pray."
		[36]He then gave them a proverb:	**Th 47:5, 4, 3**
[16]Nobody patches an old garment with a piece of unshrunken cloth, since the patch pulls away from the garment and creates a worse tear.	[21]Nobody sews a piece of unshrunk cloth on an old garment, otherwise the new, unshrunk patch pulls away from the old and creates a worse tear.	"Nobody tears a piece from a new garment and puts it on an old one, since the new one will tear and the piece from the new will not match the old.	[5]An old patch is not sewn onto a new garment, since it would create a tear.
[17]Nor do they pour new wine into old wineskins, otherwise the wineskins burst, the wine gushes out, and the wineskins are destroyed.	[22]And nobody pours new wine into old wineskins, otherwise the wine will burst the wineskins, and destroy both the wine and the wineskins.	[37]And nobody pours new wine into old wineskins, otherwise the new wine will burst the wineskins, it will gush out, and the wineskins will be destroyed.	[4]New wine is not poured into old wineskins, or they might break,
Instead, they put new wine in new wineskins and both are preserved."	Instead, ⟨put⟩ new wine into new wineskins."	[38]Instead, new wine must be put into new wineskins.	
			and aged wine is not poured into a new wineskin, or it might spoil.
		[39]Besides, nobody wants new wine after drinking aged wine. As they say, 'Aged wine is just fine!'"	[3]Nobody drinks aged wine and immediately wants to drink new wine.
9:18–26 #93, p. 72	2:23–28 #64, p. 52	6:1–5 #64, p. 52	

62. The Healing of Two Blind Men

Mt 9:27–31*	Mk	Lk
[27]And when Jesus left there, two blind men followed him, shouting, "Have mercy on us, son of David." [28]When Jesus arrived home, the blind men came to him. Jesus says to them, "Do you trust that I can do this?" They reply to him, "Yes, master." [29]Then he touched their eyes, saying, "Let it happen to you according to your trust."[30]And their eyes were opened. Then Jesus snapped at them, saying, "See that no one finds out about it." [31]But they went out and spread the news of him throughout that whole territory. 9:32–34 #69, p. 56		

* Ⓓ Mt 20:29–34 (#201, p. 152)

63. The Good Crop

Mt 9:35–38	Mk 6:6b, 34	Lk 8:1; 10:2	Th 73
[35]And Jesus went about all the towns and villages, teaching in their meeting places and proclaiming the gospel of the empire ⟨of Heaven⟩ and healing every disease and ailment. [36]When he saw the crowd, he was moved by them because they were beaten down and helpless, like sheep without a shepherd. [37]Then he said to his disciples, "The crop is good, but there are few to harvest it. [38]So beg the harvest boss to dispatch workers to the fields."* 10:1–4 #97, p. 78	[6b]And he used to go around the villages, teaching in a circuit. [34]When he came ashore, he saw a huge crowd and was moved by them, because they resembled sheep without a shepherd, and he started teaching them at length.	**Lk 8:1** And it came to pass soon afterward that he traveled through towns and villages, preaching and announcing the good news of the empire of God. The Twelve were with him, **Lk 10:2** [2]He would say to them, "The crop is good, but there are few to harvest it. So beg the harvest boss to dispatch workers to the fields.*	The crop is huge but the workers are few, so beg the boss to dispatch workers to the fields.*

* Jn 4:35 You have a saying: "It's still four months till harvest." But I'm telling you: look at the fields, they're ripe for harvesting. (#286, p. 233)

64. Picking Grain on the Sabbath

Mt 12:1–8	Mk 2:23–28	Lk 6:1–5
[1]On that occasion Jesus walked through the grainfields on the Sabbath. His disciples were hungry and began to strip heads of grain and chew them. [2]When the Pharisees saw this, they argued with him, "See here, your disciples are doing what's not permitted on the Sabbath."	[23]It so happened that he was making his way through the grainfields on the Sabbath, and his disciples began to strip heads of grain as they made their way. [24]And the Pharisees started to argue with him: "See here, why are they doing what's not permitted on the Sabbath?"	[1]It came to pass that he was walking through grainfields on a Sabbath, and his disciples would strip some heads of grain, husk them in their hands, and chew them. [2]Some of the Pharisees said, "Why are you doing what's not permitted on the Sabbath?"
[3]He said to them, "I guess you don't recall what David did when he and his companions were hungry. [4]He went into the house of God, and ate the consecrated bread, which no one is permitted to eat—not even David or his companions—except the priests alone! [5]Or haven't you read in the Law that during the Sabbath the priests violate the Sabbath in the temple and are held blameless? [6]Yet I say to you, someone greater than the temple is here. [7]And if you had known what this means, 'It's mercy I desire instead of sacrifice,' you would not have condemned those who are blameless.	[25]And he says to them: "I guess you don't recall what David did when he found it necessary, when both he and his companions were hungry. [26]He went into the house of God, when Abiathar was chief priest,[a] and ate the consecrated bread, and even gave some to his men to eat. No one is permitted to eat this bread, except the priests."	[3]And Jesus answered them, "I guess you don't recall what David did when he and his companions were hungry. [4]He went into the house of God, took and ate the consecrated bread himself, and gave some to his men to eat. No one is permitted to eat this bread except the priests alone."
	[27]And he continued, "The Sabbath was created for human beings, not human beings for the Sabbath.	[5]And he used to say to them,
[8]Remember, the Human One is master of the Sabbath."	[28]So, the Human One is master even of the Sabbath."	"The Human One is master of the Sabbath."

[a] Mk 2:26 Some mss omit *when Abiathar was chief priest* (see 1 Sam 21:1–7).

65. Healing on the Sabbath

Mt 12:9–14	Mk 3:1–6	Lk 6:6–11
[9]And when he had moved on, he went into their meeting place. [10]Just then a man with a crippled hand appeared, and they asked him, "Is it permitted to heal on the Sabbath?" so they could discredit him.*	[1]Then he went back to the meeting place, and a man with a crippled hand was there. [2]So they kept an eye on him, to see whether he would heal the man on the Sabbath, so they could denounce him.	[6]On another Sabbath it came to pass that he entered the meeting place and taught. A man was there whose right hand was crippled. [7]And the scholars and the Pharisees watched him carefully, to see if he would heal on the Sabbath, so they could find some excuse to denounce him. [8]However, he knew their motives,
[11]He asked them, "If you had only a single sheep, and it fell into a ditch on the Sabbath, wouldn't you grab it and pull it out? [12]A person is worth way more than a sheep. So, it is permitted to do good on the Sabbath!"		14:5
	[3]And he says to the man with the crippled hand, "Get up here in front of everybody." [4]Then he says to them, "On the Sabbath is it permitted to do good or to do evil, to save life or to kill?" But they remained silent. [5]And looking right at them with outrage, exasperated at their closed mindedness, he says to the man, "Hold out your hand."	and he said to the man with the crippled hand, "Get up and stand here in front of everybody." And he got to his feet and stood there. [9]Then Jesus said to them, "Let me ask you: on the Sabbath is it permitted to do good or to do evil, to save life or to destroy it?" [10]And he looked right at all of them, and said to him, "Hold out your hand!"
[13]Then he says to the man, "Hold out your hand!" He held it out and it was restored to health like the other. [14]The Pharisees went out and hatched a plot against him to destroy him.	He held it out and his hand was restored. [6]Then the Pharisees left immediately with the Herodians and hatched a plot against him, to destroy him.	He did and his hand was restored. [11]But they were filled with rage and discussed among themselves what to do with Jesus.
		6:12–16 #67, p. 55

*Lk 14:3 (#172, p. 131)

66. Jesus draws a huge crowd

Mt 12:15–21	Mk 3:7–12	Lk 6:17–19; 4:41
		Lk 6:17–19
15Aware of this, Jesus withdrew from there, and huge crowds followed him, and he healed all of them.	7Then Jesus withdrew with his disciples to the sea, and a huge crowd from Galilee followed. When they heard what he was doing, a huge crowd from Judea, 8and from Jerusalem and Idumea and across the Jordan, and from around Tyre and Sidon, collected around him. 9And he told his disciples to have a small boat ready for him on account of the crowd, so they wouldn't mob him. (10You see, he had healed so many that all who had diseases were pushing forward to touch him.)*	17On the way down with them, Jesus stopped at a level place. There was a huge crowd of his disciples and a great throng of people from all Judea and Jerusalem and the coast of Tyre and Sidon.
4:25		18They came to hear him and to be healed of their diseases. Those who were tormented by unclean spirits were cured. 19And everyone in the crowd tried to touch him, since power would flow out from him and heal them all.
	11The unclean spirits also, whenever they faced him, would kneel before him and shout out, "You son of God, you!" 12But he always warned them not to tell who he was.	**Lk 4:41** Demons would also come out of many of them screaming, and saying, "You son of God, you!" But he would rebuke them and not allow them to speak, because they knew that he was the Anointed One.
16And he warned them not to disclose his identity, 17in order to fulfill the prediction spoken through Isaiah the prophet: 18Here is my servant whom I have selected, the one I love, of whom I fully approve. I will put my spirit upon him, and he will announce judgment for gentiles. 19He will not be contentious, nor loud-mouthed, nor will anyone hear his voice on the streets. 20He is not about to break a crushed reed, and he's not one to snuff out a smoldering wick, until he brings forth a decisive victory, 21and gentiles put their hope in his name.		
12:22–24 #69, p. 56		

* Mt 14:36 / Mk 6:56 (#109, p. 90)

67. Jesus selects the Twelve

Mt 10:1–4	Mk 3:13–19	Lk 6:12–16
[1]And summoning his twelve disciples he gave them authority to drive out unclean spirits and to heal every disease and every ailment. [2]The names of the twelve apostles were these: first, Simon, also known as Rock (⟨Peter⟩), and Andrew his brother, and James the son of Zebedee and John his brother,	[13]Then he goes up on the mountain and summons those he wanted, and they came to him. [14]He formed a group of twelve[a] to be his companions, and to be sent out to preach, [15]and to have authority to drive out demons.* [16]And to Simon he gave the nickname Rock (⟨Peter⟩), [17]and to James, the son of Zebedee, and to John, his brother, he also gave a nickname, Boanerges (which means "Sons of Thunder"); [18]and	[12]During that time it came to pass that he went out to the mountain to pray, and spent the night in prayer to God. [13]The next day, he called his disciples and selected twelve of them, whom he named apostles: [14]Simon, whom he nicknamed Rock (⟨Peter⟩), and Andrew his brother, and James and John,
[3]Philip and Bartholomew, Thomas, and Matthew the toll collector, James the son of Alphaeus, and Thaddaeus,[b] [4]Simon the Zealot, and Judas of Iscariot, the one who, in the end, turned him in.	Andrew and Philip and Bartholomew and Matthew and Thomas and James, the son of Alphaeus; and Thaddeus and Simon the Zealot; [19]and Judas Iscariot, who, in the end, turned him in.	and Philip, and Bartholomew, [15]and Matthew, and Thomas, and James the son of Alphaeus, and Simon who was called the Zealot, [16]and Judas the son of James, and Judas Iscariot, who turned traitor.
10:5–15 #98, p. 79		6:17–19 #66, p. 54

* Ⓓ Mk 6:7 / Lk 9:1–2 (#96, p. 77)

[a] Mk 3:14 Some mss insert "whom he also named apostles" after *twelve*.
[b] Mt 10:3 A few mss have "Lebbaeus" instead of *Thaddaeus*. Many mss have "Lebbaeus who is called Thaddaeus."

68. Jesus' Family Troubles

Mt	Mk 3:20–21	Lk
	[20]Then he goes home, and once again a crowd gathers, so they couldn't even have a meal. [21]When his relatives heard about it, they came to take him away. (You see, they thought he was out of his mind.)	

69. With the Power of Beelzebul
SEE #373, P. 304

Mt 12:22–24	Mt 9:32–34	Mk 3:22	Lk 11:14–15
[22]Then they brought to him a blind and mute person who was demon-possessed, and he cured him so the mute could both speak and to see. [23]And the entire crowd was beside itself and was saying, "This man can't be the son of David, can he?" [24]But when the Pharisees heard of it, they said, "This guy drives out demons only with the power of Beelzebul, the head demon."	[32]Just as they were leaving, they brought to him a mute who was demon-possessed. [33]And after the demon had been driven out, the mute started to speak. And the crowd was amazed and said, "Nothing like this has ever been seen in Israel." [34]But the Pharisees would say, "He drives out demons with the power of the head demon."[a]	And the scholars who had come down from Jerusalem would say, "He is possessed by Beelzebul" and "He drives out demons with the power of the head demon."	[14]Jesus was driving out a demon that was mute, and when the demon had departed the mute man spoke. And the crowds were amazed. [15]But some of them said, "He drives out demons with the power of Beelzebul, the head demon."
12:25–28 #71, p. 57		3:23–26 #71, p. 57	11:16–20 #71, p. 57

[a] Mt 9:34 A few mss omit this verse.

70. Like Sheep without a Shepherd
SEE #366, P. 299

Mt 9:35–38	Mk 6:6b, 34	Lk 8:1a; 10:2	Th 73
[35]And Jesus went about all the towns and villages, teaching in their meeting places and proclaiming the gospel of the empire ⟨of Heaven⟩ and healing every disease and ailment. [36]When he saw the crowd, he was moved by them because they were beaten down and helpless, like sheep without a shepherd. [37]Then he said to his disciples, "The crop is good, but there are few to harvest it. [38]So beg the harvest boss to dispatch workers to the fields."	[6b]And he used to go around the villages, teaching in a circuit. [34]When he came ashore, he saw a huge crowd and was moved by them, because they resembled sheep without a shepherd, and he started teaching them at length.	**Lk 8:1a** And it came to pass soon afterward that he traveled through towns and villages, preaching and announcing the good news of the empire of God. **Lk 10:2** [2]He would say to them, "The crop is good, but there are few to harvest it. So beg the harvest boss to dispatch workers to the fields."	The crop is huge but the workers are few, so beg the boss to dispatch workers to the fields.
10:1–4 #97, p. 78			

71. A Divided Empire
SEE #373, P. 304

Mt 12:25–28	Mk 3:23–26	Lk 11:16–20
16:1	8:11	[16]Others were putting him to the test by demanding a sign from heaven. [17]But he knew what they were thinking, and said to them,
[25]But he knew how they thought, and said to them,	[23]And after calling them over, he would speak to them in riddles: "How can Satan drive out Satan? [24]After all, if an empire is divided against itself, that empire cannot survive. [25]And if a household is divided against itself, that household won't be able to survive. [26]So if Satan rebels against himself and is divided, he cannot endure but is doomed."	
"Every empire divided against itself is devastated, and no town or household divided against itself can survive. [26]So if Satan drives out Satan, he is divided against himself. In that case, how can his empire survive? [27]Suppose I do drive out demons with the power of Beelzebul, then with whose power do your own people drive ⟨them⟩ out? That's why they will be your judges. [28]But if I drive out demons with the spirit of God, then the empire of God has come for you."		"Every empire divided against itself is devastated, and a house divided against a house falls. [18]If Satan is divided against himself—since you claim I drive out demons with Beelzebul's power—how will his empire survive? [19]Suppose I do drive out demons with the power of Beelzebul, then with whose power do your own people drive ⟨them⟩ out? That's why they will be your judges. [20]But if I drive out demons with the finger of God, then the empire of God has come for you."

72. Plundering a Strong Man's House
SEE #373, P. 304

Mt 12:29–30	Mk 3:27	Lk 11:21–23	Th 35:1–2
[29]Or how can anyone enter a strong man's house and plunder his belongings, unless he first ties him up? Only then does he plunder his house.	No one can enter a strong man's house to plunder his belongings unless he first ties him up. Only then does he plunder his house.	[21]When a strong man is fully armed and guards his courtyard, his possessions are safe. [22]But when a stronger man attacks and overpowers him, he takes away the weapons on which he was relying and divides up his loot.	[1]You can't enter a strong man's house and take it by force without tying his hands. [2]Then you can loot his house.
[30]Those who aren't with me are against me, and those who don't gather with me scatter.*		[23]Those who aren't with me are against me, and those who don't gather with me scatter.*	
		11:24–26 #148, p. 118	

* Mk 9:40 / Lk 9:50b (#129, p. 108)

73. Blaspheming the Holy Spirit
SEE #383, P. 311

Mt 12:31–32	Mk 3:28–30	Lk 12:10	Th 44:1–3
[31]That's why I tell you: every offense and blasphemy will be forgiven humankind,	[28]Let me tell you: all offenses and whatever blasphemies humankind might blaspheme will be forgiven them.		[1]Whoever blasphemes against the Father will be forgiven,
but the blasphemy of the spirit won't be forgiven. [32]And the one who speaks a word against the Human One will be forgiven; but the one who speaks a word against the holy spirit won't be forgiven, neither in this age nor in the age to come.	[29]But whoever blasphemes against the holy spirit is never forgiven, but is guilty of an eternal sin"—[30]because they were saying, "He is possessed by an unclean spirit."	And everyone who utters a word against the Human One will be forgiven; but whoever blasphemes against the holy spirit won't be forgiven.	[2]and whoever blasphemes against the son will be forgiven, [3]but whoever blasphemes against the holy spirit will not be forgiven, either on earth or in heaven.
	3:31–35 #75, p. 60	12:11–12 #157, p. 124	

74. Trees and Fruits

SEE #359, P. 293

Mt 12:33–37	Mt 7:16–20	Mk	Lk 6:44, 43, 45	Th 45:1–3
[33]If you make the tree choice, its fruit will be choice; if you make the tree rotten, its fruit will be rotten.				
	[16]You'll know who they are by what they produce. Since when do people pick grapes from thorns or figs from thistles? [17]Every healthy tree produces choice fruit, but the rotten tree produces spoiled fruit. [18]A healthy tree cannot produce spoiled fruit, any more than a rotten tree can produce choice fruit. [19]Every tree that does not produce choice fruit gets cut down and tossed on the fire. [20]Remember, you'll know who they are by what they produce.		[44]Each tree is known by its fruit. Figs are not gathered from thorns, nor are grapes picked from brambles. [43]A choice tree does not produce rotten fruit, any more than a rotten tree produces choice fruit;	[1]Grapes are not harvested from thorn trees, nor are figs gathered from thistles, for they yield no fruit.
After all, the tree is known by its fruit. [34]You spawn of Satan, how can your speech be good when you are evil? As you know, the mouth gives voice to what the heart is full of. [35]The good person produces good things out of a fund of good; and the evil person produces evil things out of a fund of evil. [36]Let me tell you, on judgment day people will have to account for every thoughtless word they utter. [37]Your own words will vindicate you, and your own words will condemn you.			[45]The good person produces good from the fund of good in the heart, and the evil person produces evil from the evil within. As you know, the mouth gives voice to what the heart is full of.	[2]Good persons produce good from what they've stored up; [3]bad persons produce evil from the wickedness they've stored up in their hearts, and say evil things. For from the overflow of the heart comes evil.
12:38–42 #150, p. 119	7:21–23 #40, p. 32		6:46 #48, p. 39	

75. Jesus' True Family

Mt 12:46–50	Mk 3:31–35	Lk 8:19–21	Th 99:1–3
[46]While he was still speaking to the crowds, his mother and brothers showed up outside; they had come to speak to him. [47]Someone said to him, "Look, your mother and your brothers are outside and they want to speak to you."[a]	[31]Then his mother and his brothers arrive. While still outside, they send in and ask for him. [32]A crowd was sitting around him, and they say to him, "Look, your mother and your brothers are outside looking for you."	[19]Then his mother and his brothers came to see him, but they could not reach him because of the crowd. [20]When he was told, "Your mother and your brothers are outside and want to see you,"	[1]The disciples said to him, "Your brothers and your mother are standing outside."
[48]In response he said to the one speaking to him, "Who is my mother and who are my brothers?"	[33]In response he says to them, "Who are my mother and brothers?"		
[49]And he pointed to his disciples and said, "Here are my mother and my brothers. [50]For whoever does the will of my Father in heaven, that's my brother and sister and mother."*	[34]And looking right at those seated around him in a circle, he says, "Here are my mother and my brothers. [35]Whoever does God's will, that's my brother and sister and mother."*	[21]he replied to them, "My mother and my brothers are those who listen to God's message and do it."*	[2]He said to them, "Those here who do what my Father wants are my brothers and my mother. [3]They're the ones who will enter my Father's empire."
		8:22–25 #91, p. 69	

*GHeb 4a My mother, the holy spirit, took me by one of my hairs and brought me to Tabor, the great mountain. (#516, p. 392)

———

[a] Mt 12:47 Many mss lack v. 47.

76. The Parable of the Sower

Mt 13:1–9	Mk 4:1–9	Lk 8:4–8	Th 9:1–5
[1]That same day, Jesus left the house and sat beside the sea. [2]Huge crowds gathered around him, so he climbed into a boat and sat down, while the entire crowd stood on the sea shore. [3]He told them many things in parables:	[1]Once again he started to teach beside the sea. An enormous crowd gathers around him, so he climbs into a boat and sits there on the water facing the huge crowd on the shore. [2]He would then teach them many things in parables. In the course of his teaching he would tell them:	[4]Since a huge crowd was now gathering, and people were making their way to him from town after town, 5:1–3 he told them some such parable as this:	
This sower went out to sow. [4]While he was sowing, some seed fell along the path, and the birds came and devoured it. [5]Other seed fell on rocky ground where there wasn't much soil, and it came up right away because the soil had no depth. [6]When the sun came up it was scorched, and because it had no roots it withered. [7]Still other seed fell among thorns, and the thorns came up and choked them.	[3]Listen to this! This sower went out to sow. [4]While he was sowing, some seed fell along the path, and the birds came and devoured it. [5]Other seed fell on rocky ground where there wasn't much soil, and it came up right away because the soil had no depth. [6]But when the sun came up it was scorched, and because it had no root it withered. [7]Still other seed fell among thorns, and the thorns came up and choked it, so that it produced no fruit. [8]Finally, some seed fell on good soil and started producing fruit. The seed sprouted and grew: one part had a yield of thirty, another part sixty, and a third part one hundred.	[5]A sower went out to sow his seed; and while he was sowing, some seed fell along the path, and was trampled under foot, and the birds of the sky devoured it. [6]Other seed fell on the rock; when it grew, it withered because it lacked moisture. [7]Still other seed fell among thorns; the thorns grew with it and choked it.	[1]Look, the sower went out, took a handful ⟨of seeds⟩, and scattered ⟨them⟩. [2]Some fell on the road, and the birds came and gathered them. [3]Others fell on rock, and they didn't take root in the soil and didn't produce heads of grain. [4]Others fell on thorns, and they choked the seeds and worms ate them.
[8]Other seed fell on good soil and started producing fruit: one part had a yield of one hundred, another a yield of sixty, and a third a yield of thirty.		[8]Other seed fell on fertile soil; and when it matured, it produced fruit a hundredfold.	[5]And others fell on good soil, and it produced a good crop: it yielded sixty per measure and one hundred twenty per measure.
[9]Anyone here with ears, use 'em!*	[9]And he would say, "Anyone here with two good ears, use 'em!"*	During his discourse, he would call out, "Anyone here with two good ears, use 'em!"*	

*Mt 11:15; 13:43b; Mk 4:23; Lk 14:35b; Th 8:4; 21:10; 24:2; 63:4; 65:8; 96:3

77. The Strategy of Parables

SEE #310, P. 249

Mt 13:10–17	Mk 4:10–12	Lk 8:9–10; 10:23–24	Jn
[10]And his disciples came up and said to him, "Why do you instruct them only in parables?" [11]In response he said to them, "You've been given the privilege of knowing the secrets of the empire of Heaven, but that privilege has not been granted to anyone else. [12]In fact, to those who have, more will be given, and then some; and from those who don't have, even what they do have will be taken away. [13]That is why I tell them parables, because "When they look they don't really see and when they listen they don't really hear or understand." [14]Moreover, in them the prophecy of Isaiah is fulfilled, the one which says, "You listen closely, yet you won't ever understand, and you look intently but won't ever see. [15]For the mind of this people has grown dull, and their ears are hard of hearing, and they have shut their eyes, otherwise they might actually see with their eyes, and hear with their ears, and understand with their minds, and turn around and I would heal them." [16]How privileged are your eyes because they see, and your ears because they hear. [17]Let me tell you, many prophets and just persons longed to see what you see and never saw it, and to hear what you hear and never heard it.	[10]Whenever he went off by himself, those close to him, together with the Twelve, would ask him about the parables. [11]And he would say to them: "You have been given the secret of the empire of God; but to those outside everything is presented in parables, 4:25 [12]so that "They may look with eyes wide open but never quite see, and may listen with ears attuned but never quite understand, otherwise they might turn around and find forgiveness.	**Lk 8:9–10** [9]His disciples asked him what this parable was all about. [10]He replied, "You have been given the privilege of knowing the secrets of the empire of God; but the rest get only parables, 8:18 so that "They may look but not see, listen but not understand." **Lk 10:23–24** [23]Turning to the disciples he said privately, "How privileged are the eyes that see what you see! [24]I'm telling you, many prophets and kings wanted to see what you see, and never saw it, and to hear what you hear, and never heard it." 10:25–28 #144, p. 116	 12:40a 12:40b

78. The Interpretation of the Parable of the Sower

Mt 13:18–23	Mk 4:13–20	Lk 8:11–15
[18]You there, pay attention to the interpretation of the sower. [19]When anyone listens to the message of the empire of ⟨Heaven⟩ and does not understand it, the evil one comes and steals away what was sown in the heart: this is the one who is sown 'along the path.'	[13]Then he says to them: "You don't get this parable, so how are you going to understand other parables? [14]The 'sower' is 'sowing' the message. [15]The first group are the ones 'along the path': here the message 'is sown,' but when they hear, right away Satan comes and steals the message that has been 'sown' into them.	[11]Now this is the interpretation of the parable. The 'seed' is God's message. [12]Those 'along the path' are those who have listened to it, but then the devil comes and steals the message from their hearts, so they won't trust and be saved.
[20]The one who is sown 'on rocky ground' is the one who listens to the message and right away receives it happily. [21]However, this one lacks its own 'root' and so is short-lived. When tribulation or persecution comes because of the message, right away that person is brought down. [22]And the one sown 'into the thorns' is the one who listens to the message, but the worries of the age and the seductiveness of wealth 'choke' the message and it becomes 'fruitless.'	[16]The second group are the ones sown 'on rocky ground.' Whenever they listen to the message, right away they receive it happily. [17]Yet they do not have their own 'root' and so are short-lived. When tribulation or persecution comes because of the message, right away they are brought down. [18]And the third group are those sown 'among the thorns.' These are the ones who have listened to the message, [19]but the worries of the age and the seductiveness of wealth and the yearning for everything else come and 'choke' the message and they become 'fruitless.' [20]And the final group are the ones sown 'on good soil.' They are the ones who listen to the message and take it in and 'bear fruit, here thirty, there sixty, and there one hundred.'	[13]Those 'on the rock' are those who, when they listen to the message, receive it happily. But they 'have no root,' they trust for the moment but fall away when they are tested. [14]What 'fell into the thorns' represents those who listen, but as they continue on, they are 'choked' by the worries and wealth and pleasures of life, and they do not come to maturity.
[23]The one who is sown 'on the good soil' is the one who listens to the message and understands, who really 'bears fruit and yields here a hundred, there sixty, and there thirty.'		[15]But the seed 'in good soil' stands for those who listen to the message and hold on to it with a good and fertile heart, and 'bear fruit' through perseverance.
13:24–30 #82, p. 66		

79. Lamps go on lampstands
SEE #376, 381, 417–18 PP. 307, 310, 332

Mt 5:15; 10:26	Mk 4:21–23	Lk 8:16–17; 11:33; 12:2	Th 33:2–3; 5:2; 6:5–6
Mt 5:15 Nor do people light a lamp and put it under a bushel basket, but instead on a lamp-stand, where it sheds light for everyone in the house.	[21]And he was saying to them, "Since when is the lamp brought in to be put under the bushel basket or under the bed? It's put on the lamp-stand, isn't it?	**Lk 8:16–17** [16]No one lights a lamp and covers it with a pot or puts it under a bed; instead, one puts it on a lampstand, so that those who come in can see the light.	**Th 33:2–3** [2]No one lights a lamp and puts it under a basket, nor does one put it in a hidden place. [3]Rather, one puts it on a lampstand so that all who come and go will see its light.
	[22]After all, there is nothing hidden except to be brought to light, nor anything kept secret that won't be exposed.	[17]After all, there is nothing hidden that won't be brought to light, nor kept secret that won't be made known and exposed.	**Th 5:2 (6:5)** After all, there's nothing hidden that won't be revealed.
	[23]If anyone here has two good ears, use 'em!*	**Lk 11:33** No one lights a lamp and then puts it in a cellar or under a bushel basket, but instead on a lampstand so that those who come in can see the light.	
5:15	v. 21		33:2–3
Mt 10:26 So don't be afraid of them. After all, there is nothing covered up that won't be exposed, or hidden that won't be made known.	v. 22	**Lk 12:2** There is nothing covered up that won't be exposed, or hidden that won't be made known.	**Th 6:5–6 (5:2)** [5]After all, there's nothing hidden that won't be revealed, [6]and there's nothing covered up that will remain undis-closed.

*Mt 11:15; 13:9; 13:43b; Mk 4:9; Lk 8:8b; 14:35b; Th 8:4; 21:10; 24:2; 63:4; 65:8; 96:3

80. Reciprocal Standards

Mt 7:2; 13:12; 25:29	Mk 4:24–25	Lk 6:38; 8:18; 19:26	Th 41:1–2
	[24]And he went on to say to them,	**Lk 6:38** Give, and it'll be given to you: they'll put in your lap a full measure, packed down, sifted, and overflowing.	
Mt 7:2 Don't forget, the judgment you hand out will be the judgment you get back. And the standard you apply will be the standard applied to you.	Pay attention to what you hear! The standard you apply will be the standard applied to you, and then some.	For the standard you apply will be the standard applied to you. **Lk 8:18** So pay attention to how you're listening;	
Mt 13:12 In fact, to those who have, more will be given, and then some; and from those who don't have, even what they do have will be taken away. **Mt 25:29** In fact, to everyone who has, more will be given and then some; and from those who don't have, even what they do have will be taken away.	[25]In fact, to those who have, more will be given, and from those who don't have, even what they do have will be taken away!	in fact, to those who have, more will be given, and from those who don't have, even what they seem to have will be taken away. **Lk 19:26** I'm telling you, to everyone who has, more will be given; and from those who don't have, even what they do have will be taken away.	[1]Those who have something in hand will be given more, [2]and those who have nothing will be deprived of even the little they have.

81. The Parable of the Seed Growing by Itself

Mt	Mk 4:26–29	Lk	Th 21:9
	[26]And he was saying, "The empire of God is like this: suppose someone sows seed on the ground, [27]and sleeps and rises night and day, and the seed sprouts and matures, although the sower is unaware of it. [28]The earth produces fruit on its own, first a shoot, then a head, then mature grain on the head. [29]But when the grain ripens, right away he sends for the sickle, because it's harvest time. 4:30–32 #83, p. 66		When the crop ripened, he came quickly carrying a sickle and harvested it.

82. The Parable of the Weeds and the Wheat

Mt 13:24–30	Mk	Lk	Th 57:1–4
[24]He spun out another parable for them: The empire of Heaven is like someone who sowed good seed in his field. [25]And while everyone was asleep, his enemy came and scattered weed seed around in his wheat and stole away. [26]And when the crop sprouted and produced grain, then the weeds also appeared. [27]The owner's slaves came and asked him, "Master, didn't you sow good seed in your field? Then why are there weeds every-where?" [28]He replied to them, "Some enemy has done this." The slaves said to him, "So do you want us to go and pull the weeds?" [29]He replied, "No, otherwise you'll uproot the wheat at the same time as you pull the weeds. [30]Let them grow up together until the harvest, and at harvest time I'll say to the harvesters, 'Gather the weeds first and bind them in bundles for burning, but gather the wheat into my granary.'"			[1]The Father's empire is like someone who had [good] seed.

[2]His enemy came during the night and sowed weeds among the good seed.

[3]The man did not let the ⟨workers⟩ pull up the weeds, but said to them, "Don't, or else you might go to pull up the weeds and pull up the wheat along with them."
[4]For on the day of the harvest the weeds will be conspicuous, and will be pulled up and burned. |

83. The Parable of the Mustard

SEE #391, P. 316

Mt 13:31–32	Mk 4:30–32	Lk 13:18–19	Th 20:1–4
[31]He put another parable be-fore them with these words: The empire of Heaven is

like a mustard seed that a man took and sowed in his field.
[32]Though it is the smallest of all seeds,
when it grows up, it is the largest of garden plants, and becomes a tree,
so that the birds of the sky come and roost in its branches. | [30]And he was saying:

To what should we compare the empire of God, or what parable should we use for it?
[31]Think about the mustard seed: when it is sown on the ground, though it is the smallest of all the seeds on the earth, [32]—yet when it is sown, it comes up, and becomes the biggest of all garden plants, and produces branches,
so that the birds of the sky can nest in its shade.

4:33–34 #85, p. 67 | [18]Then he was saying,

What is the empire of God like? What does it remind me of?
[19]It's like a mustard seed that a man took and tossed into his garden.

It grew and

became a tree,
and the birds of the sky roosted in its branches. | [1]The disciples said to Jesus,

"Tell us what Heaven's empire is like."
[2]He said to them,
It's like a mustard seed. [3]⟨It's⟩ the smallest of all seeds, [4]but when it falls on prepared soil,

it produces a large branch and becomes a shelter for birds of the sky. |

84. The Parable of the Leaven

SEE #392, P. 317

Mt 13:33	Mk	Lk 13:20–21	Th 96:1–3
He told them another parable: The empire of Heaven is like leaven that a woman took and concealed in fifty pounds of flour until it was all leavened.		[20]He continued, What does the empire of God remind me of? [21]It's like leaven that a woman took and concealed in fifty pounds of flour until it was all leavened. 13:22–27 #168, p. 129	[1]The Father's empire is like [a] woman [2]who took a little leaven, [hid] it in dough, and made it into large loaves of bread. [3]Whoever has ears to hear should listen.*

* Mt 11:15; 13:9; 13:43b; Mk 4:9; 4:23; Lk 8:8b; 14:35b; Th 8:4; 21:10; 24:2; 63:4; 65:8

85. Only in Parables

Mt 13:34–35	Mk 4:33–34	Lk
[34]Jesus spoke all these things to the crowds in parables. And he would not say anything to them except by way of parable, [35]in order to fulfill the prediction spoken through the prophet:[a] "I will open my mouth in parables, I will utter secrets kept since the foundation of the world."[b]	[33]And with the help of many such parables he would speak his message to them according to their ability to comprehend. [34]Yet he would not say anything to them except by way of parable, but would explain everything in private to his own disciples. 4:35–41 #91, p. 69	

[a] Mt 13:35 A few mss have supplied the prophet Isaiah's name.
[b] Mt 13:35 Some mss do not have *of the world*.

86. The Explanation of the Parable of the Weeds and the Wheat

Mt 13:36–43	Mk	Lk
[36]Then he left the crowds and went into the house. His disciples came to him with this request: "Explain the parable about the weeds in the field to us." [37]This was his response: "The one who 'sows the good seed' is the Human One. [38]'The field' is the world and 'the good seed' are children of the empire ⟨of Heaven⟩, but 'the weeds' represent children of the evil one. [39]'The enemy' who sows ⟨the weeds⟩ is the devil, and 'the harvest' is the end of the present age; 'the harvesters' are the heavenly messengers. [40]Just as the weeds are gathered and destroyed by fire—that's how it will be at the end of the age. [41]The Human One will send his messengers and they will gather all the traps and the subverters of the Law out of his empire [42]and throw them into the fiery furnace. People in that place will weep and grind their teeth. [43]Then the virtuous will shine like the sun in my Father's empire. Anyone here with ears, use 'em!*		

* Mt 11:15; 13:9; Mk 4:9; 4:23; Lk 8:8b; 14:35b; Th 8:4; 21:10; 24:2; 63:4; 65:8; 96:3

87. The Parable of the Treasure

Mt 13:44	Mk	Lk	Th 109:1–3
The empire of Heaven is like treasure hidden in a field. When someone finds it, that person covers it up again, and out of sheer joy goes and sells every last possession and buys that field.			[1]The ⟨Father's⟩ empire is like a man who had a treasure in his field but didn't know it. [2]And [when] he died he left it to his [son]. The son [did] not know ⟨about it either⟩. He took over the field and sold it. [3]The buyer went plowing, [discovered] the treasure, and began to lend money at interest to whomever he wished.

88. The Parable of the Pearl

Mt 13:45–46	Mk	Lk	Th 76:1–2
[45]Again, the empire of Heaven is like some merchant looking for beautiful pearls. [46]When he finds one priceless pearl, he sells everything he owns and buys it.			[1]The Father's empire is like a merchant who had a supply of merchandise and then found a pearl. [2]That merchant was prudent; he sold the merchandise and bought the single pearl for himself.

89. The Parable of the Fishnet

Mt 13:47–50	Mk	Lk	Th 8:1–4
[47]The empire of Heaven is like a net that is cast into the sea and catches all kinds of fish. [48]When the net is full, they haul it ashore. Then they sit down and collect the good fish into baskets, but the worthless fish they throw away. [49]This is how the present age will end. God's messengers will go out and separate the evil from the just [50]and throw the evil into the fiery furnace. People in that place will weep and grind their teeth.			[1]The human being is like a wise fisherman who cast his net into the sea and drew it up from the sea full of little fish. [2]Among them the wise fisherman discovered a fine large fish. [3]He threw all the little fish back into the sea, and easily chose the large fish. [4]Whoever has ears to hear should listen.*

*Mt 11:15; 13:9; 13:43b; Mk 4:9; 4:23; Lk 8:8b; 14:35b; Th 21:10; 24:2; 63:4; 65:8; 96:3

90. Treasures Old and New

Mt 13:51–53	Mk	Lk
[51]"Do you understand all these things?" "Of course," they replied. [52]He said to them, "That's why every scholar who is schooled in the empire of Heaven is like some proprietor who produces from his storeroom treasures old and new." [53]And so it happened that, when Jesus had finished these parables, he moved on from there. 13:53–58 #95, p. 75		

91. Jesus calms a storm

Mt 8:18, 23–27	Mk 4:35–41	Lk 8:22–25
[18]When Jesus saw the crowds[a] around him, he gave orders to cross over to the other side. [23]When he got into a boat, his disciples followed him. [24]And just then a powerful earthquake hit the sea, so that the boat was swamped by the waves; but he was asleep. [25]And they went and woke him up, and said to him, "Master, save us! We're sinking!" [26]He says to them, "Why are you such cowards, you with your meager trust?" Then he got up and rebuked the winds and the sea, and there was a great calm. [27]And everyone was astounded, saying, "What kind of person is this? Even the winds and the sea obey him." 8:19–22 #137, p. 112	[35]Later in the day, when evening had come, he says to them, "Let's go across to the other side." [36]After sending the crowd away, they took him along since he was in the boat, and other boats accompanied him. [37]Then a great squall comes up and the waves begin to pound against the boat, so that the boat suddenly began to fill up. [38]He was in the stern, sleeping on a cushion. And they wake him up and say to him, "Teacher, don't you care? We're sinking!" [39]Then he got up and rebuked the wind and said to the sea, "Be quiet, shut up!" The wind then died down and there was a great calm. [40]He said to them, "Why are you such cowards? You still don't trust, do you?" [41]And they were completely terrified and would say to one another, "Who in the world is this? Even the wind and the sea obey him."	[22]It came to pass that Jesus and his disciples got into a boat, and he said to them, "Let's cross to the other side of the lake." So they shoved off, [23]and as they sailed he fell asleep. A squall descended on the lake; they were being swamped and were in serious danger. [24]And they went and woke him up, saying, "Master, master, we're sinking!" He got up and rebuked the wind and the rough water; and they settled down, and there was a calm. [25]Then he said to them, "Where is your trust?" Although they were terrified, they were astounded, saying to one another, "Who in the world is this? He commands even winds and water and they obey him?"

[a] Mt 8:18 Most mss report that "huge" *crowds* surrounded Jesus.

92. The Possessed Man/Men at Gerasa/Gadara

Mt 8:28–34	Mk 5:1–20	Lk 8:26–39
[28]And when he came to the other side, to the region of the Gadarenes,[a] he was met by two people possessed by demons who came out from the tombs. They were so hard to deal with that no one could pass that way.	[1]And they came to the other side of the sea, to the region of the Gerasenes.[b] [2]And when he got out of the boat, right away a man possessed by an unclean spirit came from the tombs to meet him. [3]This man made his home in the tombs, and nobody was able to bind him, not even with a chain, [4]because, though he had often been bound with shackles and chains, he would break the shackles and pull the chains apart, and nobody could subdue him. [5]And day and night he would howl among the tombs and across the hills and keep bruising himself on the stones. [6]And when he saw Jesus from a distance, he ran up and knelt before him [7]and, screaming at the top of his voice, he says,	[26]They sailed to the region of the Gerasenes,[c] which lies directly across from Galilee. [27]As he stepped out on land, this man from the town who was possessed by demons met him. For quite some time he had been going without clothes and hadn't lived in a house but stayed in the tombs instead.
[29]And just then they screamed, "What do you want with us, you son of God? Did you come here ahead of time to torment us?"	"What do you want with me, Jesus, you son of the most high God? For God's sake, don't torment me!" [8]—because he had been saying to it, "Come out of this man, you filthy spirit!"	[28]When he saw Jesus, he screamed and knelt before him, and said at the top of his voice, "What do you want with me, Jesus, you son of the most high God? I beg you, don't torment me." ([29]You see, he had ordered the unclean spirit to get out of the man. The demon had taken control of him many times; the man had been kept under guard, bound with chains and shackles, but he would break the bonds and be driven by the demon into the desert.)
	[9]And Jesus started questioning him, "What's your name?" "My name is Legion," it says, "because there are many of us." [10]And it kept begging him over and over again not to expel them from their territory.	[30]Jesus questioned him: "What is your name?" "Legion," he said, because many demons had entered him. [31]They kept begging him not to order them to depart into the abyss.
[30]And a large herd of pigs was feeding off in the distance. [31]And the demons kept bargaining with him: "If you drive us out, send us into the herd of pigs." [32]And he said to them, "Get out ⟨of him⟩!" And they came out and went into the pigs, and suddenly the whole herd stampeded down the bluff into the sea and drowned in the water. [33]The herdsmen ran off and went into town and reported everything, especially about the possessed pair. [34]And what do you know, the whole town came out to meet Jesus.	[11]Now over there by the mountain a large herd of pigs was feeding. [12]And so they bargained with him, "Send us over to the pigs so we may enter them!" [13]And he agreed. And then the unclean spirits came out and entered the pigs, and the herd stampeded down the bluff into the sea, about two thousand of them, and drowned in the sea. [14]And the herdsmen ran off and reported it in town and out in the country. And they went out to see what had happened. [15]And they come to Jesus and	[32]Now over there a large herd of pigs was feeding on the mountain; and they bargained with him to let them enter those pigs. And he agreed. [33]Then the demons came out of the man and entered the pigs, and the herd stampeded down the bluff into the lake and was drowned. [34]When the herdsmen saw what had happened, they ran off and reported it in town and out in the country. [35]And people came out to see what had happened. They came to Jesus and found

And when they saw him, they begged him to move on from their district.

9:1–8 #59, p. 48

notice the demon possessed man sitting there with his clothes on and with his wits about him, the one who had harbored Legion, and they got scared. [16]And those who had seen told them what had happened to the possessed man, and all about the pigs. [17]And they started begging him to leave their region.

[18]And as Jesus was getting into the boat, the man who had been possessed kept pleading with him to let him come along. [19]And he would not let him, but says to him, "Go home to your people and tell them what the Lord has done for you—how he has shown mercy to you."

[20]And he went away and started spreading the news in the Ten Cities about what Jesus had done for him, and everybody would marvel.

the man from whom the demons had gone, sitting at Jesus' feet, with his clothes on and his wits about him; and they got scared. [36]Those who had seen it explained to them how the possessed man had been cured. [37]Then the entire populace of the Gerasene region asked him to leave them; for they were gripped by a great fear.

So he got into a boat and went back. [38]The man from whom the demons had departed begged to go with him; but he dismissed him, saying, [39]"Return home and tell the story of what God has done for you."

And he went his way, spreading the news throughout the whole town about what Jesus had done for him.

[a] Mt 8:28 Some mss spell the name of people in the region "Gerasenes," while other mss spell it "Gergesenes."

[b] Mk 5:1 Some mss read *Gerasenes,* others "Gadarenes" or "Gergesenes."

[c] Lk 8:26 Some mss read either "Gergesenes" or "Gadarenes."

93. Jesus heals a woman and revives a girl

Mt 9:18–26	Mk 5:21–43	Lk 8:40–56
	[21]When Jesus had again crossed over to the other side, a large crowd gathered around him, and he was beside the sea. [22]And one of the synagogue officials comes, Jairus by name, and as soon as he sees him, he kneels at his feet [23]and pleads with him and begs, "My little daughter is on the verge of death, so come and put your hands on her so she may be cured and live."	[40]Now when Jesus returned, the crowd welcomed him, for they were all waiting for him. [41]Just then a man named Jairus, a synagogue official, came up to Jesus. He knelt at Jesus' feet and begged him to come to his house, [42]because his only child, a twelve-year-old daughter, was dying.
[18]Just as he was saying these things to them, one of the officials came, kept bowing down to him, and said,		
"My daughter has just died. But come and put your hand on her and she will live." [19]And Jesus got up and followed him, along with his disciples.	[24]And Jesus set out with him. And a large crowd started following and shoving against him. [25]And there was a woman who had experienced a chronic flow of blood for twelve years, [26]who had endured much under many doctors, and who had spent everything she had, but hadn't been helped at all, but instead had gotten worse. [27]When she heard about Jesus, she came up from behind in the crowd and touched his cloak. ([28]You see, she was saying, "If I could just touch his clothes, I'll be cured.") [29]And right away her flow of blood stopped, and she sensed in her body that she was cured of her illness. [30]And right away, because Jesus realized that power had drained out of him, he turned around and started asking the crowd, "Who touched my clothes?"	As Jesus was walking along, the crowd milled around him. [43]A woman who had experienced a chronic flow of blood for twelve years,[a] and had found no one able to heal her,
[20]And just then a woman who had experienced a chronic flow of blood for twelve years		
came up from behind and touched the hem of his cloak. ([21]You see, she was saying to herself, "If I only touch his cloak, I'll be cured.")		[44]came up behind him, and touched the hem of his cloak.
		Immediately her flow of blood stopped.
	[31]And his disciples said to him, "You see the crowd jostling you around and you're asking, 'Who touched me?'" [32]And he started looking around to see who had done this. [33]Although the woman got scared and started trembling, realizing what had happened to her, she came and knelt before him and told him the whole truth.	[45]Then Jesus said, "Who touched me?" When everyone denied it, Peter said, "Master, the crowds are pressing in and jostling you!" [46]But Jesus insisted, "Someone touched me; I can tell that power has drained out of me." [47]And when the woman saw that she had not escaped notice, she came forward trembling, and knelt before him. In front of all the people she explained why she had touched him, and how she had been immediately healed.
[22]When Jesus turned around and saw her, he said, "Be brave, daughter, your trust has cured you." And the woman was cured right then and there.	[34]He said to her, "Daughter, your trust has cured you. Go in peace, and be healed of your affliction."	[48]Jesus said to her, "Daughter, your trust has cured you; go in peace."
	[35]While he was still speaking, the synagogue official's people approach and say, "Your daughter has died; why keep bothering the teacher?"	[49]While he is still speaking, someone from the synagogue official's house comes and says, "Your daughter is dead; don't bother the teacher further."

²³And when Jesus came into the home of the official and saw the mourners with their flutes, and the crowd making a disturbance, ²⁴he said,

"Go away; the girl hasn't died; she's sleeping."

And they started laughing at him. ²⁵When the crowd had been thrown out,

he came in and took the little girl by the hand and raised her up.

²⁶And news of this spread all around that region.

³⁶When Jesus overheard this conversation, he says to the official, "Don't be afraid, just have trust!"

³⁷And he wouldn't let anyone follow along with him except Peter and James and John, James' brother. ³⁸When they come to the official's house, he notices a lot of clamor and people crying and wailing, ³⁹and he goes in and says to them, "Why are you carrying on like this? The child hasn't died; she's sleeping."

⁴⁰And they started laughing at him. But he throws everyone out and takes the child's father and her mother and his companions and goes in where the child is. ⁴¹And he takes the child by the hand and says to her, *"talitha kum"* (which means, "Little girl—I'm talking to you—get up!"). ⁴²And right away the little girl got up and started walking around. (You see, she was twelve years old.)

And they were downright ecstatic. ⁴³And he gave them strict orders that no one should learn about this, and he told them to give her something to eat.

6:1–6a #95, p. 75

⁵⁰When Jesus heard this, he answered him, "Don't be afraid; just have trust, and she'll be cured."

⁵¹When he arrived at the house, he wouldn't allow anyone to go in with him except Peter and John and James, and the child's father and mother. ⁵²Everyone was crying and grieving over her, but he said, "Don't cry; she hasn't died; she's sleeping."

⁵³But they started laughing at him, certain that she had died.

⁵⁴He took her by the hand and called out, "Child, get up!" ⁵⁵Her breathing returned and she immediately got up.

He ordered them to give her something to eat.

⁵⁶Her parents were quite ecstatic; but he commanded them not to tell anyone what had happened.

9:1–6 #96, p. 77

ᵃ Lk 8:43 Many mss add "and had spent her life savings on physicians" after *twelve years.*

94. Healing of the Blind Men

Mt 9:27–31	Mt 20:29–34*	Mk	Lk
[27]And when Jesus left there, two blind men followed him, shouting, "Have mercy on us, son of David." [28]When Jesus arrived home, the blind men came to him. Jesus says to them, "Do you trust that I can do this?" They reply to him, "Yes, master." [29]Then he touched their eyes, saying, "Let it happen to you according to your trust."[30]And their eyes were opened. Then Jesus snapped at them, saying, "See that no one finds out about it."[31]But they went out and spread the news of him throughout that whole territory.	[29]And as they were leaving Jericho, a huge crowd followed him. [30]There were two blind men sitting along the wayside. When they heard that Jesus was going by, they shouted, "Have mercy on us, Master, son of David." [31]The crowd yelled at them to shut up, but they shouted all the louder, "Have mercy on us, Master, son of David." [32]Jesus paused and called out to them, "What do you want me to do for you?" [33]They said to him, "Master, open our eyes!" [34]Then Jesus took pity on them, touched their eyes, and right away they regained their sight and followed him.		
9:32–34 #69, p. 56	21:1–9 #204, p. 155		

*Mk 10:46–52 / Lk 18:35–43 (#201, p. 152)

95. Jesus visits Nazareth

Mt 13:53–58	Mk 6:1–6a	Lk 4:16–30	other
[53]And so it happened that, when Jesus had finished these parables, he moved on from there. [54]And he came to his hometown and resumed teaching them in their meeting place,	[1]Then he left that place, and he comes to his hometown, and his disciples follow him. [2]When the Sabbath arrived, he started teaching in the meeting place;	[16]When he came to Nazareth, where he had been brought up, he went to the meeting place on the Sabbath, as was his custom. He stood up to do the reading [17]and was handed the scroll of the prophet Isaiah. He unrolled the scroll and found the place where it was written: "[18]The spirit of the Lord is upon me, because he has anointed me to bring good news to the poor. He has sent me to announce pardon for prisoners and recovery of sight to the blind; to set free the oppressed, [19]to proclaim the year of the Lord's amnesty." [20]After rolling up the scroll, he gave it back to the attendant, and sat down; and the attention of everyone in the meeting place was riveted on him. [21]He began by saying to them, "Today this scripture has been fulfilled as you listen."	
so they were astounded and said so: "Where did this wisdom and these miracles come from?	and many who heard him were astounded and said so: "Where's he getting all this?" and "Where'd he get all this wisdom?" and "Where'd he get the power to perform such miracles? [3]This is the carpenter, isn't it? Isn't he the son of Mary? And aren't his brothers James, Joses, Judas, and Simon? And aren't his sisters our neighbors?"	[22]And they all were responding favorably to him, and marveling at the pleasing speech that he delivered; and they were saying, "Isn't this the son of Joseph?" [23]And he said to them, "No doubt you will quote me that proverb, 'Doctor, cure yourself,' and you'll tell me, 'Do here in your hometown what we've heard you've done in Capernaum.'"	**Jn 7:15** The Judeans were taken aback, saying, "This man is uneducated; how come he's so articulate?" **Jn 6:42** They were saying, "Isn't this Jesus, son of Joseph? Don't we know both his father and his mother? How can he now say, 'I've come down from heaven'?"
[55]This is the carpenter's son, isn't it? Isn't his mother called Mary? And aren't his brothers James and Joseph and Simon and Judas? [56]And aren't all his sisters neighbors of ours? So where did he get all this?" [57]And they took offense at him.	And they took offense at him.		

Mt 13:53–58	Mk 6:1–6a	Lk 4:16–30	other
			Jn 4:44b
Jesus said to them, "No prophet is disrespected, except on his home turf and at home!"	[4]Jesus used to tell them, "No prophet is disrespected, except on his home turf and among his relatives and at home."	[24]Then he said, "Let me tell you, no prophet is welcome on his home turf.	A prophet gets no respect on his own turf.
			Th 31:1
			No prophet is welcome in his home town.
[58]And he did not perform many miracles there	[5]He was unable to perform a single miracle there, except that he did cure a few by laying hands on them, [6]though he was always shocked at their lack of trust.		
because of their lack of trust.			
		[25]I can assure you, there were many widows in Israel in Elijah's time, when the sky was dammed up for three and a half years, and a severe famine swept through the land. [26]Yet Elijah was not sent to any of them, but instead to a widow in Zarephath near Sidon. [27]There were also many lepers in Israel in the prophet Elisha's time; but none of them was made clean, except Naaman the Syrian."	
		[28]Everyone in the meeting place was filled with rage when they heard this. [29]They rose up, ran him out of town, and led him to the brow of the hill on which their town was built, intending to hurl him over the cliff.	**Jn 10:39**
		[30]But he slipped through their fingers and got away.	Again they tried to arrest him, but he escaped.
			EgerG 1:10
			So the Master himself slipped through their hands and got away.
14:1–2 #104, p. 85		4:31–37 #11, p. 17	

96. The Mission of the Twelve (a)

SEE #98, P. 79

Mt 9:35; 10:1, 9–14	Mk 6:6b–13	Lk 9:1–6*	Lk 10:1, 4a, 5–7, 10–11
Mt 9:35 And Jesus went about all the towns and villages, teaching in their meeting places and proclaiming the gospel of the empire ⟨of Heaven⟩ and healing every disease and ailment. **Mt 10:1, 9–14**	6bAnd he used to go around the villages, teaching in a circuit.		
1And summoning his twelve disciples he gave them authority to drive out unclean spirits and to heal every disease and every ailment . . .†	7Then he summoned the Twelve and started sending them out in pairs and giving them authority over unclean spirits.	1He called the Twelve together and gave them power and authority over all demons and to heal diseases. 2He sent them out to announce the empire of God and to heal the sick. 3He said to them, "Don't carry anything on the way: neither staff nor knapsack, neither bread nor money; no one is to take two shirts.	1After this the Master appointed seventy-twoa others and sent them on ahead of him in pairs to every town and place that he himself intended to visit.
9Don't get gold or silver or copper coins for spending money, 10don't take a knapsack for the road, or two shirts, or sandals, or a staff; for 'the worker deserves to be fed.'	8And he instructed them not to take anything on the way, except a staff: no bread, no knapsack, no spending money, 9but to wear sandals, and to wear no more than one shirt.		4aCarry no purse, no knapsack, no sandals.
11Whichever town or village you enter, find out who is deserving; stay there until you leave. 12When you enter a house, greet it. 13And if the house is deserving, give it your peace blessing, but if it is unworthy, withdraw your peace blessing.	10And he went on to say to them, "Wherever you enter someone's house, stay there until you leave town.	4And whichever house you enter, stay there and leave from there.	v. 7
			5Whenever you enter a house, first say, 'Peace to this house.' 6If peaceful people live there, your peace will rest on them. But if not, it will return to you. 7Stay at that one house, eating and drinking whatever they provide, for workers deserve their wages. Do not move from house to house.
14And if anyone will not welcome you, or listen to your words, as you are going out of that house or town shake the dust off your feet.	11And whatever place does not welcome you or listen to you, get out of there and shake the dust off your feet in witness against them."	5And wherever they do not welcome you, leave the town and shake the dust from your feet in witness against them."	10But whenever you enter a town and they don't welcome you, go out into its streets and say, 11"Even the dust of your town that sticks to our feet, we wipe off against you. But know this: the empire of God is arriving.'
	12So they set out and announced that people should	6And they set out and went from village to village, bringing	

Mt 9:35; 10:1, 9–14	Mk 6:6b–13	Lk 9:1–6*	Lk 10:1, 4a, 5–7, 10–11
	turn their lives around, ¹³and they were driving out demons and anointing many sick people with oil and healing them.	good news and healing everywhere.	
10:5–15 #98, p. 79		9:7–9 #104, p. 85	10:1–12 #138, p. 113

* Ⓓ Lk 10:1–12 (#138, p. 113)
† Ⓓ Mt 10:8 (#98, p. 79)

ᵃ Lk 10:1 Many mss read "seventy" rather than *seventy-two.*

97. Jesus authorizes the Twelve

Mt 10:1–4	Mk 6:7; 3:14–19	Lk 9:1; 6:13–16
¹And summoning his twelve disciples he gave them authority to drive out unclean spirits and to heal every disease and every ailment.	**Mk 6:7** Then he summoned the Twelve and started sending them out in pairs and giving them authority over unclean spirits.	**Lk 9:1** He called the Twelve together and gave them power and authority over all demons and to heal diseases.
	Mk 3:14–19 ¹⁴He formed a group of twelveᵃ to be his companions, and to be sent out to preach, ¹⁵and to have authority to drive out demons.	**Lk 6:13–16** ¹³He called his disciples and selected twelve of them, whom he named apostles:
²The names of the twelve apostles were these: first, Simon, also known as Rock ⟨(Peter)⟩, and Andrew his brother, and James the son of Zebedee and John his brother,	¹⁶And to Simon he gave the nickname Rock ⟨(Peter)⟩, ¹⁷and to James, the son of Zebedee, and to John, his brother, he also gave a nickname, Boanerges (which means "Sons of Thunder");	¹⁴Simon, whom he nicknamed Rock ⟨(Peter)⟩, and Andrew his brother, and James and John,
³Philip and Bartholomew, Thomas, and Matthew the toll collector, James the son of Alphaeus, and Thaddaeus,ᵇ ⁴Simon the Zealot, and Judas of Iscariot, the one who, in the end, turned him in.	¹⁸and Andrew and Philip and Bartholomew and Matthew and Thomas and James, the son of Alphaeus; and Thaddeus and Simon the Zealot; ¹⁹and Judas Iscariot, who, in the end, turned him in.	and Philip, and Bartholomew, ¹⁵and Matthew, and Thomas, and James the son of Alphaeus, and Simon who was called the Zealot, ¹⁶and Judas the son of James, and Judas Iscariot, who turned traitor.
	3:20–21 #68, p. 55	6:17–20a #43, p. 34

ᵃ Mk 3:14 Some mss insert "whom he also named apostles" after *twelve.*
ᵇ Mt 10:3 A few mss have "Lebbaeus" instead of *Thaddaeus.* Many mss have "Lebbaeus who is called Thaddaeus."

98. The Mission of the Twelve (b)

SEE #96, P. 77

Mt 10:5–15	Mk 6:8–11	Lk 10:9, 4, 8, 5, 10–12	Lk 9:2–5
[5]Jesus sent out these twelve after he had given them these instructions: "Don't travel foreign roads and don't enter a Samaritan town, [6]but go instead to the lost sheep of the house of Israel.* [7]Go and announce: 'The empire of Heaven has arrived.'† [8]Heal the sick, raise the dead, cleanse the lepers, drive out demons.‡ You have received freely, so freely give. [9]Don't get gold or silver or copper coins for spending money, [10]don't take a knapsack for the road, or two shirts, or sandals, or a staff; for 'the worker deserves to be fed.'	[8]And he instructed them		
		[9]Cure the sick there and tell them, 'For you, God's empire has arrived.'‡	[2]He sent them out to announce the empire of God and to heal the sick.
	not to take anything on the way, except a staff: no bread, no knapsack, no spending money, [9]but to wear sandals, and to wear no more than one shirt.	[4]Carry no purse, no knapsack, no sandals. Don't greet anyone on the road.	[3]He said to them, "Don't carry anything on the way: neither staff nor knapsack, neither bread nor money; no one is to take two shirts.
[11]Whichever town or village you enter, find out who is deserving; stay there until you leave. [12]When you enter a house, greet it. [13]And if the house is deserving, give it your peace blessing, but if it is unworthy, withdraw your peace blessing. [14]And if anyone will not welcome you, or listen to your words, as you are going out of that house or town shake the dust off your feet.	[10]And he went on to say to them, "Wherever you enter someone's house, stay there until you leave town. [11]And whatever place does not welcome you or listen to you, get out of there and shake the dust off your feet in witness against them."	[8]Whenever you enter a town and they welcome you, eat whatever they offer you. [5]Whenever you enter a house, first say, 'Peace to this house.' [6]If peaceful people live there, your peace will rest on them. But if not, it will return to you. [10]But whenever you enter a town and they don't welcome you, go out into its streets and say, [11]'Even the dust of your town that sticks to our feet, we wipe off against you. But know this: the empire of God is arriving.' [12]I'm telling you, on that day Sodom will be better off than that town.	[4]And whichever house you enter, stay there and leave from there. [5]And wherever they do not welcome you, leave the town and shake the dust from your feet in witness against them.
[15]Let me tell you, the land of Sodom and Gomorrah will be better off on judgment day than that town.			
6:6b–13 #96, p. 77		10:1–12 #138, p. 113	9:1–6 #96, p. 77

* Mt 15:24 (#112, p. 93)

† Mt 3:2 (#3, p. 10); 4:17 (#9, p. 16)

‡ Th 14:4 When you go into any region and walk about in the countryside, when people take you in, eat what they serve you and care for the sick among them. (#425, p. 336)

99. What to Do When They Come for You

SEE #313, 319, 357, 383, PP. 251, 255, 292, 311

Mt 10:16–25	Mk 13:9, 11–13	Lk 10:3; 21:12–19: 6:40	other
[16]Look, I'm sending you out like sheep to a pack of wolves. Therefore you must be as sly as snakes and as simple as pigeons.		**Lk 10:3** Get going; look, I'm sending you out like lambs into a pack of wolves.	**Th 39:3** As for you, be as sly as snakes and as simple as pigeons.
		Lk 21:12–19 [12]But before all these things happen, they'll manhandle you, and persecute you, and turn you over to synagogues and deliver you to prisons, and you'll be hauled up before kings and governors on account of my name. [13]This will give you a chance to make your case.	
[17]And beware of people, for they'll turn you over to Jewish councils and flog you in synagogues.* [18]And you'll be hauled up before governors and even kings on my account so you can make your case to them and to the gentiles. [19]And when they lock you up, don't worry about how you should speak or what you should say. It will occur to you at that moment what to say.	[9]But you look out for yourselves. They'll turn you over to Jewish councils, and beat you in synagogues, and haul you up before governors and kings on my account, so you can make your case to them. [11]And when they take you away to turn you in, don't be worried about what you should say. Instead, whatever occurs to you at the moment, say that.	[14]So make up your minds not to rehearse your defense in advance, [15]for I will give you the wit and wisdom which none of your adversaries will be able to resist or refute.	**Lk 12:11–12** [11]And when they make you appear in front of synagogues and haul you up before rulers and authorities, don't worry about how or in what way you should defend yourself or what you should say. [12]The holy spirit will teach you at that very moment what you ought to say.
[20]For it's not you who are speaking but your Father's spirit speaking through you. [21]One brother will turn in another to be put to death, and a father his child, and children will turn against their parents and kill them. [22]And you'll be universally hated because of me.†	For it's not you who are speaking but the holy spirit. [12]And one brother will turn in another to be put to death, and a father his child, and children will turn against their parents and kill them. [13]And you'll be universally hated because of me.	[16]You'll be turned in, even by parents and brothers and relatives and friends; and they'll put some of you to death. [17]And you'll be universally hated because of me. [18]Yet not a single hair on your head will be harmed.‡ [19]By your perseverance you will secure your lives.	
But those who hold out to the end will be saved. [23]When they persecute you in this town, flee to another.[a] Let me tell you, you certainly won't have gone through the towns of Israel before the Human One comes.	Those who hold out to the End will be saved.		

		Lk 6:40	
[24]Students are not above their teachers,		Students are not above their teachers.	
			Jn 13:16a Slaves are never better than their masters.
nor slaves above their masters.			**Jn 15:20** Slaves are never better than their masters.
[25]It's enough for students to become like their teachers and slaves to be like their masters. If they have dubbed the master of the house "Beelzebul," aren't they even more likely to malign the members of his household?		But those who are fully taught will be like their teachers.	If they persecuted me, they'll surely persecute you. If they follow my teaching, they'll also follow yours.
	13:14–20 #225, p. 174		

* Ⓓ Mt 24:9 (#224, p. 173)
† Ⓓ Mt 24:13 (#224, p. 173)
‡ Lk 12:7 / Mt 10:30 (#155, p. 123)

[a] Mt 10:23 At this point in the verse, a few mss add: "And when they persecute you in another, flee to yet another one."

100. Cover ups will be exposed
SEE #381, P. 310

Mt 10:26–27	Mk 4:22	Lk 8:17; 12:2–3	Th 5:2; 6:5–6; 33:1
26So don't be afraid of them. After all, there is nothing covered up that won't be exposed,	There is nothing hidden except to be brought to light,	**Lk 8:17** There is nothing hidden that won't be brought to light, nor kept secret that won't be made known and exposed.	**Th 5:2** For there's nothing hidden that won't be revealed.
or hidden that won't be made known.	nor anything kept secret that won't be exposed.	**Lk 12:2–3** 2There is nothing covered up that won't be exposed, or hidden that won't be made known.	**Th 6:5–6** 5After all, there's nothing hidden that won't be revealed, 6and there's nothing covered up that will remain undisclosed.
27What I say to you in the dark, say in the light, and what you hear whispered in your ear,		3And so whatever you've said in the dark will be heard in the light, and what you've whispered behind closed doors will be announced from the rooftops.	**Th 33:1** What you will hear in your ear,[a]
announce from the rooftops.	4:21–23 #79, p. 64		proclaim from your rooftops.

[a] Th 33:1 Between *ear* and *proclaim* the Coptic has "in the other ear." This is very likely a scribal error (dittography, the inadvertent repetition of a phrase). It is therefore omitted from the translation.

101. Whom to Fear
SEE #382, 383, PP. 310, 311

Mt 10:28–33	Mk	Lk 12:4–9
28Don't fear those who kill the body but cannot kill the soul; instead, you ought to fear the one who can destroy both the soul and the body in Gehenna.		4I'm telling you, my friends, don't fear those who kill the body, and after that can do no more. 5I'll show you whom you ought to fear: fear the one who can kill and then has authority to cast into Gehenna. Believe me, that's the one you should fear!
29What do two sparrows cost? A couple of bucks? Yet not one of them will fall to the ground without your Father's consent. 30As for you, even the hairs on your head have all been counted.* 31So, don't be so timid; you're worth more than a flock of sparrows. 32Everyone who acknowledges me in public, I too will acknowledge before my Father in the heavens. 33But the one who disowns me in public, I too will disown in front of my Father in the heavens.		6What do five sparrows cost? Five bucks? Yet not one of them is overlooked by God. 7In fact, even the hairs of your head have all been counted.* Don't be so timid; you're worth more than a flock of sparrows. 8I'm telling you, everyone who acknowledges me in public, the Human One will acknowledge in front of God's messengers. 9But whoever disowns me in public will be disowned in front of God's messengers.† 12:10 #73, p. 58

*Lk 21:18 (#224, p. 173)
†Mk 8:38 / Lk 9:26 (#121, p. 102)

102. Discipleship trumps family
SEE #398, 399, PP. 320, 321

Mt 10:34–39	Mk	Lk 12:51–53; 14:26–27; 17:33	other
		Lk 12:51–53	**Th 16:1–3**
[34]Don't get the idea that I came to bring peace on earth. I didn't come to bring peace, but a sword!		[51]Do you think I came here to bring peace on earth? No, I'm telling you, on the contrary: conflict. [52]As a result, from now on in any given house there will be five in conflict, three against two and two against three. [53]Father will be pitted against son and son against father, mother against daughter and daughter against mother, mother-in-law against daughter-in-law and daughter-in-law against mother-in-law.	[1]Perhaps people think that I've come to cast peace upon the world. [2]They don't know that I've come to sow conflict upon the earth: fire, sword, war.* [3]For there'll be five in a house: there'll be three against two and two against three, father against son and son against father.
[35]After all, I've come to pit a man against his father, a daughter against her mother, and a daughter-in-law against her mother-in-law.	13:12		
[36]Your enemies live under your own roof.			
			Th 101:1
		Lk 14:26–27	Whoever does not hate [father] and mother as I do cannot be my [disciple].
[37]If you love your father and mother more than me, you're not worthy of me, and if you love your son or daughter more than me, you're not worthy of me.		[26]If any of you comes to me and does not hate your own father and mother and wife and children and brothers and sisters—yes, even your own life—you cannot be my disciple.	**Th 55:1–2** [1]Whoever does not hate father and mother cannot be my disciple, [2]and whoever does not hate brothers and sisters, and carry the cross as I do, will not be worthy of me.
[38]Unless you take your cross and come along with me, you're not worthy of me.†		[27]Unless you carry your own cross and come along with me, you cannot be my disciple.†	
		Lk 17:33	**Jn 12:25**
[39]By finding your life, you'll lose it, but by losing your life for my sake, you'll find it.‡		Whoever tries to hang on to life will lose it, but whoever loses it will preserve it.‡	If you love your life you'll lose it, but if you hate your life in this world you'll preserve it for unending life.

* Th 82:1–2 [1]'Whoever is near me is near the fire, [2]and whoever is far from me is far from the ⟨Father's⟩ empire. (#474, p. 356)

† Mt 16:24 / Mk 8:34 / Lk 9:23 (#121, p. 102)

‡ Mt 16:25 / Mk 8:35 / Lk 9:24 (#121, p. 102)

103. You, Me, and the One Who Sent Me

SEE #127, 311, 131, 368, PP. 107, 250, 109, 301

Mt 10:40–11:1	Mk 9:37b, 41	Lk 10:16	Jn 13:20; 15:23; 5:23
[40]The one who welcomes you is welcoming me, and the one who welcomes me is welcoming the one who sent me.*	[37b]Whoever welcomes me is not so much welcoming me as the one who sent me.*	Whoever hears you hears me,	**Jn 13:20** If they receive anyone I send, they are receiving me; and if they receive me, they are receiving the one who sent me. **Jn 15:23** Those who hate me also hate my Father. **Jn 5:23** Whoever does not respect the son does not respect the Father who sent him.
		and whoever rejects you rejects me, and whoever rejects me rejects the one who sent me.	
[41]The one who welcomes a prophet as a prophet will be treated like a prophet; and the one who welcomes a just person as a just person will be treated like a just person. [42]And whoever gives so much as a cup of cool water to one of these little ones, because the little one is a follower of mine, let me tell you, such a person certainly won't go unrewarded." **11** [1]And so it happened that, when Jesus had finished instructing his twelve disciples, he moved on from there to teach and proclaim in their towns.	[41]You see, whoever gives you a cup of water to drink because you carry the name of the Anointed One, let me tell you: such a person certainly won't go unrewarded.		
11:2–6 #54, p. 44		10:17–20 #140, p. 115	

*Mt 18:5 / Lk 9:48 (#127, p. 107)

104. John the Baptizer Raised from the Dead?

Mt 14:1–2	Mk 6:14–16	Lk 9:7–9
[1]On that occasion Herod the tetrarch heard the rumor about Jesus [2]and said to his servants, "This is John the Baptizer. He's been raised from the dead; that's why miraculous powers are at work in him."	[14]King Herod heard about it—by now, Jesus' fame had spread—and people kept saying that John the Baptizer had been raised from the dead and that's why miraculous powers were at work in him. [15]But others were saying that he was Elijah, and others that he was a prophet like one of the ⟨old time⟩ prophets. [16]When Herod got wind of it, he started declaring, "John, the one I beheaded, has been raised!"	[7]Now Herod the tetrarch heard about everything that was happening. He was perplexed because some were saying that John had been raised from the dead, [8]some that Elijah had appeared, and others that one of the ancient prophets had come back to life. [9] Herod said, "John I beheaded; but this one about whom I hear such things—who is he?" And he was curious to see him. 9:10–11 #106, p. 87

105. The Murder of John the Baptizer

Mt 14:3–12	Mk 6:17–29	Lk 3:19–20
[3]Herod, remember, had arrested John, put him in chains, and thrown him in prison on account of Herodias, his brother Philip's wife. [4]John, for his part, had said to him, "It is not right for you to have her."	[17]Earlier Herod himself had sent someone to arrest John and put him in chains in a dungeon, on account of Herodias, his brother Philip's wife, because he had married her. ([18]You see, John had said to Herod, "It is not right for you to have your brother's wife.")	[19]But Herod the tetrarch, who had been denounced by John over the matter of Herodias, his brother's wife, [20]topped off all his other crimes by shutting John up in prison.
[5]And while Herod wanted to kill him, he was afraid of the crowd because they regarded John as a prophet.	[19]So Herodias nursed a grudge against him and wanted to eliminate him, but she couldn't manage it, [20]because Herod was afraid of John. He knew that he was an upright and holy man, and so protected him, and, although he listened to him frequently, he was very confused, yet he listened to him eagerly.	
[6]On Herod's birthday, the daughter of Herodias danced for them and captivated Herod, [7]so he swore an oath and promised to give her whatever she asked.	[21]Now a festival day came, when Herod gave a banquet on his birthday for his courtiers, and his commanders, and the leading citizens of Galilee. [22]And the daughter of Herodias came in and captivated Herod and his dinner guests by dancing. The king said to the girl, "Ask me for whatever you wish and I'll grant it to you!" [23]Then he swore an oath to her: "I'll grant you whatever you ask for, up to half my domain!" [24]She went out and said to her mother, "What should I ask for?" And she replied, "The head of John the Baptizer!"	
[8]Prompted by her mother, she said, "Give me the head of John the Baptizer right here on a platter." [9]The king was sad, but because of his oath and his dinner guests, he ordered that it be done. [10]And he sent and had John beheaded in prison.	[25]Right away she hurried back and made her request: "I want you to give me the head of John the Baptizer on a platter, right now!" [26]The king grew regretful, but because of his oaths and the dinner guests, he didn't want to refuse her. [27]So right away the king sent for the executioner and commanded him to bring his head. And he went away and beheaded ⟨John⟩ in prison.	
[11]⟨John's⟩ head was brought on a platter and presented to the girl, and she gave it to her mother. [12]Then his disciples came and got his body and buried him. Then they went and told Jesus.	[28]He brought his head on a platter and presented it to the girl, and the girl gave it to her mother. [29]When his disciples heard about it, they came and got his body and put it in a tomb.	
		3:19–22 #6, p. 13

106. Jesus is pursued by crowds

Mt 14:13–14; 9:36	Mk 6:30–34	Lk 9:10–11
Mt 14:13–14 ¹³When Jesus got word of ⟨John's death⟩, he sailed away quietly to an isolated place. The crowds got wind of ⟨his departure⟩ and followed him on foot from the towns. ¹⁴As he stepped ashore and saw this huge crowd, he was moved by them, and healed their sick. **Mt 9:36** When he saw the crowd, he was moved by them because they were beaten down and helpless, like sheep without a shepherd.	³⁰Then the apostles regroup around Jesus and they reported to him everything that they had done and taught. ³¹And he says to them, "You come by yourselves to an isolated place and rest a little." (You see, many were coming and going and they didn't even have a chance to eat.) ³²So they went away in the boat privately to an isolated place. ³³But many noticed them leaving and figured it out and raced there on foot from all the towns and got there ahead of them. ³⁴When he came ashore, he saw a huge crowd and was moved by them, because they resembled sheep without a shepherd, and he started teaching them at length.	¹⁰On their return the apostles reported to him what they had done. Taking them along, Jesus withdrew privately to a town called Bethsaida. ¹¹But the crowds found this out and followed him. He welcomed them, spoke to them about the empire of God, and cured those in need of treatment.

107. Bread and Fish for 5,000

SEE #293, P. 238

Mt 14:15–21*	Mk 6:35–44*	Lk 9:12–17	Jn 6:4–13
¹⁵When it was evening the disciples approached him and said, "This place is deserted and it's already late. Send the crowd away so that they can go to the villages and buy food for themselves." ¹⁶Jesus said to them, "They don't need to leave; give them something to eat yourselves!"	³⁵And as the hour had already grown late, his disciples were approaching him and saying, "This place is deserted and it's late. ³⁶Send them away so that they can go to the farms and villages around here to buy something to eat." ³⁷But in response he said to them, "Give them something to eat yourselves." And they say to him, "Are we supposed to go out and buy two hundred denarii worth of bread and donate it for their meal?" ³⁸So he says to them, "How many loaves do you have? Go look."	¹²As the day began to draw to a close, the Twelve approached him and said, "Send the crowd away, so that they can go to the villages and farms around here and find food and lodging; for we are in a deserted place here." ¹³But he said to them, "Give them something to eat yourselves."	⁴It was about time for the Jewish festival of Passover. ⁵Jesus looks up and sees a big crowd approaching him, and he says to Philip, "Where are we going to buy enough bread to feed these people?" (⁶He was saying this to test him; you see, Jesus already knew what he was going to do.) ⁷"Two hundred denarii wouldn't buy enough bread for everyone to have a bite," Philip said. ⁸One of his disciples, Andrew, Simon Peter's brother, says to him,

Mt 14:15–21*	Mk 6:35–44*	Lk 9:12–17	Jn 6:4–13
[17]But they say to him, "We have nothing here except five loaves and two fish."	And when they find out, they say, "Five, and two fish."	They said, "All we have are five loaves and two fish—unless we go ourselves and buy food for all these people." ([14]There were about five thousand men.)	[9]"There's a kid here with five loaves of barley bread and two fish; but what does that amount to for so many?"
v. 21	v. 44		
[18]He said, "Bring them here to me." [19]And he told the crowd to recline on the grass,	[39]Next he instructed them all to recline to eat, some over here, some over there, on the green grass. [40]So they sat down group by group, in hundreds and in fifties.	He said to his disciples, "Have them recline in groups of about fifty." [15]They did so and got them reclined.	[10]Jesus said, "Have the people sit down." (They were in a grassy place.) So they sat down. (The men ⟨alone⟩ numbered about five thousand.)
and he took the five loaves and two fish, and looking up to the sky he gave a blessing, and breaking it apart he gave the bread to the disciples, and the disciples gave it to the crowd.	[41]And he took the five loaves and the two fish, looked up to the sky, gave a blessing, and broke the bread apart, and started giving it to his disciples to pass around to them; and even the two fish they shared with everybody.	[16]Then he took the five loaves and two fish, looked up to the sky, gave a blessing, and broke them, and started handing them out to the disciples to pass around to the crowd.	[11]Jesus took the loaves, gave thanks, and passed them around to the people sitting there, along with the fish,
[20]And everybody had more than enough to eat.	[42]Everybody had more than enough to eat.	[17]And everybody had more than enough to eat.	and all of them had as much as they wanted. [12]And when they had eaten their fill, he says to his disciples, "Gather up the leftovers so that nothing goes to waste."
Then they picked up twelve baskets full of leftovers.	[43]Then they picked up twelve baskets full of leftovers, including some fish.	Then the leftovers were collected, twelve baskets full.	[13]So they gathered them up and filled twelve baskets with scraps from the five barley loaves—from what was left over.
[21]The number of people who had eaten came to about five thousand, not counting women and children.	[44]And the number of men who had some bread came to five thousand.	v. 14	
		9:18–20 #119, p. 100	

* ⒟ Mt 15:32–39 / Mk 8:1–10 (#115, p. 95)

108. Jesus walks on the sea
SEE #294, P. 240

Mt 14:22–33	Mk 6:45–52	Lk	Jn 6:16–21
[22]And right away he made the disciples get in a boat and go ahead of him to the other side, while he dispersed the crowds. [23]After he had dispersed the crowds, he went up to the mountain privately to pray. He remained there alone well into the evening.	[45]And right away he made his disciples embark in the boat and go ahead to the opposite shore toward Bethsaida, while he himself dispersed the crowd. [46]And once he got away from them, he went off to the mountain to pray.		[16]As evening approached, his disciples went down to the sea. [17]They boarded a boat and were trying to cross the sea to Capernaum. It had already gotten dark, and Jesus still had not joined them.
[24]By this time the boat was already some distance from land and was being pounded by waves because the wind was against them.	[47]When evening came, the boat was in the middle of the sea, and he was alone on the land. [48]When he saw they were having a rough time making headway, because the wind was against them,		[18]A strong wind began to blow and the sea was getting rough. [19]When they had rowed about three or four miles,
[25]About three o'clock in the morning he came toward them walking on the sea.	at about three o'clock in the morning he comes toward them walking on the sea and intending to go past them.		they catch sight of Jesus walking on the sea and coming toward the boat.
[26]But when the disciples saw him walking on the sea, they were terrified. "It's a ghost," they said, and cried out in fear. [27]Right away Jesus spoke to them, saying, "Be brave; it's me! Don't be afraid."	[49]But when they saw him walking on the sea, they thought he was a ghost and they cried out, [50]because they all saw him and were terrified. But right away he spoke with them and says to them, "Take heart, it's me! Don't be afraid."		They were frightened, [20]but he says to them, "Don't be afraid! It's me."
[28]In response Peter said, "Master, if it's really you, order me to come across the water to you." [29]He said, "Come on." And Peter got out of the boat and walked on the water and came toward Jesus. [30]But with the strong wind in his face, he started to panic. And when he began to sink, he cried out, "Master, save me." [31]Jesus immediately held out his hand and took hold of him and says to him, "You with your meager trust! Why did you hesitate?"[32]And by the time they had climbed into the boat, the wind had died down.			
[33]Then those in the boat paid homage to him, saying, "You really are God's son."	[51]And he climbed into the boat with them, and the wind died down. By this time they were completely dumbfounded. (|[52]You see, they hadn't understood about the loaves; their minds were closed.)		[21]Then they would have taken him on board, but the boat instantly arrived at the shore they had been making for.

109. Healings at Gennesaret

Mt 14:34–36	Mk 6:53–56	Lk	Jn
			6:22–24
³⁴Once they had crossed over they landed at Gennesaret.	⁵³Once they had crossed over to land, they landed at Gennesaret and moored. ⁵⁴As soon as they had gotten out of the boat, people immediately recognized him, ⁵⁵and they ran around over the whole area and started bringing those who were ill on mats to wherever he was rumored to be. ⁵⁶And wherever he would go, into villages, or towns, or onto farms, they would lay out the sick in the marketplaces and beg him to let them touch the fringe of his cloak. And all those who managed to touch it were cured.		
³⁵And the local people recognized him and sent word into the whole surrounding area and brought him all who were ill.			
³⁶And they begged him just to let them touch the fringe of his cloak. And all those who managed to touch it were cured.			

110. Controversy over Washing Hands

Mt 15:1–9	Mk 7:1–13	Lk	EgerG 3:6
¹Then the Pharisees and scholars from Jerusalem come to Jesus, and say,	¹The Pharisees gather around him, along with some of the scholars, who had come from Jerusalem. ²When they notice some of his disciples eating their meal with defiled hands, that is to say, without washing their hands (³you see, the Pharisees and the Jews never eat without first washing their hands in a particular way, always observing the tradition of the elders, ⁴and they won't eat when they get back from the marketplace without washing again, and there are many other traditions they cherish, such as the washing of cups and jugs and kettles), ⁵the Pharisees and the scholars start questioning him: "Why don't your disciples live up to the tradition of the elders, instead of eating bread with defiled hands?"		
²"Why do your disciples deviate from the traditions of the elders? For instance, they don't wash their hands before they eat bread." ³In response he asked them, "Why do you also break God's commandment because of your tradition? ⁴For example, God said, 'Honor your father and mother' and 'Those who curse their father or mother absolutely must die.' ⁵But you say, 'If people say to their	vv. 9–13		

father or mother, "Whatever I might have spent to support you has been consecrated to God," [6]they need not honor their father.' So you end up invalidating God's word because of your tradition.

[7]How accurately Isaiah prophesied about you phonies when he said, [8]"This people honors me with their lips, but their heart stays far away from me. [9]Their worship of me is empty, because they insist on teachings that are human regulations."

vv. 3–6

[6]And he answered them, "How accurately Isaiah foretold you phonies when he wrote, "This people honors me with their lips, but their heart stays far away from me. [7]Their worship of me is empty, because they insist on teachings that are human regulations." [8]You have set aside God's commandment and hold fast to human tradition."

[9]Or he would say to them, "How expert you've become at putting aside God's commandment to establish your own tradition. [10]For example, Moses said, 'Honor your father and your mother' and 'Those who curse their fathers or mothers absolutely must die.' [11]But you say, 'If people say to their fathers or mothers, "Whatever I might have spent to support you is *korban*"' (which means "consecrated to God"), [12]you no longer let those persons do anything for their fathers or mothers. [13]So you end up invalidating God's word with your own tradition, which you then perpetuate. And you do all kinds of other things like that."

How accurately Isaiah prophesied about you when he said, "This people honors me with their lips, but their heart stays far away from me. Their worship of me is empty, [because they insist on teachings that are human] regulations."

111. What Defiles You

SEE #357, P. 292

Mt 15:10–20	Mk 7:14–23	Lk 6:39	Th 14:5; 34
[10]And he summoned the crowd and said to them, "Listen and try to understand.	[14]Once again he summoned the crowd and would say to them, "Listen to me, all of you, and try to understand.		
[11]What goes into your mouth doesn't defile you; what comes out of your mouth does."	[15]What goes into you can't defile you; what comes out of you can. [16]If anyone here has two good ears, use 'em!"*[a]		**Th 14:5** What goes into your mouth won't defile you; what comes out of your mouth will.
[12]The disciples came and said to him, "Don't you realize that the Pharisees who heard this remark were offended by it?" [13]He responded, "Every plant which my heavenly Father does not plant will be rooted out. [14]Never mind them. They are blind guides of blind people![b] If one blind person guides another, both will end up in some ditch."		Can one blind person guide another? Won't they both end up in some ditch?	**Th 34** If a blind person leads a blind person, both of them will fall into a hole.
	[17]When he entered a house away from the crowd, his disciples started questioning him about the riddle. [18]And he says to them, "Are you as dim-witted as the rest? Don't you realize that nothing from outside can defile by going into a person, [19]because it doesn't get to the heart but passes into the stomach, and comes out in the outhouse?" (This is how everything we eat is purified.)		
[15]Then Peter replied, "Explain the riddle to us." [16]He said, "Are you still as dim-witted as the rest? [17]Don't you realize that everything that goes into the mouth passes into the stomach and comes out in the outhouse?	[20]And he went on to say, "It's what comes out of a person that defiles. [21]For from out of the human heart issue wicked intentions: sexual immorality, thefts, murders, [22]adulteries, greed, wickedness, deceit, promiscuity, an evil eye, blasphemy, arrogance, lack of good sense.		
[18]But the things that come out of the mouth come from the heart, and those things defile a person. [19]For out of the heart emerge evil intentions: murders, adulteries, sexual immorality, thefts, false testimonies, blasphemies.			

[20]These are what defile you. Eating with unwashed hands doesn't defile anybody."	[23]All these evil things come from the inside out and defile you."	
	6:37–42 #46, p. 37	

*Mt 11:15; 13:9; 13:43b; Mk 4:9; 4:23; Lk 8:8b; 14:35b; Th 8:4; 21:10; 24:2; 63:4; 65:8; 96:3

[a] Mk 7:16 This entire verse is missing in some early mss.
[b] Mt 15:14 Some mss omit *of blind people*.

112. Jesus and the Foreign Woman

Mt 15:21–28	Mk 7:24–30	Lk
[21]So Jesus left there, and withdrew to the district of Tyre and Sidon.	[24]From there he got up and went away to the regions of Tyre. Whenever he visited a house he wanted no one to know, but he could not escape notice. [25]But right away a woman whose daughter had an unclean spirit heard about him, and came and knelt at his feet. [26]The woman was a Greek, by race a Phoenician from Syria, and she started asking him to drive the demon out of her daughter.	
[22]Just then this Canaanite woman from those parts showed up and started shouting, "Have mercy on me, sir, you son of David. My daughter is severely possessed." [23]But he did not respond at all. And his disciples came and began to complain, "Get rid of her; she's badgering us." [24]But in response he said, "I was sent only to the lost sheep of the house of Israel." [25]She came and bowed down to him, saying, "Sir, please help me." [26]In response he said, "It's not right to take bread out of children's mouths and throw it to the dogs." [27]But she said, "Of course, sir, but even the dogs eat the scraps that fall from their master's table." [28]Then in response Jesus said to her, "My good woman, your trust is enormous! Your wish is as good as fulfilled." And her daughter was cured at that moment.	[27]He was saying to her, "Let the children be fed first, since it isn't good to take bread out of children's mouths and throw it to the dogs!" [28]But she answered him, "Sir, even the dogs under the table get to eat scraps ⟨dropped by⟩ children!" [29]Then he said to her, "For that insightful answer, be on your way, the demon has come out of your daughter." [30]She returned home and found the child lying on the bed and the demon gone.	
15:29–31 #114, p. 94		

113. The Healing of a Deaf-Mute

Mt	Mk 7:31–37	Lk
15:29	[31]Then he left the regions of Tyre and traveled through Sidon to the Sea of Galilee, through the middle of the region known as the Ten Cities. [32]And they bring him a deaf-mute and plead with him to lay his hand on him. [33]Taking him aside from the crowd in private, he stuck his fingers into the man's ears and spat and touched his tongue. [34]And looking up to the sky, he groaned and says to him, *"ephphatha"* (which means, "Be opened"). [35]And right away his ears opened up and his speech impediment was removed and he started speaking properly. [36]Then he ordered them to tell no one. But the more he ordered them not to, they more they spread it around. [37]And they were completely dumbfounded. "He's done everything and done it well," they said; "He even makes the deaf hear and the mute speak!" 8:1–10 #115, p. 95	

114. Mass Healings

Mt 15:29–31	Mk	Lk
[29]Then Jesus left there and went to the sea of Galilee. And he climbed up the mountain and sat there. [30]And huge crowds came to him and brought with them the lame, the blind, the maimed, the mute, and many others, and they crowded around his feet and he healed them. [31]As a result, the crowd was astonished when they saw the mute now speaking, the maimed made whole, the lame walking, and the blind seeing. And they gave all the credit to the God of Israel.	7:31	

115. Bread and Fish for 4,000

Mt 15:32–39*	Mk 8:1–10*	Lk
[32]Then Jesus called his disciples aside and said, "I feel sorry for the crowd because they have already spent three days with me and now they've run out of food. And I don't want to send these people away hungry, for fear they'll collapse on the way." [33]And the disciples say to him, "How can we get enough bread here in this desert place to feed so many people?" [34]Jesus says to them, "How many loaves do you have?" They replied, "Seven, plus a few fish." [35]And he ordered the crowd to sit down on the ground. [36]And he took the seven loaves and the fish and gave thanks and broke them into pieces, and started giving them to the disciples, and the disciples ⟨started giving them⟩ to the crowds. [37]And everyone had more than enough to eat. Then they picked up seven baskets full of leftovers. [38]Those who had eaten numbered four thousand, not counting women and children. [39]And after he sent the crowds away, he got into the boat and went to the Magadan region.	[1]And in those days, there was again a huge crowd without anything to eat, so he calls the disciples aside and says to them, [2]"I feel sorry for the crowd, because they have already spent three days with me and now they've run out of food. [3]If I send these people home hungry, they will collapse on the way and some of them have come from quite a distance." [4]And his disciples answered him, "How can anyone feed these people bread out here in this desert place?" [5]And he started asking them, "How many loaves do you have?" They replied, "Seven." [6]Then he orders the crowd to sit down on the ground. And he took the seven loaves, gave thanks, and broke them into pieces, and started giving them to his disciples to hand out; and they passed them around to the crowd. [7]They also had a few small fish. When he had blessed them, he told them to hand those out as well. [8]They had more than enough to eat. Then they picked up seven big baskets of leftover scraps. [9]There were about four thousand people there. Then he started sending them away. [10]And right away he got into the boat with his disciples and went to the Dalmanutha district.	

* Ⓓ Mt 14:15–21 / Mk 6:35–44 / Lk 9:12–17 (#107, p. 87)

116. Demanding a Sign

Mt 16:1–4	Mt 12:38–39	Mk 8:11–13
[1]And the Pharisees and Sadducees came, and they put him to the test by asking him to show them a sign from heaven.	[38]Then some of the scholars and Pharisees responded to him, "Teacher, we would like to see a sign from you."	[11]The Pharisees came out and started to argue with him. To put him to the test, they demanded a sign from heaven.
[2]In response he said to them, "When it's evening, you say, 'It'll be fair weather because the sky looks red.' [3]Early in the morning you say, 'The day will bring winter weather because the sky looks red and dark.'[a] You know how to read the face of the sky, but you can't discern the signs of the times.		
	[39]In response he said to them,	[12]He groaned under his breath and says,
[4]An evil and adulterous generation demands a sign, yet no sign will be given it	"An evil and adulterous generation demands a sign, and no sign will be given it—	"Why does this generation demand a sign? Let me tell you, this generation won't get any sign!"
except the sign of Jonah." And he turned his back on them and walked away.	except the sign of Jonah the prophet!"	[13]And turning his back on them, he got back in the boat and crossed over to the other side.
	12:38–42 #150, p. 119	

[a] Mt 16:2b–3 Some mss do not have these verses.

Lk 11:16; 12:54–56; **11:29**	other
Lk 11:16 Others were putting him to the test by demanding a sign from heaven. **Lk 12:54–56** [54]He would also say to the crowds, "When you see a cloud rising in the west, right away you say that it's going to rain; and so it does. [55]And when the wind blows from the south, you say we're in for scorching heat; and we are. [56]You phonies! You know the lay of the land and can read the face of the sky, so why don't you know how to interpret the present time?" **Lk 11:29** As more and more people were crowding around him, he began to say, "This generation is an evil generation. It demands a sign, but it will be given no sign— except the sign of Jonah!	**Jn 6:30** They asked him, "What sign are you going to perform so we can see it and come to believe in you? What 'work' are you going to do?" **Th 91:2** You examine the face of heaven and earth, but you have not come to know the one who is in your presence, and you don't know how to examine the present moment.

117. The Leaven of Jesus' Opponents

Mt 16:5–12	Mk 8:14–21	Lk 12:1
		Meanwhile, a crowd of many thousands had thronged together and were trampling each other.
[5]And the disciples came to the opposite shore, but they forgot to bring any bread. [6]Jesus said to them, "Look, be careful: guard against the leaven of the Pharisees and Sadducees."	[14]They forgot to bring any bread and had nothing with them in the boat except one loaf. [15]Then he started warning them, "Look, watch out for the leaven of the Pharisees and the leaven of Herod."[a]	He began to speak first to his disciples: "Be on guard against the leaven of the Pharisees" (that is, their hypocrisy).
[7]Now they began arguing among themselves, saying, "We didn't bring any bread."	[16]They began discussing with one another that they had no bread. [17]And because he was aware of this, he says to them, "Why are you talking about bread you don't have? You still don't get it, do you? You still haven't got the point, have you? Are you just closed-minded? [18]You have eyes, but you still don't see, and you have ears, but you still don't hear. Don't you even remember [19]how many baskets full of scraps you picked up when I broke up the five loaves for the five thousand?"	
[8]Because Jesus was aware of this, he said, "Why are you puzzled that you don't have any bread, you with your meager trust? [9]You still don't get it, do you?		
You don't remember the five loaves for the five thousand and how many baskets you carried away, do you?		
	"Twelve," they reply to him.	
[10]Nor the seven loaves for four thousand and how many big baskets you filled?	[20]"When I broke up the seven loaves for the four thousand, how many big baskets full of scraps did you pick up?" And they say, "Seven." [21]And he repeats, "You still don't understand, do you?"	
[11]How can you possibly think I was talking to you about bread? Just be on guard against the leaven of the Pharisees and Sadducees." [12]Then they understood that he was not talking about guarding against the leaven in bread but against the teaching of the Pharisees and Sadducees.		
16:13–19 #119, p. 100		12:2–3 #100, p. 82

[a] Mk 8:15 Some mss read "the Herodians" in place of *Herod*.

118. Jesus heals a blind man in two stages

Mt	Mk 8:22–26	Lk
	22They come to Bethsaida, and they bring him a blind man, and plead with him to touch him. 23He took the blind man by the hand and led him out of the village. And he spat into his eyes, and placed his hands on him, and started questioning him, "Do you see anything?" 24And he looked up and began to say, "I see human figures, as though they were trees walking around." 25Then he put his hands on his eyes a second time. And he opened his eyes, and his sight was restored, and he saw everything clearly. 26And he sent him home, saying, "Don't even go into the village."	

119. Who do you say I am?

SEE #343, P. 281

Mt 16:13–19	Mk 8:27–29	Lk 9:18–20	other
[13]When Jesus came to the region of Caesarea Philippi, he started questioning his disciples, asking, "What are people saying about the Human One?" [14]They said, "Some ⟨say⟩ 'John the Baptizer,' but others, 'Elijah,' and others, 'Jeremiah or one of the prophets.'" [15]He says to them, "What about you, who do you say I am?" [16]And Simon Peter responded, "You are the Anointed One, the son of the living God!"* [17]And in response Jesus said to him, "You are to be congratulated, Simon bar Jonah, because flesh and blood did not reveal this to you but my Father who is in heaven. [18]Let me tell you, you are Peter, ⟨'the Rock,'⟩ and on this very rock I will build my congregation, and the gates of Hades will not be able to overpower it. [19]I will give you the keys of the empire of Heaven, and whatever you uphold on earth will be upheld in heaven, and whatever you dismiss on earth will be dismissed in heaven."†	[27]Jesus and his disciples set out for the villages of Caesarea Philippi. On the way he started questioning his disciples, asking them, "What are people saying about me?" [28]And they told him, "⟨Some say,⟩ 'John the Baptizer,' and others, 'Elijah,' but others, 'One of the prophets.'" [29]But he kept pressing them, "What about you, who do you say I am?" Peter responds to him, "You are the Anointed One!"*	[18]And it came to pass, when Jesus was praying alone, that the disciples were with him; and he questioned them asking, "What are the crowds saying about me?" [19]They said in response, "⟨Some say⟩ 'John the Baptizer,' while others, 'Elijah,' and still others, 'One of the ancient prophets has come back to life.'" [20]Then he said to them, "What about you, who do you say I am?" And Peter responded, "God's Anointed One!"*	**Th 13:1–2** [1]Jesus said to his disciples, "Compare me to something and tell me what I'm like." [2]Simon Peter said to him, "You are like a just angel." *Jn 6:67–69* **Jn 20:23** If you cancel anyone's sins, they are cancelled; if you retain them, they are retained.

*Jn 1:40–41 (#281, p. 230)

† Ⓓ Mt 18:18 (#132, p. 110)

120. First Passion Prediction

Mt 16:20–23	Mk 8:30–33	Lk 9:21–22
[20]Then he ordered the disciples to tell no one that he was the Anointed One. [21]From that time on Jesus[a] started to make it clear to his disciples that he was destined to go to Jerusalem, and endure much at the hands of the elders and chief priests and scholars, and be killed and, on the third day, be raised. [22]And Peter took him aside and began to lecture him, saying, "God forbid, master; there's no way that can happen to you." [23]But he turned and said to Peter, "Get out of my sight, you Satan, you. You're getting in my way because you're not thinking in God's terms, but in human terms."	[30]And he warned them not to tell anyone about him. [31]He started teaching them that the Human One was destined to endure much, and be rejected by the elders and the chief priests and the scholars, and be killed, and after three days rise. [32]And he was putting this in plain language. And Peter took him aside and began to lecture him. [33]But he turned, noticed his disciples, and reprimanded Peter verbally: "Get out of my sight, you Satan, you, because you're not thinking in God's terms, but in human terms."	[21]Then he warned them, and forbade them to tell this to anyone, [22]adding, "The Human One is destined to endure much, be rejected by the elders and chief priests and scholars, and be killed and, on the third day, be raised."

[a] Mt 16:21 A few mss have *Jesus* "the Anointed."

121. Pick up your cross

SEE #309, P. 247

Mt 16:24–28	Mk 8:34–9:1	Lk 9:23–27	other
[24]Then Jesus said to his disciples,	[34]After he called the crowd together with his disciples, he said to them,	[23]He would say to everyone,	**Th 55:1–2** [1]Whoever does not hate father and mother cannot be my disciple, [2]and whoever does not hate brothers and sisters, and carry the cross as I do, will not be worthy of me.
"If any of you wants to come after me you should deny yourself, pick up your cross, and follow me!*	"If any of you wants to come after me, you should deny yourself, pick up your cross, and follow after me.	"If any of you wants to come after me, you should deny yourself, pick up your cross every day, and follow me!*	**Jn 12:25** If you love your life you'll lose it, but if you hate your life in this world you'll preserve it for unending life.
[25]Remember, if you try to save your life you'll lose it, but if you lose your life for my sake, you'll find it.†	[35]Remember, if you try to save your life, you'll lose it, but if you lose your life for the sake of the good news, you'll save it.	[24]Remember, if you try to save your life you'll lose it, but if you lose your life for my sake, you'll save it.†	
[26]After all, what good will it do if you acquire the whole world but forfeit your life? Or what will you give in exchange for your life?	[36]After all, what good does it do to acquire the whole world and forfeit your life? [37]Or, what would you give in exchange for life?	[25]After all, what good does it do to acquire the whole world and lose or forfeit yourself?	
	[38]Moreover, if any of you are ashamed of me and my message in this adulterous and sinful generation, of you	[26]Moreover, if any of you are ashamed of me and of my message,	
[27]Remember, the Human One is going to come in the glory of his Father with his messengers, and then he will reward everyone according to their deeds.	the Human One will likewise be ashamed when he comes in his Father's glory accompanied by the holy heavenly messengers."	the Human One will be ashamed of you when he comes in his glory and the glory of the Father and of the holy messengers.‡	
[28]Let me tell you, some of those standing here won't ever taste death before they see the Human One arriving with full imperial power."	9 [1]And he was telling them, "Let me tell you, some of those standing here won't ever taste death before they see the empire of God arriving in force."	[27]I'm telling you the truth: some of those standing here won't ever taste death before they see the empire of God."	

* Ⓓ Mt 10:38 / Lk 14:27 (#176, p. 134)
† Ⓓ Mt 10:39 / Lk 17:33 (#190, p. 142)
‡ Ⓓ Lk 12:9 (#156, p. 123)

122. Jesus is transformed

Mt 17:1–8	Mk 9:2–8	Lk 9:28–36
[1]Six days later, Jesus takes Peter and James and his brother John along and he leads them off by themselves to a lofty mountain. [2]He was transformed in front of them and his face shone like the sun, and his clothes turned as white as light. [3]The next thing you know, Moses and Elijah appeared to them and were conversing with Jesus.	[2]Six days later, Jesus takes Peter and James and John along and leads them off by themselves to a lofty mountain. He was transformed in front of them, [3]and his clothes became an intensely brilliant white, whiter than any laundry on earth could make them. [4]Elijah appeared to them, with Moses, and they were conversing with Jesus.	[28]About eight days after these sayings it came to pass that Jesus took Peter and John and James along with him and climbed up the mountain to pray. [29]And it came to pass as he was praying that his face took on a strange appearance, and his clothing turned dazzling white. [30]The next thing you know, two men were talking with him, Moses and Elijah, [31]who appeared in glory and were discussing his departure, which he was destined to accomplish in Jerusalem.
		[32]Now Peter and those with him were half asleep at the time. But they came wide awake when they saw his glory and the two men standing next to him.
[4]Peter said to Jesus, "Master, it's a good thing we're here. If you want, I'll set up three tents here, one for you, one for Moses, and one for Elijah."	[5]Peter responds by saying to Jesus, "Rabbi, it's a good thing we're here. How about we set up three tents, one for you and one for Moses and one for Elijah?" ([6]You see, he didn't know what else to say, since they were terrified.)	[33]And it came to pass as the men were leaving him that Peter said to Jesus, "Master, it's a good thing we're here. How about we set up three tents, one for you, one for Moses, and one for Elijah?" (He didn't know what he was saying.)
[5]While he was still speaking, there was a bright cloud that cast a shadow over them. And just then a voice spoke from the cloud:	[7]And a cloud moved in and cast a shadow over them, and a voice came out of the cloud:	[34]While he was still speaking, a cloud moved in and cast a shadow over them. And their fear increased as they entered the cloud. [35]And out of the cloud a voice spoke:
"This is my son, the one I love—I fully approve of him. Listen to him!"* [6]And as the disciples listened, they knelt with their faces on the ground, and were frightened out of their wits. [7]And Jesus came and touched them and said, "Get up; don't be afraid." [8]Looking up they saw no one except Jesus by himself.	"This is my son, the one I love, listen to him!"*	"This is my son, my chosen one.[a] Listen to him!"*
	[8]Suddenly, as they looked around, they saw no one, but were alone with Jesus.	[36]When the voice had spoken, Jesus was perceived to be alone. And they were speechless and told no one back then anything of what they had seen.
		9:37–43a #124, p. 104

* Jn 12:27–30 (#309, p. 247)

---

[a] Lk 9:35 Many mss read "the one I love" in place of *my chosen one.*

123. Elijah has come

Mt 17:9–13	Mk 9:9–13	Lk
[9]And as they came down from the mountain, Jesus ordered them, "Don't tell anyone about this vision until the Human One has been raised from the dead."	[9]And as they were walking down the mountain he instructed them not to describe what they had seen to anyone, until the Human One rises from the dead. [10]And they kept it to themselves, puzzling over what this could mean, this 'rising from the dead.'	
[10]And the disciples questioned him, "So why do the scholars claim that Elijah must come first?"	[11]And they started questioning him, "The scholars claim, don't they, that Elijah must come first?"	
[11]In response he said, "Elijah does come and will restore everything. [12]But I'm telling you, Elijah has already come, and they did not recognize him but they did to him whatever they wanted. So the Human One is also going to suffer at their hands."	[12]He was responding to them, "Of course Elijah comes first to restore everything. So, how does scripture claim that the Human One will endure much and be treated with contempt? [13]But take my word for it: Elijah did in fact arrive, just as the scriptures said he would, and they did to him whatever they pleased."	
[13]Then the disciples understood that he had been talking to them about John the Baptizer.		

124. Exorcism of an Epileptic Boy

Mt 17:14–20	Mk 9:14–29	Lk 9:37–43a; 17:6
		Lk 9:37–43a
	[14]When they rejoined the disciples, they saw a huge crowd surrounding them and scholars arguing with them. [15]And right away, when the whole crowd caught sight of him, they were amazed and rushed up to meet him. [16]He asked them, "Why are you bothering to argue with them?"	[37]It came to pass on the next day, when they came down from the mountain, that a huge crowd met him.
[14]And when they rejoined the crowd, a person approached and knelt before him [15]and said, "Master, have mercy on my son, because he suffers terribly from epilepsy. For example, he often falls into the fire and just as often into the water.	[17]And someone from the crowd answered him, "Teacher, I brought my son to you, because he has a mute spirit. [18]Whenever it takes him over, it knocks him down, and he foams at the mouth and grinds his teeth and stiffens up.	[38]Suddenly a man from the crowd shouted, "Teacher, I beg you to take a look at my son, for he is my only child. [39]Without warning a spirit gets hold of him, and all of a sudden he screams; it throws him into convulsions, causing him to foam at the mouth; and it leaves him only after abusing him.
[16]So I brought him to your disciples, but they couldn't heal him."	I asked your disciples to drive it out, but they couldn't."	[40]I begged your disciples to drive it out, but they couldn't."
[17]In response Jesus said, "You distrustful and perverted lot, how much longer do I have to be around you? How much longer do I have to put up with you? Bring him here."	[19]In response he says, "You distrustful generation, how much longer do I have to be around you? How much longer do I have to put up with you? Bring him over here!"	[41]In response Jesus said, "You distrustful and perverted generation, how much longer do I have to be around you and put up with you?

Bring your son here." |
| | [20]And they brought him over to him. And when the spirit noticed him, right away it threw him into convulsions, and | [42]But as the boy approached, the demon knocked him down and threw him into convulsions. |

he fell to the ground, and kept rolling around, foaming at the mouth. ²¹And Jesus asked his father, "How long has he been like this?"

He replied, "Ever since he was a child. ²²It has frequently tried to destroy him by throwing him into fire and into water. So if you can do anything, take pity on us and help us!"

²³Jesus said to him, "What do you mean, 'If you can'? Anything is possible for those who trust."

²⁴Right away the father of the child cried out and said, "I do trust! Help my lack of trust!"

¹⁸And Jesus rebuked the demon

²⁵When Jesus saw that the crowd was about to mob them, he rebuked the unclean spirit, commanding it, "Deaf and mute spirit, I command you, get out of him and don't ever go back inside him!"

Jesus rebuked the unclean spirit, healed the boy, and gave him back to his father.

and it came out of him and the child was healed at that precise moment.

²⁶And after he shrieked and went into a series of convulsions, it came out. And he took on the appearance of a corpse, so that the rumor went around that he had died. ²⁷But Jesus took hold of his hand and raised him, and there he stood.

⁴³And everybody was astounded at the majesty of God.

¹⁹Later the disciples came to Jesus privately and asked, "Why couldn't we drive it out?"

²⁸And when he had gone home, his disciples started questioning him privately, "Why couldn't we drive it out?"

²⁹He said to them, "The only thing that can drive this kind out is prayer."

²⁰So he says to them, "Because of your meager trust. Let me tell you, even if you have trust no bigger than a mustard seed, you will say to this mountain, 'Move from here to there,' and it will move. And nothing will be impossible for you."ᵃ*

Lk 17:6
If you had trust no bigger than a mustard seed, you could tell this mulberry tree, 'Uproot yourself and plant yourself in the sea,' and it would obey you.

---

* Ⓓ Mt 21:21 / Mk 11:23 (#209, p. 159)

ᵃ Mt 17:20 Some mss add a v. 21, "This kind does not come out except with prayer and fasting."

125. The Second Passion Prediction

Mt 17:22–23	Mk 9:30–32	Lk 9:43b–45
[22]And when they had been reunited in Galilee, Jesus said to them, "The Human One is destined to be turned over to his enemies, [23]and they will kill him, and on the third day he'll be raised." And they were very upset.	[30]They left there and started going through Galilee, and he did not want anyone to know. [31]You see, he was instructing his disciples and telling them, "The Human One will be turned over to his enemies, and they will kill him. And three days after he is killed he will rise." [32]They didn't understand this instruction and they dreaded asking him about it.	[43b]While they all were marveling at everything he was doing, he said to his disciples, [44]"Mark well these words: the Human One is destined to be turned over to his enemies." [45]But they didn't understand this instruction. It was couched in veiled language, so they would not get its meaning. And they always dreaded to ask him about this remark.
	9:33–37 #127, p. 107	9:46–48 #127, p. 107

126. The Temple Tax

Mt 17:24–27	Mk	Lk

[24]And when they came to Capernaum, those who collect the temple tax came to Peter and said, "Your teacher pays his temple tax, doesn't he?" [25]He said, "That's right."
    And when he got home, Jesus anticipated what was on Peter's mind. "What are you thinking, Simon? On whom do earthly kings levy taxes and tolls? Do they levy them on their own people or on foreigners?"
    [26]Peter said, "On foreigners."
Jesus responded to him, "Then their own people are exempt. [27]Still, we don't want to get in trouble with them, so go down to the sea, cast your line in, and take the first fish you catch. Open its mouth and you'll find a coin. Take it and pay them for both of us."		

127. Who is greatest?

SEE #103, 311, 314, PP. 84, 250, 251

Mt 18:1–5	Mk 9:33–37	Lk 9:46–48	other
[1]At that moment the disciples approached Jesus with the question: "Who is greatest in the empire of Heaven?"	[33]And they came to Capernaum. When he got home, he started questioning them, "What were you arguing about on the way?" [34]And they fell silent, because on the way they had been bickering about who was greatest.	[46]Now an argument broke out among them over which of them was greatest.	
20:26–27; 23:11	[35]He sat down and called the Twelve and says to them, "If any of you wants to be 'number one,' you have to be last of all and servant of all."*	22:26	
[2]And he called a child over, had her stand in front of them, [3]and said,	[36]And he took a child and had her stand in front of them, and he put his arm around her, and he said to them,	[47]But Jesus, knowing what was on their minds, took a child and had her stand next to him. [48]He said to them,	
"Let me tell you, if you don't turn yourself around and become like children, you'll never enter the empire of Heaven.† [4]Therefore, those who lower themselves to this child's level are greatest in the empire of Heaven.	10:15	18:17	Th 46:2
[5]And whoever welcomes one such child in my name is welcoming me.	[37]"Whoever welcomes a child like this in my name is welcoming me. And whoever welcomes me is not so much welcoming me as the one who sent me."‡	"Whoever welcomes this child in my name is welcoming me. And whoever welcomes me is welcoming the one who sent me.‡ Don't forget, the one who is least among you is the one who is great."	**Jn 13:20** Let me tell you this: if they receive anyone I send, they are receiving me; and if they receive me, they are receiving the one who sent me.‡
10:40			
18:6–10 #131, p. 109			

*Mk 10:43–44 (#200, p. 151)

†Mt 19:13–15 / Mk 10:13–16 / Lk 18:15–17 / Th 22:1–2 (#195, p. 146)

‡Jn 12:44–45 (#311, p. 250)

128. An Unauthorized Exorcist

Mt	Mk 9:38–39	Lk 9:49–50
	³⁸John said to him, "Teacher, we saw someone driving out demons in your name, so we tried to stop him, because he wasn't one of our followers." ³⁹Jesus responded, "Don't stop him. You see, no one who performs a miracle in my name will then turn around and curse me."	⁴⁹John said in response, "Master, we saw someone driving out demons in your name, and we tried to stop him because he isn't one of your followers." ⁵⁰But he said to him, "Don't stop him; for whoever is not against you is on your side." 9:51–56 #136, p. 112

129. For and Against

Mt 12:30	Mk 9:40	Lk 9:50b; 11:23	GOxy 1224 6:1b–2
	For whoever is not against us is on our side.	**Lk 9:50b** Whoever is not against you is on your side. **Lk 11:23** Those who aren't with me are against me, and those who don't gather with me scatter.	¹ᵇWhoever is not [against y]ou is on your side. ²[Whoever today i]s at a distance, tomorrow will [b]e [near you] and in [. . .] of the advers[ary]
Those who aren't with me are against me, and those one who don't gather with me scatter. 12:31–32 #73, p. 58			

130. A Cup of Water

Mt 10:42	Mk 9:41	Lk
Whoever gives so much as a cup of cool water to one of these little ones, because the little one is a follower of mine, let me tell you: such a person certainly won't go unrewarded. 10:40–11:1 #103, p. 84	You see, whoever gives you a cup of water to drink because you carry the name of the Anointed One, let me tell you: such a person certainly won't go unrewarded.	

131. Don't exploit the little ones
SEE #404, P. 322

Mt 18:6–10	Mk 9:42–48	Lk 17:1–2
[6]Any of you who entraps and exploits one of these little ones who trusts me would be better off having a millstone hung around your neck and being drowned in the deepest part of the sea! [7]Damn the world for the snares it sets! It's inevitable that traps will be set; but still, damn those who set them! [8]If your hand or your foot gets you into trouble, cut it off and throw it away! It's better for you to enter life maimed or lame than to be thrown into the eternal fire with both hands and both feet.	[42]And any of you who entraps and exploits one of these little trusting souls would be better off if you had a millstone tied around your neck and were thrown into the sea! [43]And if your hand gets you into trouble, cut it off! It's better for you to enter life maimed than to wind up in Gehenna, in the unquenchable fire, with both hands![a] [45]And if your foot gets you into trouble, cut it off! It's better for you to enter life lame than to be thrown into Gehenna with both feet![a]	[1]He said to his disciples, "There's no way that traps won't be set; but still, damn those who set them! [2]You'd be better off if you had a millstone tied around your neck and were dumped into the sea than to entrap and exploit one of these little ones.
[9]And if your eye gets you into trouble, rip it out and throw it away! After all, it's better for you to enter life one-eyed than to be thrown into Gehenna's fire with both eyes.*	[47]And if your eye gets you into trouble, rip it out! It's better for you to enter God's empire one-eyed than to be thrown into Gehenna with both eyes, [48]where the worm never dies and the fire never goes out!	
[10]See that you don't disdain one of these little ones. For I'm telling you, their guardian angels constantly gaze on the face of my Father in heaven.[b]		
18:12–14 #177, p. 135	9:49–50 #18, p. 21	

* Ⓓ Mt 5:29–30 (#21, p. 23)
___
[a] Mk 9:43, 45 Many mss add a v. 44 and a v. 46, both of which repeat v. 48.
[b] Mt 18:10 Some mss add a v. 11, "The Human One came to save the lost."

132. Dealing with an Errant Companion

SEE #271, P. 221

Mt 18:15–18	Mk	Lk 17:3	Jn 20:23
[15]And if some companion does wrong,[a] go have it out between the two of you privately. If that person listens to you, you have won your companion over. [16]And if he or she doesn't listen, take one or two people with you so that 'every fact may be supported by two or three witnesses.' [17]Then if he or she refuses to listen to them, report it to the congregation. If he or she refuses to listen even to the congregation, treat that companion like you would a pagan or toll collector. [18]Let me tell you, whatever you uphold on earth will be upheld in heaven, and whatever you dismiss on earth will be dismissed in heaven.*		If your companion does wrong, scold that person; if there is a change of heart, forgive the person.	If you cancel anyone's sins, they are cancelled; if you retain them, they are retained.
		17:4 #134, p. 111	

* Ⓓ Mt 16:19 (#119, p. 100)

[a] Mt 18:15 Some mss made the condition more specific by inserting a "you:" *if some companion does* "you" *wrong.*

133. Two or Three Gathered

Mt 18:19–20	Mk	Lk	Th 30:2[a]
[19]Again I assure you, if two of you on earth agree on anything you ask for, it will be done for you by my Father in heaven. [20]In fact, wherever two or three are gathered together in my name, I will be there among them."			Where there are two or one, I am with that one.

[a] Th 30:2 The Coptic version of this saying is deficient, based perhaps on a scribal error. The Greek version is closer to the original: "Where there are [three, they are without] God, and where there is only [one,] I say, I am with that one."

134. Forgiving 7 / 77 Times
SEE #407, P. 324

Mt 18:21–22	Mk	Lk 17:4	GNaz 5:1
		If someone wrongs you seven times a day, and seven times turns around and says to you, "I'm sorry," you must forgive that person.	If your brother or sister has wronged you verbally and made amends, welcome him or her seven times a day.
²¹Then Peter came up and asked him, "Master, how many times can a companion wrong me and still expect my forgiveness? As many as seven times?" ²²Jesus replies to him, "My advice to you is not seven times, but seventy-seven times.			His disciple Simon said to him, "Seven times a day?" The Master answered him, "That's right; in fact, up to seventy times seven times."
		17:5–6 #186, p. 140	

135. The Parable of the Unforgiving Debtor

Mt 18:23–35	Mk	Lk
²³This is why the empire of Heaven should be compared to a human ruler who decided to settle accounts with his slaves. ²⁴When the process began, this debtor was brought to him who owed a gazillion dollars. ²⁵Since he couldn't pay it back, the ruler ordered him sold, along with his wife and children and everything he had, so he could recover his money. ²⁶At this prospect, the slave knelt down and groveled before him: "Be patient with me and I'll pay you back in full." ²⁷Because he was compassionate, the master of that slave let him go and canceled the debt. ²⁸As soon as he got out, that same slave collared one of his fellow slaves who owed him five thousand dollars, and grabbed him by the neck and demanded, "Pay back what you owe!" ²⁹His fellow slave knelt down and begged him, "Be patient with me and I'll pay you back." ³⁰But he wasn't interested; instead, he went out and threw him in prison until he paid the debt. ³¹When his fellow slaves realized what had happened, they were terribly upset and went and reported to their master everything that had happened. ³²At that point, his master summoned him. "You wicked slave," he says to him, "I canceled your entire debt because you begged me. ³³Wasn't it only fair for you to treat your fellow slave with the same consideration as I treated you?" ³⁴And the master was so angry he turned him over to the torturers until he paid back everything he owed. ³⁵That's what my heavenly Father will do to you, unless you find it in your heart to forgive each one of your brothers and sisters.* 19:1–9 #193, p. 145		

*Mt 6:15 (#28, p. 27)

136. Samaritans snub Jesus

Mt	Mk	Lk 9:51–56
		[51]It came to pass, as the deadline for him to be taken up was fast approaching, that he set his sights on Jerusalem. [52]He sent messengers on ahead of him. They entered a Samaritan village, to get things ready for him. [53]But the Samaritans would not welcome him, because he had made up his mind to go on to Jerusalem. [54]When his disciples James and John realized this, they said, "Master, do you want us to call down fire from heaven and annihilate them?" [55]But he turned and reprimanded them. [56]Then they continued on to another village.

137. Demands of Discipleship

SEE #365, P. 299

Mt 8:19–22	Mk	Lk 9:57–62	Th 86:1–2
[19]And one scholar came forward and said to him, "Teacher, I'll follow you wherever you go." [20]And Jesus says to him, "Foxes have dens, and birds of the sky have nests, but the Human One has nowhere to rest his head." [21]Another of his disciples said to him, "Master, first let me go and bury my father." [22]But Jesus says to him, "Follow me, and leave it to the dead to bury their own dead."		[57]As they were going along the road, someone said to him, "I'll follow you wherever you go." [58]And Jesus said to him, "Foxes have dens, and birds of the sky have nests, but the Human One has nowhere to rest his head." [59]To another he said, "Follow me." But he said, "First, let me go and bury my father." [60]Jesus said to him, "Leave it to the dead to bury their own dead; but you, go out and announce the empire of God." [61]Another said, "I'll follow you, sir; but let me first say good-bye to my people at home." [62]Jesus said to him, "No one who puts his hand to the plow and looks back is qualified for the empire of God."	[1][Foxes have] their dens and birds have their nests, [2]but the human being has no place to lie down and rest.
8:18, 23–27 #91, p. 69			

138. The Mission of the Seventy-Two
SEE #366, P. 299

Mt 9:37–38; 10:16, 9–10a, 11–13, 10b, 7–8a, 14–15	Mk 6:7–11	Lk 10:1–12*	Th 73; 39:3; 14:4
	7Then he summoned the Twelve and started sending them out in pairs and giving them authority over unclean spirits.	1After this the Master appointed seventy-twoa others and sent them on ahead of him in pairs to every town and place that he himself intended to visit. 2He would say to them,	
Mt 9:37–38 37Then he said to his disciples, "The crop is good, but there are few to harvest it.† 38So beg the harvest boss to dispatch workers to the fields."		"The crop is good, but there are few to harvest it.† So beg the harvest boss to dispatch workers to the fields.	**Th 73** The crop is huge but the workers are few,† so beg the boss to dispatch workers to the fields.
Mt 10:16 Look, I'm sending you out like sheep to a pack of wolves. Therefore you must be as sly as snakes and as simple as pigeons.		3Get going; look, I'm sending you out like lambs into a pack of wolves.	**Th 39:3** Be as sly as snakes and as simple as pigeons.
Mt 10:9–10a 9Don't get gold or silver or copper coins for spending money, 10don't take a knapsack for the road, or two shirts, or sandals, or a staff.	8And he instructed them not to take anything on the way, except a staff: no bread, no knapsack, no spending money, 9but to wear sandals, and to wear no more than one shirt.	4Carry no purse, no knapsack, no sandals.	
Mt 10:11–13 11Whichever town or village you enter, find out who is deserving; stay there until you leave. 12When you enter a house, greet it. 13And if the house is deserving, give it your peace blessing, but if it is unworthy, withdraw your peace blessing.	10And he went on to say to them, "Wherever you enter someone's house, stay there until you leave town.	Don't greet anyone on the road. 5Whenever you enter a house, first say, 'Peace to this house.' 6If peaceful people live there, your peace will rest on them. But if not, it will return to you. 7Stay at that one house, eating and drinking whatever they provide,	
Mt 10:10b for "the worker deserves to be fed."		for workers deserve their wages. Do not move from house to house. 8Whenever you enter a town and they welcome you, eat whatever they offer you. 9Cure the sick there and tell them, 'For you, God's empire has arrived.'	**Th 14:4** When you go into any region and walk about in the countryside, when people take you in, eat what they serve you and care for the sick among them.
Mt 10:7–8a 7Go and announce: "The empire of Heaven has arrived." 8aHeal the sick, raise the dead, cleanse the lepers, drive out demons.			

Mt 9:37–38; 10:16, 9–10a, 11–13, 10b, 7–8a, 14–15	Mk 6:7–11	Lk 10:1–12*	Th 73; 39:3; 14:4
Mt 10:14–15 ¹⁴And if anyone will not welcome you, or listen to your words, as you are going out of that house or town shake the dust off your feet. 10:7 ¹⁵Let me tell you, the land of Sodom and Gomorrah will be better off on judgment day than that town.	¹¹And whatever place does not welcome you or listen to you, get out of there and shake the dust off your feet in witness against them." 6:6b–13 #96, p. 77	¹⁰But whenever you enter a town and they don't welcome you, go out into its streets and say, ¹¹'Even the dust of your town that sticks to our feet, we wipe off against you. But know this: the empire of God is arriving.' ¹²I'm telling you, on that day Sodom will be better off than that town.	

* ⓓ Lk 9:2–6 (#96, p. 77)
† Jn 4:35–36 (#286, p. 233)

ᵃ Lk 10:1 Many mss read "seventy" rather than *seventy-two*.

139. Damn you, Chorazin and Bethsaida
SEE #367, P. 301

Mt 11:20–24	Mk	Lk 10:13–15
²⁰Then he began to insult the towns where he had performed most of his miracles, because they had not changed their ways. ²¹"Damn you, Chorazin! Damn you, Bethsaida! If the miracles done in you had been done in Tyre and Sidon, they would have ⟨sat⟩ in sackcloth and ashes and changed their ways long ago. ²²So I'm telling you, Tyre and Sidon will be better off on judgment day than you. ²³And you, Capernaum, you don't think you'll be exalted to heaven, do you? No, you'll go to hell. Because if the miracles done within your boundaries had been done in Sodom, Sodom would still be around. ²⁴So I'm telling you, the land of Sodom will be better off on judgment day than you. 11:25–27 #141, p. 115		¹³Damn you, Chorazin! Damn you, Bethsaida! If the miracles done in you had been done in Tyre and Sidon, they would have sat in sackcloth and ashes and changed their ways long ago. ¹⁴But Tyre and Sidon will be better off at the judgment than you. ¹⁵And you, Capernaum, you don't think you'll be exalted to heaven, do you? No; you'll go to hell. 10:16 #103, p. 84

140. Satan falls like lightning
SEE #309, P. 247

Mt	Mk	Lk 10:17–20	Jn
		[17]The seventy-two[a] returned joyfully, saying, "Master, even the demons submit to us when we invoke your name!"	
	16:17–18	[18]And he said to them, "I was watching Satan fall like lightning from heaven. [19]Look, I have given you authority to trample on snakes and scorpions, and over the full force of the enemy; nothing will ever harm you. [20]However, don't rejoice that the spirits submit to you; rejoice instead that your names have been inscribed in heaven."	*12:31*

[a] Lk 10:17 Many mss read "seventy" rather than *seventy-two*.

141. Son and Father
SEE #284, 369, PP. 232, 302

Mt 11:25–27	Mk	Lk 10:21–22	other
[25]At that point, Jesus responded, "I praise you, Father, master of earth and sky, because you have hidden these things from the wise and the learned but revealed them to the unsophisticated; [26]yes indeed, Father, because that is the way you want it.		[21]At that moment Jesus was overjoyed by the holy spirit and said, "I praise you, Father, master of earth and sky, because you have hidden these things from the wise and the learned but revealed them to the unsophisticated; yes indeed, Father, because that's the way you want it.	**Th 61:3b** I have been given some of the things of my Father. **Jn 3:35** The Father loves the son and has entrusted everything to him. **Jn 13:3** Jesus could tell that the Father had left everything up to him and that he had come from God and was going back to God. **Jn 10:15a** The Father knows me and I know the Father.
[27]My Father has turned everything over to me.		[22]My Father has turned everything over to me.	
No one knows the son except the Father, nor does anyone know the Father except the son—and anyone to whom the son wishes to reveal him.		No one knows who the son is except the Father, or who the Father is except the son—and anyone to whom the son wishes to reveal him.	
		10:23–24 #143, p. 116	

142. The Comfortable Yoke

Mt 11:28–30	Mk	Lk	Th 90:1–2
[28]All you who toil and are overloaded come to me, and I will refresh you. [29]Take my yoke upon you and learn from me, because I am gentle and modest and your lives will find rest. [30]For my yoke is comfortable and my load is light. 12:1–8 #64, p. 52			[1]Come to me, for my yoke is comfortable and my authority is gentle, [2]and you will find rest for yourselves.

143. Privileged Eyes

SEE #370, P. 302

Mt 13:16–17	Mk	Lk 10:23–24
[16]How privileged are your eyes because they see, and your ears because they hear. [17]Let me tell you, many prophets and just persons have longed to see what you see and never saw it, and to hear what you hear and never heard it.* 13:18–23 #78, p. 63		[23]Turning to the disciples he said privately, "How privileged are the eyes that see what you see! [24]I'm telling you, many prophets and kings wanted to see what you see, and never saw it, and to hear what you hear, and never heard it."*

*Th 38:1–2 [1]You've often wanted to hear these sayings that I am speaking to you, and you have no one else from whom to hear them. [2]There will be days when you'll seek me and you won't find me." (#444, p. 342)

144. How to Inherit Eternal Life

Mt 22:34–39	Mk 12:28–31	Lk 10:25–28	Th 25:1–2
[34]When the Pharisees learned that he had silenced the Sadducees, they conspired against him. [35]And one of them, a legal expert, put him to the test: [36]"Teacher, which commandment in the Law is the greatest?" [37]He replied to him,	[28]And one of the scholars approached when he heard them arguing, and because he saw how skillfully Jesus answered them, he asked him, "Of all the commandments, which is the most important?" [29]Jesus answered, "The first is, 'Hear, Israel, the Lord your God is one Lord,	[25]On one occasion, a legal expert stood up to put him to the test with a question: "Teacher, what do I have to do to inherit eternal life?" [26]He said to him, "How do you read what is written in the Law?" [27]And he answered,	
"'You shall love the Lord your God with all your heart and all your soul and all your mind.'	[30]and you shall love the Lord your God with all your heart and all your soul and all your mind and with all your strength.'	"You shall love the Lord your God with all your heart and all your soul and all your strength and with all your mind;	

³⁸This commandment is first and foremost. ³⁹And the second is like it: 'You shall love your neighbor as yourself.'	³¹The second is this: 'You shall love your neighbor as yourself.'	and your neighbor as your-self." ²⁸Jesus said to him, "You're right; do this and you will have life."	¹Love your friends like your own soul, ²protect them like the pupil of your eye.
22:34–40 #215, p. 166	12:28–34 #215, p. 166		

145. The Parable of the Good Samaritan

Mt	Mk	Lk 10:29–37
		²⁹But trying to justify himself, ⟨a legal expert⟩ said to Jesus, "But who is my neighbor?" ³⁰Jesus replied, "This man was on his way from Jerusalem down to Jericho when he fell into the hands of bandits. They stripped him, beat him, and went off, leaving him half dead. ³¹Now by coincidence a priest was going down that road; when he caught sight of him, he went out of his way to avoid him. ³²In the same way, when a Levite came to the place, he took one look at him and crossed the road to avoid him. ³³But this Samaritan was traveling that way. When he came to where he was and caught sight of him, his heart went out to him. ³⁴He went up to him and bandaged his wounds, pouring olive oil and wine on them. He hoisted him onto his own animal, brought him to an inn, and looked after him. ³⁵The next day he took out two denarii, which he gave to the innkeeper, and said, 'Look after him, and on my way back I'll reimburse you for any extra expense you've had.' ³⁶"Which of these three, in your opinion, acted like a neighbor to the man who fell into the hands of the bandits?" ³⁷He said, "The one who showed him compassion." Jesus said to him, "Then go and do the same yourself."

146. Martha and Mary

Mt	Mk	Lk 10:38–42
		[38]Now as they went along, he came to this village where a woman named Martha welcomed him into her home. [39]And she had a sister named Mary, who sat at the Master's feet and listened to his words. [40]But Martha kept getting distracted because she was doing all the serving. So she went up to Jesus and said, "Master, doesn't it matter to you that my sister has left me with all the serving? Tell her to give me a hand." [41]But the Master answered her, "Martha, Martha, you are worried and upset about a lot of things. [42]But only one thing is necessary. Mary has made the better choice and it's something she will never lose." 11:1–4 #28, p. 27

147. The Parable of the Annoying Friend at Midnight

Mt	Mk	Lk 11:5–8
		[5]Jesus said to them, "Suppose you have a friend who comes to you in the middle of the night and says to you, 'Friend, lend me three loaves, [6]for a friend of mine on a trip has just shown up and I have nothing to offer him.' [7]And suppose you reply, 'Stop bothering me. The door is already locked and my children and I are in bed. I can't get up to give you anything.' [8]I'm telling you, even though you won't get up and give him anything out of friendship, you will get up and give him whatever he needs because of his shameless behavior." 11:9–13 #36, p. 31

148. One demon brings back seven more

SEE #374, P. 305

Mt 12:43–45	Mk	Lk 11:24–26
[43]When an unclean spirit leaves a person, it wanders through waterless places in search of a place to rest. When it doesn't find one, [44]it then says, 'I will return to the home I left.' It then returns and finds the place empty, swept, and put in order. [45]Next, it goes out and brings back with it seven other spirits more vile than itself, who enter and settle in there. So that person ends up worse off than when he or she started. That's how it will be for this evil generation. 12:46–50 #75, p. 60		[24]When an unclean spirit leaves a person, it wanders through waterless places in search of a place to rest. When it doesn't find one, it says, 'I will go back to the home I left.' [25]It then returns, and finds the place swept and put in order. [26]Next, it goes out and brings back seven other spirits more vile than itself, who enter and settle in there. So that person ends up worse off than when he or she started.

149. Congratulations to the Womb that Carried Jesus

Mt	Mk	Lk 11:27–28	Th 79:1–2
		²⁷And it came to pass, as he was making these remarks, that a woman from the crowd raised her voice and said to him, "Congratulations to the womb that carried you and the breasts that nursed you!" ²⁸"Rather," he replied, "congratulations to those who hear the word of God and keep it."*	¹A woman in the crowd said to him, "Congratulations to the womb that carried you and the breasts that fed you." ²He said to [her], "Congratulations to those who've heard the word of the Father and have truly kept it."

* Lk 8:21 (#75, p. 60)

150. The Sign of Jonah
SEE #375, P. 306

Mt 12:38–42	Mk 8:11–12	Lk 11:29–32
³⁸Then some of the scholars and Pharisees responded to him, "Teacher, we would like to see a sign from you."* ³⁹In response he said to them, "An evil and adulterous generation demands a sign, and no sign will be given it—except the sign of Jonah the prophet!† ⁴⁰You see, just as 'Jonah was in the belly of a sea monster for three days and three nights,' so the Human One will be in the heart of the earth for three days and three nights. ⁴¹On judgment day, the citizens of Nineveh will come back to life along with this generation and condemn it, because they had a change of heart in response to Jonah's message. Yet take note: what is right here is greater than Jonah. ⁴²On judgment day, the queen of the south will be brought back to life along with this generation, and she will condemn it, because she came from the ends of the earth to listen to Solomon's wisdom. Yet take note: what is right here is greater than Solomon." v. 41 12:43–45 #148, p. 118	¹¹The Pharisees came out and started to argue with him. To put him to the test, they demanded a sign from heaven.* ¹²He groaned under his breath and says, "Why does this generation demand a sign? Let me tell you, this generation won't get any sign!" 8:11–13 #116, p. 96	11:16 ²⁹As more and more people were crowding around him, he began to say, "This generation is an evil generation. It demands a sign, but it will be given no sign—except the sign of Jonah! ³⁰You see, just as Jonah became a sign for the Ninevites, so the Human One will be a sign for this generation." v. 32 ³¹On judgment day, the queen of the south will be brought back to life along with members of this generation, and she will condemn them, because she came from the ends of the earth to listen to Solomon's wisdom. Yet take note: what is right here is greater than Solomon. ³²On judgment day, the citizens of Nineveh will come back to life along with this generation and condemn it, because they had a change of heart in response to Jonah's message. Yet take note: what is right here is greater than Jonah.

* Jn 6:30 They asked him, "What sign are you going to perform so we can see it and come to believe in you? What 'work' are you going to do?" (see #296, p. 241)

† Ⓓ Mt 16:4 (#116, p. 96)

151. Lamps go on lampstands

SEE #376, P. 307

Mt 5:15	**Mk 4:21**	**Lk 11:33***	**Th 33:2–3**
People do not light a lamp and put it under a bushel basket,	Since when is the lamp brought in to be put under the bushel basket or under the bed?	No one lights a lamp and then puts it in a cellar or under a bushel basket,[a]	[2]After all, no one lights a lamp and puts it under a basket, nor does one put it in a hidden place.
but instead on a lampstand, where it sheds light for everyone in the house.	It's put on the lampstand, isn't it?	but instead on a lampstand so that those who come in can see the light.	[3]Rather, one puts it on a lampstand so that all who come and go will see its light.
5:13–16 #18, p. 21	4:21–23 #79, p. 64		

* Ⓓ Lk 8:16 (#79, p. 64)

[a] Lk 11:33 A few mss omit *or under a bushel basket.*

152. The eye is the body's lamp

SEE #377, P. 307

Mt 6:22–23	Mk	**Lk 11:34–36**	Th 24:3; 61:5
[22]The eye is the body's lamp. It follows that if your eye is clear, your whole body will be flooded with light. [23]If your eye is clouded, your whole body will be shrouded in darkness. If, then, the light within you is darkness, how dark that can be!		[34]Your eye is the body's lamp. When your eye is clear, your whole body is flooded with light. When your eye is clouded, your body is shrouded in darkness. [35]Take care, then, that the light within you is not darkness.	**Th 24:3** There is light within a person of light, and it shines on the whole world. If it does not shine, it is dark.
		[36]So if your whole body is flooded with light, and no corner of it is darkness, it will be completely illuminated as when a lamp's rays engulf you.	**Th 61:5** If anyone becomes unwavering, they will be filled with light, but if anyone becomes divided, they will be filled with darkness.
6:24 #32, p. 28			

153. Damn you, Pharisees!

SEE #378–380, PP. 308–9

Mt 23 (various verses)	Mk	Lk 11:37–54	Th 89:1–2; 39:1–2
		[37]While he was speaking, a Pharisee invites him to dinner at his house. So he came and reclined ⟨at the table⟩. [38]The Pharisee was astonished to see that he did not first wash his hands before the meal. [39]But the Master said to him,	
[25]You scholars and Pharisees, you impostors! Damn you! You wash the outside of cups and plates, but inside they are full of greed and self-indulgence.		"You Pharisees clean the outside of cups and dishes, but inside you are full of greed and evil. [40]You fools! Did not the one who made the outside also make the inside? [41]Still, donate what is inside to charity, and then you'll see how everything comes clean for you.	**Th 89:1–2** [1]Why do you wash the outside of the cup? [2]Don't you understand that the one who made the inside is also the one who made the outside?
[26]You blind Pharisee, first clean the inside of the cup and then the outside will be clean too. [23]You scholars and Pharisees, you impostors! Damn you! You pay tithes on mint and dill and cumin too, but ignore the really important matters of the Law, such as justice and mercy and trust. It's these you should have practiced without ignoring the others.		[42]Damn you, Pharisees! You pay tithes on mint and rue and every herb, but neglect justice and the love of God. It's these you should have practiced without neglecting the others.	
[6]They love the best couches at banquets and the prominent seats in synagogues [7]and respectful greetings in marketplaces and having everyone call them 'Rabbi.' [27]You scholars and Pharisees, you impostors! Damn you! You're like whitewashed tombs: on the outside they look beautiful, but inside they are full of dead bones and every kind of decay.		[43]Damn you, Pharisees! You love the prominent seat in synagogues and respectful greetings in marketplaces.* [44]Damn you! You're like unmarked graves that people walk on without realizing it."	
		[45]One of the legal experts says to him in reply, "Teacher, when you say these things you're insulting us, too." [46]And he said, "Damn you legal experts too! You load people down with crushing burdens, but you yourselves don't lift a finger to help carry them.	
[4]They invent heavy burdens and lay them on folks' shoulders, but they themselves won't lift a finger to move them. [29]You scholars and Pharisees, you impostors! Damn you! You build the tombs of the prophets and decorate the graves of the just [30]and claim, 'If we had lived in the days of our ancestors, we wouldn't have		[47]Damn you! You build monuments to the prophets whom your ancestors murdered. [48]You are therefore witnesses to and approve of the deeds of your ancestors: they	

Mt 23 (various verses)	Mk	Lk 11:37–54	Th 89:1–2; 39:1–2
joined them in spilling the prophets' blood.' [31]So, you witness against yourselves: you are descendants of those who murdered the prophets, [32]and you're the spitting image of your ancestors. [34]Look, that is why I send you prophets and sages and scholars. Some you're going to kill and crucify, and some you're going to flog in your synagogues and hound from town to town. [35]And so all the innocent blood that has ever been shed on the earth will be on you, from the blood of innocent Abel to the blood of Zechariah, son of Baruch, whom you murdered between the temple and the altar. [36]Let me tell you, all these things are going to rain down on this generation. [13]You scholars and Pharisees, you impostors! Damn you! You slam the door of the empire of Heaven in people's faces. You yourselves don't go in, and you block the way of those trying to go in.[a]†		killed ⟨the prophets⟩ and you build ⟨monuments⟩ to them. [49]'That's why the Wisdom of God has said, 'I will send them prophets and apostles, and some of them they are always going to kill and persecute.' [50]So, this generation will have to answer for the blood of all the prophets that has been shed since the world was founded, [51]from the blood of Abel to the blood of Zechariah, who perished between the altar and the sanctuary. Yes, I'm telling you, this generation will have to answer for it. [52]You legal experts, damn you! You've taken away the key of knowledge. You yourselves haven't gone in and you have blocked the way of those trying to go in."† [53]By the time he had left there, the scholars and Pharisees began to resent him bitterly and to harass him with all kinds of questions, [54]conspiring to trap him with his own words.	**Th 39:1–2** [1]The Pharisees and the scholars have taken the keys of knowledge and hidden them. [2]They have not entered, nor have they allowed those who want to enter to do so.†

* Ⓓ Mk 12:38–39 / Lk 20:46 (#217, p. 167)

† Th 102 Damn the Pharisees! They are like a dog sleeping in the cattle's feeding trough: the dog neither eats nor [lets] the cattle eat." (#487, p. 361)

[a] Mt 23:13 Some mss add a v. 14: "Damn you, you scholars and Pharisees, impostors! You prey on widows and their families, and recite long prayers for appearance sake. Therefore, you will get a stiff sentence."

154. The Leaven of the Pharisees

Mt 16:6	Mk 8:15	Lk 12:1
Look, be careful: guard against the leaven of the Pharisees and Sadducees.	Look, watch out for the leaven of the Pharisees and the leaven of Herod.	Meanwhile, a crowd of many thousands had thronged together and were trampling each other. He began to speak first to his disciples: "Be on guard against the leaven of the Pharisees" (that is, their hypocrisy).
16:5–12 #117, p. 98	8:14–21 #117, p. 98	12:2–3 #100, p. 82

155. What do sparrows cost?

SEE #382, P. 310

Mt 10:28–31	Mk	Lk 12:4–7
[28]Don't fear those who kill the body but cannot kill the soul; instead, you ought to fear the one who can destroy both the soul and the body in Gehenna. [29]What do two sparrows cost? A couple of bucks? Yet not one of them will fall to the ground without your Father's consent. [30]As for you, even the hairs on your head have all been counted.* [31]So, don't be so timid; you're worth more than a flock of sparrows.		[4]I'm telling you, my friends, don't fear those who kill the body, and after that can do no more. [5]I'll show you whom you ought to fear: fear the one who can kill and then has authority to cast into Gehenna. Believe me, that's the one you should fear! [6]What do five sparrows cost? Five bucks? Yet not one of them is overlooked by God. [7]In fact, even the hairs of your head have all been counted.* Don't be so timid; you're worth more than a flock of sparrows.

*Lk 21:18 (#224, p. 173)

156. Acknowledging Jesus in Public

SEE #383, P. 311

Mt 10:32–33	Mk	Lk 12:8–9
[32]Everyone who acknowledges me in public, I too will acknowledge before my Father in the heavens. [33]But the one who disowns me in public, I too will disown in front of my Father in the heavens.		[8]I'm telling you, everyone who acknowledges me in public, the Human One will acknowledge in front of God's messengers. [9]But whoever disowns me in public will be disowned in front of God's messengers.*
10:34–39 #102, p. 83		12:10 #73, p. 58

*Mk 8:38 / Lk 9:26 (#121, p. 102)

157. Don't worry about what to say
SEE #383, P. 311

Mt 10:19–20	Mk 13:9–11	Lk 12:11–12
[19]And when they lock you up,	[9]But you look out for yourselves. They'll turn you over to Jewish councils, and beat you in synagogues, and haul you up before governors and kings on my account, so you can make your case to them. [10]Yet the good news must first be announced to all peoples.	[11]And when they make you appear in front of synagogues and haul you up before rulers and authorities,
don't worry about how you should speak or what you should say.	[11]And when they take you away to turn you in, don't be worried about what you should say.	don't worry about how or in what way you should defend yourself or what you should say.
It will occur to you at that moment what to say. [20]For it's not you who are speaking but your Father's spirit speaking through you.	Instead, whatever occurs to you at the moment, say that. For it's not you who are speaking but the holy spirit.	[12]The holy spirit will teach you at that very moment what you ought to say.*
10:16–25 #99, p. 80	13:9–13 #224, p. 173	

* Ⓓ Lk 21:14–15 (#224, p. 173)

158. The Parable of the Rich Fool

Mt	Mk	Lk 12:13–21	Th 72:1–3; 63:1–3
		[13]Someone in the crowd said to him, "Teacher, tell my brother to divide the inheritance with me." [14]But Jesus said to him, "Mister, who appointed me your judge or arbiter?"	**Th 72:1–3** [1]A [person said] to him, "Tell my brothers to divide my father's possessions with me." [2]He said to the person, "Mister, who made me a divider?" [3]He turned to his disciples and said to them, "I'm not a divider, am I?"
		[15]Then he said to them, "Watch out! Be on guard against greed in all its forms; after all, possessions, even in abundance, don't guarantee you life." [16]Then he told them a parable: There was a rich man whose fields produced a bumper crop. [17]"What do I do now?" he asked himself, "since I don't have any place to store my crops. [18]I know!" he said, "I'll tear down my barns and build larger ones so I can store all my grain and my goods. [19]Then I'll say to myself, 'You have plenty put away for years to come. Take it easy; eat, drink, and enjoy yourself.'" [20]But God said to him, "You fool! This very night your life will be demanded back from you. All this stuff you've collected—whose will it be now?" [21]That's the way it is with those who save up for themselves, but aren't rich where God is concerned.	**Th 63:1–3** [1]There was a rich man who had a great deal of money. [2]He said, "I shall invest my money so that I may sow, reap, plant, and fill my storehouses with produce, that I may lack nothing." [3]These were the things he was thinking in his heart, but that very night he died.
		12:22–31 #33, p. 29	

159. Waiting for the Master

Mt	Mk	Lk 12:35–38
25:1–13	13:33–37	[35]Keep your belts fastened and your lamps lit. [36]Imitate those who are waiting for their master to come home from a wedding, ready to open the door for him as soon as he arrives and knocks. [37]Those slaves the master finds alert when he arrives are to be congratulated. Let me tell you, he will put on an apron, have them recline at the table, and proceed to wait on them. [38]If he gets home around midnight, or even around 3 a.m., and finds them so, they are to be congratulated!

160. Anticipating the Burglar

SEE #386, P. 313

Mt 24:43–44	Mk	Lk 12:39–40	Th 21:5	Th 103
[43]Mark this well: if the homeowner had known when the burglar was coming, he would have been on guard and not have allowed anyone to break into his house.		[39]Mark this well: if the homeowner had known what time the burglar was coming,[a] he would not have let anyone break into his house.	For this reason I say, if the owners of a house know that a thief is coming, they will be on guard before the thief arrives, and won't let the thief break into their house and steal their possessions.	Congratulations to the one who knows where the brigands are going to attack. [He] can take action, mobilize his kingdom, and be prepared before the brigands invade.
[44]Therefore, you too should be prepared. Remember, the Human One is coming when you least expect it.	13:35–36	[40]You too should be prepared. Remember, the Human One is coming when you least expect it.		

[a] Lk 12:39 Many mss insert "he would have watched and" after *coming*.

161. The Trustworthy Slave and the Dismembered Slave

SEE #387, P. 314

Mt 24:45–51	Mk	Lk 12:41–48
[45]Who then is the trustworthy and prudent slave to whom the master assigns responsibility for his household, to provide them with food at the right time? [46]Congratulations to the slave who's on the job when his master arrives. [47]Let me tell you, he'll put him in charge of all his property. [48]But suppose that worthless slave says to himself, 'My master is taking his time,' [49]and begins to beat his fellow slaves, and starts eating and drinking with drunks, [50]that slave's master will show up on the day he least expects and at an hour he doesn't suspect. [51]He'll cut him to pieces, and assign him a fate among the impostors, where they'll weep and grind their teeth.	13:35	[41]Peter said, "Master, are you telling this parable just for us or for the benefit of everyone?" [42]The Master said, "Who then is the trustworthy and prudent manager to whom the master assigns responsibility for his household staff, to dole out their food allowance at the right time? [43]Congratulations to the slave who's on the job when his master arrives. [44]I'm telling you the truth: he'll put him in charge of all his property. [45]But suppose that slave says to himself, 'My master is taking his time getting here,' and begins to beat the servants and the maids, and to eat and drink and get drunk, [46]that slave's master will show up on the day he least expects and at an hour he doesn't suspect. He'll cut him to pieces and assign him a fate among the disloyal. [47]And the slave who knew what his master wanted, but didn't get things ready or act properly, will be flogged severely. [48]On the other hand, the slave who didn't know what his master wanted, yet did things that deserve punishment, will be flogged lightly. A great deal will be required of everyone to whom much is given; yet even more will be demanded from the one to whom a great deal has been entrusted.
25:1–13 #232, p. 178		

162. Jesus brings fire and conflict
SEE #388, P. 315

Mt 10:34–36	Mk 10:38	Lk 12:49–53	Th 10; 16:1–3
		⁴⁹I came to set the earth on fire, and how I wish it were already ablaze!*	**Th 10** I have cast fire upon the world, and look, I'm guarding it until it blazes.*
20:22b	Can you drink the cup that I'm drinking, or go through the baptism I'm going through?"	⁵⁰I have a baptism to be baptized with, and what pressure I'm under until it's over!	
³⁴Don't get the idea that I came to bring peace on earth. I didn't come to bring peace, but a sword!		⁵¹Do you think I came here to bring peace on earth? No, I'm telling you, on the contrary: conflict. ⁵²As a result, from now on in any given house there will be five in conflict, three against two and two against three. ⁵³Father will be pitted against son and son against father, mother against daughter and daughter against mother, mother-in-law against daughter-in-law and daughter-in-law against mother-in-law.	**Th 16:1–3** ¹Perhaps people think that I've come to cast peace upon the world. ²They don't know that I've come to sow conflict upon the earth: fire, sword, war. ³For there'll be five in a house: there'll be three against two and two against three, father against son and son against father.
³⁵After all, I've come to pit a man against his father, a daughter against her mother,	*13:12*		
and a daughter-in-law against her mother-in-law. ³⁶Your enemies live under your own roof.			
10:34–39 #102, p. 83	10:34–45 #200, p. 151		

* Th 82:1–2 ¹Whoever is near me is near the fire, ²and whoever is far from me is far from the ⟨Father's⟩ empire. (#474, p. 356)

163. Reading the Face of the Sky
SEE #389, P. 315

Mt 16:2–3	Mk	Lk 12:54–56	Th 91:2
²In response he said to them, "When it's evening, you say, 'It'll be fair weather because the sky looks red.' ³Early in the morning you say, 'The day will bring winter weather because the sky looks red and dark.' You know how to interpret the face of the sky, but you can't ⟨do that for⟩ the signs of the times.		⁵⁴He would also say to the crowds, "When you see a cloud rising in the west, right away you say that it's going to rain; and so it does. ⁵⁵And when the wind blows from the south, you say we're in for scorching heat; and we are. ⁵⁶You phonies! You know the lay of the land and can read the face of the sky, so why don't you know how to read the present time?	You examine the face of heaven and earth, but you have not come to know the one who is in your presence, and you don't know how to examine the present moment.
16:1–4 #116, p. 96			

164. Settle out of court
SEE #390, P. 316

Mt 5:25–26	Mk	Lk 12:57–59
[25]You should settle quickly with your accuser while you are both on the way ⟨to court⟩, or else your accuser will turn you over to the judge, and the judge to the bailiff, and you are thrown in jail. [26]Let me tell you, you'll never get out of there until you've paid the last dime. 5:27–30 #21, p. 23		[57]Why can't you decide for yourselves what is right? [58]When you're about to appear with your accuser before the magistrate, do your best to settle with him on the way, or else he might drag you up before the judge, and the judge turn you over to the jailer, and the jailer throw you in prison. [59]I'm telling you, you'll never get out of there until you've paid every last cent.

165. Change or Doom

Mt	Mk	Lk 13:1–5
		[1]Some who were there at the time told him about the Galileans, about how Pilate had mixed their own blood with their sacrifices. [2]He answered them, "Do you suppose that these Galileans were the worst sinners in Galilee, because they suffered this? [3]Hardly. However, let me tell you, if you don't have a change of heart, you'll all meet your doom in the same way. [4]Or how about those eighteen in Siloam, who were killed when that tower fell on them—do you suppose that they were any guiltier than the whole population of Jerusalem? [5]Hardly. However, let me tell you, if you don't have a change of heart, all of you will meet your doom in a similar fashion."

166. The Parable of the Patient Vinekeeper

Mt	Mk	Lk 13:6–9

		[6]Then he told this parable:
		    A man had a fig tree growing in his vineyard; he came looking for fruit on it but didn't find any. [7]So he said to the vinekeeper, "See here, for three years in a row I've come looking for fruit on this tree, and haven't found any. Cut it down. Why should it suck the nutrients out of the soil?"
		    [8]In response he says to him, "Let it stand, sir, one more year, until I get a chance to dig around it and work in some manure. [9]Maybe it will produce next year; but if it doesn't, we can go ahead and cut it down."

167. Exorcism of the Woman with a Bent Spine

Mt	Mk	Lk 13:10–17
		[10]Now he was teaching in one of the meeting places on the Sabbath. [11]A woman showed up who for eighteen years had been afflicted by a spirit; she was bent over and unable to straighten up even a little. [12]When Jesus noticed her, he called her over and said, "Woman, you are freed from your affliction." [13]He laid hands on her, and immediately she stood up straight and began to praise God.
		[14]The leader of the meeting place was indignant, however, because Jesus had healed on the Sabbath. He said to the crowd, "There are six days which we devote to work; so come on one of those days and be healed, but not on the Sabbath."
		[15]But the Master answered him, "You phonies! Every last one of you unties your ox or your donkey from the feeding trough on the Sabbath and leads it off to water, don't you?* [16]This woman, a daughter of Abraham whom Satan has kept in bondage for eighteen long years—should she not be released from these bonds just because it is the Sabbath?" [17]As he said this, all his adversaries were put to shame, but most folks rejoiced at all the wonderful things he was doing.
		13:18–19 #83, p. 66

*Mt 12:11 / Lk 14:5 (#172, p. 131)

168. The Narrow Door

SEE #393, P. 317

Mt 7:13–14; 25:10b–12; 7:22–23	Mk	Lk 13:22–27
		[22]On his journey he passed through towns and villages, teaching and making his way toward Jerusalem. [23]And someone asked him, "Sir, is it true that only a few are going to be saved?" He said to them, [24]"Struggle to get in through the narrow door;
Mt 7:13–14 [13]Get in through the narrow gate. Wide and smooth is the road that leads to destruction. Many are taking that route. [14]Narrow and rough is the road that leads to life. Only a few discover it.*		I'm telling you, many will try to get in, but won't be able.*
Mt 25:10b–12 [10b]The bridegroom arrived and those who had come prepared accompanied him to the wedding; then the door was closed. [11]The other maidens finally come and say, "Master, master, open the door for us." [12]He responded, "Let me tell you, I don't recognize you."		[25]Once the master of the house gets up and bars the door, you'll be left standing outside and knocking at the door: 'Master, open up for us.' But he'll answer you, 'I don't know where you come from.'
Mt 7:22–23 [22]On that day many will say to me, 'Master, master, didn't we use your name when we prophesied? Didn't we use your name when we exorcised demons? Didn't we use your name when we performed all those miracles?' [23]Then I will tell them honestly, 'I never knew you; get away from me, you subverters of the Law!'		[26]Then you'll start saying, 'We ate and drank with you, and you taught in our streets.' [27]But he'll reply, 'I don't know where you come from; get away from me, all you evildoers!'

*Th 75 There are many standing at the door, but those who are solitary will enter the wedding hall. (#468, p. 354)

169. Thrown out of the Patriarchs' Banquet
SEE #394, P. 318

Mt 8:11–12	Mk	Lk 13:28–29
[11]Many will come from east and west and dine with Abraham and Isaac and Jacob in the empire of Heaven, [12]but those who think the empire of Heaven belongs to them will be thrown out into the utter darkness. There'll be weeping and grinding of teeth out there. 8:5–13 #52, p. 42		[28]There'll be weeping and grinding of teeth out there when you see Abraham and Isaac and Jacob and all the prophets in God's empire and yourselves thrown out. [29]And people will come from east and west, from north and south, and dine in God's empire.

170. The first will be last
SEE #394, P. 318

Mt 19:30; 20:16	Mk 10:31	Lk 13:30	Th 4:2
Mt 19:30 Many of the first will be last, and many of the last will be first. **Mt 20:16** The last will be first and the first last.	Many of the first will be last, and many of the last will be first. 10:32–34 #199, p. 150	And remember, those who will be first are last, and those who will be last are first.	For many of the first will be last.

171. Herod the Fox

Mt	Mk	Lk 13:31–33
		[31]About that time some Pharisees approached and warned him, "Get out of here! Herod wants to kill you." [32]He replied to them, "Go tell that fox, 'Look here, today and tomorrow I'll be driving out demons and healing people, and the third day I'll be finished.' [33]Still, today and tomorrow and the day after, I have to move on, because it's impossible for a prophet to die outside of Jerusalem." 13:34–35 #220, p. 171

172. Is it permissible to heal on the Sabbath?

Mt 12:11	Mk	Lk 14:1–6*
		[1]And it came to pass one Sabbath, when Jesus was having dinner at the house of a prominent Pharisee, that they were keeping an eye on him. [2]This man who had dropsy suddenly showed up.
		[3]Jesus addressed the legal experts and Pharisees: "Is it permitted to heal on the Sabbath, or not?"
		[4]But they were silent.
		So he took the man, healed him, and sent him on his way.
If you had only a single sheep, and it fell into a ditch on the Sabbath, wouldn't you grab it and pull it out?		[5]Then he said to them, "Suppose your son[a] or your ox falls down a well, would any of you hesitate for a second to pull him out on the Sabbath?"
12:9–14 #65, p. 53		[6]And they had no response to this.

* Mt 12:9–14 / Mk 3:1–6 / Lk 6:6–11 (#65, p. 53)
———
[a] Lk 14:5 Some mss read "donkey" in place of *son*.

173. Banquet Wisdom
SEE #396, P. 318

Mt 23:12	Mk	Lk 14:7–11
		[7]He would tell a parable for the guests, when he noticed how they were choosing the places of honor.
		He said to them, [8]"When someone invites you to a wedding banquet, don't take the place of honor, in case someone more important than you has been invited. [9]Then the one who invited you both will come and say to you, 'Make room for this person,' and you'll be embarrassed to have to take the lowest place. [10]Instead, when you're invited, go take the lowest place, so when the host comes he'll say to you, 'Friend, come up higher.' Then you'll be honored in front of all those reclining ⟨around the table⟩ with you.
Those who promote themselves will be demoted and those who demote themselves will be promoted.		[11]Those who promote themselves will be demoted, and those who demote themselves will be promoted."*
23:1–12 #218, p. 168		

* Ⓓ Lk 18:14 (#192, p. 144)

174. Invite those who can't repay you

Mt	Mk	Lk 14:12–14
		[12]Then he said also to his host, "When you give a lunch or a dinner, don't invite your friends, or your brothers and sisters, or relatives, or rich neighbors. They might invite you in return and so you would be repaid. [13]Instead, when you throw a dinner party, invite the poor, the crippled, the lame, and the blind. [14]In that case, you are to be congratulated, since they cannot repay you. You will be repaid at the resurrection of the just."

175. The Parable of the Dinner Guests Who Had Excuses

SEE #397, P. 319

Mt 22:1–14	Mk	Lk 14:15–24	Th 64:1–12
[1]Jesus again responded to them and told them parables. [2]The empire of Heaven is like a king who gave a wedding celebration for his son. [3]Then he sent his slaves to summon those who had been invited to the wedding, but they declined to attend.		[15]When one of his fellow guests heard this, he said to him, "Congratulations to those who will eat bread in the empire of God!" [16]Jesus told him: Someone was giving a big dinner and invited many guests. [17]At the dinner hour the host sent his slave to tell the guests, "Come, it's ready now." [18]But one by one they all began to make excuses. The first said to him, "I just bought a farm and I have to go and inspect it; please excuse me." [19]And another said, "I just bought five pairs of oxen and I'm on my way to check them out; please excuse me." [20]And another said, "I just got married and so I cannot attend." [21]So the slave came back and reported these ⟨excuses⟩ to his master.	[1]A man was receiving guests. When he had prepared the dinner, he sent his slave to invite the guests. [2]The slave went to the first and said, "My master invites you." [3]He replied, "Some merchants owe me money; they're coming to me tonight. I have to go and give them instructions. Please excuse me from dinner." [4]The slave went to another and said, "My master has invited you." [5]He said to him, "I've bought a house and I've been called away for a day. I won't have any time." [6]He went to another and said, "My master invites you." [7]He said to him, "My friend is to be married and I have to arrange the banquet. I won't be able to come. Please excuse me from dinner." [8]He went to another and said, "My master invites you." [9]He said to him, "I've bought an estate and I'm going to collect the rent. I won't be able to come. Please excuse me." [10]The slave returned and said to his master, "Those whom you invited to dinner have asked to be excused."

⁴He sent additional slaves with the instructions: "Tell those invited, 'Look, the feast is ready, the oxen and fat calves have been slaughtered, and everything is set. Come to the wedding.'"

⁵But they couldn't be bothered and went off, one to his own farm, one to his business, ⁶while the rest seized his slaves, attacked and killed them.

⁷Now the king was outraged and sent his armies to destroy those murderers and burn their city. ⁸Then he tells his slaves, "The wedding celebration is ready, but those we've invited didn't deserve it. ⁹So go to the city gates and invite anybody you find to the wedding."

¹⁰Those slaves then went out into the streets and collected everybody they could find, the good and bad alike. And the wedding hall was full of guests.

¹¹The king came in to see the guests for himself and noticed this one man without proper attire. ¹²And he says to him, "Look pal, how'd you get in here without dressing for the occasion?"

And he was speechless.

¹³Then the king ordered his waiters, "Bind him hand and foot and throw him out into the utter darkness. They'll weep and grind their teeth out there. ¹⁴After all, many are called but few are chosen."

22:15–22 #213, p. 164

Then the master of the house was outraged

and instructed his slave, "Quick! Go out into the streets and alleys of the town, and usher in the poor, and crippled, the blind, and the lame."
²²And the slave said, "Master, your orders have been carried out, and there's still room."
²³And the master said to the slave, "Then go out into the roads and the country lanes, and force people to come in so my house will be filled.
²⁴For I'm telling you, not one of those who were invited will taste my dinner."

¹¹The master said to his slave, "Go out on the roads and bring back whomever you find to have dinner."

¹²Buyers and merchants [will] not enter the places of my Father.

176. Counting the Cost
SEE #398, P. 320

Mt 10:37–39	Mk	Lk 14:25–33	Th 101:1; 55:1–2
[37]If you love your father and mother more than me, you're not worthy of me, and if you love your son or daughter more than me, you're not worthy of me.		[25]Once when hordes of people were traveling with him, he turned and addressed them: [26]"If any of you comes to me and does not hate your own father and mother and wife and children and brothers and sisters—yes, even your own life—you cannot be my disciple.	**Th 101:1** Whoever does not hate [father] and mother as I do cannot be my [disciple]. **Th 55:1–2** [1]Whoever does not hate father and mother cannot be my disciple, [2]and whoever does not hate brothers and sisters, and carry the cross as I do,
[38]Unless you take your cross and come along with me, you're not worthy of me.* [39]By finding your life, you'll lose it, but by losing your life for my sake, you'll find it.		[27]Unless you carry your own cross and come along with me, you cannot be my disciple.*	will not be worthy of me.
		17:33	
		[28]Think about it: if you plan to build a tower, don't you first sit down and calculate whether you can afford to complete it? [29]Otherwise you might lay the foundation and not be able to finish, and all the onlookers would begin to make fun of you: [30]'That guy started to build but couldn't finish.' [31]Or if a king was going to war against another king, wouldn't he first sit down and figure out whether he would be able with ten thousand men to engage an enemy coming against him with twenty thousand? [32]If he decided he couldn't, he would send an envoy to ask for terms of peace while the enemy was still a long way off. [33]It's just like that: if you don't say good-bye to everything that belongs to you, you cannot be my disciple.	
10:40–11:1 #103, p. 84		14:34–35 #18, p. 21	

*Mt 16:24 / Mk 8:34 / Lk 9:23 (#121, p. 102)

177. The Parable of the Lost-and-Found Sheep

SEE #405, P. 323

Mt 18:12–14	Mk	Lk 15:1–7	other
		[1]Now the toll collectors and sinners kept crowding around Jesus so they could hear him. [2]But the Pharisees and the scholars would complain to each other, "This guy welcomes sinners and eats with them."*	**GOxy 1224 5:1** When the scholars an[d Pharise]es and priests observ[ed hi]m, they were indignant [because he reclined ⟨at table⟩ in the com]pany of sin[ners].
		[3]So he told them this parable:	
[12]What do you think about this? If someone has a hundred sheep and one of them wanders off, won't he leave the ninety-nine in the hills and go look for the one that wandered off? [13]And if he should find it, let me tell you, he'll rejoice over it more than over the ninety-nine that didn't wander off.		[4]Is there any one of you who owns a hundred sheep and one of them gets lost, who wouldn't leave the ninety-nine in the wild and go after the one that got lost until he finds it? [5]And when he finds it, he is happy and hoists it onto his shoulders. [6]Once he gets home, he invites his friends and his neighbors over, and says to them, "Celebrate with me, because I've found my lost sheep."	**Th 107:1–3** [1]The ⟨Father's⟩ empire is like a shepherd who had a hundred sheep. [2]One of them, the largest, went astray. He left the ninety-nine and looked for the one until he found it. [3]After he had struggled, he said to the sheep, "I love you more than the ninety-nine."
[14]And so it is the intention of your Father in heaven that not one of these little ones be lost.		[7]I'm telling you, it'll be just like that in heaven: there'll be more celebrating over one sinner who has a change of heart than over ninety-nine virtuous people who have no need to change their hearts.	
18:15–18 #132, p. 110			

*Mt 9:11 / Mk 2:16 / Lk 5:30 (#60, p. 49)

178. The Parable of the Lost-and-Found Coin

SEE #406, P. 323

Mt	Mk	Lk 15:8–10
		[8]Or again, is there any woman with ten drachmas, who if she loses one, wouldn't light a lamp and sweep the house and search high and low until she finds it? [9]When she finds it, she invites her friends and neighbors over and says, "Celebrate with me, because I've found the drachma I lost."
		[10]I'm telling you, it's just like that among God's messengers: they celebrate when one sinner has a change of heart.

179. The Parable of the Man and His Two Sons

Mt	Mk	Lk 15:11–32
		[11]Then he said: Once there was this man who had two sons. [12]The younger of them said to his father, "Father, give me the share of the property that's coming to me." So he divided his resources between them. [13]Not too many days later, the younger son got all his things together and left home for a faraway country, where he squandered his resources by living recklessly. [14]Just when he had spent it all, a serious famine swept through that country, and he began to do without. [15]So he went and hired himself out to one of the citizens of that country, who sent him out to his farm to feed the pigs. [16]He longed to satisfy his hunger with the carob pods, which the pigs usually ate; but no one offered him anything. [17]Coming to his senses he said, "Lots of my father's hired hands have more than enough to eat, while here I am starving to death! [18]I'll get up and go to my father and I'll say to him, 'Father, I have sinned against Heaven and against you. [19]I no longer deserve to be called your son; treat me like one of your hired hands.'" [20]And he got up and returned to his father. But while he was still a long way off, his father caught sight of him and was moved to compassion. He went running out to him, threw his arms around his neck, and kissed him. [21]And the son said to him, "Father, I have sinned against Heaven and against you. I no longer deserve to be called your son." [22]But the father said to his slaves, "Hurry up! Bring out the finest robe and put it on him; put a ring on his finger and sandals on his feet. [23]Fetch the fat calf and slaughter it; let's have a feast and celebrate, [24]because this son of mine was dead and has come back to life; he was lost and now is found." And they started celebrating. [25]Now his elder son was out in the field; and as he got closer to the house, he heard music and dancing. [26]He called one of the servant boys over and asked what was going on. [27]He told him, "Your brother has come home and your father has slaughtered the fat calf, because he has him back safe and sound." [28]But he was angry and refused to go in. So his father came out and began to plead with him. [29]But he answered his father, "See here, all these years I have slaved for you. I never once disobeyed any of your orders; but you never once let me have a kid goat so I could celebrate with my friends. [30]But when this son of yours shows up, the one who has devoured your assets with whores—for him you slaughter the fat calf." [31]But ⟨the father⟩ said to him, "My child, you are always at my side. Everything that's mine is yours. [32]But we just had to celebrate and rejoice, because this brother of yours was dead and has come back to life; he was lost and now is found."

180. The Parable of the Dishonest Manager

Mt	Mk	Lk 16:1–9
		[1]Jesus would say to the disciples: There was this rich man whose manager had been maliciously accused of squandering his master's property. [2]He called him in and said, "What's this I hear about you? Turn in your record books; you're no longer working here." [3]Then the manager said to himself, "What am I going to do? My master is firing me. I'm not able to dig ditches and I'm ashamed to beg. [4]I've got it! I know what I'll do so doors will open for me when I'm removed from management." [5]So he called in each of his master's debtors. He said to the first, "How much do you owe my master?" [6]He said, "Five hundred gallons of olive oil." And he said to him, "Here is your invoice; sit down right now and make it two hundred and fifty." [7]Then he said to another, "And how much do you owe?" He said, "A thousand bushels of wheat." He says to him, "Here is your invoice; make it eight hundred." [8]The master praised the dishonest manager because he had acted prudently. For the children of this world are more prudent in dealing with their own kind than are the children of light. [9]And I'm telling you, make use of your ill-gotten mammon to make friends for yourselves, so that when the bottom falls out they are there to welcome you into eternal dwelling places.

181. God and Mammon

SEE #401, P. 321

Mt 6:24	Mk	Lk 16:10–13	Th 47:2
		[10]Those who can be trusted in trivial matters can also be trusted with large amounts; and those who cheat in trivial matters will also cheat where large amounts are concerned. [11]So if you can't be trusted with ill-gotten mammon, who will trust you with real wealth? [12]And if you can't be trusted with something that belongs to somebody else, who will give you property of your own?	
No one can be a slave to two masters. That slave will either hate one and love the other, or be devoted to one and disdain the other. You can't be enslaved to both God and Mammon.		[13]No servant can be a slave to two masters. That slave will either hate one and love the other, or be devoted to one and disdain the other. You can't be enslaved to both God and mammon.	And a slave cannot serve two masters, otherwise that slave will honor the one and offend the other.
6:25–34 #33, p. 29			

182. Greedy Pharisees

Mt	Mk	Lk 16:14–15
		[14]The Pharisees, who were money grubbers, heard all this and sneered at him. [15]But he said to them, "You're the type who justify yourselves to others, but God reads your hearts. What people rank highest is detestable in God's estimation."

183. Violence and God's Empire

SEE #402, P. 321

Mt 11:12–13, 14–15; 5:18	Mk	Lk 16:16–17
Mt 11:12–15 [12]From the time of John the Baptizer until now the empire of Heaven has been breaking in violently, and violent men are trying to seize it. [13]You see, the Prophets and the Law predicted everything up to John's time. [14]And if you are willing to admit it, John is the Elijah who was to come. [15]Anyone here with ears, use 'em!*		[16]Right up to John's time you have the Law and the Prophets; since then God's empire has been proclaimed as good news and everyone is breaking into it violently.
Mt 5:18 Let me tell you, before earth and sky pass away,† not one iota, not one serif, will disappear from the Law, until it all happens.		[17]But it's easier for earth and sky to pass away† than for one serif of the Law to drop out. 16:18 #22, p. 23

* Mt 13:9; 13:43b; Mk 4:9; 4:23; Lk 8:8b; 14:35b; Th 8:4; 21:10; 24:2; 63:4; 65:8; 96:3

† Th 11:1 This heaven will pass away and the one above it will pass away. (#422, p. 335)

184. The Parable of the Rich Man and Lazarus

Mt	Mk	Lk 16:19–31
		[19]There was this rich man, who wore clothing fit for a king and who dined lavishly every day. [20]This poor man, named Lazarus, languished at his gate, all covered with sores. [21]He longed to eat what fell from the rich man's table. Dogs even used to come and lick his sores. [22] It came to pass that the poor man died and was carried by the heavenly messengers to be with Abraham. The rich man died too, and was buried. [23]From Hades, where he was being tortured, he looked up and saw Abraham a long way off and Lazarus with him. [24]He called out, "Father Abraham, have pity on me! Send Lazarus to dip the tip of his finger in water and cool my tongue, for I am in torment in these flames." [25]But Abraham said, "My child, remember that you had good fortune in your lifetime, while Lazarus had it bad. Now he is being comforted here, and you are in torment. [26]And besides all this, a great chasm has been set between us and you, so that even those who want to cross over from here to you cannot, and no one can cross over from that side to ours." [27]But he said, "Father, I beg you then, send him to my father's house [28]—after all, I have five brothers—so he can warn them not to wind up in this place of torture." [29]But Abraham says, "They have Moses and the prophets; why don't they listen to them?" [30]"But they won't do that, father Abraham," he said. "But, if someone appears to them from the dead, they'll have a change of heart." [31]Abraham said to him, "If they won't listen to Moses and the prophets, they won't be convinced even if someone were to rise from the dead." 17:1–2 #131, p. 109

185. Serial Forgiving

SEE #407, P. 324

Mt 18:15, 21–22	Mk	Lk 17:3–4	GNaz 5:1
[15]If some companion does wrong, go have it out between the two of you privately. If that person listens to you, you have won your companion over. [21]Then Peter came up and asked him, "Master, how many times can a companion wrong me and still expect my forgiveness? As many as seven times?" [22]Jesus replies to him, "My advice to you is not seven times, but seventy-seven times." 18:23–35 #135, p. 111		[3]So be on your guard. If your companion does wrong, scold that person; if there is a change of heart, forgive the person. [4]If someone wrongs you seven times a day, and seven times turns around and says to you, "I'm sorry," you must forgive that person."	If your brother or sister has wronged you verbally and made amends, welcome him or her seven times a day. His disciple Simon said to him, "Seven times a day?" The Master answered him, "That's right; in fact, up to seventy times seven times."

186. How to Move Mountains and Trees

SEE #408, P. 324

Mt 17:20b; 21:21	Mk 11:23	Lk 17:5–6	Th 48; 106:2
Mt 17:20b Let me tell you, even if you have trust no bigger than a mustard seed, you will say to this mountain, "Move from here to there," and it will move. **Mt 21:21** Let me tell you, if you have trust and do not doubt, not only can you do this to a fig tree but you can even say to this mountain, "Up with you and into the sea!" and that's what will happen.	Let me tell you, those who say to this mountain, "Up with you and into the sea!" and do not waver in their conviction, but trust that what they say will happen, that's the way it will be. 11:20–25 #209, p. 159	[5]The apostles said to the Master, "Make our trust grow!" [6]And the Master said, "If you had trust no bigger than a mustard seed, you could tell this mulberry tree, 'Uproot yourself and plant yourself in the sea,' and it would obey you."	**Th 48** If two make peace with each other in a single house, they will say to the mountain, "Move from here!" and it will move. **Th 106:2** When you say, "Mountain, move from here!" it will move.

187. "We're worthless slaves"

Mt	Mk	Lk 17:7–10
		[7]If you had a slave plowing or herding sheep and he came in from the fields, would any of you tell him, "Come right in and recline ⟨at the table⟩"? [8]Wouldn't you say to him instead, "Get my dinner ready, put on your apron, and serve me while I eat and drink. You can eat and drink later"? [9]He wouldn't thank the slave because he did what he was told to do, would he? [10]The same goes for you: when you've done everything you've been told to do, say, "We're worthless slaves; we've only done our job."

188. Ten Lepers Healed

Mt	Mk	Lk 17:11–19
		[11]And it came to pass on the way to Jerusalem that he was passing between Samaria and Galilee. [12]As he was coming into this village, he was met by ten lepers, who kept their distance. [13]They shouted, "Jesus, Master, have mercy on us!" [14]When he saw them, he told them, "Go show yourselves to the priests." And it came to pass as they departed that they were made clean. [15]Then one of them, realizing that he had been healed, came back. He praised God out loud, [16]knelt with his face to the ground at Jesus' feet, and thanked him. (Incidentally, this man was a Samaritan.) [17]But Jesus said, "Ten were cured, weren't they? What became of the other nine? [18]Didn't any of them return to praise God besides this foreigner?" [19]And he said to him, "Get up and be on your way; your trust has cured you."

189. Empire of God Among You

SEE #190, 409, PP. 142, 324

Mt	Mk	Lk 17:20–21	Th 113:1–4	Th 3:1–3
		[20]When asked by the Pharisees when the empire of God would come, he answered them, "You won't be able to observe the coming of the empire of God. [21]People won't be able to say, 'Look, here it is!' or 'Over there!'* On the contrary, the empire of God is among you."	[1]His disciples said to him, "When will the ⟨Father's⟩ empire come?" [2]"It won't come by watching for it. [3]It won't be said, 'Look, here!' or 'Look, there!'* [4]Rather, the Father's empire is spread out upon the earth, and people don't see it."	[1]If your leaders say to you, "Look, the ⟨Father's⟩ empire is in the sky," then the birds of the sky will precede you. [2]If they say to you, "It's in the sea," then the fish will precede you. [3]Rather, the ⟨Father's⟩ empire is inside you and outside you.

*Mt 24:23 / Mk 13:21 (#226, p. 175)

190. The Day of the Human One

SEE #309, 410, PP. 247, 325

Mt 24 (various verses) + 10:39	Mk 13:21, 15–16	Lk 17:22–37	other
			Th 113:1–4 [1]His disciples said to him, "When will the ⟨Father's⟩ empire come?"
		[22]And he said to the disciples, "There'll come a time when you will yearn to see one of the days of the Human One, and you won't see it.	
Mt 24:23, 26–27, 37–39, 17–18 [23]Then if someone says to you, "Look, here's the Anointed One" or "over here," don't count on it! [26]In fact, if they should say to you, "Look, he's in the desert," don't go out there; or "Look, he's in one of the inner rooms," don't count on it. [27]For just as lightning comes out of the east and is visible all the way to the west, that's what the coming of the Human One will be like.	[21]And then if someone says to you, "Look, here's the Anointed One," or "Look, there he is!" don't count on it!	[23]And they'll be telling you, 'Look, there it is!' or 'Look, here it is!' Don't rush off; don't pursue it.	[2]"It won't come by watching for it. [3]It won't be said, 'Look, here!' or 'Look, there!'
		[24]For just as lightning flashes and lights up the sky from one end to the other, that's what the Human One will be like in his day.[a] [25]But first he is destined to endure much and be rejected by this present generation.	[4]Rather, the Father's empire is spread out upon the earth, and people don't see it."
[37]The Human One's coming will be just like the days of Noah. [38]That's how people behaved then before the flood came: they ate and drank, married and were given in marriage, until the day Noah boarded the ark, [39]and they were oblivious until the flood came and swept them all away.		[26]And just as it was in the days of Noah, that's how it will be in the days of the Human One. [27]They ate, drank, got married, and were given in marriage, until the day Noah boarded the ark. Then the flood came and destroyed them all.	
		[28]That's also the way it was in the days of Lot. Everyone ate, drank, bought, sold, planted, and built. [29]But on the day Lot left Sodom, fire and sulfur rained down from the sky and destroyed them all. [30]It will be like that on the day the Human One is revealed.	
That's how it will be when the Human One comes. [17]No one on the roof should go downstairs to retrieve anything;	[15]No one on the roof should go downstairs, no one should enter the house to retrieve anything,	[31]On that day, if any are on the roof and their things are in the house, they had better not go down to fetch them.	

¹⁸and no one in the field should turn back to get a coat. **Mt 10:39** ³⁹By finding your life, you'll lose it, but by losing your life for my sake, you'll find it. **Mt 24:40–41, 28** ⁴⁰Then two men will be in the field; one will be taken and one will be left. ⁴¹Two women will be grinding at the mill; one will be taken and one left. ²⁸For wherever there's a corpse, that's where vultures gather.	¹⁶and no one in the field should turn back to get a coat.	The same goes for those in the field: they had better not turn back for anything left behind. ³²Remember Lot's wife. ³³Whoever tries to hang on to life will lose it, but whoever loses it will preserve it.* ³⁴I'm telling you, on that night there will be two on one couch; one will be taken and the other left. ³⁵There will be two women grinding together; one will be taken and the other left."ᵇ ³⁷Then they asked him, "Taken where, Master?" And he said to them, "Vultures collect wherever there's a carcass."	**Jn 12:25** If you love your life you'll lose it, but if you hate your life in this world you'll preserve it for unending life. **Th 61:1** Two will recline on a couch; one will die, one will live.

* Mt 16:25 / Mk 8::35 / Lk 9:24 (#121, p. 102)

ᵃ Lk 17:24 Some mss omit *in his day.*
ᵇ Lk 17:35 Some mss add another verse, traditionally numbered 17:36: "Two will be in the fields; one will be taken, the other left."

191. The Parable of the Judge and the Widow

Mt	Mk	Lk 18:1–8
		¹He told them a parable about the need to pray at all times and never to lose heart. ²This is what he said: Once there was a judge in this town who neither feared God nor had any respect for people. ³In that same town was a widow who kept coming to him and demanding, "Give me a ruling against my opponent." ⁴For a while he refused; but eventually he said to himself, "I don't fear God and I have no respect for people, ⁵but this widow keeps pestering me. So I'm going to rule in her favor, or else she'll keep coming back until she wears me down." ⁶And the Master said, "Don't you hear what this corrupt judge is saying? ⁷Do you really think God won't hand out justice to his chosen ones—those who call on him day and night? Do you really think he'll put them off? ⁸I'm telling you, he'll give them justice and give it quickly. Still, when the Human One comes, will he find any trust on the earth?"

192. The Parable of the Pharisee and the Toll Collector

Mt	Mk	Lk 18:9–14
		[9]Then for those who were confident of their own moral superiority and who held everyone else in contempt, he had this parable: [10]Two men went up to the temple to pray, one a Pharisee and the other a toll collector. 　[11]The Pharisee stood up and prayed silently as follows: "I thank you, God, that I'm not like everybody else, thieving, unjust, adulterous, and especially not like that toll collector over there. [12]I fast twice a week; I donate ten percent of everything that I acquire." 　[13]But the toll collector stood off by himself and didn't even dare to look up, but struck his chest, saying, "God, have mercy on me, sinner that I am." 　[14]Let me tell you, the second man went back home vindicated but the first one did not. For those who promote themselves will be demoted, but those who demote themselves will be promoted.* 18:15–17　#195, p. 146

* Ⓓ　Mt 23:12 / Lk 14:11 (#173, p. 131)

193. On Divorce
SEE #403, 525, PP. 322, 398

Mt 19:1–9	Mk 10:1–12	Lk
[1]And so it happened that, when Jesus had finished this instruction, he took leave of Galilee and went to the territory of Judea across the Jordan. [2]And large crowds followed him and he healed them there. [3]And the Pharisees approached him and, to test him, they ask, "Is ⟨a man⟩ permitted to divorce his wife for any reason?" v. 7 v. 8 [4]In response he said to them, "Haven't you read that in the beginning the Creator 'made them male and female,' [5]and that further on it says, 'for this reason, a man will leave his father and mother and be united with his wife, and the two will be one body'? [6]That's why they are longer two but 'one body.' Therefore, those whom God has coupled together, no one else should separate." [7]They say to him, "Then why did Moses order 'a certificate of separation and divorce'?" [8]He says to them, "Because you are headstrong Moses permitted you to divorce your wives, but it wasn't like that originally. [9]Now I say to you, whoever divorces his wife, except for immorality, and marries another commits adultery."*	[1]And from there he gets up and goes to the territory of Judea and across the Jordan, and again crowds gather around him. And again, as usual, he started teaching them. [2]And Pharisees approach him and, to test him, they ask whether a husband is permitted to divorce his wife. [3]In response he said to them, "What did Moses command you?" [4]They replied, "Moses allowed a man to get a divorce by preparing a certificate of separation." [5]Jesus said to them, "He gave you this injunction because you are headstrong. [6]But in the beginning, at the creation, 'God made them male and female.' [7]'For this reason, a man will leave his father and mother and be united with his wife, [8]and the two will be one body.' That's why they are no longer two, but 'one body.' [9]Therefore those whom God has coupled together, no one else should separate." v. 4 v. 5 [10]And once again, as usual, when they got home, the disciples questioned him about this. [11]And he says to them, "Whoever divorces his wife and marries another commits adultery against her; [12]and if she divorces her husband and marries another, she commits adultery." 10:13–16 #195, p. 146	Lk

* Ⓓ Mt 5:32 But I tell you, anyone who divorces his wife (except in the case of immorality) forces her into adultery; and whoever marries a divorced woman commits adultery.

Lk 16:18 Everyone who divorces his wife and marries another commits adultery; and the one who marries a woman divorced from her husband commits adultery. (#22, p. 23)

194. Castrated Men

Mt 19:10–12	Mk	Lk
[10]The disciples say to him, "If that's the way a man has to treat wife, it's better not to marry." [11]Then he said to them, "Not everyone can accept this teaching, only those for whom it was intended. [12]After all, there are castrated men who were born that way, and there are castrated men who were castrated by others, and there are castrated men who castrated themselves because of the empire of Heaven. If you can accept this ⟨teaching⟩, do so."		

195. Children and the Empire of God

Mt 19:13–15	Mk 10:13–16	Lk 18:15–17	Th 22:1–2
[13]Then children were brought to him so he could lay his hands on them and pray, but the disciples scolded them.	[13]And they would bring children to him so he could bless them with his hands, but the disciples scolded them.	[15]They would even bring him their babies so he could bless them with his hands. But when the disciples noticed it, they scolded them.	
	[14]Then Jesus grew indignant when he saw this and said to them,		
[14]Now Jesus said,		[16]Jesus called for the babies and said,	[1]Jesus saw some babies nursing. [2]He said to his disciples,
"Let the children alone. Don't try to stop them from coming up to me. After all,	"Let the children come up to me; don't try to stop them. After all,	"Let the children come up to me, and don't try to stop them. After all,	"These nursing babies are like those who enter
the empire of Heaven belongs to people like these."	the empire of God belongs to people like these.	the empire of God belongs to people like these.	the ⟨Father's⟩ empire."
18:3	[15]Let me tell you, whoever doesn't welcome the empire of God the way a child would, will never set foot in ⟨his empire⟩."	[17]Let me tell you, whoever doesn't welcome the empire of God the way a child would, will never enter it."	Th 46:2
[15]And he laid his hands on them and left that place.	[16]After he put his arms around them, he blesses them, laying his hands on them.		

196. The Young Man with a Fortune

Mt 19:16–22	Mk 10:17–22	Lk 18:18–23	GNaz 6:1–4
[16]And just then someone came and asked him, "Teacher, what good do I have to do to have eternal life?"	[17]As he was traveling along the way, someone ran up, knelt before him, and started questioning him, "Good teacher, what do I have to do to inherit eternal life?"	[18]Someone from the ruling class asked him, "Good teacher, what do I have to do to inherit eternal life?"	[1]The second rich man said to him, "Teacher, what good do I have to do to live?"
[17]He said to him, "Why ask me about the good? There is only One who is good. If you want to enter life, observe the commandments."	[18]Jesus said to him, "Why do you call me good? No one is good except God alone. [19]You know the commandments:	[19]Jesus said to him, "Why do you call me good? No one is good except God alone. [20]You know the commandments:	[2]He said to him, "Mister, follow the Law and the Prophets."
[18]He says to him, "Which ones?" Jesus replied, "'You shall not murder, you shall not commit adultery, you shall not steal, you shall not give false testimony, [19]you shall honor your father and mother, and you shall love your neighbor as yourself.'"	'You shall not murder, you shall not commit adultery, you shall not steal, you shall not give false testimony, you shall not defraud, and you shall honor your father and mother.'"	'You shall not commit adultery, you shall not murder, you shall not steal, you shall not give false testimony, and you shall honor your father and mother.'"	
[20]The young man says to him, "I have observed all these; what am I missing?"	[20]He said to him, "Teacher, I have observed all these things since I was a child."	[21]And he said, "I have observed all these since I was a child."	He answered, "I've done that."
[21]Jesus said to him, "If you want to be perfect, make your move, sell your belongings, and give ⟨the money⟩ to the poor and you will have treasure in heaven. And then come on, follow me!"	[21]Jesus looked at him and loved him and said to him, "You are missing one thing: make your move, sell whatever you have, and give ⟨the money⟩ to the poor, and you will have treasure in heaven. And then come on, follow me!"	[22]When Jesus heard this, he said to him, "You are still short one thing. Sell everything you have and distribute ⟨the money⟩ among the poor, and you will have treasure in heaven. And then come on, follow me!"	He said to him, "Go sell everything you own and give it away to the poor and then come on, follow me."
[22]When the young man heard this advice, he went away dejected since he had a fortune.	[22]But stunned by this advice, he went away dejected, since he had a fortune.	[23]But when he heard this, he became very sad, for he was extremely rich.	[3]But the rich man didn't want to hear this and began to scratch his head. And the Master said to him, "How can you say that you follow the Law and the Prophets? In the Law it says: 'Love your neighbor as yourself.' [4]Look around you: many of your brothers and sisters, sons and daughters of Abraham, are living in filth and dying of hunger. Your house is full of good things and not a thing of yours manages to get out to them."
22:39	12:31	10:27b	
		16:19–31	

197. A Camel and the Eye of a Needle

SEE #412, P. 328

Mt 19:23–30	Mk 10:23–31	Lk 18:24–30; 22:28–30; 13:30	other
		Lk 18:24–28	
	[23]After looking around, Jesus says to his disciples, "How difficult it is for those with money to enter God's empire!" [24]The disciples were amazed at his words.	[24]When Jesus observed that he had become very sad, he said, "How difficult it is for those with money to enter God's empire!	
[23]Jesus said to his disciples, "Let me tell you, it's difficult for the wealthy to enter the empire of Heaven.	In response Jesus says again, "Children, how difficult it is to enter God's empire!		
[24]I'm telling you again, it's easier for a camel to squeeze through the eye of a needle than for the wealthy to get into the empire of God."	[25]It's easier for a camel to squeeze through the eye of a needle than for the wealthy to get into the empire of God!"	[25]It's easier for a camel to squeeze through the eye of a needle than for the wealthy to get into the empire of God."	**GNaz 6:5b** It's easier for a camel to squeeze through the eye of a needle than for a wealthy person to get into the empire of Heaven.
[25]When the disciples heard this, they were very amazed and said, "Well then, who can be saved?"	[26]And they were totally amazed, saying to each other, "Well then, who can be saved?"	[26]Those who heard this said, "Well then, who can be saved?"	
[26]Jesus looked them in the eye, and said to them, "For humans this is impossible; for God everything's possible."	[27]Jesus looks them in the eye and says, "For humans it's impossible, but not for God; you see, everything's possible for God."	[27]But he said, "What's impossible for humans is possible for God."	
[27]In response Peter said to him, "Look at us, we left everything to follow you! What do we get out of it?"	[28]Peter began telling him, "Look at us, we left everything to follow you!"	[28]Then Peter said, "Look at us! We have left what we had to follow you."	
[28]Jesus told them, "Let me tell you, you who have followed me, when the Human One is seated on his throne of glory in the renewal ⟨of creation⟩, you also will be seated on twelve thrones and sit in judgment on the twelve tribes of Israel.		**Lk 22:28–30** [28]You are the ones who have stuck by me in my ordeals. [29]And I confer on you the right to rule, just as surely as my Father conferred that right on me, [30]so you may eat and drink at my table in my empire, and be seated on thrones and sit in judgment on the twelve tribes of Israel.	
		Lk 18:29–30	
[29]And everyone who for my sake has left homes or brothers or sisters or father or mother or children or farms, will receive a hundred times	[29]Jesus said, "Let me tell you, there is no one who has left home or brothers or sisters or mother or father or children or farms on my account	[29]And he told them, "Let me tell you, there is no one who has left home or wife or brothers or parents or children for the sake of the empire of God, [30]who won't	

as much and inherit eternal life.	and on account of the good news, ³⁰who won't receive a hundred times as much now, in the present time: homes and brothers and sisters and mothers and children and farms—including persecutions—and in the age to come, eternal life.	receive many times as much in the present age, and in the age to come, eternal life."	
			Th 4:2–3 ²For many of the first will be last, ³and will become a single one.
³⁰Many of the first will be last, and many of the last will be first."*	³¹Many of the first will be last, and many of the last will be first."	**Lk 13:30** Those who will be first are last, and those who will be last are first.	
	10:32–34 #199, p. 150	18:31–34 #199, p. 150	

* Ⓓ Mt 20:16 (#198, p. 149)

198. The Parable of the Workers in the Vineyard

Mt 20:1–16	Mk	Lk
¹The empire of Heaven is like a landowner who went out first thing in the morning to hire workers for his vineyard. ²After agreeing with the workers for a denarius a day he sent them into his vineyard. ³And coming out around 9 a.m. he saw others loitering in the marketplace ⁴and he said to them, "You go into the vineyard too, and I'll pay you whatever is fair." ⁵So they went. Around noon he went out again, and at 3 p.m. he repeated the process. ⁶About 5 p.m. he went out and found others loitering about and says to them, "Why did you stand around here idle the whole day?" ⁷They reply, "Because no one hired us." He tells them, "You go into the vineyard as well." ⁸When evening came the owner of the vineyard tells his foreman, "Call the workers and pay them their wages starting with those hired last and ending with those hired first." ⁹Those hired at 5 p.m. came up and received a denarius each. ¹⁰Those hired first approached thinking they would receive more. But they also got a demarius apiece. ¹¹They took it and began to grumble against the owner: ¹²"These guys hired last worked only an hour but you have made them equal to us who did most of the work during the heat of the day." ¹³In response he said to one of them, "Friend, did I wrong you? You did agree with me for a denarius, didn't you? ¹⁴Take what's yours and go! I choose to treat the man hired last the same as you. ¹⁵Is there some law against my doing what I please with my own money? Or are you envious because I am generous?" ¹⁶"The last will be first and the first last."*		

* Ⓓ Mt 19:30 (#197, p. 148)

199. The Third Passion Prediction

Mt 20:17–19	Mk 10:32–34	Lk 18:31–34
[17]As he was going up to Jerusalem, Jesus took the Twelve aside privately and said to them as they walked along, [18]"Listen, we're going up to Jerusalem, and the Human One will be turned over to the chief priests and scholars, and they will sentence him to death, [19]and turn him over to foreigners to be made fun of and flogged and crucified. But on the third day he will be raised."	[32]On the way up to Jerusalem, Jesus was leading the way; they were anxious, and those following were afraid. Once again he took the Twelve aside and started telling them what was going to happen to him. [33]"Listen, we're going up to Jerusalem, and the Human One will be turned over to the chief priests and the scholars, and they will sentence him to death, and turn him over to foreigners, [34]and they will make fun of him, and spit on him, and flog him, and kill ⟨him⟩. But after three days he will rise."	[31]Jesus took the Twelve aside and said to them, "Listen, we're going up to Jerusalem, and everything written by the prophets about the Human One will come true. [32]For he will be turned over to the gentiles, and will be made fun of and insulted. They will spit on him [33]and flog him and kill him, and on the third day he will rise." [34]But they did not understand any of this; this remark was obscure to them, and they never did figure out what it meant. 18:35–43 #201, p. 152

200. How To Be Great

Mt 20:20–28	Mk 10:35–45	Lk 12:50; **22:24–27**
[20]Then the mother of the sons of Zebedee came up to him with her sons, bowed down before him, and asked him for a favor.	[35]Then James and John, the sons of Zebedee, come up to him, and say to him, "Teacher, we want you to do for us whatever we ask."	
[21]He said to her, "What do you want?"	[36]He said to them, "What do you want me to do for you?"	
She said to him, "Give me your word that these two sons of mine may sit, one at your right hand and one at your left, in your empire."	[37]They reply to him, "In your glory, let one of us sit at your right hand, and the other at your left."	
[22]In response Jesus said, "You have no idea what you're asking for. Can you drink the cup that I'm about to drink?"	[38]Jesus said to them, "You have no idea what you're asking for. Can you drink the cup that I'm drinking, or go through the baptism I'm going through?"	**Lk 12:50** I have a baptism to be baptized with, and what pressure I'm under until it's over!
They said to him, "We can!"	[39]They said to him, "We can!"	
[23]He says to them, "You'll be drinking my cup,	Jesus said to them, "The cup I'm drinking you'll be drinking, and the baptism I'm going through you'll go through, [40]but as for sitting at my right or my left, that's not mine to grant, but belongs to those for whom it has been reserved."	
but as for sitting at my right or my left, that's not up to me; it's for those for whom it's been reserved by my Father."		
[24]And when the other ten heard of it, they were incensed with the two brothers. [25]And calling them aside, Jesus said, "You know how foreign rulers lord it over their subjects, and how their strong men tyrannize them.	[41]When the other ten heard of it, they were incensed with James and John. [42]Calling them aside, Jesus says to them, "You know how those who supposedly rule over foreigners lord it over them, and how their strong men tyrannize them. [43]But it's not going to be like that with you. With you, whoever wants to become great must be your servant,	**Lk 22:24–27** [24]Then they got into an argument over which of them should be considered the greatest. [25]He said to them, "Among the foreigners, it's the kings who lord it over everyone, and those in power are addressed as 'benefactors.' [26]But not so with you; rather, the greatest among you must behave as a beginner, and the leader as one who serves. [27]Who is the greater, after all: the one reclining ⟨at a banquet⟩ or the one doing the serving? Isn't it the one who reclines? But here among you I am the one doing the serving.
[26]It's not going to be like that with you! With you, whoever wants to become great will be your slave, [27]and whoever among you wants to be 'number one' is to be your slave.	[44]and whoever among you wants to be 'number one' must be everybody's slave.	
[28]After all, the Human One didn't come to be served, but to serve and to give his life as a ransom for many."	[45]You see, the Human One didn't come to be served, but to serve and to give his life as a ransom for many."	
		22:24–30 #240, p. 185

22:24–30 #240, p. 185

201. Healing of the Blind Man/Men of Jericho

Mt 20:29–34*	Mk 10:46–52	Lk 18:35–43
[29]And as they were leaving Jericho, a huge crowd followed him. [30]There were two blind men sitting along the wayside. When they heard that Jesus was going by, they shouted, "Have mercy on us, Master,[a] son of David." [31]The crowd yelled at them to shut up, but they shouted all the louder, "Have mercy on us, Master, son of David." [32]Jesus paused and called out to them, "What do you want me to do for you?" [33]They said to him, "Master, open our eyes!" [34]Then Jesus took pity on them, touched their eyes, and right away they regained their sight and followed him. 21:1–9 #204, p. 155	[46]Then they come to Jericho. As he was leaving Jericho with his disciples and a good-sized crowd, Bartimaeus, a blind beggar, the son of Timaeus, was sitting by the wayside. [47]When he heard that it was Jesus the Nazarene, he began to shout, "Son of David, Jesus, have mercy on me!" [48]And many kept yelling at him to shut up, but he shouted all the louder, "Son of David, have mercy on me!" [49]Jesus paused and said, "Call him over here!" They called to the blind man, "Be brave, get up, he's calling you!" [50]So he threw off his cloak, and jumped to his feet, and went over to Jesus. [51]In response Jesus said, "What do you want me to do for you?" The blind man said to him, "Rabbi, I want to see again." [52]And Jesus said to him, "Get going; your trust has cured you." And right away he regained his sight, and he started following him on the way. 11:1–10 #204, p. 155	[35]It came to pass, as he was coming into Jericho, that this blind man was sitting by the wayside begging. [36]Hearing a crowd passing through, he asked what was going on. [37]They told him, "Jesus the Nazarene is going by." [38]Then he shouted, "Jesus, son of David, have mercy on me!" [39]Those in the lead kept yelling at him to shut up, but he kept shouting all the louder, "Son of David, have mercy on me!" [40]Jesus paused and ordered them to guide the man over. When he came near, Jesus asked him, [41]"What do you want me to do for you?" He said, "Master, I want to see again." [42]Jesus said to him, "Then see again; your trust has cured you." [43]And immediately he regained his sight, and began to follow him, praising God all the while. And everyone who saw it gave God the praise.

* Ⓓ Mt 9:27–31 (#94, p. 74)

---

[a] Mt 20:30 Some mss omit *Master* from the blind men's shout, while a few mss substitute "Jesus."

202. Jesus and Zacchaeus

Mt	Mk	Lk 19:1–10
		[1]Then he entered Jericho and was making his way through it. [2]Now a man named Zacchaeus lived there who was a chief toll collector and a rich man. [3]He was trying to see who Jesus was, but couldn't, because of the crowd, since he was short. [4]So he ran on ahead to a point Jesus was to pass and climbed a sycamore tree to get a view of him. [5]When Jesus reached that spot, he looked up at him and said, "Zacchaeus, hurry up and climb down; I have to stay at your house today." [6]So he scurried down and welcomed him warmly. [7]Everyone who saw this complained, "He's going to spend the day with some sinner!" [8]But Zacchaeus stood his ground and said to the Master, "Look, sir, I'll give half of what I own to the poor, and if I have extorted anything from anyone, I'll pay back four times as much." [9]Jesus said to him, "Today salvation has come to this house. This man is a real son of Abraham. [10]Remember, the Human One came to seek out and to save what was lost."

203. The Parable of the Ruthless Master

SEE #411, P. 326

Mt 25:14–30	Mk	Lk 19:11–27
		[11]While they were still paying attention to this exchange, he proceeded to tell a parable, because he was near Jerusalem and it seemed to them that God's empire was about to appear at any moment. [12]So he said,
[14]You know, it's like a man going on a trip who called his slaves and turned his property over to them. [15]To the first he gave five talents' worth of silver, to the second two talents' worth, and to the third one talent's worth, to each in proportion to his ability. Then he left.	*13:34*	A nobleman went off to a distant land intending to acquire a kingship for himself and then return. [13]Calling ten of his slaves, he gave them ten minas and told them, "Do business with this while I'm away."
		[14]His fellow citizens, however, hated him and sent a delegation right on his heels, with the petition: "We don't want this man to rule us."
[16]The one who had received five talents' worth of silver went right out and put the money to work; he doubled his investment.		
[17]The second also doubled his money.		
[18]But the third, who had received the smallest amount, went out, dug a hole, and hid his master's silver.		
[19]After a long absence, the master of those slaves returned to settle accounts with them. [20]The first, who had received five talents' worth of silver, came and produced an additional five, with this report: "Master, you handed me five talents of silver; as you can see, I've made you five more."		[15]And it came to pass that he got the kingship and returned. He had those slaves summoned to whom he had given the money, in order to find out what profit they had made.
[21]His master commended him: "Well done, you competent and trustworthy slave. You've been trustworthy in a little, so I'll put you in charge of a lot. Come celebrate with your master."		[16]The first came in and reported, "Master, your mina has increased ten times over."
		[17]He said to him, "Well done, you competent slave! Because you've been trustworthy in this small matter, you are to be in charge of ten towns."
[22]The one with two talents of silver also came and reported, "Master, you handed me two talents of silver; as you can see, I've made you two more."		[18]The second came in and reported, "Master, your mina has increased five times over."
[23]His master commended him: "Well done, you competent and trustworthy slave. You've been trustworthy in a little, so I'll put you in charge of a lot. Come celebrate with your master."		[19]And he said to him, "And you are to be in charge of five towns."
[24]The one who had received one talent's worth of silver also came and reported, "Master, I know that you are ruthless, reaping where you didn't sow and gathering where you didn't scatter. [25]Since I was afraid, I went out and buried your money in the ground. Look, here it is!"		[20]Then the other ⟨slave⟩ came in and said, "Master, here is your money. I kept it tucked away safe in a handkerchief. [21]You see, I was afraid of you, because you're a demanding man: you withdraw what you didn't deposit and reap what you didn't sow."
[26]But his master replied to him, "You incompetent and timid slave! So you knew that I reap where I didn't sow and gather where I didn't scatter, did you? [27]Then you should have taken my money to the bankers. Then when I returned I would have recovered what's mine, plus interest.		[22]He said to him, "You incompetent slave! Your own words convict you. So you knew I was a demanding man, did you? That I withdraw what I didn't deposit and reap what I didn't sow? [23]So why didn't you put my money in the bank? Then I could have collected it with interest when I got back."
[28]So take the talent away from this guy and give it to the one who has ten.		[24]Then he said to his attendants, "Take the mina away from this guy and give it to the one who has ten."

<table>
<tr><td>

²⁹In fact, to everyone who has, more will be given and then some; and from those who don't have, even what they do have will be taken away.*
³⁰And throw this worthless slave out into the utter darkness, where they'll weep and grind their teeth."

25:31–46 #233, p. 179

</td><td>

²⁵"But master," they said to him, "he already has ten minas."

²⁶He replied, "I'm telling you, to everyone who has, more will be given; and from those who don't have, even what they do have will be taken away.*
²⁷But now, about those enemies of mine, the ones who didn't want me to rule them: bring them here and slaughter them in front of me."

</td></tr>
</table>

* Ⓓ Mt 13:12 / Mk 4:25 / Lk 8:18 / Th 41:1–2 (#80, p. 65)

204. Jesus rides into Jerusalem
SEE #308, P. 246

Mt 21:1–9	Mk 11:1–10	Lk 19:28–40	Jn 12:12–15
		²⁸When he had finished the parable, he walked on ahead, on his way up to Jerusalem.	
¹When they got close to Jerusalem, and came to Bethphage at the Mount of Olives, then Jesus sent two disciples ahead ²with these instructions:	¹When they get close to Jerusalem, near Bethphage and Bethany at the Mount of Olives, he sends off two of his disciples ²with these instructions:	²⁹And it came to pass as he got close to Bethphage and Bethany, at the mountain called Olives, that he sent off two of the disciples ³⁰with these instructions:	
"Go into the village across the way, and right away you will find a donkey tied up, and a colt alongside her. Untie them and bring them to me. ³And if anyone says anything to you, just say, 'The Master needs them and he'll send them back right away.'"	"Go into the village across the way, and after you enter it, right away you'll find a colt tied up, one that has never been ridden. Untie it and bring it here. ³If anyone says, 'Why are you doing this?' just say, 'The master needs it and he will send it back here right away.'"	"Go into the village across the way. As you enter, you will find a colt tied there, one that has never been ridden. Untie it and bring it here. ³¹If anyone asks you, 'Why are you untying it?' just say, 'The Master needs it.'"	
⁴This happened in order to fulfill the prediction spoken through the prophet: "⁵Tell the daughter of Zion, "Look, your king comes to you gently, mounted on a donkey and on a colt, the foal of a pack animal."			vv. 14–15
⁶Then the disciples went and did as Jesus instructed them,	⁴They set out and found a colt tied up at the door out on the street, and they untie it. ⁵Some of the people standing around started saying to them, "What	³²So those who were sent went off and found it exactly as he had described. ³³Just as they were untying the colt, its owners said to them, "What are you doing	

Mt 21:1–9	Mk 11:1–10	Lk 19:28–40	Jn 12:12–15
	do you think you're doing, untying that colt?" ⁶But they said just what Jesus had told them to say, so they left them alone.	untying that colt?" ³⁴So they said, "The Master needs it."	
⁷and brought the donkey and colt and they placed their cloaks on them, and he sat on top of them.	⁷So they bring the colt to Jesus, and they throw their cloaks over it; then he got on it.	³⁵So they brought it to Jesus. They threw their cloaks on the colt and helped Jesus mount it. ³⁶And as he rode along, people would spread their cloaks on the road. ³⁷As he approached the slope of the Mount of Olives, the entire throng of his disciples began to cheer and shout praise to God for all the miracles they had seen. ³⁸They kept repeating,	¹²The next day the huge crowd that had come for the festival heard that Jesus was coming into Jerusalem.
⁸The enormous crowd spread their cloaks on the road, and others cut branches from the trees and spread them on the road.	⁸And many people spread their cloaks on the road, while others cut leafy branches from the fields.		¹³They got palm fronds and went out to meet him.
⁹The crowds leading the way and those following kept shouting, "Hosanna to the son of David! Blessed is the one who comes in the name of the Lord! Hosanna in the highest ⟨heaven⟩."	⁹Those leading the way and those following kept shouting, "Hosanna! Blessed is the one who comes in the name of the Lord! ¹⁰Blessed is the coming kingdom of our father David! Hosanna in the highest ⟨heaven⟩!"	"Blessed is the king who comes in the name of the Lord! Peace in heaven and glory in the highest ⟨heaven⟩!"	They began to shout, "Hosanna! Blessed is the one who comes in the name of the Lord! ⟨Blessed is⟩ the King of Israel!"
vv. 4–5			¹⁴Then Jesus found a young donkey and rode on it, as scripture puts it: ¹⁵"Fear not, daughter of Zion. Look, your king comes riding on a donkey's colt."
		³⁹But some of the Pharisees, also in the crowd, said to him, "Teacher, restrain your disciples." ⁴⁰But he responded, "Take my word for it: if these folks were to keep quiet, these stones would shout."	
21:10–17 #206, p. 157	11:11 #206, p. 157		

205. Jesus weeps over Jerusalem

Mt	Mk	Lk 19:41–44
		[41]When he got close enough to catch sight of the city, he wept over it. [42]"If you—yes, you—had only recognized the path to peace even today! But as it is, it is hidden from your eyes. [43]The time will come down on you when your enemies will throw up a rampart against you and surround you, and hem you in on every side, [44]and then smash you to the ground, you and your children with you. They will not leave one stone on top of another within you, because you failed to recognize the time of your visitation." 19:45–48 #208, p. 158

206. Jesus visits/disrupts the Temple
SEE #208, P. 158

Mt 21:10–17	Mk 11:11	Lk
[10]And when he entered Jerusalem the whole city was shaken, saying, "Who is this?" [11]The crowds said, "This is the prophet Jesus from Nazareth in Galilee!" [12]And Jesus went into God's[a] temple and threw all the vendors and customers out of the temple area; and he knocked over the currency exchange tables, along with the chairs of the dove merchants. [13]Then he says to them, "It is written, 'My house shall be designated a house of prayer, but you're turning it into 'a hideout for bandits'!" [14]And some blind and lame people came to him in the temple area, and he healed them. [15]Then the chief priests and scholars saw the remarkable feats he performed, and the children who kept cheering in the temple area, shouting, "Hosanna to the son of David," and they were infuriated. [16]And they said to him, "Do you hear what these people are saying?" Jesus says to them, "Of course. Have you never read the verse, 'Out of the mouths of babies and nursing infants you brought forth praise for yourself'?" [17]And leaving them behind, he went outside the city to Bethany and spent the night there.	And he went into Jerusalem to the temple area and took stock of everything, 11:15–17 but, since the hour was already late, he returned to Bethany with the Twelve.	19:45–46

[a] Mt 21:12 Some mss omit *God's* as a modifier of *temple*.

207. Jesus curses a fig tree

Mt 21:18–19	Mk 11:12–14	Lk
[18]Early in the morning, as he was returning to the city, he was hungry. [19]And so when he spotted a single fig tree on the way, he went up to it, and found nothing on it, only leaves, and he says to it, "You'll never bear fruit again!" And the fig tree withered right then and there. 21:20–22 #209, p. 159	[12]On the next day, as they were leaving Bethany, he was hungry. [13]So when he spotted a fig tree in the distance with leaves on it, he went up to it hoping to find something on it. But when he got up next to it, he found nothing on it, only leaves. (You see, it wasn't "time" for figs.) [14]And he reacted by saying to it, "May no one so much as taste your fruit again!" And his disciples were listening.	

[a] Mt 21:12 Some mss omit *God's* as a modifier of *temple*.

208. Jesus disrupts the temple

SEE #282, P. 231

Mt 21:12–13	Mk 11:15–19	Lk 19:45–48	Jn 2:13–16
[12]And Jesus went into God's temple and threw all the vendors and customers out of the temple area;	[15]They come to Jerusalem. And he went into the temple and began throwing the vendors and the customers out of the temple area,	[45]Then he entered the temple area and began throwing the vendors out.	[13]It was almost time for the Jewish Passover festival, so Jesus went up to Jerusalem. [14]In the temple area he found people selling oxen and sheep and doves, and others exchanging currency. [15]He made a whip out of rope and drove them all out of the temple area, sheep and oxen; then he knocked over the exchange tables and scattered the coins. [16]And to the dove merchants he said, "Get these birds out of here!
and he knocked over the currency exchange tables, along with the chairs of the dove merchants.	and he knocked over the currency exchange tables, along with the chairs of the dove merchants, [16]and he wouldn't even let anyone carry a container through the temple area. [17]Then he started teaching and saying to them,		
[13]Then he says to them, "It is written, 'My house shall be designated a house of prayer,'	"Don't the scriptures say, 'My house shall be designated a house of prayer for all peoples?'	[46]He says to them, "It is written, 'My house shall be a house of prayer.'	
But you're turning it into 'a hideout for bandits'!"	But you have turned it into 'a hideout for bandits'!" [18]And the chief priests and the scholars heard this	But you have turned it into 'a hideout for bandits'!" [47]Every day he would teach in the temple area. The chief priests and the scholars, along with the leaders of the people,	How dare you use my Father's house as a public market."
	and kept looking for a way to destroy him. (You see, they were afraid of him because the	kept looking for some way to destroy him. [48]But they never figured out how to do	

	whole crowd was astonished at his teaching.) ¹⁹And when it grew dark, they were leaving the city.	it, because all the people hung on his every word.	
21:10–17 #206, p. 157		20:1–8 #210, p. 160	

209. How to Move Mountains
SEE #317, 321, PP. 253, 256

Mt 21:20–22; 6:14	Mk 11:20–25	Lk	other
Mt 21:20–22 ²⁰And when the disciples saw this, they expressed amazement: "How could the fig tree wither so quickly?" ²¹In response Jesus said to them, "Let me tell you, if you have trust and do not doubt, not only can you do this to a fig tree but you can even say to this mountain, 'Up with you and into the sea!' and that's what will happen;*	²⁰As they were walking along early in the morning, they saw the fig tree withered from the roots up. ²¹And Peter remembered and says to him, "Rabbi, look, the fig tree you cursed has withered!" ²²In response Jesus says to them, "Have trust in God. ²³Let me tell you, those who say to this mountain, 'Up with you and into the sea!' and do not waver in their conviction, but trust that what they say will happen, that's the way it will be.		**Th 48** If two make peace with each other in a single house, they will say to the mountain, "Move from here!" and it will move. **Th 106:1–2** ¹When you make the two into one, you will become children of Adam, ²and when you say, "Mountain, move from here!" it will move. **Jn 15:7** If you stay attached to me and my words live in you, ask whatever you want and it will happen to you. **Jn 16:23** Let me tell you this: if you ask the Father for anything using my name, he will grant it to you.†
²²and everything you ask for in prayer you'll get if you trust."	²⁴This is why I keep telling you, trust that you will receive everything you pray and ask for, and that's the way it will turn out.		
Mt 6:14 For if you forgive the offenses of others, your heavenly Father will also forgive yours.	²⁵And when you stand up to pray, if you are holding anything against anyone, forgive them, so your Father in heaven may forgive your transgressions."ᵃ ‡	6:37c	

* ⒟ Mt 17:20 / Lk 17:6 (#186, p. 140)

† Jn 14:13–14; 15:16 (#317, p. 253)

‡ Mt 5:23–24 (#20, p. 22)

ᵃ Mk 11:25 Many mss include a v. 26: "But if you do not forgive, neither will your father in heaven forgive your misdeeds."

210. By What Authority?

Mt 21:23–27	Mk 11:27–33	Lk 20:1–8
[23]And when he came to the temple area, the chief priests and elders of the people approached him while he was teaching, and asked, "Where'd you get the authority to do these things?" and "Who gave you this authority?"	[27]Again they come to Jerusalem. As he walks around in the temple area, the chief priests and scholars and elders come up to him [28]and start questioning him: "Where'd you get the authority to do these things?" or, "Who gave you the authority to do these things?"	[1]And it came to pass one day, as he was teaching the people in the temple area and speaking of the good news, that the chief priests and the scholars approached him along with the elders, [2]and put this question to him: "Tell us where you got the authority to do these things? Who's the one who gave you this authority?"
[24]In response Jesus said to them, "I also have one question for you. If you answer me, I'll tell you by what authority I do these things. [25]The baptism of John, where did it come from? From Heaven or from humans?"	[29]But Jesus said to them, "I have one question for you. If you answer me, then I'll tell you by what authority I do these things. [30]Tell me, was the baptism of John from Heaven or was it of from humans? Answer me that."	[3]In response Jesus said to them, "I also have a question for you: tell me, [4]was John's baptism from Heaven or from humans?"
And they conferred among themselves, saying, "If we say 'from Heaven,' he'll say to us, 'Then why didn't you believe him?' [26]And if we say 'From humans! . . .' We're afraid of the crowd." (Remember, everybody considered John a prophet.) [27]So they answered Jesus by saying, "We can't tell."	[31]And they conferred among themselves, saying, "If we say 'from Heaven,' he'll say, 'Then why didn't you trust him?' [32]But if we say 'From humans! . . .'" They were afraid of the crowd. (You see, everybody considered John a genuine prophet.) [33]So they answered Jesus by saying, "We can't tell."	[5]And they started conferring among themselves, reasoning as follows: "If we say, 'From Heaven,' he'll say, 'Then why didn't you trust him?' [6]But if we say, 'From humans,' the people will all stone us." (Remember, ⟨the people⟩ were convinced John was a prophet.) [7]So they answered that they couldn't tell where it came from.
He replied to them in kind: "Then I'm not going to tell you by what authority I do these things.	And Jesus says to them, "Then I'm not going to tell you by what authority I do these things!"	[8]And Jesus said to them, "Then I'm not going to tell you by what authority I do these things."
	12:1–12 #212, p. 162	20:9–19 #212, p. 162

211. The Parable of the Sons Who Had Second Thoughts

Mt 21:28–32	Mk	Lk 7:29–30
[28]Now what do you think? A man had two sons. He went to the first, and said, "Son, go and work in the vineyard today." [29]He answered, "I'm on it, master," but he didn't move. [30]Then he went to the second and said the same thing. He responded, "I don't want to," but later on he thought better of it and went ⟨to work⟩. [31]"Which of the two did what the father wanted?" They said, "The second."[a] Jesus said to them, "Let me tell you, toll collectors and prostitutes will get into God's empire, but you will not. [32]After all, John came to you walking in the way of God, but you didn't believe him; yet toll collectors and prostitutes believed him. Even after you observed ⟨this⟩, you didn't think better of it later and believe him.		[29]All the people, even the toll collectors, who were listening and had been baptized by John, vindicated God's plan; [30]but the Pharisees and the legal experts, who had not been baptized by him, subverted God's plan for themselves.

[a] Mt 21:29–31 The textual transmission of the parable is very confusing. Some mss adopt the version printed above; many mss had the first son say "no," but then change his mind, while the second son says "yes," and then doesn't go. In this case the audience responds "the first." A few mss even have the first son say "no," but change his mind; the second say "yes," but not go; and the audience answer the "the second."

212. The Parable of the Tenants

Mt 21:33–46	Mk 12:1–12	Lk 20:9–19	Th 65:1–8; 66
[33]Listen to another parable. There once was a landlord who planted a vineyard, put a hedge around it, dug a winepress in it, built a tower, leased it out to some farmers, and went abroad. [34]Now when harvest time arrived, he sent his slaves to the farmers to collect his crop. [35]And the farmers grabbed his slaves, and one they beat and another they killed, and another they stoned.	[1]And he began to speak to them in parables. A man planted a vineyard, put a hedge around it, dug a winepress, built a tower, leased it out to some farmers, and went abroad. [2]In due time he sent a slave to the farmers to collect his share of the vineyard's crop from them. [3]But they grabbed him, beat him, and sent him away empty-handed.	[9]Then he began to tell the people this parable. A man planted a vineyard, leased it out to some farmers, and went abroad for an extended time. [10]In due course he sent a slave to the farmers, so they could pay him his share of the vineyard's crop. But the farmers beat him and sent him away empty-handed.	**Th 65:1–8** [1]A [greedy][a] man owned a vineyard and rented it to some farmers, so they could work it and he could collect its crop from them. [2]He sent his slave so the farmers would give him the vineyard's crop. [3]They grabbed him, beat him, and almost killed him, and the slave returned and told his master. [4]His master said, "Perhaps he didn't know them."[b]
[36]Again he sent other slaves, more than the first group, and they did the same thing to them.	[4]And again he sent another slave to them, but they attacked him and abused him. [5]Then he sent another, and this one they killed; many others followed, some of whom they beat, others of whom they killed.	[11]He repeated his action by sending another slave; but they beat him up too, and humiliated him, and sent him away empty-handed. [12]And he sent yet a third slave; but they injured him and threw him out.	[5]He sent another slave, and the farmers beat that one as well.
[37]Then finally he sent his son to them, with the thought, "They'll show my son respect."	[6]Finally he sent his son, whom he loved. He said to himself, "They will show this son of mine some respect."	[13]Then the owner of the vineyard asked himself, "What should I do now? I'll send my son, the one I love. They'll probably show him some respect."	[6]Then the master sent his son and said, "Perhaps they'll show my son some respect."
[38]But when the farmers recognized the son they said to one another, "This guy's the heir! Come on, let's kill him and we'll have his inheritance!" [39]And they grabbed him, dragged him outside the vineyard, and killed him.	[7]But those farmers said to one another, "This guy's the heir! Come on, let's kill him and the inheritance will be ours!" [8]So they grabbed him, and killed him, and threw him outside the vineyard.	[14]But when the farmers recognized him, they talked it over, and concluded, "This guy's the heir. Let's kill him so the inheritance will be ours." [15]So they dragged him outside the vineyard and killed him.	[7]Because the farmers knew that he was the heir to the vineyard, they grabbed him and killed him. [8]Whoever has ears to hear should listen.*
[40]When the owner of the vineyard comes, what will he do to those farmers then? [41]They say to him, "He'll massacre those scum and lease the vineyard out to other farmers who will deliver their produce to him at the proper time."	[9]What will the owner of the vineyard do? He will come in person, and massacre those farmers, and give the vineyard to others.	So what will the owner of the vineyard do to them? [16]He will come in person, massacre those farmers, and give the vineyard to others.	

[42]Jesus says to them,

"It seems you haven't read in scripture:
'A stone that the builders threw away has ended up as the keystone. It was the Lord's doing, something we find amazing.'

[43]So take my word for it: God's empire will be taken away from you and given to a people that bears its fruit."[c]
[45]And when the chief priests and Pharisees heard his parable, they understood that he was talking about them.
[46]They wanted to seize him, but were afraid of the crowds, because everyone thought he was a prophet.

22:1–14 #175, p. 132

[10]It seems you haven't read in scripture:
"A stone that the builders threw away has ended up as the keystone. [11]It was the Lord's doing, something we find amazing."

They kept looking for some opportunity to seize him, but they were afraid of the crowd because they understood that he had aimed the parable at them. So they left him there and went away.

When they heard this, they said, "God forbid!"
[17]But Jesus looked them straight in the eye and said, "What can this scripture possibly mean:
'A stone that the builders threw away has ended up as the keystone'?

[18]Everyone who falls over that stone will be smashed to bits, and anyone on whom it falls will be crushed."

[19]The scholars and the chief priests wanted to lay hands on him then and there, but they were afraid of the people because they understood he had aimed this parable at them.

Th 66
Show me the stone that the builders rejected: that is the keystone.

---

* Mt 11:15; 13:9; 13:43b; Mk 4:9; 4:23; Lk 8:8b; 14:35b; Th 8:4; 21:10; 24:2; 63:4; 96:3

[a] Th 65:1 A lacuna in the papyrus makes the Coptic here uncertain; the hole can be filled in to read either "good man" or "greedy man."

[b] Th 65:4 *Perhaps he didn't know them*: Some scholars believe that the text should be emended here to read: "Perhaps they didn't know him."

[c] Mt 21:43 Many mss add a v. 44: "The one who falls over this stone will be smashed to pieces, and anyone on whom it falls will be crushed."

213. God and Caesar

Mt 22:15-22	Mk 12:13–17	Lk 20:20–26	other
[15]Then the Pharisees went and conferred on how to trap him with a riddle.	[13]And they send some of the Pharisees and the Herodians to him to trap him with a riddle.	[20]So they kept him under surveillance, and sent spies, who feigned sincerity, so they could twist something he said and turn him over to the authority and jurisdiction of the governor.	
			EgerG 3:1–4 [1]They come to him and interrogate him as a way of putting him to the test. [2]They ask,
[16]And they send their disciples to him along with the Herodians to say, "Teacher, we know that you are honest and that you teach God's way forthrightly, and that you are impartial, because you pay no attention to appearances. [17]So tell us what you think:	[14]They come and say to him, "Teacher, we know that you are honest and impartial, because you pay no attention to appearances, but instead you teach God's way forthrightly.	[21]They asked him, "Teacher, we know that what you speak and teach is correct, that you show no favoritism, but instead teach God's way forthrightly.	"Teacher, Jesus, we know that you are [from God], since the things you do put you above all the prophets.
is it permissible to pay the poll tax to Caesar or not?"	Is it permissible to pay the poll tax to Caesar or not? Should we pay or should we not pay?"	[22]Is it permissible for us to pay taxes to Caesar or not?"	[3]Tell us, then, is it permissible to pay to rulers what is due them? Should we pay them or not?"
[18]Jesus knew how devious they were, and said, "Why do you provoke me, you phonies? [19]Show me the money used to pay the poll tax." And they handed him a denarius.	[15]But he saw through their trap, and said to them, "Why do you provoke me like this? Let me have a look at a denarius." [16]They handed him one,	[23]But he saw through their duplicity, and said to them, [24]"Show me a denarius.	[4]Jesus knew what they were up to, and became indignant. **Th 100:1–4** [1]They showed Jesus a gold coin and said to him, "Caesar's people demand taxes from us."
[20]And he says to them, "Whose image is this? Whose name is on it?"	and he says to them, "Whose image is this? Whose name is on it?"	Whose image and inscription is on it?"	
[21]They say to him, "Caesar's." Then he says to them, "Pay to Caesar what belongs to Caesar, and to God what belongs to God!"	They replied, "Caesar's." [17]Jesus said to them, "Pay to Caesar what belongs to Caesar, and to God what belongs to God."	They said, "Caesar's." [25]So he said to them, "Then pay to Caesar what belongs to Caesar, and to God what belongs to God!"	[2]He said to them, "Give Caesar what belongs to Caesar, [3]give God what belongs to God, [4]and give me what is mine."
[22]When they heard his reply, they were dumbfounded. And they withdrew from him and went away.	And they were dumbfounded at him.	[26]And so they were unable to catch him in anything he said in front of the people; they were dumbfounded at his answer and fell silent.	

214. A Woman with Seven Husbands

Mt 22:23–33	Mk 12:18–27	Lk 20:27–40
[23]That same day, some Sadducees, who maintain there is no resurrection, came up to him and questioned him. [24]"Teacher," they said, "Moses said, 'If someone dies without children, his brother shall marry the widow and produce offspring for his brother.'	[18]And some Sadducees—those who maintain there is no resurrection—come up to him and they start questioning him. [19]"Teacher," they said, "Moses wrote for our benefit, 'If someone's brother dies and leaves his widow childless, his brother shall take the widow as his wife and produce offspring for his brother.' [20]There were seven brothers; now the first took a wife but left no children when he died. [21]So the second married her but died without leaving offspring, and the third likewise. [22]In fact, all seven ⟨married her but⟩ left no offspring. Finally, the wife died too. [23]In the resurrection, after they rise, whose wife will she be, since all seven had her as a wife?"	[27]Some of the Sadducees—those who argue there is no resurrection—came up to him [28]and put a question to him. "Teacher," they said, "Moses wrote for our benefit, 'If someone's brother dies, leaving behind a wife but no children, his brother shall take the widow as his wife and produce offspring for his brother.' [29]Now let's say there were seven brothers; the first took a wife, and died childless. [30]Then the second [31]and the third married her, and so on. All seven ⟨married her but⟩ left no children when they died.
[25]We knew these seven brothers. Now the first married and died, and since he left no children, he left his widow to his brother. [26]The second brother did the same thing, and the third, and so on, through the seventh brother.		
[27]Finally the wife died. [28]So then, in the resurrection, whose wife, of the seven, will she be, since they had all married her?"		[32]Finally, the wife died too. [33]So then, in the 'resurrection' whose wife will the woman be, since all seven had her as a wife?"
[29]In response Jesus said to them, "You've missed the point; you ignore both the scriptures and the power of God.	[24]Jesus said to them, "Isn't this the reason you've missed the point: that you ignore both the scriptures and the power of God?	[34]And Jesus said to them, "The children of this age marry and are given in marriage; [35]but those who are considered worthy of participating in the age to come, which means 'in the resurrection from the dead,' do not marry. [36]They can no longer die, since they are the equivalent of heavenly messengers; they are children of God and children of the resurrection. [37]Moses proved that the dead are raised in the passage about the bush: he calls the Lord 'the God of Abraham, the God of Isaac, and the God of Jacob.' [38]So this is not the God of the dead, but of the living, since to him they are all alive."
[30]You see, at the resurrection people do not marry but resemble heaven's messengers. [31]As for the resurrection of the dead, I guess you haven't read God's word to you:	[25]You see, when men and women rise from the dead, they do not marry, but resemble heaven's messengers. [26]As for whether or not the dead are raised, I guess you haven't read in the book of Moses in the passage about the bush, how God spoke to him:	
[32]'I am the God of Abraham and the God of Isaac and the God of Jacob.' This is not the God of the dead, but of the living."	'I am the God of Abraham and the God of Isaac and the God of Jacob.' [27]This is not the God of the dead, but of the living—you're constantly missing the point."	
[33]And when the crowd heard, they were stunned by his teaching.		[39]And some of the scholars answered, "Well put, Teacher." ([40]You see, they no longer dared to ask him about anything else.)
		20:41–44 #216, p. 167

215. The Most Important Commandment(s)

Mt 22:34–40	Mk 12:28–34	Lk 10:25–28	Th 25:1–2
[34]When the Pharisees learned that he had silenced the Sadducees, they conspired against him. [35]And one of them, a legal expert, put him to the test: [36]"Teacher, which commandment in the Law is the greatest?"	[28]And one of the scholars approached when he heard them arguing, and because he saw how skillfully Jesus answered them, he asked him, "Of all the commandments, which is the most important?"	[25]On one occasion, a legal expert stood up to put him to the test with a question: "Teacher, what do I have to do to inherit eternal life?"	
[37]He replied to him,	[29]Jesus answered, "The first is, 'Hear, Israel, the Lord your God is one Lord,	[26]He said to him, "How do you read what is written in the Law?" [27]And he answered,	
"'You shall love the Lord your God with all your heart and all your soul and all your mind.' [38]This commandment is first and foremost. [39]And the second is like it: 'You shall love your neighbor as yourself.'	[30]and you shall love the Lord your God with all your heart and all your soul and all your mind and all your strength.' [31]The second is this: 'You shall love your neighbor as yourself.'	"You shall love the Lord your God with all your heart and all your soul and all your strength and all your mind; and your neighbor as yourself."	[1]Love your friends like your own soul, [2]protect them like the pupil of your eye.
[40]Everything in the Law and the Prophets hangs on these two commandments."	There is no other commandment greater than these."		
		[28]Jesus said to him, "You're right; do this and you will have life."	
	[32]And the scholar said to him, "That's a fine answer, Teacher. You have correctly said that God is one and there is no other beside him. [33]And 'to love him with all one's heart and with all one's mind and with all one's strength' and 'to love one's neighbor as oneself' is greater than all the burnt offerings and sacrifices put together." [34]And when Jesus saw that he answered him sensibly, he said to him, "You are not far from God's empire."	*20:39*	
22:46b	And from then on no one dared question him.	*20:40*	
		10:29–37 #145, p. 117	

216. How can the Anointed be David's son?

Mt 22:41–46	Mk 12:35–37	Lk 20:41–44
[41]When the Pharisees gathered around, Jesus asked them, [42]"What do you think about the Anointed One? Whose son is he?" They said to him, "David's." [43]He said to them, "Then how can David call him 'lord,' while speaking under the influence of the spirit: [44]"The Lord said to my lord, "Sit here at my right, until I make your enemies grovel at your feet"? [45]If David actually called him 'lord,' how can he be his son?" [46]And no one could come up with an answer to his riddle. And from that day on no one dared ask him a question. 23:1–12 #218, p. 168	[35]And while Jesus was teaching in the temple area, he was asking this question: "How can the scholars claim that the Anointed One is the son of David? [36]David himself said under the influence of the holy spirit, "The Lord said to my lord, "Sit here at my right, until I make your enemies grovel at your feet." [37]David himself calls him 'lord,' so how can he be his son?" And a huge crowd was listening to him with delight. *12:34b*	[41]Then he asked them, "How can they say that the Anointed One is the son of David? [42]Remember, David himself says in the book of Psalms, "The Lord said to my lord, "Sit here at my right, [43]until I make your enemies grovel at your feet." [44]Since David calls him 'lord,' how can he be his son?" *20:40*

217. Beware of scholars

Mt 23:6–7	Mk 12:38–40	Lk 20:45–47
[6]They love the best couches at banquets and the prominent seats in synagogues [7]and respectful greetings in marketplaces and having everyone call them 'Rabbi.'	[38]In his teaching he was saying, "Look out for the scholars who like to parade around in long robes, and ⟨insist on⟩ respectful greetings in the marketplaces [39]and the prominent seats in the synagogues and the best couches at banquets. [40]They are the ones who prey on widows and their families, and then recite long prayers just to look good. These people will get what's coming to them, and more!	[45]Within earshot of the people Jesus said to the disciples, [46]"Be on guard against the scholars who like to parade around in long robes, and who love respectful greetings in the marketplaces and the prominent seats in the synagogues and the best couches at banquets. [47]They are the ones who prey on widows and their families, and then recite long prayers just to look good. These people will get what's coming to them, and more!" 21:1–4 #221, p. 171

218. Beware of scholars (and Pharisees)

SEE #379, 396, PP. 309, 318

Mt 23:1–12	Mk 12:38–40	Lk 20:45; 11:46; 20:46; 18:14b/14:11; 20:47
[1]Then Jesus said to the crowds and to his disciples, [2]"The scholars and Pharisees occupy the chair of Moses. [3]So do everything they tell you, but don't do what they do; they don't practice what they preach. [4]They invent heavy burdens[a] and lay them on folks' shoulders, but they themselves won't lift a finger to move them. [5]Everything they do, they do for show. So they widen their phylacteries and enlarge their tassels.	[38]In his teaching he was saying,	**Lk 20:45** [45]Within earshot of the people Jesus said to the disciples, **Lk 11:46** Damn you legal experts too! You load people down with crushing burdens, but you yourselves don't lift a finger to help carry them.
[6]They love the best couches at banquets and the prominent seats in synagogues [7]and respectful greetings in marketplaces and having everyone call them 'Rabbi.' [8]But none of you are to be called 'Rabbi'; after all, you only have one teacher, and all of you belong to the same family. [9]And don't call anyone on earth 'father,' since you have only one Father, and he is in heaven. [10]You are not to be called 'instructors,' because you have only one instructor, the Anointed One. [11]Now whoever is greater than you will be your slave.†	"Look out for the scholars who like to parade around in long robes, and ⟨insist on⟩ respectful greetings in the marketplaces [39]and the prominent seats in the synagogues and the best couches at banquets.	**Lk 20:46** Be on guard against the scholars who like to parade around in long robes, and who love respectful greetings in the marketplaces and the prominent seats in the synagogues and the best couches at banquets.*
[12]Those who promote themselves will be demoted, and those who demote themselves will be promoted."		**Lk 18:14b** Those who promote themselves will be demoted, but those who demote themselves will be promoted. **Lk 14:11** Those who promote themselves will be demoted, and those who demote themselves will be promoted.
	[40]They are the ones who prey on widows and their families, and then recite long prayers just to look good. These people will get what's coming to them, and more!"	**Lk 20:47** They are the ones who prey on widows and their families, and then recite long prayers just to look good. These people will get what's coming to them, and more!
	12:41–44 #221, p. 171	

* Ⓓ Lk 11:43 (#153, p. 121)

† Mk 9:35 / Lk 9:48 (#127, p. 107)

[a] Mt 23:4 Some mss add "that are hard to bear" after *heavy burdens*.

219. Damn you, scholars and Pharisees and legal experts!

SEE #380, P. 309

Mt 23:13–36	Mk	Lk 11:52, 42, 39–41, 44, 47–51	Th 39:1–2; 89:1–2
[13]You scholars and Pharisees, you impostors! Damn you! You slam the door of the empire of Heaven in people's faces. You yourselves don't go in, and you block the way of those trying to go in.[a] [15]You scholars and Pharisees, you impostors! Damn you! You scour land and sea to make one convert, and when you do, you make that person twice as much a child of Gehenna than you. [16]Damn you, you blind guides who claim, 'When you swear by the temple, it doesn't matter, but when you swear by the treasure in the temple, it is binding.' [17]You blind fools, which is greater, the treasure or the temple that makes the gold sacred? [18]You go on, 'When you swear by the altar, it doesn't matter, but when you swear by the offering that lies on the altar, it is binding.' [19]You are so blind! Which is greater, the offering or the altar that makes the offering sacred? [20]So when you swear by the altar, you swear by the altar and everything on it. [21]And anyone who swears by the temple, swears by the temple and the one who makes it home, [22]and anyone who swears by heaven swears by the throne of God and the one who occupies it. [23]You scholars and Pharisees, you impostors! Damn you! You pay tithes on mint and dill and cumin too, but ignore the really important matters of the Law, such as justice and mercy and trust. It's these you should have practiced without ignoring the others. [24]You blind leaders! You strain out a gnat and gulp down a camel! [25]You scholars and Pharisees, you impostors! Damn you! You wash the outside of cups and plates, but inside they are full of greed and self-indulgence. [26]You blind Pharisee, first clean the inside of the cup and then		[52]You legal experts, damn you! You've taken away the key of knowledge. You yourselves haven't gone in and you have blocked the way of those trying to go in. [42]Damn you, Pharisees! You pay tithes on mint and rue and every herb, but neglect justice and the love of God. It's these you should have practiced without neglecting the others. [39]You Pharisees clean the outside of cups and dishes, but inside you are full of greed and evil. [40]You fools! Did not the one who made the outside also make the inside? [41]Still, donate what is inside to charity, and	**Th 39:1–2** [1]The Pharisees and the scholars have taken the keys of knowledge and hidden them. [2]They have not entered, nor have they allowed those who want to enter to do so.* **Th 89:1–2** [1]Why do you wash the outside of the cup? [2]Don't you understand that the one who made the inside is also the one who made the outside?

Mt 23:13–36	Mk	Lk 11:52, 42, 39–41, 44, 47–51	Th 39:1–2; 89:1–2

Mt 23:13–36

the outside will be clean too.

27You scholars and Pharisees, you impostors! Damn you! You're like whitewashed tombs: on the outside they look beautiful, but inside they are full of dead bones and every kind of decay. 28So you too look like upright people on the outside, but on the inside you are doing nothing but posturing and subverting the Law.

29You scholars and Pharisees, you impostors! Damn you! You build the tombs of the prophets and decorate the graves of the just 30and claim, 'If we had lived in the days of our ancestors, we wouldn't have joined them in spilling the prophets' blood.' 31So, you witness against yourselves: you are descendants of those who murdered the prophets, 32and you're the spitting image of your ancestors. 33You serpents! You spawn of Satan! How are you going to escape Gehenna's judgment?†

34Look, that is why I send you prophets and sages and scholars. Some you're going to kill and crucify, and some you're going to flog in your synagogues and hound from town to town. 35And so all the innocent blood that has ever been shed on the earth will be on you, from the blood of innocent Abel to the blood of Zechariah, son of Baruch, whom you murdered between the temple and the altar. 36Let me tell you, all these things are going to rain down on this generation.

Lk 11:52, 42, 39–41, 44, 47–51

then you'll see how everything comes clean for you.

44Damn you! You're like unmarked graves that people walk on without realizing it."

47Damn you! You build monuments to the prophets whom your ancestors murdered.

48You are therefore witnesses to and approve of the deeds of your ancestors: they killed ⟨the prophets⟩ and you build ⟨monuments⟩ to them.

49That's why the Wisdom of God has said, 'I will send them prophets and apostles, and some of them they are always going to kill and persecute.'

50So, this generation will have to answer for the blood of all the prophets that has been shed since the world was founded, 51from the blood of Abel to the blood of Zechariah, who perished between the altar and the sanctuary. Yes, I'm telling you, this generation will have to answer for it.

*Th 102 Damn the Pharisees! They are like a dog sleeping in the cattle's feeding trough: the dog neither eats nor [lets] the cattle eat. (#487, p. 361)

† ⒟ Mt 3:7 / Lk 3:7 (#4, p. 11)

ªMt 23:13 Some mss add a v. 14: "Damn you, you scholars and Pharisees, impostors! You prey on widows and their families, and recite long prayers for appearance sake. Therefore, you will get a stiff sentence."

220. Jerusalem, Murderer of Prophets

SEE #395, P. 318

Mt 23:37–39	Mk	Lk 13:34–35
[37]Jerusalem, Jerusalem, you murder the prophets and stone those sent to you! How often I wanted to gather your children as a hen gathers her chicks under her wings, but you wouldn't let me. [38]Can't you see, your house is being abandoned as a ruin? [39]I'm telling you, you certainly won't see me again until you say, 'Blessed is the one who comes in the name of the Lord.'"		[34]Jerusalem, Jerusalem, you murder the prophets and stone those sent to you! How often I wanted to gather your children as a hen ⟨gathers⟩ her own chicks under her wings, but you wouldn't let me. [35]Can't you see, your house is being abandoned? I'm telling you, you certainly won't see me until the time comes when you say, 'Blessed is the one who comes in the name of the Lord.'"
24:1–2 #222, p. 171		14:1–6 #172, p. 131

221. The Widow's Pittance

Mt	Mk 12:41–44	Lk 21:1–4
	[41]And he sat across from the temple treasury and was observing the crowd dropping money into the collection box. And many wealthy people would drop large amounts in. [42]Then one poor widow came and put in two quarters, which is a pittance. [43]And he motioned his disciples over and said to them, "Let me tell you, this poor widow has contributed more than all those who dropped something into the collection box. [44]You see, they were all donating out of their surplus, whereas she, out of her poverty, was contributing all she had, her whole livelihood."	[1]He looked up and observed the rich dropping their donations into the collection box. [2]Then he noticed that a needy widow put in two quarters, [3]and he observed, "I'm telling you the truth: this poor widow has contributed more than all of them. [4]You see, they all made donations out of their surplus, whereas she, out of her poverty, was contributing everything she had to live on."

222. Not One Stone on Another

Mt 24:1–2	Mk 13:1–2	Lk 21:5–6
[1]Jesus was leaving the temple area on his way out, when his disciples came to him and called his attention to the sacred buildings. [2]In response he said to them, "Yes, take a good look at all this! Let me tell you, not one single stone will be left on top of another! Every last one will be knocked down!"	[1]And as he was going out of the temple area, one of his disciples remarks to him, "Teacher, look, what magnificent masonry! What wonderful buildings!" [2]And Jesus replied to him, "Take a good look at these monumental buildings! Not a single stone will be left on top of another! Every last one will certainly be knocked down!"	[5]When some were remarking about how the temple was adorned with fine masonry and ornamentation, he said, [6]"As for these things that you now admire, the time will come when not one stone will be left on top of another! Every last one will be knocked down!"

223. The Sign of the End

Mt 24:3–8	Mk 13:3–8	Lk 21:7–11
³As he was sitting on the Mount of Olives, the disciples came to him privately, and said,	³And as he was sitting on the Mount of Olives across from the temple, Peter was asking him privately, as would James and John and Andrew,	⁷And they asked him,
"Tell us, when are these things going to happen, and what will be the sign of your coming and of the culmination of the age?"	⁴"Tell us, when are these things going to happen, and what will be the sign to show when all these things are about to culminate?"	"Teacher, when are these things going to happen? What will be the sign to show when these things are about to occur?"
⁴And in response Jesus said to them, "Stay alert, or else someone might deceive you. ⁵You know, many will come using my name, and claim, 'I'm the Anointed One!' and they will deceive many people. ⁶You're going to hear about wars and rumors of wars. See that you are not afraid.	⁵And Jesus began to say to them, "Stay alert, or else someone might deceive you. ⁶You know, many will come using my name and claim, 'I'm the one!' and they will deceive many people. ⁷When you hear of wars and rumors of wars, don't be afraid.	⁸He said, "Stay alert! Don't be deceived. You know, many will come using my name and claim, 'I'm the one!' and 'The time has arrived!' Don't go running after them! ⁹And when you hear of wars and insurrections, don't panic.
For these are inevitable, but it is not yet the End.	These are inevitable, but it is not yet the End.	It's inevitable that these things happen first, but that doesn't mean the End is imminent." ¹⁰Then he went on to tell them,
⁷For nation will rise up against nation and empire against empire; and there will be famines and earthquakes everywhere. ⁸Now all these things mark the beginning of the birth pangs.	⁸For nation will rise up against nation and empire against empire; there will be earthquakes everywhere; there will be famines. These things mark the beginning of the birth pangs.	"Nation will rise up against nation, and empire against empire. ¹¹There will be powerful earthquakes, and famines and plagues all over the place; there will be dreadful events and spectacular signs from heaven.

224. How to Face the Coming Persecution

Mt 10:17–23; 24:9–14	Mk 13:9–13	Lk 21:12–19
Mt 10:17–22 [17]And beware of people, for they'll turn you over to Jewish councils and flog you in synagogues. [18]And you'll be hauled up before governors and even kings on my account so you can make your case to them and to the gentiles. [19]And when they lock you up, don't worry about how you should speak or what you should say. It will occur to you at that moment what to say. [20]For it's not you who are speaking but your Father's spirit speaking through you. [21]One brother will turn in another to be put to death, and a father his child, and children will turn against their parents and kill them. [22]And you'll be universally hated because of me.†	[9]But you look out for yourselves. They'll turn you over to Jewish councils, and beat you in synagogues, and haul you up before governors and kings on my account, so you can make your case to them. [10]Yet the good news must first be announced to all peoples. [11]And when they take you away to turn you in, don't be worried about what you should say. Instead, whatever occurs to you at the moment, say that. For it's not you who are speaking but the holy spirit. [12]And one brother will turn in another to be put to death, and a father his child, and children will turn against their parents and kill them. [13]And you'll be universally hated because of me.	[12]But before all these things happen, they'll manhandle you, and persecute you, and turn you over to synagogues and deliver you to prisons, and you'll be hauled up before kings and governors on account of my name. [13]This will give you a chance to make your case. [14]So make up your minds not to rehearse your defense in advance, [15]for I will give you the wit and wisdom which none of your adversaries will be able to resist or refute.* [16]You'll be turned in, even by parents and brothers and relatives and friends; and they'll put some of you to death.
[23]When they persecute you in this town, flee to another.ᵃ Let me tell you, you certainly won't have gone through the towns of Israel before the Human One comes.		[17]And you'll be universally hated because of me.
But those who hold out to the end will be saved.§	Those who hold out to the End will be saved.	[18]Yet not a single hair on your head will be harmed.‡ [19]By your perseverance you will secure your lives.
Mt 24:9–14 [9]At that time they will turn you in to be tortured, and will kill you, and you'll be universally hated because of me. [10]And then many will fall away, and they will turn one another in and hate each other. [11]And many phony prophets will appear and will deceive many. [12]And as lawlessness spreads, many people's love will grow cold. [13]Those who hold out to the End will be saved. [14]And this good news of the empire of Heaven will have been proclaimed in the whole inhabited world, so you can make your case to all peoples. And then the End will come.	v. 13a v. 13b	v. 17 v. 19

* ⅅ Lk 12:11–12 (#157, p. 124)
† ⅅ Mt 24:9b (above)
‡ Lk 12:7 / Mt 10:30 (#155, p. 123)
§ ⅅ Mt 24:13 (above)

ᵃ Mt 10:23 A few mss add: "And when they persecute you in another, flee to yet another one."

225. The Coming Tribulation

Mt 24:15–22	Mk 13:14–20	Lk 21:20–24; 17:31
[15]So when you see the "devastating desecration" (as described by Daniel the prophet) standing "in the holy place" —the lector had better figure out what this means— [16]then the people in Judea should head for the hills;	[14]When you see the "devastating desecration" standing where it should not —the lector had better figure out what this means—then the people in Judea should head for the hills.	**Lk 21:20–21** [20]When you see Jerusalem surrounded by armies, know then that its destruction is just around the corner. [21]Then the people in Judea should head for the hills, and those inside the city flee, and those out in the countryside not re-enter.
[17]no one on the roof should go downstairs to retrieve anything;	[15]No one on the roof should go downstairs, no one should enter the house to retrieve anything,	**Lk 17:31** On that day, if any are on the roof and their things are in the house, they had better not go down to fetch them. The same goes for those in the field: they had better not turn back for anything left behind.
[18]and no one in the field should turn back to get a coat.	[16]and no one in the field should turn back to get a coat.	**Lk 21:22–24** [22]For these are days of vengeance, when everything that was predicted will be fulfilled.
[19]It'll be too bad for pregnant women and nursing mothers in those days! [20]Pray that you don't have to flee during the winter or on the Sabbath. [21]For there will be great tribulation, the likes of which has not occurred since the world began until now, and will never occur again. [22]And if those days had not been cut short, no human being would have survived. But for the sake of the chosen people, those days will be cut short.	[17]It'll be too bad for pregnant women and nursing mothers in those days! [18]Pray that none of this happens in winter! [19]For those days will see tribulation the likes of which has not occurred since God created the world until now, and will never occur again. [20]And if the Lord had not cut short the days, no human being would have survived. But he did shorten the days for the sake of the chosen people whom he selected.	[23]It'll be too bad for pregnant women and for nursing mothers in those days! There will be utter misery throughout the land and wrath ⟨will fall⟩ upon this people.
		[24]They will fall by the edge of the sword, and be hauled off as prisoners to all the foreign countries, and Jerusalem will be overrun by pagans, until the period allotted to the pagans has run its course.
		21:25–28 #227, p. 175

226. Warning against Phony Messiahs

SEE #410, P. 325

Mt 24:23–28	Mk 13:21–23	Lk 17:23–24, 37b
[23]Then if someone says to you, "Look, here's the Anointed One" or "over here," don't count on it!* [24]After all, phony messiahs and phony prophets will show up, and they'll provide spectacular signs and omens in an attempt to deceive, if possible, even the chosen people. [25]Look, I have warned you in advance. [26]In fact, if they should say to you, "Look, he's in the desert," don't go out there; or "Look, he's in one of the inner rooms," don't count on it. [27]For just as lightning comes out of the east and is visible all the way to the west, that's what the coming of the Human One will be like. [28]For wherever there's a corpse, that's where vultures gather.	[21]And then if someone says to you, "Look, here's the Anointed One," or "Look, there he is!" don't count on it!* [22]After all, phony messiahs and phony prophets will show up, and they'll provide signs and omens in an attempt to deceive, if possible, the chosen people. [23]But you be on your guard. I have warned you about everything in advance.	[23]And they'll be telling you, "Look, there it is!" or "Look, here it is!" Don't rush off; don't pursue it. [24]For just as lightning flashes and lights up the sky from one end to the other, that's what the Human One will be like in his day. [37b]Vultures collect wherever there's a carcass. 17:22–37 #190, p. 142

*Th 113:1–3 [1]His disciples said to him, "When will the ⟨Father's⟩ empire come?" [2]"It won't come by watching for it. [3]It won't be said, 'Look, here!' or 'Look, there!'" (#494, p. 363)

227. The Coming of the Human One

Mt 24:29–31	Mk 13:24–27	Lk 21:25–28
[29]Right after the tribulation of those days the sun will be darkened, and the moon will not give off her glow; the stars will fall from the sky, and the heavenly forces will be shaken. [30]And then the sign of the Human One will appear in the sky, and every tribe of the earth will lament, and they'll see the Human One coming on the clouds of the sky with great power and splendor. [31]And he'll send out his messengers with a blast on the trumpet, and they'll gather his chosen people from the four winds, from one end of the sky to the other.	[24]But in those days, after that tribulation, the sun will be darkened, and the moon will not give off her glow; [25]the stars will fall from the sky, and the heavenly forces will be shaken. [26]And then they will see the Human One coming on the clouds with great power and splendor. [27]And then he will send out messengers and will gather the chosen people from the four winds, from the ends of the earth to the edge of the sky.	[25]And there will be omens in the sun and moon and stars, and on the earth nations will be anguished in their confusion at the roar of the surging sea. [26]People will faint from terror at the prospect of what is coming over the civilized world, for the heavenly forces will be shaken. [27]And then they will see the Human One coming a cloud with great power and splendor. [28]Now when these things begin to happen, stand tall and hold your heads high, because your deliverance is just around the corner!

228. Taking a Cue from the Fig Tree

Mt 24:32–36	Mk 13:28–32	Lk 21:29–33
32Take a cue from the fig tree. When its branch is already in bud and leaves come out, you know that summer is near.	28Take a cue from the fig tree. When its branch is already in bud and leaves come out, you know that summer is near.	29Then he told them a parable: "Observe the fig tree, or any tree, for that matter. 30Once it puts out foliage, you can see for yourselves that summer is near.
33So, when you see all these things, you should realize that he is near, just outside your door.	29So, when you see these things happen, you should realize that he is near, just outside your door.	31So, when you see these things happening, you should realize that the empire of God is near.
34Let me tell you, this generation certainly won't pass away before all these things happen!*	30Let me tell you, this generation certainly won't pass away before all these things happen!*	32Let me tell you, this generation certainly won't pass away before it all happens.*
35The earth will pass away and so will the sky, but my words will never pass away.	31The earth will pass away and so will the sky, but my words will never pass away.	33The earth will pass away and so will the sky, but my words will never pass away!
36As for that exact day and hour, no one knows, not even Heaven's messengers, nor even the son[a]—no one, except the Father alone.	32As for that exact day or hour, no one knows, not even heaven's messengers, nor even the son—no one, except the Father.	
24:37–42 #231, p. 177		21:34–38 #230, p. 177

* Ⓓ Mt 16:28 / Mk 9:1 / Lk 9:27 (#121, p. 102)

[a]Mt 24:36 *Nor even the son* is omitted by many mss, but it is present in the best early mss.

229. Stay Alert
SEE #386, P. 313

Mt 25:13–15; 24:42, 44	Mk 13:33–37	Lk 19:12–13; 12:40
Mt 25:13–15 13So stay alert because you don't know either the day or the hour. 14You know, it's like a man going on a trip who called his slaves and turned his property over to them. 15To the first he gave five talents' worth of silver, to the second two talents' worth, and to the third one talent's worth, to each in proportion to his ability. Then he left.	33Be on guard! Stay alert! For you never know what time it is. 34It's like a person who takes a trip and puts slaves in charge, each with a task, and orders the doorkeeper to be alert.	**Lk 19:12–13** 12A nobleman went off to a distant land intending to acquire a kingship for himself and then return. 13Calling ten of his slaves, he gave them ten minas and told them, "Do business with this while I'm away."
Mt 24:42 So stay alert! You never know on what day your master returns.	35Therefore, stay alert! For you never know when the master of the house returns, maybe at dusk, or at midnight, or when the rooster crows, or maybe early in the morning. 36He may return suddenly and find you asleep. 37What I'm telling you, I say to everyone: stay alert!	
Mt 24:44 Therefore, you too should be prepared. Remember, the Human One is coming when you least expect it.		**Lk 12:40** You too should be prepared. Remember, the Human One is coming when you least expect it.
	14:1–2 #234, p. 180	

230. Pray for strength

Mt	Mk	Lk 21:34–38
		[34]So watch yourselves so your minds won't be dulled by hangovers and drunkenness and the worries of everyday life, and so that day won't spring upon you suddenly like some trap you weren't expecting. [35]It will come down for sure on all who inhabit the earth. [36]Stay alert! Pray constantly that you may have the strength to escape all these things that are on their way and the strength to stand before the Human One. [37]During the day he would teach in the temple area, and in the evening he would go and spend the night on the mountain called Olives. [38]And all the people would get up early to come to the temple area to hear him. 22:1–2 #234, p. 180

231. Like the Days of Noah

SEE #410, P. 325

Mt 24:37–42	Mk	Lk 17:26–27, 30, 34–35	Th 61:1
[37]The Human One's coming will be just like the days of Noah. [38]That's how people behaved then before the flood came: they ate and drank, married and were given in marriage, until the day Noah boarded the ark, [39]and they were oblivious until the flood came and swept them all away. That's how it will be when the Human One comes. [40]Then two men will be in the field; one will be taken and one will be left. [41]Two women will be grinding at the mill; one will be taken and one left. [42]So stay alert! You never know on what day your master returns. 24:43–44 #160, p. 125	13:35	[26]And just as it was in the days of Noah, that's how it will be in the days of the Human One. [27]They ate, drank, got married, and were given in marriage, until the day Noah boarded the ark. Then the flood came and destroyed them all. [30]It will be like that on the day the Human One is revealed. [34]I'm telling you, on that night there will be two on one couch; one will be taken and the other left. [35]There will be two women grinding together; one will be taken and the other left.[a] 17:22–37 #190, p. 142	Two will recline on a couch; one will die, one will live.

[a] Lk 17:35 Some mss add another verse, traditionally numbered 17:36: "Two will be in the fields; one will be taken, the other left."

232. The Parable of the Foolish and Prudent Maidens

SEE #393, P. 317

Mt 25:1–13	Mk 13:33, 35, 37	Lk 12:35–36, 38; 13:25; 12:40
[1]When the time comes, the empire of Heaven will be like ten maidens who took their lamps and went out to meet the bridegroom. [2]Five of them were foolish and five were prudent. [3]You see, the foolish maidens took their lamps but failed to take oil with them, [4]while the prudent ones took flasks of oil along with their lamps. [5]When the bridegroom was delayed, they all dozed off and fell asleep.		**Lk 12:35–36, 38** [35]Keep your belts fastened and your lamps lit. [36]Imitate those who are waiting for their master to come home from a wedding, ready to open the door for him as soon as he arrives and knocks.
[6]Then in the middle of the night there was a shout: "Look, the bridegroom is coming! Let's go out to meet him." [7]Then the maidens all got up and trimmed their lamps.	13:35–37	[38]If he gets home around midnight, or even around 3 a.m., and finds them so, they are to be congratulated!
[8]The foolish said to the prudent ones, "Let us have some of your oil because our lamps are going out."		
[9]But the prudent maidens responded, "We can't do that in case there isn't enough for both of us. You'd better go to the merchants and buy some for yourselves."		
[10]While they were gone to get some, the bridegroom arrived and those who had come prepared accompanied him to the wedding; then the door was closed.		
[11]The other maidens finally come and say, "Master, master, open the door for us."		**Lk 13:25** Once the master of the house gets up and bars the door, you'll be left standing outside and knocking at the door: 'Master, open up for us.' But he'll answer you, 'I don't know where you come from.'
[12]He responded, "Let me tell you, I don't recognize you."		
[13]So stay alert because you don't know either the day or the hour.*	[33]Be on guard! Stay alert! For you never know what time it is. [35]Therefore, stay alert! For you never know when the master of the house returns, maybe at dusk, or at midnight, or when the rooster crows, or maybe early in the morning. [37]What I'm telling you, I say to everyone: stay alert!	
25:14–30 #203, p. 154	14:1–2 #234, p. 180	

* Mt 24:44 / Lk 12:40 (#229, p. 176)

233. The Judgment of the Sheep and the Goats

Mt 25:31–46	Mk	Lk
³¹When the Human One comes in his glory, accompanied by all his messengers,* he'll be seated on his glorious throne. ³²Then all peoples will be assembled before him, and he will separate them into groups, much as a shepherd separates sheep from goats. ³³He'll place the sheep to his right and the goats to his left. ³⁴Then the king will say to those at his right, "Come, you who have the blessing of my Father, inherit the empire prepared for you from the foundation of the world. ³⁵For I was hungry and you gave me something to eat; I was thirsty and you gave me something to drink; I was a foreigner and you offered me hospitality; ³⁶I was naked and you clothed me; I was ill and you visited me; I was in prison and you came to see me." ³⁷Then the righteous will say to him, "Master, when did we see you hungry and feed you or thirsty and give you a drink? ³⁸When did we notice that you were a foreigner and offer you hospitality? Or naked and clothe you? ³⁹When did we find you ill or in prison and come to visit you?" ⁴⁰And the king will respond to them, "Let me tell you, whatever you did for the least of my brothers and sisters, you did for me." ⁴¹Next, he will say to those at his left, "You, condemned to the everlasting fire prepared for the devil and his messengers, get away from me! ⁴²For I was hungry and you didn't give me anything to eat; I was thirsty and you refused me a drink; ⁴³I was a foreigner and you failed to offer me hospitality; naked and you didn't clothe me; ill and in prison and you didn't visit me." ⁴⁴Then they will give him a similar reply, "Master, when did we notice that you were hungry or thirsty or a foreigner or naked or ill or in prison and not take care of you?" ⁴⁵He will then respond, "Let me tell you, whatever you didn't do for the least of my brothers and sisters, you didn't do for me." ⁴⁶The second group will then head for everlasting punishment, but the righteous for everlasting life.†		

* Mt 16:27 / Mk 8:38 / Lk 9:26 (#121, p. 102)

† Jn 5:28–29 ²⁸The time is coming when all who are in their graves will hear his voice ²⁹and come out—those who have done good will be raised to life, and those who have done vile deeds raised to stand trial. (#291, p. 236)

234. The Conspiracy to Arrest Jesus
SEE #306, P. 244

Mt 26:1–5	Mk 14:1–2	Lk 22:1–2
[1]And so it happened that, when Jesus had concluded his discourse, he told his disciples, [2]"You know that Passover comes in two days, and the Human One will be turned over to be crucified."	[1]Now it was two days until Passover and the festival of Unleavened Bread.	[1]The festival of Unleavened Bread, known as Passover, was approaching.
[3]Then the chief priests and elders of the people gathered in the courtyard of the chief priest, whose name was Caiaphas, [4]and they conspired to seize Jesus by trickery and kill him.*	And the chief priests and the scholars were looking for some way to seize him by trickery and kill him.*	[2]The chief priests and the scholars were still looking for some way to get rid of Jesus,*
[5]They were saying, "Not during the festival or else the people will riot."	[2]For they were saying, "Not during the festival, otherwise the people will riot."	but they feared the people.
		22:3–6 #236, p. 181

* Jn 11:47, 53 [47]So the chief priests and Pharisees called the Council together and posed this question to them: "What are we going to do now that this man performs so many signs? . . . [53]So from that day on they began plotting how to kill him. (#306, p. 244)

235. A Woman anoints Jesus
= #307, P. 244

Mt 26:6–13	Mk 14:3–9	Lk 7:36–39	Jn 12:1–8
			[1]Six days before Passover Jesus came to Bethany, where Lazarus lived, the one Jesus had raised from the dead. [2]There they gave a dinner for him; Martha did the serving, and Lazarus was one of those who ate with him.
[6]While Jesus was in Bethany at the house of Simon the leper,	[3]When he was in Bethany at the house of Simon the leper,	[36]One of the Pharisees invited him to dinner; he entered the Pharisee's house, and reclined ⟨for the meal⟩. [37]A local woman, who was a sinner, found out that he was having dinner at the Pharisee's house. She suddenly showed up with an alabaster jar of aromatic ointment,	
[7]a woman who had an alabaster jar of very expensive aromatic ointment came up to him and poured it over his head while he was reclining ⟨at table⟩.	he was just reclining there, and a woman came in carrying an alabaster jar of aromatic ointment made from pure and expensive nard. She broke the jar and poured ⟨the ointment⟩ on his head.	[38]and stood there behind him weeping at his feet. Her tears wet his feet, and she wiped them dry with her hair; she kissed his feet, and anointed them with the ointment.	[3]Mary brought in a pound of expensive aromatic ointment made from pure nard and anointed Jesus' feet and wiped them with her hair. And the house was filled with the ointment's fragrance.
		[39]The Pharisee who had invited him saw this and said to himself, "If this man were a prophet, he would know who this is and what kind of woman is touching him, since she is a sinner."	
[8]When they saw this, the disciples were annoyed, and said, "What good is this waste?	[4]Now some were annoyed ⟨and thought⟩ to themselves, "What good does it do to waste this ointment? [5]She		[4]Judas Iscariot, the disciple who was going to turn him in, says,

[Column 1]

⁹She could have sold it for a good price

and given ⟨the money⟩ to the poor."

¹⁰But Jesus knew what was going on and said to them, "Why are you giving this woman a hard time?

v. 12
After all, she has done a good deed for me. ¹¹Remember, the poor will always be around;

but I won't always be around. ¹²After all, by pouring this ointment on my body she has prepared me for burial. ¹³Let me tell you, wherever this good news is announced in all the world, the story of what she's done will be told in her memory."

[Column 2]

could have sold the ointment for more than three hundred denarii
and given ⟨the money⟩ to the poor."
And they were angry with her.

⁶Then Jesus said, "Let her alone! Why are you giving her a hard time?

v. 8
She has done a good deed for me. ⁷Remember, the poor will always be around, and whenever you want you can do good for them, but I won't always be around. ⁸She did what she could; she has planned ahead by anointing my body for burial. ⁹Let me tell you, wherever the good news is announced in all the world, the story of what she's done will be told in her memory."

[Column 4]

⁵"Why wasn't this ointment sold? It would bring three hundred denarii, and the money could have been given to the poor."

(⁶He didn't say this because he cared about the poor, but because he was a thief. He was in charge of the common purse and now and again would pilfer money put into it.)
⁷"Leave her alone," Jesus said.

"Let her keep it for the day of my burial.

⁸There will always be poor around,

but I won't always be around."ᵃ

v. 7b

ᵃJn 12:8 A few mss lack this verse.

236. Judas agrees to turn Jesus over

Mt 26:14–16	Mk 14:10–11	Lk 22:3–6
¹⁴Then one of the Twelve, Judas Iscariot by name, went to the chief priests ¹⁵and said, "What are you willing to pay me if I turn him over to you?" They agreed on thirty silver coins.	¹⁰And Judas Iscariot, one of the Twelve, went off to the chief priests to turn him over to them.	³Then Satan took possession of Judas,* the one called Iscariot, who was a member of the Twelve. ⁴He went off to negotiate with the chief priests and ⟨temple⟩ police how to turn Jesus over to them.
¹⁶And from that moment he started looking for a good opportunity to turn him in.	¹¹When they heard, they were delighted, and promised to pay him in silver. And he started looking for a good opportunity to turn him in.	⁵They were delighted and agreed to pay him in silver. ⁶And Judas accepted the deal and began looking for a good opportunity to turn him in when a crowd was not around.

*Jn 13:27 (#315, p. 252)

237. Preparations for the Passover

Mt 26:17–19	Mk 14:12–16	Lk 22:7–13
[17]On the first ⟨day⟩ of Unleavened Bread	[12]On the first day of Unleavened Bread, when they would sacrifice the Passover lamb,	[7]The festival of Unleavened Bread arrived, when the Passover ⟨lambs⟩ had to be sacrificed. [8]So Jesus sent Peter and John, with these instructions: "Go get things ready for us to eat the Passover." [9]They said to him,
the disciples came to Jesus and said, "Where do you want us to get things ready for you to celebrate Passover?"	his disciples say to him, "Where do you want us to go and get things ready for you to celebrate Passover?"	"Where do you want us to get things ready?"
[18]He said, "Go into the city to a certain guy	[13]He sends two of his disciples and says to them, "Go into the city, and a man carrying a water pot will meet you. Follow him, [14]and whatever place he enters say to the head of the house, 'The Teacher asks,	[10]He said to them, "Look, when you enter the city, a man carrying a waterpot will meet you. Follow him into the house he enters, [11]and say to the head of the house, 'The Teacher asks you,
and tell him, 'The Teacher says, "My time is near; I will observe Passover at your place with my disciples."'"	"Where is my guest room where I can celebrate Passover with my disciples?"' [15]And he'll show you a large upstairs room that has been arranged. That's the place where you should get ready for us."	"Where is the guest room where I can celebrate Passover with my disciples?"' [12]And he will show you a large upstairs room that's been arranged; that's the place where you should get things ready."
[19]And the disciples did as Jesus instructed them and they got things ready for Passover.	[16]And the disciples left, went into the city, and found it exactly as he had told them; and they got things ready for Passover.	[13]They set off and found things exactly as he had told them; and they got things ready for Passover.

238. The Betrayer's Identity

SEE #315, P. 252

Mt 26:20–25	Mk 14:17–21	Lk 22:14–23	Jn 13:21–27
[20]When it was evening, he was reclining ⟨for the meal⟩ with his twelve disciples.	[17]When evening comes, he arrives with the Twelve.	[14]When the time came, he took his place ⟨at the meal⟩, and the apostles joined him. [15]He said to them, "I have looked forward with all my heart to celebrating this Passover with you before my ordeal begins. [16]For I'm telling you, I certainly won't eat it again until everything is fulfilled in God's empire." [17]Then he took a cup, gave thanks, and said, "Take this and share it among yourselves. [18]For I'm telling you, I certainly won't drink any of the fruit of the vine from now on until God's empire is established!"	
26:29	14:25		

		¹⁹And he took a loaf, gave thanks, broke it into pieces, offered it to them, and said, "This is my body, which is offered for you. Do this as my memorial."	
26:26	14:22		
26:27	14:23	²⁰And, in the same manner, he took the cup after dinner and said, "This cup is the new covenant in my blood, which is poured out for you."	
²¹And as they were eating, he said,	¹⁸And as they reclined ⟨for dinner⟩ and were eating, Jesus said,		²¹When he had said all this, Jesus became agitated. He declared,
"Let me tell you, one of you is going to turn me in."	"Let me tell you, one of you eating with me is going to turn me in!"	²¹"But look! Right here with me at this very table is the one who is going to turn me in. ²²The Human One goes to meet his destiny; and yet damn the one responsible for turning him in!"	"Let me tell you this: one of you will turn me in."
v. 24	v. 21		
²²And they were very upset and each one said to him in turn, "I'm not the one, am I, Master?"	¹⁹They got very upset and said to him one after another, "I'm not the one, am I?"	²³And they began to ask one another which of them could possibly attempt such a thing.	²²The disciples stole glances at each other, at a loss to understand who it was he was talking about. ²³One of them, the disciple Jesus loved, was reclining next to him. ²⁴So Simon Peter leans over to ask that disciple who it was Jesus was talking about. ²⁵He, in turn, leans back on Jesus' chest and asks him, "Master, who is it?" ²⁶Jesus answers, "I am going to dip this piece of bread, and the one I give it to is the one."
²³In response he said, "The one who dips his hand in the bowl with me—that's who's going to turn me in. ²⁴The Human One departs just as the scriptures predict, but damn the one responsible for turning the Human One in! That man would be better off if he'd never been born!" ²⁵Judas, the one who was going to turn him in, responded, "You can't mean me, can you, Rabbi?"	²⁰But he said to them, "It's one of the Twelve, the one who is dipping into the bowl with me. ²¹The Human One departs just as the scriptures predict, but damn the one responsible for turning the Human One in! That man would be better off if he'd never been born!"	v. 22	So he dips the piece of bread and gives it to Judas, son of Simon Iscariot. ²⁷The moment ⟨he had given Judas⟩ the piece of bread, Satan took possession of him. Then Jesus says to him, "Go ahead and do what you're going to do."
		v. 3	
		v. 4	
		22:24–30 #240, p. 185	

239. Jesus' Body and Blood

Mt 26:26–29	Mk 14:22–25	Lk 22:19–20, 18
[26]As they were eating, Jesus took a loaf, gave a blessing, and broke it into pieces. And he offered it to the disciples, and said, "Take some and eat; this is my body."	[22]And as they were eating, he took a loaf, gave a blessing, broke it into pieces, and offered it to them. And he said, "Take some; this is my body!"	[19]And he took a loaf, gave thanks, broke it into pieces, offered it to them, and said, "This is my body, which is offered for you.[a] Do this as my memorial."
[27]He also took a cup and gave thanks and offered it to them, saying, "Drink from it, all of you, [28]for this is my blood of the covenant, which has been poured out for many for the forgiveness of sins.*	[23]He also took a cup, gave thanks, and offered it to them, and they all drank from it. [24]And he said to them, "This is my blood of the covenant, which has been poured out for many.*	[20]And, in the same manner, he took the cup after dinner and said, "This cup is the new covenant in my blood, which is poured out for you.*
[29]Now I'm telling you, from now on I won't touch a drop of this fruit of the vine, until that day when I drink it for the first time with you in my Father's empire!"	[25]Let me tell you, I'll never touch a drop of the fruit of the vine until that day when I drink it for the first time in God's empire."	[18]For I'm telling you, I certainly won't drink any of the fruit of the vine from now on until God's empire is established!"
26:30–35 #241, p. 186	14:26–31 #241, p. 186	22:14–23 #238, p. 182

* 1 Cor 11:23–25 [23]I received from the lord the same thing I passed on to you, that on the night when he was handed over, the lord Jesus took bread [24]and after he gave thanks he broke it and said, "This is my body broken for you. Do this to remember me." [25]And in the same way he took the wine cup after the meal and said, "This cup is the new covenant ratified by my blood. Whenever you drink this, do it to remember me." (#526, p. 400)

———
[a] Lk 22:19–20 A few mss omit *which is offered for you* and all of v. 20.

240. What it Means to be Greatest
SEE #412, P. 328

Mt 20:24–28; 19:28	Mk 10:41–45	Lk 22:24–30
Mt 20:24–28 24And when the other ten heard of it, they were incensed with the two brothers. 25And calling them aside, Jesus said, "You know how foreign rulers lord it over their subjects, and how their strong men tyrannize them. 26It's not going to be like that with you! With you, whoever wants to become great will be your servant, 27and whoever among you wants to be 'number one' is to be your slave. 28After all, the Human One didn't come to be served, but to serve and to give his life as a ransom for many." **Mt 19:28** Let me tell you, you who have followed me, when the Human One is seated on his throne of glory in the renewal ⟨of creation⟩, you also will be seated on twelve thrones and sit in judgment on the twelve tribes of Israel.	41When the other ten heard of it, they were incensed with James and John. 42Calling them aside, Jesus says to them, "You know how those who supposedly rule over foreigners lord it over them, and how their strong men tyrannize them. 43But it's not going to be like that with you. With you, whoever wants to become great must be your servant, 44and whoever among you wants to be 'number one' must be everybody's slave. 45You see, the Human One didn't come to be served, but to serve and to give his life as a ransom for many."	24Then they got into an argument over which of them should be considered the greatest. 25He said to them, "Among the foreigners, it's the kings who lord it over everyone, and those in power are addressed as 'benefactors.' 26But not so with you; rather, the greatest among you must behave as a beginner, and the leader as one who serves. 27Who is the greater, after all: the one reclining ⟨at a banquet⟩ or the one doing the serving? Isn't it the one who reclines? But here among you I am the one doing the serving. 28You are the ones who have stuck by me in my ordeals. 29And I confer on you the right to rule, just as surely as my Father conferred that right on me, 30so you may eat and drink at my table in my empire, and be seated on thrones and sit in judgment on the twelve tribes of Israel."
20:29–34 #201, p. 152	10:46–52 #201, p. 152	

241. Peter's Denial Predicted

SEE #316, P. 253

Mt 26:30–35	Mk 14:26–31	Lk 22:39, 31–34	Jn 13:36–38
[30]And they sang a hymn and left for the Mount of Olives.	[26]And they sang a hymn and left for the Mount of Olives.	[39]Then he left and walked, as usual, over to the Mount of Olives; and the disciples followed him.	
[31]Then Jesus says to them,	[27]And Jesus says to them,		
"All of you will be shaken and fall away this night because of me. Remember, it is written, "I will strike the shepherd and the sheep of the flock will be scattered."	"You will all be shaken and fall away. Remember, scripture says, "I will strike the shepherd and the sheep will be scattered."	[31]"Simon, Simon, look out: Satan is after all of you, to sift you like wheat. [32]But I have prayed for you that your trust won't give out. And once you've recovered, you are to shore up these brothers of yours."	[36]Simon Peter says to him, "Master, where are you going?" Jesus answered, "For now you can't follow me where I'm going; you'll follow later."
[32]But after I'm raised I'll go ahead of you to Galilee." [33]In response Peter said to him, "Even if everyone else is shaken and falls away because of you, I never will."	[28]But after I'm raised I'll go ahead of you to Galilee." [29]Peter said to him, "Even if everyone else is shaken and falls away, I won't!"	[33]He said to him, "Master, I'm prepared to follow you not only to prison but all the way to death."	[37]Peter says to him, "Master, why can't I follow you now? I'd give my life for you."
[34]Jesus said to him, "Let me tell you, tonight before the rooster crows you will disown me three times."	[30]And Jesus says to them, "Let me tell you, tonight before the rooster crows twice you will disown me three times." [31]But he repeated it with more bluster: "Even if they condemn me to die with you, I will never disown you!" And so said they all.	[34]He said, "Let me tell you, Peter, the rooster will not crow tonight until you deny three times that you know me."	[38]Jesus responded, "You'd give your life for me? Let me tell you this: the rooster won't crow before you disown me three times."
[35]Peter says to him, "Even if they condemn me to die with you, I will never disown you!" And all the disciples said the same thing.			
26:36–46 #243, p. 187	14:32–42 #243, p. 187		

242. Two swords is plenty

Mt	Mk	Lk 22:35–38
		[35]And he said to them, "When I sent you out with no purse or knapsack or sandals, you weren't short of anything, were you?" They said, "Not a thing." [36]He said to them, "But now, if you have a purse, take it along; and the same goes for a knapsack. And if you don't have a sword, sell your coat and buy one. [37]For I'm telling you, this scripture, 'And he was considered a criminal,' is destined to be completed in my life; for what is written about me is reaching completion." [38]And they said, "Look, Master, here are two swords." And he said to them, "That's plenty."

243. Jesus' Anguished Prayer

SEE #309, 322, PP. 247, 257

Mt 26:36–46	Mk 14:32–42	Lk 22:39–46	Jn 18:1; 12:27; 18:11b
[36]Then Jesus goes with them to a place called Gethsemane,	[32]And they go to a place named Gethsemane,	[39]Then he left and walked, as usual, over to the Mount of Olives; and the disciples followed him. [40]When he arrived at his usual place, he said to them, "Pray that you won't be put to the test."	**Jn 18:1** When he had said all this, Jesus went out with his disciples across the Kidron valley. There was a garden there where he and his disciples went.
and he says to the disciples, "Sit down here while I go over there and pray."	and he says to his disciples, "Sit down here while I pray."		
[37]And taking Peter and the two sons of Zebedee, he began to feel dejected and full of anguish. [38]He says to them, "I'm so sad I could die. You stay here with me and be alert!"	[33]And he takes Peter and James and John along with him, and he grew apprehensive and full of anguish. [34]He says to them, "I'm so sad I could die. You stay here and be alert."		
[39]And he went a little farther, knelt with his face to the ground, and prayed,	[35]And he would move on a little, lay facedown on the ground, and pray that he might avoid the crisis, if possible. [36]And he was saying, "*Abba* (Father), all things are possible for you.	[41]And he withdrew from them about a stone's throw away, got down on his knees, and began to pray,	**Jn 12:27** Now my life is in turmoil, but should I say, "Father, rescue me from this moment"?
"My Father, if it's possible, take this cup away from me. But it's your will that matters, not mine."	Take this cup away from me. But it's your will that matters, not mine."	[42]"Father, if you so choose, take this cup away from me! Yet not my will, but yours, be done."[a]	No, it was to face this moment that I came. **Jn 18:11b** I have to drink from the cup my Father has given me, don't I?
[40]And he returns to the disciples and finds them sleeping, and says to Peter, "Couldn't you stay awake with me for one hour? [41]Be alert, and pray that you won't be put to the test.	[37]And he returns and finds them sleeping, and says to Peter, "Simon, are you sleeping? Couldn't you stay awake for one hour? [38]Be alert and pray that you won't be put to the test.	[45]And when he got up from his prayer and returned to the disciples, he found them asleep, weary from grief. [46]He said to them, "What are you doing asleep? Get up and pray that you won't be put to the test."	
The spirit is willing, but the flesh is weak."	The spirit is willing, but the flesh is weak."		
[42]Again for a second time he went away and prayed, "My Father, if it's not possible for me to avoid drinking from this cup, then your will be done."	[39]And once again he went away and prayed, saying the same thing.		
[43]And once again he came and found them sleeping, since their eyes had grown heavy. [44]And leaving them again, he went away and	[40]And once again he came and found them sleeping, since their eyes had grown very heavy, and they didn't know what to say to him.		

Mt 26:36–46	Mk 14:32–42	Lk 22:39–46	Jn 18:1; 12:27; 18:11b
prayed, repeating the same words for a third time. ⁴⁵Then he comes to the disciples and says to them, "Are you still sleeping and taking a rest? Look, the time has arrived! The Human One is being turned over to sinners. ⁴⁶Get up, let's go! See for yourselves! Here comes the one who is going to turn me in."	⁴¹And he comes a third time and says to them, "You may as well sleep on now and get your rest. It's all over! The time has come! Look, the Human One is being turned over to sinners. ⁴²Get up, let's go! See for yourselves! Here comes the one who is going to turn me in."		

ᵃ Lk 22:42 Many mss add another two verses, traditionally numbered 22:43–44: ⁴³"An angel from heaven appeared to him and gave him strength. ⁴⁴In his anxiety he prayed more fervently, and it so happened that his sweat fell to the ground like great drops of blood." (It is very doubtful that these verses were part of the original text.)

244. Jesus is arrested

SEE #322, P. 257

Mt 26:47–56	Mk 14:43–52	Lk 22:47–53	Jn 18:1–11
[47] And while he was still speaking, suddenly Judas, one of the Twelve, arrived and with him a great crowd wielding swords and clubs, dispatched by the chief priests and elders of the people.	[43] And right away, while he was still speaking, Judas, one of the Twelve, shows up, and with him a crowd, dispatched by the chief priests and the scholars and the elders, wielding swords and clubs.	[47] Suddenly, while he was still speaking, a crowd appeared with the one called Judas, one of the Twelve, leading the way.	When he had said all this, Jesus went out with his disciples across the Kidron valley. There was a garden there where he and his disciples went. [2] But because Jesus had often gone there with his disciples, Judas, who was about to turn him in, knew the place too. [3] So it wasn't long before Judas arrives, bringing with him the battalion ⟨of Roman soldiers⟩ and some of the police from the chief priests and the Pharisees, with their lanterns and torches and weapons.
[48] Now the one who was to turn him in had arranged a sign with them, saying, "The one I'm going to kiss is the one you want. Arrest him!"	[44] Now the one who was to turn him in had arranged a signal with them, saying, "The one I'm going to kiss is the one you want. Arrest him and escort him safely away."		
[49] And right away he came up to Jesus and said, "Hello, Rabbi," and kissed him. [50] But Jesus said to him, "Friend, do what you came to do." Then they came and laid hands on Jesus and seized him.	[45] And right away he arrives, comes up to him, and says, "Rabbi," and kissed him. [46] And they laid hands on him and seized him.	He stepped up to Jesus to give him a kiss. [48] But Jesus said to him, "Judas, would you turn in the Human One with a kiss?" v. 54	
			[4] Jesus, of course, knew just what would happen to him, so he went right up to them and says, "Who is it you're looking for?" [5] "Jesus the Nazarene," was their reply. "I am," says Jesus. (And all the while Judas, who was turning him in, was standing there with them.) [6] But as soon as he said, "I am," they all retreated and fell to the ground. [7] So Jesus asked them again, "Who is it you're looking for?" "Jesus the Nazarene," they said. [8] "I told you that I am," Jesus answered, "so if it's me you're looking for, let the others go." (⟨9⟩ This was so the prediction

Mt 26:47–56	Mk 14:43–52	Lk 22:47–53	Jn 18:1–11
			he had made would be fulfilled: "I haven't lost one—not one of those you gave me.")
		[49]And when those around him realized what was coming next, they said, "Master, should we use our swords?" [50]And one of them struck the chief priest's slave and cut off his right ear.	
[51]All of a sudden one of those with Jesus lifted his hand, drew his sword, struck the chief priest's slave, and cut off his ear. [52]Then Jesus says to him, "Put your sword back where it belongs. For everyone who takes up the sword will be destroyed by the sword.	[47]One of those standing around drew his sword and swung at the chief priest's slave and cut off his ear.	[51]But Jesus responded, "Stop! That's enough!"	[10]Simon Peter had brought along a sword, and now he drew it, slashed at the chief priest's slave, who was called Malchus, and cut off his right ear. [11]"Put the sword back in its scabbard," Jesus told Peter. "I have to drink from the cup my Father has given me, don't I?"
		And he touched his ear and healed him.	
[53]Or don't you think I can call on my Father, who would put more than twelve legions of heavenly messengers at my disposal? [54]But then how would the scriptures that say these things are inevitable be fulfilled?" [55]At that moment Jesus said to the crowds,	[48]In response Jesus said to them,	[52]Then Jesus addressed the chief priests and temple police and elders who had come out after him:	
"Have you come to arrest me with swords and clubs as you would an insurgent? I used to sit there in the temple area day after day teaching, and you didn't seize me."*	"Have you come to arrest me with swords and clubs as you would an insurgent? [49]I was with you in the temple area day after day teaching and you didn't seize me.*	"Have you come with swords and clubs to arrest me as you would an insurgent? [53]When I was with you day after day in the temple area, you didn't lay a hand on me.* But it's your turn now, and the authority of darkness is on your side."	
[56]All of this happened so the writings of the prophets would be fulfilled. Then all the disciples deserted him and ran away.	But the scriptures must be fulfilled!" [50]And they all deserted him and ran away. [51]And a young man was following him, wearing a shroud over his nude body, and they grab him. [52]But he dropped the shroud and ran away naked.		

*Jn 18:20 I have spoken openly to anyone and everyone. I've always taught in meeting places and in the temple area, in places where all Jewish people gather. I've said nothing in secret. (#325, p. 260)

245. Jesus on Trial before the Chief Priest
SEE #283, 323, 324, PP. 232, 258, 259

Mt 26:57–68	Mk 14:53–65	Lk 22:54–71	other
			Jn 18:12–13, 15a, 18 12Then the battalion and their captain, with the Judean police, arrested Jesus and bound him. 13They took him first to Annas. (Annas was the father-in-law of that year's chief priest, Caiaphas.
57Those who had arrested Jesus brought him before Caiaphas the chief priest, where the scholars and elders had assembled.	53And they brought Jesus before the chief priest, and all the chief priests and elders and scholars assemble.	54They arrested him and marched him away to the house of the chief priest.	
58But Peter followed him at a distance as far as the courtyard of the chief priest.	54Peter followed him at a distance until he was inside the courtyard of the chief priest,	Peter followed at a distance.	15aSimon Peter and another disciple were trailing along behind Jesus.
He went inside and sat with the attendants to see how things would turn out.	and was sitting with the attendants and keeping warm by the fire.	55When they had started a fire in the middle of the courtyard and were sitting around it, Peter joined them.	18Meanwhile, since it was cold, the slaves and police had made a charcoal fire and were standing around it, trying to keep warm. Peter was standing there too, warming himself.
v. 69	vv. 66–67	56Then a slave woman noticed him sitting there in the glow of the fire. She stared at him, then spoke up, "This guy was with him too."	Jn 18:25
v. 70	v. 68	57He denied it. "Lady," he said, "I don't know him."	
vv. 71–72	v. 69	58A little later someone else noticed him and said, "You're one of them too." "Not me, mister," Peter replied.	Jn 18:26
v. 73	v. 70	59About an hour went by and someone else insisted, "No question about it; this guy's also one of them; he's even a Galilean!"	Jn 18:27
v. 74	vv. 71–72a	60But Peter said, "Mister, I don't know what you're talking about." And all of a sudden, while he was still speaking, a rooster crowed. 61And the Master turned and looked straight at Peter. And Peter	
v. 75	v. 72b	remembered what the Master had told him: "Before the rooster crows tonight, you will disown me three times." 62And he went outside and wept bitterly.	

Mt 26:57–68	Mk 14:53–65	Lk 22:54–71	other
		[63]Then the men who were holding Jesus in custody began to make fun of him and rough him up. [64]They blindfolded him and demanded: "Prophesy! Guess who hit you!" [65]And this was only the beginning of their insults.	
vv. 67–68	v. 65		
		[66]When day came, the elders of the people convened, along with the chief priests and scholars. They had him brought before their Council,	
27:1	15:1		
[59]The chief priests and the whole Council were looking for false testimony against Jesus so they might issue a death sentence; [60]but they couldn't find many perjurers to come forward.	[55]The chief priests and the whole Council were looking for evidence against Jesus in order to issue a death sentence, but they couldn't find any. [56]Although many gave false evidence against him, their stories didn't agree. [57]And some people stood up and testified falsely against him, [58]"We have heard him saying, 'I'll destroy this temple made with hands and in three days I'll build another, not made with hands!'" [59]Yet even then their stories did not agree.		
Finally, two men came forward [61]and said, "This man said, 'I can destroy the temple of God and rebuild it within three days.'"			**Jn 2:19** Destroy this temple and I'll raise it in three days. **Th 71** I will destroy [this] house, and no one will be able to build it [. . .].
[62]Then the chief priest got up and questioned him, "Don't you have something to say? Why do these people testify against you?" [63]But Jesus was silent.	[60]And the chief priest got up and questioned Jesus, "Don't you have anything to say? Why do these people testify against you?" [61]But he was silent and refused to answer.	where they interrogated him: [67]"If you are the Anointed One, tell us."	
And the chief priest said to him, "I ask you under oath before the living God: tell us if you are the Anointed One, the son of God!" [64]Jesus says to him, "If you say so.	Once again the chief priest questioned him and says to him, "Are you the Anointed One, the son of the Blessed One?" [62]Jesus replied, "I am!	But he said to them, "If I tell you, there's no way you'll believe me. [68]If I ask you a question, there's no way you'll answer.	
But I'm telling you, from now on you will see the Human One sitting at the right hand of Power and coming on the clouds of the sky."*	And you will see the Human One sitting at the right hand of Power and coming with the clouds of the sky!"*	[69]But from now on the Human One will be seated at the right hand of the power of God." [70]And they all said, "So you, are you the son of God?" He said to them, "You're	

⁶⁵Then the chief priest tore his vestment and said, "He has blasphemed! Why do we still need witnesses? See, now you have heard the blasphemy. ⁶⁶What do you think?"

In response they said, "He deserves to die!"

⁶⁷Then they spit in his face, and beat him and slapped him, ⁶⁸saying, "Prophesy for us, you Anointed One, you! Guess who hit you!"

⁶³Then the chief priest tore his vestments and says, "Why do we still need witnesses? ⁶⁴You have heard the blasphemy! What do you think?"

And they all concurred in the death penalty.

⁶⁵And some began to spit on him, and to put a blindfold on him, and beat him, and say to him, "Prophesy!" And the guards slapped him around as they took him into custody.

the ones who say so."

⁷¹And they said, "Why do we still need witnesses? We have heard it ourselves from his own mouth."

vv. 63–64

23:1 #247, p. 195

Pt 3:4
And others standing about would spit in his eyes, and others slapped his face, while others poked him with a rod. Some kept flogging him as they said, "Let's pay proper respect to the son of God."

* Ⓓ Mt 24:30 / Mk 13:26 (#227, p. 175)

246. Peter denies Jesus
= #326, P. 261

Mt 26:69–75	Mk 14:66–72	Lk 22:56–62	Jn 18:25–27
[69]Meanwhile Peter was sitting outside in the courtyard,	[66]And while Peter was below in the courtyard,		[25]Meanwhile, Simon Peter was still standing outside, keeping warm.
and one slave woman came up to him,	one of the chief priest's slave women comes over, [67]and sees Peter warming himself; she looks at him closely and says,	[56]Then a slave woman noticed him sitting there in the glow of the fire. She stared at him, then spoke up,	The others there said to him,
and said, "You too were with Jesus the Galilean."	"You too were with that Nazarene, Jesus."	"This guy was with him too."	"You're not one of his disciples too, are you?"
[70]But he denied it in front of everyone, saying, "I don't know what you're talking about."	[68]But he denied it, saying, "I haven't the slightest idea what you're talking about." And he went outside into the forecourt.	[57]He denied it. "Lady," he said, "I don't know him."	He denied it. "No, I'm not," he said.
[71]After Peter went out to the entrance, another slave woman saw him and says to those there,	[69]And when the slave woman saw him, she once again began to say to those standing nearby,	[58]A little later someone else noticed him and said,	[26]One of the chief priest's slaves, a relative of the one whose ear Peter had cut off, says,
"This guy was with that Nazarean, Jesus."	"This guy is one of them."	"You're one of them too."	"I saw you in the garden with him, didn't I?"
[72]And again he denied it with an oath: "I don't know the man!"	[70]But once again he denied it.	"Not me, mister," Peter replied.	[27]Once again Peter denied it.
[73]A little later those standing around came and said to Peter, "You really are one of them; even the way you talk gives you away!"	And a little later, those standing nearby were saying to Peter, "You really are one of them, since you also are a Galilean."	[59]About an hour went by and someone else insisted, "No question about it; this guy's also one of them; he's even a Galilean!"	
[74]Then he began to curse and swear: "I don't know the man!"	[71]But he began to curse and swear, "I don't know this man you're talking about!"	[60]But Peter said, "Mister, I don't know what you're talking about."	
And just then a rooster crowed.	[72]And just then a rooster crowed a second time,	And all of a sudden, while he was still speaking, a rooster crowed. [61]And the Master turned and looked straight at Peter.	At that very moment a rooster crowed.
[75]And Peter remembered what Jesus had said: "Before the rooster crows you will disown me three times." And he went outside and wept bitterly.	and Peter remembered what Jesus had told him: "Before a rooster crows twice you will disown me three times." And he broke down and started to cry.	And Peter remembered what the Master had told him: "Before the rooster crows tonight you will disown me three times." [62]And he went outside and wept bitterly.	

247. Jesus is turned over to Pilate

SEE #327, P. 262

Mt 27:1–2	Mk 15:1	Lk 23:1	Jn 18:28a
[1]When morning came, all the chief priests and elders of the people plotted against Jesus to put him to death. [2]And they bound him and led him away and turned him over to Pilate the ⟨Roman⟩ governor.	And right away, at daybreak, the chief priests, after consulting with the elders and scholars and the whole Council, bound Jesus and led him away and turned him over to Pilate. 15:2–5 #249, p. 196	At this point the whole assembly got up and took him before Pilate. 23:2–4 #249, p. 196	 They then take Jesus from Caiaphas' place to the governor's residence. By now it was early morning.

248. Judas kills himself

Mt 27:3–10	Mk	Lk
[3]Then Judas, who had turned him in, realizing that Jesus had been condemned, was overcome with remorse and returned the thirty silver coins to the chief priests and elders. [4]He said, "I've made a serious mistake in turning in this blameless man." But they said, "What do we care? That's your business." [5]And hurling the silver into the temple he slunk off, and went out and hanged himself. [6]The chief priests took the silver and said, "It wouldn't be right to put this into the temple treasury, since it's blood money." [7]So they devised a plan and bought the potter's field as a burial ground for foreigners. [8]As a result, that field has been called Bloody Field even to this day. [9]Then the prediction spoken through Jeremiah the prophet was fulfilled: "And they took the thirty silver coins, the price put on a man's head (this is the price they put on him among the Israelites), [10]and they donated it for the potter's field, as my Lord commanded me."		

249. Pilate interrogates Jesus

SEE #327, P. 262

Mt 27:11–14	Mk 15:2–5	Lk 23:2–4	Jn 18:33, 37–38
		[2]They introduced their accusations by saying, "We have found this man to be a corrupting influence on our people, opposing the payment of taxes to Caesar and claiming that he himself is an anointed king."	18:29–30
[11]Jesus stood before the 〈Roman〉 governor, and the governor questioned him: "*You* are 'the King of the Judeans'?"	[2]And Pilate questioned him: "*You* are 'the King of the Judeans'?"	[3]Pilate questioned him, "*You* are 'the King of the Judeans'?"	[33]Then Pilate went back into his residence. He summoned Jesus and asked him, "*You* are 'the King of the Judeans'?" . . . [37]"So you are a king!" said Pilate.
Jesus said, "If you say so."	And in response he says to him, "If you say so."	In response he said to him, "If you say so."	"You're the one saying I'm a king," responded Jesus. "This is what I was born for, and this is why I came into the world: to testify to the truth. Everyone who belongs to the truth listens to my voice." [38]"What is the truth?" says Pilate.
[12]And while he was being accused by the chief priests and elders, he said absolutely nothing. [13]Then Pilate says to him, "Don't you have anything to say to the long list of charges they bring against you?" [14]But he did not respond to him, not to a single charge, so the governor was very astonished.	[3]And the chief priests started a long list of accusations against him. [4]Again Pilate tried questioning him: "Don't you have some answer to give? Look at the long list of charges they bring against you!" [5]But Jesus still did not respond, so Pilate was astonished.	*23:10*	
		[4]And Pilate said to the chief priests and the crowds, "In my judgment there is no case against this man."	When he had said this, he again went out to the Judeans. "In my judgment there is no case against him," he says to them.
27:15–26 #252, p. 198	15:6–15 #252, p. 198		

250. Jesus before Herod

Mt	Mk	Lk 23:5–12
27:12	15:3	[5]But they persisted, saying, "He foments unrest among the people by going around teaching everywhere in Judea and as far away as Galilee and everywhere between." [6]When Pilate heard this, he asked whether the man were a Galilean. [7]And once he confirmed that he was from Herod's jurisdiction, he sent him on to Herod, who happened to be in Jerusalem at the time. [8]Now Herod was delighted to see Jesus. In fact, he had been eager to see him for quite some time, since he had heard so much about him, and was hoping to see him perform some sign. [9]So Herod plied him with questions; but Jesus would not answer him at all. [10]All this time the chief priests and the scholars were standing around, hurling accusation after accusation against him. [11]Herod and his soldiers treated him with contempt and made fun of him; they put a magnificent robe around him, then sent him back to Pilate. [12]That very day Herod and Pilate became friends; prior to this they had been constantly at odds.

251. Pilate declares Jesus innocent

Mt	Mk	Lk 23:13–16
		[13]Pilate then called together the chief priests, the rulers, and the people, [14]and addressed them. "You brought this man to me because you claim he's been corrupting the people. Now look, after interrogating him in your presence, I have found in this man no grounds at all for your charges against him. [15]Nor has Herod, since he sent him back to us. In fact, he has done nothing to deserve death. [16]So I will teach him a lesson and set him free."[a]

[a] 23:16 Many mss add another verse, traditionally numbered 23:17: "He was required to release one man to them during the festival." A few mss place this verse after 23:19.

252. Jesus or Barabbas

SEE #327, 328, PP. 262, 263

Mt 27:15–26	Mk 15:6–15	Lk 23:18–25	other
[15]At each festival it was the custom for the governor to set one prisoner free for the crowd, whichever one they wanted. [16]⟨The Romans⟩ were then holding a notorious prisoner named Jesus[a] Barabbas.	[6]At each festival it was the custom for ⟨the Roman governor⟩ to set one prisoner free for them, whichever one they requested. [7]And one called Barabbas was being held with the insurgents who had committed murder during the insurrection.		**Jn 18:39–40** [39]⟨Pilate said,⟩ "It's your privilege at Passover to have me free one prisoner for you.
[17]When the crowd had gathered,	[8]And when the crowd arrived, they began to demand that he do what he usually did for them.		
Pilate said to them, "Do you want me to set Jesus[a] Barabbas free for you or Jesus who is known as 'the Anointed One'?"	[9]And in response Pilate said to them, "Do you want me to set 'the King of the Judeans' free for you?"		So, do you want me to free 'the King of the Judeans' for you?"
		[18]But they all cried out in unison, "Do away with this man, and set Barabbas free." ([19]This man had been thrown into prison for murder and for an act of insurrection carried out in the city.)	[40]At this they shouted back, "Not this guy—Barabbas!" (Barabbas was an insurgent.)
([18]You see, he knew that they had turned him over out of envy.) [19]While he was sitting on the judgment seat, his wife sent a message to him: "Don't have anything to do with that innocent man, because I have agonized a great deal today over a dream about him." [20]The chief priests and the elders induced the crowds to ask for Barabbas but to have Jesus executed. [21]In response ⟨to their request⟩ the governor said to them, "Which of the two do you want me to set free for you?" They said, "Barabbas!"	([10]You see, he realized that the chief priests had turned him over out of envy.) [11]But the chief priests incited the crowd to get Barabbas set free for them instead.		
[22]Pilate says to them, "What should I do with Jesus, known as 'the Anointed One'?"	[12]But in response Pilate again said to them, "What do you want me to do with the man you call 'the King of the Judeans'?"	[20]But Pilate, who wanted to set Jesus free, addressed them again,	

Everyone responded, "Have him crucified!" ²³But he said, "Why? What has he done wrong?"	¹³And they in turn shouted, "Crucify him!" ¹⁴Pilate kept saying to them, "Why? What has he done wrong?"	²¹but they shouted out, "Crucify, crucify him!" ²²For the third time he said to them, "Why? What has he done wrong? In my judgment there is no capital case against him. So, I will teach him a lesson and set him free."	**Jn 18:38b** "In my judgment there is no case against him," ⟨Pilate⟩ says to them.
But they would shout all the louder, "Have him crucified!" ²⁴Now when Pilate could see that he was getting nowhere, but that a riot was starting instead, he took water and washed his hands in full view of the crowd and said, "I'm not responsible for this man's blood. That's your business!" ²⁵In response all the people said, "So, smear his blood on us and on our children."	But they shouted all the louder, "Crucify him!"	²³But they kept up the pressure, shouting their demands that he be crucified. And their shouts were prevailing,	**Pt 11:4** Pilate responded by saying, "I am clean of the blood of the son of God; this was all your doing."
²⁶Then he set Barabbas free for them,	¹⁵And because Pilate was always looking to satisfy the crowd, he set Barabbas free for them,	²⁴so Pilate ruled that their demand should be carried out. ²⁵He set free the man they had asked for, who had been thrown into prison for insurrection and murder;	
but had Jesus flogged,	had Jesus flogged,		**Jn 19:1** Then Pilate had Jesus taken away and flogged. **Jn 19:16** And so, in the end, Pilate turned him over to them to be crucified.
and then turned him over to be crucified.	and then turned him over to be crucified.	but he turned over Jesus to their will. 23:26 #254, p. 200	**Pt 2:5** And he turned him over to the people on the day before their festival, known as Unleavened Bread, began.

ᵃ Mt 27:16; 17 Many texts omit *Jesus.*

253. Soldiers humiliate Jesus

Mt 27:27–31a	Mk 15:16–20a	Lk
[27]Then the governor's soldiers took Jesus into the governor's residence and surrounded him with the whole cohort ⟨of Roman troops⟩. [28]They stripped him and dressed him in a crimson cloak, [29]and they wove a crown out of thorns and put it on his head. They placed a stick in his right hand, and bowing down before him, they made fun of him, saying, "Greetings, 'King of the Judeans'!" [30]And spitting on him, they took the stick and hit him on the head. [31a]And when they had made fun of him, they stripped off the cloak and put his own clothes back on him	[16]And the ⟨Roman⟩ soldiers led him away to the courtyard of the governor's residence, and they summoned the whole company ⟨of troops⟩. [17]And they dressed him in purple and crowned him with a garland woven of thorns. [18]And they began to salute him: "Greetings, 'King of the Judeans'!" [19]And they kept striking him on the head with a stick, and spitting on him; and they were getting down on their knees and bowing down to him. [20a]And when they had made fun of him, they stripped off the purple and put his own clothes back on him.	

254. Jesus is led to crucifixion
SEE #331, P. 268

Mt 27:31b–32	Mk 15:20b–21	Lk 23:26	Jn 19:16b–17a
[31b]And they led him out to crucify him. [32]As they were going out, they came across a Cyrenian named Simon. This man they conscripted to carry his cross. 27:33–37 #256, p. 202	[20b]And they lead him out to crucify him. [21]And they conscript someone named Simon of Cyrene, who was coming in from the country, the father of Alexander and Rufus, to carry his cross. 15:22–26 #256, p. 202	And as they were marching him away, they grabbed someone named Simon, a Cyrenian, as he was coming in from the country. They loaded the cross on him, to carry behind Jesus.	[16b]So they took Jesus, [17a]who carried the cross by himself.

255. Jesus and the Weeping Women

Mt	Mk	Lk 23:27–31	Th 79:3
		[27]A huge crowd of the people followed him, including women who mourned and lamented him. [28]Jesus turned to them and said, "Daughters of Jerusalem, do not weep for me. Weep instead for yourselves and for your children. [29]Look, the time is coming when they will say, 'Congratulations to those who are infertile, to the wombs that never gave birth, and to the breasts that never nursed!' [30]Then they will beg the mountains, 'Fall on us,' and the hills, 'Bury us.' [31]If they behave this way when the wood is green, what will happen when it dries out?"	There will be days when you will say, "Congratulations to the womb that has not conceived and the breasts that have not given milk."

Jn 19:2–3	Pt 3:1–4
[2]And the soldiers wove a crown out of thorns and put it on his head; they also dressed him up in a purple robe. [3]They began marching up to him and saying, "Greetings, 'King of the Judeans,'" as they slapped him in the face.	They took the Master and kept pushing him along as they ran; and they were saying, "Let's drag the son of God along, since we have him in our power." [2]And they threw a purple robe around him and sat him upon the judgment seat and said, "Judge justly, king of Israel." [3]And one of them brought a crown of thorns and set it on the head of the Master. [4]And others standing about would spit in his eyes, and others slapped his face, while others poked him with a rod. Some kept flogging him as they said, "Let's pay proper respect to the son of God."

256. Jesus is crucified

Mt 27:33–37	Mk 15:22–26	Lk 23:32–34, 38
		[32]Two others, who were criminals, were also taken away with him to be executed. [33]And when they reached the place
[33]And when they reached the place known as Golgotha (which means "Place of the Skull"), [34]they gave him a drink of wine mixed with gall, but once he tasted it, he didn't want to drink it. [35]After crucifying him,	[22]And they bring him to the place Golgotha (which means "Place of the Skull"). [23]And they tried to give him wine mixed with myrrh, but he didn't take it. [24]And they crucify him,	called "The Skull,"
		they crucified him there along with the criminals, one on his right and the other on his left.[a]
v. 28	v. 27	
they divided up his clothes by casting lots.	and they divide up his clothes, casting lots to see who would get what.	[34]They divided up his clothes after they cast lots ⟨for them⟩.
[36]And they sat down there and kept guard over him.		
	[25]It was nine o'clock in the morning when they crucified him. [26]And the placard, on which the charge against him was inscribed, read,	
[37]And over his head they put an inscription that identified his crime: "This is Jesus, the King of the Judeans."	"The King of the Judeans."	[38]There was also this placard over him: "This is the King of the Judeans."[b]

[a] Lk 23:34 Many mss add "And Jesus said, 'Father, forgive them because they don't know what they're doing.'"

[b] Lk 23:38 Many mss add that the notice "was written in Greek, Latin, and Hebrew."

Jn 19:16b–18, 23–24a, 19	Pt 4:1, 3, 2
So they took Jesus, [17]who carried the cross by himself, out to the place called Skull (known in Hebrew as *Golgotha*).	
v. 29 [18]There they crucified him, and with him two others—one on each side, with Jesus in the middle.	[1]And they brought two criminals and crucified the Master between them. But he himself remained silent, as if in no pain.
[23]When the soldiers had crucified Jesus, they took his clothes and divided them into four shares, one share for each soldier. But his shirt was woven continuously without seam. [24a]So they said to each other, "Let's not tear it, but toss to see who gets it."	[3]And they piled his clothes in front of him; then they divided them among themselves and gambled for them.
[19]Pilate also had a notice written and posted it on the cross; it read: "Jesus the Nazorean, the King of the Judeans."	[2]And when they set up the cross, they put an inscription on it, "This is the king of Israel."

257. Jesus is taunted

Mt 27:38–43	Mk 15:27–32a	Lk 23:35–38	Jn 19:18, 29
[38]Then they crucified two insurgents with him, one on his right and one on his left.	[27]And with him they crucify two insurgents, one on his right and one on his left.[a]	v. 33b	[18]There they crucified him, and with him two others—one on each side, with Jesus in the middle.
[39]Those passing by kept taunting him, wagging their heads, and saying, [40]"You were going to destroy the temple and rebuild it in three days? Save yourself! If you're God's son, come down from the cross!"	[29]Those passing by kept taunting him, wagging their heads, and saying, "Well, well, well! *You're* the one who was going to destroy the temple and rebuild it in three days! [30]Save yourself and come down from that cross."	[35]And the people stood around looking on.	
[41]Likewise the chief priests made fun of him along with the scholars and elders; they were saying, [42]"He saved others, but he can't even save himself!	[31]Likewise the chief priests had made fun of him to one another, along with the scholars; they were saying, "He saved others, but he can't even save himself!	And the rulers kept sneering at him, "He saved others; he should save himself if he is God's Anointed One, the Chosen One!"	
v. 48	v. 36	[36]The soldiers also made fun of him. They would come up and offer him sour wine,*	[29]A bowl of sour wine was sitting there, and so they filled a sponge with wine, stuck it on some hyssop, and held it to his mouth.
He's the King of Israel; he should come down from the cross here and now and then we'll believe him. [43]He trusted God, so God should rescue him now if he cares about him. After all, he said, 'I'm God's son.'"	[32]"The Anointed One,' 'the King of Israel,' should come down from the cross here and now, so that we can see for ourselves and believe!"	[37]and they would say, "If you're the King of the Judeans, why not save yourself?"	
v. 37	v. 26	[38]There was also this placard over him: "This is the King of the Judeans."[b]	Jn 19:19

* Pt 5:2 (#500, p. 372)

———

[a] Mk 15:27 Some mss add a verse here, traditionally numbered 15:28: "And the scripture that says, 'And he was considered one of the lawless' was fulfilled."

[b] Lk 23:38 Many mss add that the notice "was written in Greek, Latin, and Hebrew."

258. The Men Crucified with Jesus

Mt 27:44	Mk 15:32b	Lk 23:39–43	Pt 4:4
In the same way, the insurgents who were crucified with him were also insulting him.	Even those being crucified along with him were insulting him.	[39]One of the criminals hanging there kept taunting him: "Aren't you supposed to be the Anointed One? Save yourself and us!" [40]But the other ⟨criminal⟩ rebuked the first: "Don't you even fear God, since you're under the same sentence? [41]We are getting justice, since we are getting what we deserve. But this man has done nothing wrong." [42]And he implored, "Jesus, remember me when you come into your empire." [43]And Jesus said to him, "Let me tell you, today you'll be with me in Paradise."	But one of those criminals reproached them and said, "We're suffering for the evil that we've done, but this man, who has become a savior of humanity, what wrong has he done to you?"

259. Jesus dies

SEE #337, P. 272

Mt 27:45–50	Mk 15:33–37	Lk 23:44–46
[45]Beginning at noon darkness blanketed the entire land until mid-afternoon.	[33]And when noon came, darkness blanketed the whole land until mid-afternoon.	[44]It was already about noon, and darkness blanketed the whole land until mid-afternoon, [45]during an eclipse of the sun. The curtain of the temple was torn down the middle.
v. 51	v. 35	
[46]And about three o'clock in the afternoon Jesus shouted at the top of his voice, *"Eli, Eli, lema sabachthani"* (which means "My God, my God, why have you abandoned me?")	[34]And at three o'clock in the afternoon Jesus shouted at the top of his voice, *"Eloi, Eloi, lema sabachthani"* (which means "My God, my God, why have you abandoned me?").	[46]Then Jesus shouted at the top of his voice, "Father, into your hands I entrust my spirit!"
[47]When some of those standing there heard this, they said, "This guy's calling Elijah!"	[35]And when some of those standing nearby heard, they were saying, "Listen, he's calling Elijah!"	
[48]And right then one of them ran and took a sponge filled with sour wine and stuck it on a stick and offered him a drink.	[36]And someone ran and filled a sponge with sour wine, stuck it on a stick, and offered him a drink,	
[49]But the rest were saying, "Wait! Let's see if Elijah comes to rescue him."	saying, "Let's see if Elijah comes to rescue him!"	
[50]Jesus again shouted at the top of his voice and surrendered the spirit.	[37]But Jesus let out a great shout and breathed his last.	Having said this, he breathed his last.

*GHeb 1:7 After they had raised him on the cross, the Father took him up into heaven to himself. (#513, p. 391)

Jn 19:28–30	Pt 5:1a, 2, 5
	[1a]It was midday and darkness covered the whole of Judea.
	5:6
[28]Then, since Jesus knew that everything was now completed, he says (in order to fulfill the scripture), "I'm thirsty."	
[29]A bowl of sour wine was sitting there, and so they filled a sponge with wine, stuck it on some hyssop, and held it to his mouth.	[2]And one of them said, "Give him vinegar mixed with something bitter to drink." And they mixed it and gave it to him to drink.
[30]When Jesus had taken some wine, he said, "Now it's complete."	[5]And the Master cried out, saying, "My power, ⟨my⟩ power, you have abandoned me."
v. 29	v. 2
Lowering his head, he handed over the spirit.	When he said this, he was taken up.*

260. Omens and Responses

Mt 27:51–54	Mk 15:38–39	Lk 23:47–48	Pt 5:6; 8:1b
			Pt 5:6
[51]And suddenly the curtain of the temple was torn in two from top to bottom, and the earth quaked, rocks were split apart, [52]and tombs were opened and many bodies of sleeping saints came back to life. [53]And they came out of the tombs after his resurrection and went into the holy city, where they appeared to many. [54]The Roman officer and those with him keeping watch over Jesus witnessed the sign and what had happened, and were terrified, and said, "This man really was God's son."	[38]And the curtain of the temple was torn in two from top to bottom! [39]When the Roman officer in charge saw that he had died like this, he said, "This man really was God's son!"	v. 45 [47]Now when the Roman officer saw what happened, he praised God and said, "This man really was innocent!" [48]And when the throng of people that had gathered for this spectacle observed what had transpired, they all returned home beating their chests.	And at that moment, the curtain of the Jerusalem temple was torn in two. **Pt 8:1b** all the people were moaning and beating their chests, and saying, "If his death has produced these overwhelming signs, he must have been completely innocent!"

261. The Women Who Watched Jesus Die
= #336, P. 272

Mt 27:55–56	Mk 15:40–41	Lk 23:49	Jn 19:25–27
[55]Many women were there observing from a distance—those who had followed Jesus from Galilee to minister to him, [56]among whom were Mary of Magdala, and Mary the mother of James and Joseph, and the mother of the sons of Zebedee.	[40]Now some women were observing from a distance, among whom were Mary of Magdala, and Mary the mother of James the younger and Joses, and Salome. [41]These women had regularly followed and assisted him when he was in Galilee, along with many other women who had come up to Jerusalem in his company.	And all his acquaintances, including the women who had followed him from Galilee, were standing off at a distance watching these events.	[25]Meanwhile, Jesus' mother, his mother's sister, Mary the wife of Klopas, and Mary of Magdala were standing near his cross. [26]When Jesus saw his mother, and the disciple he loved standing nearby, he says to his mother, "Lady, here is your son." [27]Then he says to the disciple, "Here is your mother." And from that moment the disciple made her part of his family.

262. Jesus is buried

Mt 27:57–61	Mk 15:42–47	Lk 23:50–56
	[42]And since it was the preparation day (the day before the Sabbath), and already getting dark, [43]Joseph of Arimathea, a respected Council member,	
[57]It was dark when a rich man from Arimathea, by the name of Joseph,		[50]There was a man named Joseph, a Council member, a decent and upright man, [51]who had not endorsed their decision or gone along with their action. He was from the town of Arimathea in Judea, and he lived in anticipation of the empire of God.
who himself was a follower of Jesus,	who himself was anticipating the empire of God,	
showed up [58]and went to Pilate and requested the body of Jesus.	came forward and dared to go to Pilate to request the body of Jesus.	[52]This man went to Pilate and requested the body of Jesus.
	[44]And Pilate was surprised that he had died so soon. He summoned the Roman officer and asked him whether he had been dead for long. [45]And when he had been briefed by the officer, he granted the body to Joseph. [46]And he bought a shroud and took him down	
Then Pilate ordered it to be turned over to him. [59]And taking the body,		[53]Then he took it down
Joseph wrapped it in a clean linen shroud	and wrapped him in the shroud,	and wrapped it in a shroud,
[60]and put it in his new tomb, which had been cut in the rock. He rolled a huge stone across the opening of the tomb and left.	and placed him in a tomb that had been hewn out of rock, and rolled a stone up against the opening of the tomb.	and laid him in a tomb cut from the rock, where no one had ever been buried.
		[54]It was the day of preparation, and the Sabbath was about to begin. [55]The women who had come with him from Galilee followed. They kept an eye on the tomb, to see how his body was laid to rest. [56]Then they went home to prepare spices and ointments. On the Sabbath they rested in observance of the commandment.
[61]But Mary of Magdala and the other Mary stayed there, sitting across from the tomb.	[47]And Mary of Magdala and Mary the mother of Joses noted where he had been laid to rest.	
	16:1–4 #264, p. 214	24:1–2 #264, p. 214

Jn 19:38–42	Pt 2:1–2; 6:3a, 4
[38]After all this, Joseph of Arimathea—	**Pt 2:1–2** [1]Joseph, the friend of Pilate and the Master, stood there. When he realized that they were about to crucify him,
a disciple of Jesus, but a secret one because he was afraid of the Judeans—asked Pilate's permission to take Jesus' body down.	he went to Pilate and asked for the Master's body for burial. [2]And Pilate sent to Herod and asked for his body.
Pilate agreed,	**Pt 6:3a, 4** [3]Now the Judeans rejoiced and gave his body to Joseph so that he might bury it. [4]⟨Joseph⟩ took the Master,
so Joseph came and took his body down. [39]Nicodemus, the one who had first gone to him at night, came too, bringing a mixture of myrrh and aloes weighing about seventy-five pounds. [40]So they took Jesus' body, and wound it up in strips of burial cloth along with the spices, as the Jews customarily do to bury their dead. [41]Now there was a garden in the place where he had been crucified, and a new tomb in the garden where no one had ever been laid to rest.	washed ⟨his body⟩ and wound a linen ⟨shroud⟩ around him,
[42]Since this tomb was handy and because it was the Jewish day of preparation, it was here that they laid Jesus.	and brought him to his own tomb, called "Joseph's Garden."
vv. 39–40	

263. Guards are posted at Jesus' tomb

Mt 27:62–66	Mk	Lk	Pt 8:1–6
⁶²On the next day, which is the day after preparation,			¹When the scholars and the Pharisees and the priests had gathered together, and when they heard that all the people were moaning and beating their breasts, and saying, "If his death has produced these overwhelming signs, he must have been completely innocent!" ²They became frightened and went to Pilate and begged him, ³"Give us soldiers so that ⟨we⟩ can guard his tomb for three [days], in case his disciples come and steal his body and the people assume that he is risen from the dead and do us harm."
		23:48	
the chief priests and the Pharisees met with Pilate. ⁶³"Your Excellency, we remember what that deceiver said while he was still alive: 'After three days I'm going to be raised up.' ⁶⁴So order the tomb sealed for three days so his disciples won't come and steal his body and tell everyone, 'He has been raised from the dead.' If that were to happen, the last deception will be worse than the first."			
⁶⁵Pilate replied to them, "You have guards; go and secure it as you think best."			⁴So Pilate gave them the officer Petronius with soldiers to guard the tomb. And elders and scholars went with them to the tomb. ⁵And all who were there ⟨with⟩ the officer and the soldiers helped roll a large stone against the entrance to the tomb. ⁶And they put seven seals on it. Then they pitched a tent there and kept watch.
⁶⁶They went and secured the tomb by sealing ⟨it with a⟩ stone and posting a guard.			

264. The Discovery that Jesus' Tomb is Open

SEE #340, P. 278

Mt 28:1–4	Mk 16:1–4	Lk 24:1–2
[1]After the Sabbath, at first light on Sunday, Mary of Magdala and the other Mary came to inspect the tomb.	[1]And when the Sabbath was over, Mary of Magdala and Mary the mother of James and Salome bought spices so they could go and anoint him. [2]And very early on Sunday they got to the tomb just as the sun was coming up. [3]And they had been asking themselves, "Who will help us roll the stone away from the opening of the tomb?"	[1]On Sunday, at daybreak, they made their way to the tomb, bringing the spices they had prepared.
[2]And just then there was a strong earthquake. You see, a messenger of the Lord had come down from the sky, arrived ⟨at the tomb⟩, rolled away the stone, and was sitting on it. [3]The messenger gave off a dazzling light and wore clothes as white as snow. [4]Now those who kept watch were quaking with fear and looked like corpses themselves.		
	[4]Then they look up and discover that the stone has been rolled away. (You see, the stone was very large.)	[2]They found the stone rolled away from the tomb.

Jn 20:1	Pt 12:1a, 2, 4a; 9:2–4; 13:1a; 12:5a
Early on Sunday, while it was still dark, Mary of Magdala	**Pt 12:1a, 2, 4a** [1a]Early on the Lord's day, Mary of Magdala, [2]took her friends with her and went to the tomb where he had been laid. [4a]⟨saying,⟩ "Who will roll away the stone for us, the one placed at the entrance of the tomb? **Pt 9:2–4** [2]But during the night before the Lord's day dawned, while the soldiers were on guard, in pairs during each watch, a loud noise came from the sky, [3]and they saw the skies open up and two men come down from there in a burst of light and approach the tomb. [4]The stone that had been pushed against the entrance began to roll by itself and moved away to one side; then the tomb opened up and both young men went inside.
comes to the tomb and sees that the stone has been moved away.	**Pt 13:1a** And they went and found the tomb open. **Pt 12:5a** (Remember, it was a huge stone.)

265. "He is not here"

Mt 28:5–8	Mk 16:5–8	Lk 24:3–11	Pt 13:1b–3
	[5]And when they went into the tomb,	[3]but when they went inside they did not find the body of the Master Jesus.	[1b]They went up to ⟨the tomb⟩, stooped down,
	they saw a young man sitting on the right, wearing a white robe, and they grew apprehensive.	[4]And it came to pass, while they were still uncertain about what to do, that two men in dazzling clothes suddenly appeared and stood beside them. [5]They were terrified and knelt with their faces to the ground. The men said to them, "Why are you looking for the living among the dead?	and saw a young man sitting there ⟨in⟩ the middle of the tomb; he was handsome and wore a splendid robe.
[5]In response the messenger said to the women, "Don't be afraid! I know you are looking for Jesus who was crucified.	[6]He says to them, "Don't be alarmed. You are looking for Jesus the Nazarene who was crucified. He was raised,		He said to them, [2]"Why have you come? Who are you looking for? Surely not the one who was crucified? He is risen and gone. If you don't believe it, stoop down and take a look at the place where
[6]He is not here. You see, he was raised, just as he said. Come here; look at the spot where he was lying.	he is not here. Look at the spot where they put him.	[6]He is not here—he was raised.[a] Remember what he told you while he was still in Galilee: [7]the Human One is destined to be turned over to sinners, to be crucified, and on the third day to rise.'" [8]Then they recalled what he had said.	he lay—he's not there. You see, he is risen and has gone back to the place he was sent from."
[7]Go quickly and tell his disciples that he has been raised from the dead. Don't forget, he is going ahead of you to Galilee. There you will see him. That's what I came to tell you."	[7]But go and tell his disciples, including 'Rock,' 'He is going ahead of you to Galilee. There you will see him, just as he told you.'"		
[8]And they hurried away from the tomb, afraid and filled with joy,	[8]And once they got outside, they ran away from the tomb, because great fear and excitement got the better of them. And they didn't breathe a word of it to anyone: talk about terrified . . .[b]		[3]Then the women fled in fear.
and ran to tell his disciples.		[9]And returning from the tomb, they related everything to the Eleven and to everybody else.* [10]The group included Mary of Magdala and Joanna and Mary the mother of James, and the rest of the women companions. They related their story to the apostles; [11]but their story	

		seemed nonsense to them, so they refused to believe the women.	
	Longer Ending #272, p. 222 Shorter Ending #273, p. 223	24:12 #268, p. 219	

*Jn 20:2 ⟨Mary of Magdala⟩ runs and comes to Simon Peter and the other disciple, the one that Jesus loved, and tells them, "They've taken the Master from the tomb, and we don't know where they've put him." (#340 p. 278)

-----

[a] Lk 24:6 A few mss omit *He is not here—he was raised.*

[b] Mk 16:8 The best ancient mss conclude the Gospel of Mark with this verse. Other mss supply lengthier narrative endings. See "Mark's Shorter Ending" and "Mark's Longer Ending." (#273, 272, pp. 223, 222)

266. The two Marys meet Jesus

Mt 28:9–10	Mk	Lk

[9] Just then Jesus met ⟨Mary of Magdala and the other Mary⟩ and said, "Hello!"
 	
    They came up and grabbed his feet and paid him homage.
    [10] Then Jesus says to them, "Don't be afraid. Go tell my friends so they can leave for Galilee, where they will see me."
 	
28:11–15 #269, p. 219		

267. Jesus appears to Mary of Magdala
= #342, P. 280

Mt	Mk 16:9–11	Lk	Jn 20:11–18
			[11]Mary, however, stood crying outside, and in her tears she stooped to look into the tomb, [12]and she sees two heavenly messengers in white seated where Jesus' body had lain, one at the head and the other at the feet.
			[13]"Lady, why are you crying?" they ask her.
			"They've taken my master away," she tells them, "and I don't know where they've put him."
	[9]Now after he arose at daybreak on Sunday, he appeared first to Mary of Magdala, from whom he had driven out seven demons.		[14]No sooner had she said this than she turned around and sees Jesus standing there—but she didn't realize that it was Jesus.
			[15]"Lady," Jesus says to her, "why are you crying? Who is it you're looking for?"
			Thinking that he was the gardener, she says to him, "Please, mister, if you've moved him, tell me where you've put him so I can take him away."
			[16]"Mary," says Jesus.
			She turns around and exclaims in Hebrew, "*Rabbuni!*" (which means "Teacher").
			[17]"Let go of me," Jesus tells her, "because I have not yet ascended to the Father. But go to my brothers and tell them this: 'I'm ascending to my Father and your Father—to my God and your God.'"
	[10]She went and told those who were close to him, who were mourning and weeping.		[18]Mary of Magdala goes and reports to the disciples, "I've seen the Master," and relates everything he had told her.
	[11]But when those folks heard that he was alive and had been seen by her, they did not believe it.		
	16:9–20 #272, p. 222		

268. Peter (and the other disciple) see the tomb
= #341, P. 278

Mt	Mk	Lk 24:12[a]	Jn 20:3–10
		But Peter got up and ran to the tomb.	[3]So Peter and the other disciple went out and they make their way to the tomb. [4]The two of them were running along together, but the other disciple ran faster than Peter and was the first to reach the tomb. [5]Stooping down, he could see the strips of burial cloth lying there; but he didn't go in. [6]Then Simon Peter comes along behind him and went in. He too sees the strips of burial cloth there, [7]and also the cloth they had used to cover his head, lying not with the strips of burial cloth but rolled up by itself. [8]Then the other disciple, who had been the first to reach the tomb, came in. He saw all this, and he believed. [9]But since neither of them yet understood the prophecy that he was destined to rise from the dead, [10]these disciples went back home.
		He peeked in and saw only the linen wrappings,	
		and returned home, marveling at what had happened.	
		24:13–35 #270, p. 220	

[a] Lk 24:12 A few mss omit this verse.

269. The Cover Up by Jewish Authorities

Mt 28:11–15*	Mk	Lk
[11]While ⟨Mary of Magdala and the other Mary⟩ were on their way, some of the guards returned to the city and reported to the chief priests everything that had happened. [12]They met with the elders and hatched a plan. They bribed the soldiers with an adequate amount of money [13]and ordered them, "Tell everybody, 'His disciples came at night and stole his body while we were asleep.' [14]If the governor should hear about this, don't worry; we'll deal with him." [15]They took the money and did as they had been instructed. And this story has been passed around in the Jewish community until this very day. 28:16–20 #274, p. 223		

* Pt 11:3, 5–7 [3]When those in the officer's unit saw this, they rushed out into the night to Pilate, leaving the tomb that they were supposed to be guarding. And as they were recounting everything they had seen, they became deeply disturbed and cried, "He really was God's son!"

[5]Then they all crowded around ⟨Pilate⟩ and began to beg and urge him to order the officer and his soldiers to tell no one what they had seen. [6]"You see," they said, "it's better for us to be guilty of the greatest sin before God than to fall into the hands of the Judean people and be stoned."

[7]Pilate then ordered the officer and the soldiers to say nothing. (#505 p. 380)

270. On the Road to Emmaus

Mt	Mk	Lk 24:13–35
	16:12	¹³Now, that same day a couple of them were traveling to a village named Emmaus, about seven miles from Jerusalem.* ¹⁴They were engaged in conversation about all that had taken place. ¹⁵And it came to pass, during the course of their discussion, that Jesus himself approached and began to walk along with them. ¹⁶But they couldn't recognize him.
		¹⁷He said to them, "What were you discussing as you walked along?"
		Then they paused, looking depressed. ¹⁸One of them, named Kleopas, said to him in reply, "Are you the only visitor to Jerusalem who doesn't know what's happened there these last few days?"
		¹⁹And he said to them, "What are you talking about?"
		And they said to him, "About Jesus of Nazareth, who was a prophet powerful in word and deed in the eyes of God and all the people, ²⁰and about how our chief priests and rulers turned him in to be sentenced to death, and crucified him. ²¹We were hoping that he would be the one who was going to ransom Israel. And as if this weren't enough, it's been three days now since all this happened. ²²Meanwhile, some women from our group gave us quite a shock. They were at the tomb early this morning ²³and didn't find his body. They came back claiming even to have seen a vision of heavenly messengers, who said that he was alive. ²⁴Some of those with us went to the tomb and found it exactly as the women had described; but nobody saw him."
		²⁵And he said to them, "You people are so dim, so reluctant to trust everything the prophets have said! ²⁶Wasn't the Anointed One destined to endure these things and enter into his glory?" ²⁷Then, starting with Moses and all the prophets, he interpreted for them every passage of scripture that referred to himself.
		²⁸They had gotten close to the village to which they were headed, and he acted as if he were going on. ²⁹But they insisted, "Stay with us; it's almost evening, the day is practically over." So he went in to stay with them.
		³⁰And it came to pass, as soon as he took his place at table with them, that he took a loaf, and gave a blessing, broke it, and started passing it out to them. ³¹Then their eyes were opened and they recognized him, but he vanished from their sight. ³²They said to each other, "Weren't our hearts burning within us while he was talking to us on the way, and explaining the scriptures to us?" ³³And they got up at once and returned to Jerusalem.
	16:13	And when they found the Eleven and those with them gathered together, ³⁴they said, "The Master really has been raised, and has appeared to Simon!" ³⁵Then they described what had happened on the road, and how they came to recognize him in the breaking of bread.

* Pt 14:1–2 ¹Now it was the last day of Unleavened Bread, and many began to return to their homes because the festival was over. ²But we, the twelve disciples of the Master, continued to weep and mourn, and each one, still grieving because of what had happened, left for his own home. (#508, p. 384)

271. Jesus appears to the disciples

Mt 16:19	Mk	Lk 24:36–49	Jn 20:19–23
	16:14	³⁶While they were talking about this, he himself appeared among them and says to them, "Peace be with you."ᵃ ³⁷But they were terrified and frightened, and figured that they were seeing a ghost. ³⁸And he said to them, "Why are you upset? Why do such thoughts run through your minds? ³⁹You can see from my hands and my feet that it's really me. Touch me and see—a ghost doesn't have flesh and bones as you can see that I have."ᵇ	¹⁹Now that Sunday evening, the disciples had locked the doors out of fear of the Judeans, but Jesus came and stood in front of them and he greets them: "Peace."

28:18–20

I will give you the keys of the empire of Heaven, and whatever you uphold on earth will be upheld in heaven, and whatever you dismiss on earth will be dismissed in heaven.*

²⁰Then he showed them his hands and his side.

The disciples were delighted to see the Master.

²¹Jesus greets them again: "Peace," he says. "Just as the Father sent me, so now I'm sending you." ²²And at this he breathed over them and says, "Here's some holy spirit. Take it. ²³If you cancel anyone's sins, they are cancelled; if you retain them, they are retained."

⁴¹And while for sheer joy they still didn't know what to believe and were bewildered, he said to them, "Is there anything here to eat?" ⁴²They offered him a piece of grilled fish, ⁴³and he took it and ate it in front of them.
⁴⁴Then he said to them, "This is the message I gave you while I was still with you: everything written about me in the Law of Moses and the Prophets and the Psalms is destined to be fulfilled."
⁴⁵Then he prepared their minds to understand the scriptures. ⁴⁶He said to them, "This is what is written: the Anointed One will suffer and rise from the dead on the third day. ⁴⁷And all peoples will be called on to change their hearts for the forgiveness of sins, beginning from Jerusalem. ⁴⁸You are witnesses to

Mt 16:19	Mk	Lk 24:36–49	Jn 20:19–23
		this. [49]And be prepared: I'm sending down on you what my Father promised. Stay here in the city until you are invested with power from on high."	
		24:50–53 #275, p. 223	

* Ⓓ Mt 18:18 (#132, p. 110)

───────

[a] Lk 24:36 A few mss omit *and says to them, "Peace be with you."*

[b] Lk 24:39 Many mss add a v. 40, "As he said this, he showed them his hands and his feet," taken from John 20:20.

272. Mark's Longer Ending

Mt	Mk 16:9–20	Lk	Jn
	[9]Now after he arose at daybreak on Sunday, he appeared first to Mary of Magdala, from whom he had driven out seven demons. [10]She went and told those who were close to him, who were mourning and weeping. [11]But when those folks heard that he was alive and had been seen by her, they did not believe it.		20:14–18
	[12]A little later he appeared to two of them in a different guise as they were walking along, on their way to the country. [13]And these two returned and told the others. They did not believe them either.	24:13–16	
	[14]Later he appeared to the Eleven as they were reclining ⟨at a meal⟩. He reproached them for their close-mindedness and lack of trust, because they did not believe those who had seen him after he had been raised. [15]And he said to them: "Go out into the whole world and announce the good news to every creature.	24:35 24:36	
28:19	[16]Whoever trusts and is baptized will be saved, but whoever lacks trust will be condemned. [17]These are the signs that will accompany those who have trust: they'll drive out demons in my name; they'll speak in new tongues; [18]they'll pick up snakes with their hands; and even if they swallow poison, it'll never harm them; they'll lay their hands on the sick, and they'll get well."		
	[19]The Lord Jesus, after he said these things, was taken up into the sky and sat down at the right hand of God. [20]Those ⟨to whom he had spoken⟩ went out and made their announcement everywhere, and the Lord worked with them and certified what they said by means of accompanying signs.	24:51	

273. Mark's Shorter Ending

Mt	Mk—Shorter Ending (16:21)	Lk
	They promptly reported to Peter and his companions all the instructions they had been given. Afterwards Jesus himself, using them as agents, broadcast the sacred and imperishable message of eternal salvation from one end of the earth to the other.	

274. "Make disciples of all peoples"

Mt 28:16–20	Mk	Lk	Jn
[16]The eleven disciples went to the mountain in Galilee where Jesus had told them to go. [17]And when they saw him, they paid him homage; but some were dubious. [18]And Jesus approached them and spoke these words: "All authority has been given to me in heaven and on earth. [19]You shall go and make disciples of all peoples, baptizing them in the name of the Father and the son and the holy spirit. [20]Teach them to observe everything I commanded you. I'll be with you day in and day out, as you'll see, until the culmination of the age."	16:15–16	24:47	20:21

275. Jesus is carried into the sky

Mt	Mk 16:19	Lk 24:50–53	Pt 5:5
	The Lord Jesus, after he said these things, was taken up into the sky and sat down at the right hand of God. 16:9–20 #272, p. 222	[50]Then he led them out as far as Bethany, and lifting up his hands he blessed them. [51]And while he was blessing them, it came to pass that he departed from them, and was carried up into the sky.[a]* [52]And they paid homage to him and[b] returned to Jerusalem full of joy, [53]and were continually in the temple blessing God.	And the Master cried out, saying, "My power, <my> power, you have abandoned me." When he said this, he was taken up.†

*Acts 1:3, 9 [3]After his suffering he presented himself to them in many ways that proved he was alive, appearing to them over a forty-day period and speaking about the empire of God. . . . [9]As they were watching he was lifted up and a cloud carried him up until they could no longer see him. (#527, p. 401)

† GHeb 1:7 After they had raised him on the cross, the Father took him up into heaven to himself. (#513, p. 391)

---

[a] Lk 24:51 Some mss omit *and was carried up into the sky.*

[b] Lk 24:52 A few mss omit *paid homage to him and.*

The Gospel of John

276. Prologue to the Gospel (Jn)

SEE #1, P. 8

Mt	Mk	Lk	Jn 1:1–18
1:1	*1:1*	*1:1–4*	¹In the beginning there was the divine word and wisdom.

The divine word and wisdom was there with God,
and it was what God was.
²It was there with God from the beginning.
³Everything came to be by means of it;
and without it not one thing that exists came to be.
⁴In it was life,
and this life was the light of humanity.
⁵Light was shining in darkness,
and darkness did not master it.
⁶There appeared a man sent from God named John.
⁷He came to testify—to testify about the light—so everyone would believe through him. ⁸He was not the light; he came only to testify about the light.
⁹Genuine light—the kind that enlightens everyone
—was coming into the world.
¹⁰Although it was in the world,
and the world came to be through it,
the world did not recognize it.
¹¹It came to its own place,
but its own people were not receptive to it.
¹²But to all who did embrace it,
to those who believed in it,
it gave the right to become children of God.
¹³They were born not from blood,
not from physical desire,
nor from male desire;
they were born out of God.
¹⁴The divine word and wisdom became human
and resided among us.
We have seen its glory,
glory appropriate
to a Father's only son,
brimming with generosity and truth.
¹⁵John testifies about him and has called out, "This is the one I was talking about when I said, 'The one who's coming after me ranks ahead of me, because he was before I was.'"
¹⁶From his richness
all of us benefited—
one gift after another.
¹⁷The Law was given through Moses;
mercy and truth came through Jesus the
Anointed One.
¹⁸No one has ever seen God;
the only son, close to the Father's heart—he has disclosed ⟨him⟩.

277. The Identity of John the Baptizer (Jn)

SEE #3, P. 10

Mt 3:1–3	Mk 1:4, 1–3	Lk 3:2b–6	Jn 1:19–23
[1]In due course John the Baptizer appears in the Judean desert,	[4]So, John the Baptizer appeared in the desert	[2b]The word of God came to John, son of Zechariah, in the desert. [3]And he went into the whole region around the Jordan, calling for baptism and a change of heart that lead to forgiveness of sins.	
[2]calling out, "change your ways because the empire of Heaven is arriving."	calling for baptism and a change of heart that lead to forgiveness of sins.		
			[19]This is John's testimony when the Judeans sent priests and Levites from Jerusalem to ask him, "Who are you?" [20]He made it clear—he wouldn't deny it—"I'm not the Anointed One." [21]And they asked him, "Then what are you? Are you Elijah?" And he replies, "I am not." "Are you the Prophet?" He answered, "No." [22]So they said to him, "Tell us who you are so we can report to those who sent us. What have you got to say for yourself?"
[3]No doubt this is the person described by Isaiah the prophet:	[1]The good news of Jesus the Anointed begins [2]with something Isaiah the prophet wrote: "Here is my messenger, whom I send on ahead of you to prepare your way! [3]A voice of someone shouting in the desert, 'Make ready the way of the Lord; make his paths straight.'"	[4]As is written in the book of the sayings of Isaiah the prophet:	
"A voice of someone shouting in the desert, 'Make ready the way of the Lord; make his paths straight.'"		"The voice of someone shouting in the desert: 'Make ready the way of the Lord; make his paths straight.	[23]He replied, "I am 'the voice of someone shouting in the desert, "Make the way of the Lord straight"'— that's how Isaiah the prophet put it."
		[5]Every valley will be filled, and every mountain and hill leveled. What is crooked will be made straight, and the rough ways smooth. [6]Then the whole human race will see the salvation of God.'"	

278. The One Coming after John (Jn)

SEE #5, P. 12

Mt 3:11–12	Mk 1:8, 7b	Lk 3:15–17	Jn 1:24–28
			([24]It was the Pharisees who had sent them.) [25]"So," they persisted, "why are you baptizing if you're not the Anointed One, not Elijah, and not the Prophet?"
		[15]The people were filled with expectation and everyone was trying to figure out whether John might be the Anointed One. [16]John's answer was the same to everyone:	
[11]I baptize you with water for a change of heart,	[8]I've been baptizing you with water, but he will baptize you with holy spirit.	"I baptize you with water;	[26]John answered them, "I baptize, yes, but only with water. Right there with you is someone you don't yet recognize; [27]he's the one who is coming after me. I don't even deserve to untie his sandal straps."
but someone more powerful than I will succeed me. I'm not fit to take off his sandals. He'll baptize you with holy spirit and fire. [12]His pitchfork is in his hand, and he'll make a clean sweep of his threshing floor, and gather the wheat into his granary, but the chaff he'll burn in a fire that can't be put out.	[7b]Someone more powerful than I will succeed me, whose sandal straps I am not fit to bend down and untie.	but someone more powerful than I is coming. I'm not fit to untie his sandal straps. He'll baptize you with holy spirit and fire. [17]His pitchfork is in his hand, to make a clean sweep of his threshing floor and to gather the wheat into his granary, but the chaff he'll burn in a fire that can't be put out."	
			[28]All this took place in Bethany on the far side of the Jordan, where John was baptizing.

279. The Lamb of God (Jn)

Mt	Mk	Lk	Jn 1:29–31
			[29]The next day John sees Jesus approaching and says, "Look, there's the lamb of God, who takes away the sin of the world. [30]This is the one I was talking about when I said, 'A man is coming after me who ranks ahead of me, because he was before I was.' [31]Even I didn't know who he was, although it was my mission to baptize with water so he would be revealed to Israel."

280. John sees the spirit over Jesus (Jn)*
SEE #6, P. 13

Mt 3:16–17	Mk 1:9–11	Lk 3:21–22	Jn 1:32–34
	[9]During that same period Jesus came from Nazareth, Galilee, and was baptized in the Jordan by John. [10]And right away as he got up out of the water,	[21]And it came to pass when all the people were baptized, and after Jesus had been baptized and while he was praying,	
[16]Right after Jesus had been baptized, he got up out of the water, and—amazingly—the skies opened up and he saw God's spirit coming down on him like a dove, perching on him,	he saw the skies torn open and the spirit coming down toward him like a dove.	that the sky opened up, [22]and the holy spirit came down on him in bodily form like a dove,	[32]And John continued his testimony: "I have seen the spirit coming down like a dove out of the sky, and it hovered over him. [33]I wouldn't have recognized him, but the very one who sent me to baptize with water told me, 'When you see the spirit come down and hover over someone, that's the one who baptizes with holy spirit.' [34]I have seen this and I have testified: this is the son of God."
[17]and—listen!—there was a voice from the skies, which said,	[11]There was also a voice from the skies:	and a voice came from the sky,	
"This is my son, the one I love—I fully approve of him."	"You are my son, the one I love—I fully approve of you."	"You are my son; today I have fathered you."[a]	

* GHeb 3:2–4 (#515, p. 392)

---

[a] Lk 3:22 Most mss read "You are my son, the one I love—I fully approve of you" (as in Mark 1:11).

281. Jesus recruits his first disciples (Jn)

Mt	Mk	Lk	Jn 1:35–51
			[35]The next day John was standing there again with two of his disciples. [36]When he noticed Jesus walking by, he says, "Look, there's the lamb of God."
			[37]His two disciples heard him ⟨say this⟩, and they followed Jesus. [38]Jesus turned around, saw them following, and says to them, "What are you looking for?"
			They said to him, "Rabbi" (which means "Teacher"), "where do you live?"
			[39]He says to them, "Come and see."
			They went and saw where he was staying and spent ⟨the rest of⟩the day with him. It was about four in the afternoon.
			[40]Andrew, Simon Peter's brother, was one of the two who followed Jesus after hearing John ⟨speak about him⟩. [41]First he goes and finds his brother Simon and tells him, "We have found the Messiah" (which is translated "Anointed One"), [42]and he led him to Jesus.
16:16	8:29	9:20	
16:17–18	3:16	6:14a	Jesus looked straight at him and said, "You're Simon, son of John; you're going to be called Kephas" (which means Peter ⟨or Rock⟩).
			[43]The next day Jesus decided to leave for Galilee. He finds Philip and says to him, "Follow me."
			[44]Philip was from Bethsaida, the hometown of Andrew and Peter. [45]Philip finds Nathanael and tells him, "We've found the one Moses wrote about in the Law, and the prophets mention too: Jesus, son of Joseph, from Nazareth."
			[46]"From Nazareth?" Nathanael said to him. "Can anything good come from that place?"
			Philip replies to him, "Come and see."
			[47]Jesus saw Nathanael coming toward him, and he remarks about him: "There's a genuine Israelite—not a trace of deceit in him."
			[48]"Where do you know me from?" Nathanael asks him.
			Jesus replied, "I saw you under the fig tree before Philip invited you ⟨to join us⟩."
			[49]Nathanael responded to him, "Rabbi, you are the son of God! You are King of Israel!"
			[50]Jesus replied, "Do you believe just because I told you I saw you under the fig tree? You're going to see a lot more than that."
			[51]Then he adds, "Let me tell you this: you'll see the sky split open and God's messengers ascending and descending on the Human One."

282. Jesus disrupts the temple (Jn)

SEE #208, P. 158

Mt 21:12–13	Mk 11:15–17	Lk 19:45–46	Jn 2:13–17
[12]And Jesus went into God's temple	[15]They come to Jerusalem. And he went into the temple	[45]Then he entered the temple area	[13]It was almost time for the Jewish Passover festival, so Jesus went up to Jerusalem. [14]In the temple area he found people selling oxen and sheep and doves, and others exchanging currency. [15]He made a whip out of rope and drove them all
and threw all the vendors and customers out of the temple area;	and began throwing the vendors and the customers out of the temple area,	and began throwing the vendors out.	out of the temple area, sheep and oxen;
and he knocked over the currency exchange tables, along with the chairs of the dove merchants.	and he knocked over the currency exchange tables, along with the chairs of the dove merchants, [16]and he wouldn't even let anyone carry a container through the temple area. [17]Then he started teaching and saying to them,		then he knocked over the exchange tables and scattered the coins. [16]And to the dove merchants he said, "Get these birds out of here!
[13]Then he says to them, "It is written,	"Don't the scriptures say,	[46]He says to them, "It is written,	
'My house shall be designated a house of prayer,'	'My house shall be designated a house of prayer for all peoples?'	'My house shall be a house of prayer.'	
But you're turning it into 'a hideout for bandits'!"	But you have turned it into 'a hideout for bandits'!"	But you have turned it into 'a hideout for bandits'!"	How dare you use my Father's house as a public market." [17]His disciples were reminded of the words of scripture: "Zeal for your house will eat me alive."

283. Jesus will raise the temple (Jn)

SEE #245, P. 191

Mt 26:59–61	Mk 14:57–58	Lk	Jn 2:18–22	Th 71
			[18]To this the Judeans responded, "What sign can you show us to justify doing all this?"	
[59]The chief priests and the whole Council were looking for false testimony against Jesus so they might issue a death sentence; [60]but they couldn't find many perjurers to come forward. Finally, two men came forward [61]and said, "This man said, 'I can destroy the temple of God and rebuild it within three days.'"	[57]And some people stood up and testified falsely against him, [58]"We have heard him saying, 'I'll destroy this temple made with hands and in three days I'll build another, not made with hands!'"		[19]Jesus replied, "Destroy this temple and I'll raise it in three days." [20]"It has taken forty-six years to build this temple," the Judeans said, "and you're going to raise it in three days?" ([21]However, he was referring to his body as a temple. [22]When he had been raised from the dead his disciples remembered that he had made this claim, and so they came to believe both the word of scripture and the word Jesus had spoken.)	I will destroy [this] house, and no one will be able to build it [. . .].

284. The Father entrusts everything to Jesus (Jn)

SEE #141, P. 115

Mt 11:27a	Mk	Lk 10:22a	Jn 3:35*	Th 61:3
My Father has turned everything over to me.		My Father has turned everything over to me.	The Father loves the son and has entrusted everything to him.	I am the one who comes from the one who is unwavering. I have been given some of the things of my Father.

*Jn 13:3 (#312, p. 250)

285. Jesus baptizes—but not really (Jn)

Mt	Mk	Lk	Jn 4:1–3
			[1]Jesus was aware of the rumor that had reached the Pharisees: that he is recruiting and baptizing more disciples than John. ([2]Actually, Jesus himself didn't baptize anyone; his disciples did the baptizing.) [3]So he left Judea again for Galilee.
4:12	*1:14*	*4:14a*	

286. Time for Harvest (Jn)

SEE #63, P. 51

Mt 9:37–38	Mk	Lk 10:2	Jn 4:35	Th 73
[37]The crop is good, but there are few to harvest it. [38]So beg the harvest boss to dispatch workers to the fields.		The crop is good, but there are few to harvest it. So beg the harvest boss to dispatch workers to the fields.	You have a saying: "It's still four months till harvest." But I'm telling you: look at the fields, they're ripe for harvesting.	The crop is huge but the workers are few, so beg the boss to dispatch workers to the fields.

287. A Prophet Without Respect (Jn)

SEE #95, P. 75

Mt 13:57b	Mk 6:4	Lk 4:24	Jn 4:44b	Th 31:1
No prophet is disrespected, except on his home turf and at home	No prophet is disrespected, except on his home turf and among his relatives and at home.	Let me tell you, no prophet is welcome on his home turf.	A prophet gets no respect on his own turf.	No prophet is welcome in his home town

288. An official's boy is healed (Jn)

SEE #52, P. 42

Mt 8:5–6	Mk	Lk 7:1–3	Jn 4:46b–54
7:28 ⁵When he had entered Capernaum, a Roman officer approached him and pleaded with him, ⁶"Sir, my servant boy was struck down with paralysis and is in terrible pain."		¹After he had completed all he had to say to his audience, he went into Capernaum. ²A Roman officer had a slave he was very fond of but who was sick and about to die. ³So when he heard about Jesus, the officer sent some elders of the Jewish community to him, and asked him to come and cure his slave.	⁴⁶ᵇIn Capernaum there was a government official whose son was sick. ⁴⁷When he heard that Jesus had returned to Galilee from Judea, he approached him and pleaded with him to come down and cure his son, who was about to die.
			⁴⁸Jesus said to him, "You people refuse to believe unless you see signs and omens." ⁴⁹The official responds, "Sir, please come down before my child dies."
vv. 7–12		*vv. 6–9*	⁵⁰Jesus says, "Go home, your son will live." The man believed what Jesus told him and went home. ⁵¹While he was still on his way home, his slaves met him and told him that his boy was
v. 13		v. 10	alive. ⁵²So he asked them when he had begun to recover, and they told him, "The fever broke yesterday at one o'clock." ⁵³Then the father realized that one o'clock was precisely the time Jesus had said to him, "Your son will live." And he believed, as did his whole household. ⁵⁴Jesus performed this second sign after he had returned from Judea to Galilee.

289. The Healing of the Crippled Man (Jn)

SEE #59, P. 48

Mt 9:6–7	Mk 2:10–12	Lk 5:24–25	Jn 5:1–9a
			¹After these events, on the occasion of a Jewish festival, Jesus went up to Jerusalem. ²In Jerusalem, by the Sheep ⟨Gate⟩, there is a pool, called *Bethzatha* in Hebrew. It has five colonnades, ³among which numerous invalids—blind, lame, paralyzed—were usually lying around. ⁵One man had been crippled for thirty-eight years. ⁶Jesus observed him lying there and realized he had been there a long time.
9:1–5	2:1–9	5:17–23	"Do you want to get well?" he asks him.
			⁷The crippled man replied, "Sir, I don't have anyone to put me in the pool when the water is agitated; while I'm trying to get in someone else beats me to it."
⁶But just so you realize that on earth the Human One has authority to forgive sins"—he then says to the paralytic—	¹⁰But just so you realize that on earth the Human One has authority to forgive sins"—he says to the paralytic— ¹¹"You there, get up, pick up your mat and go home!"	²⁴But just so you realize that on earth the Human One has authority to forgive sins"—he said to the paralyzed man— "You there, get up, pick up your pallet and go home."	
"Get up, pick up your bed and go home."			⁸"Get up, pick up your mat, and walk around," Jesus tells him.
⁷And he got up and went home.	¹²And he got up, picked his mat right up, and walked out as everyone looked on.	²⁵And immediately he stood up in front of them, picked up what he had been lying on, and went home praising God.	⁹ᵃAnd at once the man recovered; he picked up his mat and started walking.

290. Respecting the Son and the Father (Jn)

SEE #103, P. 84

Mt	Mk	Lk 10:16	Jn 5:19–23
			[19]Let me tell you this: the son can't do anything on his own, but only what he sees the Father doing. Whatever the Father does, the son does as well. [20]The Father loves the son, and shows him everything he does. He is going to show him even greater works, so that you'll be amazed. [21]Just as the Father raises the dead and gives them life, the son also gives life to everyone he wants. [22]Not that the Father condemns anyone; rather, he has turned all such decisions over to the son, [23]so that everyone will respect the son, just as they respect the Father. Whoever does not respect the son does not respect the Father who sent him.*
		Whoever hears you hears me, and whoever rejects you rejects me, and whoever rejects me rejects the one who sent me.	

*Jn 15:23 (#319, p. 255)

291. Resurrection for Judgment (Jn)

SEE #233, P. 179

Mt	Mk	Lk	Jn 5:24–29
			[24]Let me tell you this: those who hear my word and believe the one who sent me have unending life and do not come up for trial. No, they have passed through death into life. [25]Let me tell you this: the time is coming—in fact, it's already here—for the dead to hear the voice of God's son and, because they've heard it, to live. [26]Just as the Father is himself the source of life, he has also made the son to be the source of life. [27]And he has given him the authority to do the judging, because he is the Human One. [28]Don't be surprised; the time is coming when all who are in their graves will hear his voice [29]and come out—those who have done good will be raised to life, and those who have done vile deeds raised to stand trial.
25:31–46			

292. The Scriptures, Moses, and Jesus (Jn)

Mt	Mk	Lk	Jn 5:39–46	EgerG 1:2b–6
			³⁹You pore over the scriptures, because you imagine that in them there's unending life to be had. They do indeed give evidence on my behalf, ⁴⁰yet you refuse to come to me to have life. ⁴¹I'm not interested in any human praise; ⁴²but I also know that you have none of God's love in you. ⁴³I've come in my Father's name, and you don't welcome me; if others come in their own name, you'll welcome them. ⁴⁴How can you believe, since you accept praise from each other but don't even consider the praise that comes from the only God?	²ᵇPore over the scriptures. You imagine that in them there's life to be had. They do indeed give evidence on my behalf.
			⁴⁵Don't suppose that I'll be your accuser before the Father. You have an accuser, and it's Moses—the one you were relying on.	³Don't suppose that I've come to be your accuser before my Father. The one accusing you is Moses, the one you were relying on."
			9:29	⁴They say, "We know God spoke to Moses. But you—we don't know [where you come from."] ⁵Jesus replied: "Now you stand accused for not trusting those who are [commended by ⟨Moses⟩.]
			⁴⁶But if you really believed Moses, you'd believe me; after all, I'm the one he wrote about. ⁴⁷But since you don't really believe what he wrote, how are you going to believe what I say?	⁶If you had believed Moses, you would've believed me; after all, he [wrote] about me to your ancestors."

293. Bread and Fish for 5,000 (Jn)

SEE #107, P. 87

Mt 14:15–21*	Mk 6:35–44*	Lk 9:12–17	Jn 6:1–15
			[1]After these events, Jesus crossed to the far side of the Sea of Galilee, ⟨also known as the Sea of⟩ Tiberias. [2]A huge crowd was following him, because they wanted to see the signs he was performing for the sick. [3]Jesus climbed up the mountain, and he sat down there with his disciples. [4]It was about time for the Jewish festival of Passover.
14:13–14	*6:30–34*	*9:10–11*	
[15]When it was evening the disciples approached him and said, "This place is deserted and it's already late. Send the crowd away so that they can go to the villages and buy food for themselves."	[35]And as the hour had already grown late, his disciples were approaching him and saying, "This place is deserted and it's late. [36]Send them away so that they can go to the farms and villages around here to buy something to eat."	[12]As the day began to draw to a close, the Twelve approached him and said, "Send the crowd away, so that they can go to the villages and farms around here and find food and lodging; for we are in a deserted place here."	[5]Jesus looks up and sees a big crowd approaching him, and he says to Philip,
[16]Jesus said to them, "They don't need to leave; give them something to eat yourselves!"	[37]But in response he said to them, "Give them something to eat yourselves."	[13]But he said to them, "Give them something to eat yourselves."	"Where are we going to buy enough bread to feed these people?" ([6]He was saying this to test him; you see, Jesus already knew what he was going to do.)
	And they say to him, "Are we supposed to go out and buy two hundred denarii worth of bread and donate it for their meal?" [38]So he says to them, "How many loaves do you have? Go look."		[7]"Two hundred denarii wouldn't buy enough bread for everyone to have a bite," Philip said. [8]One of his disciples, Andrew, Simon Peter's brother, says to him,
[17]But they say to him, "We have nothing here except five loaves and two fish."	And when they find out, they say, "Five, and two fish."	They said, "All we have are five loaves and two fish—unless we go ourselves and buy food for all these people." ([14]There were about five thousand men.)	[9]"There's a kid here with five loaves of barley bread and two fish; but what does that amount to for so many?"
[18]He said, "Bring them here to me." [19]And he told the crowd to recline on the grass,	[39]Next he instructed them all to recline to eat, some over here, some over there, on the green grass. [40]So they	He said to his disciples, "Have them recline in groups of about fifty." [15]They did so and got them reclined.	[10]Jesus said, "Have the people sit down." (They were in a grassy place.) So they sat down. (The men ⟨alone⟩

and he took the five loaves and two fish, and looking up to the sky he gave a blessing, and breaking it apart he gave the bread to the disciples, and the disciples gave it to the crowd.	sat down group by group, in hundreds and in fifties. ⁴¹And he took the five loaves and the two fish, looked up to the sky, gave a blessing, and broke the bread apart, and started giving it to his disciples to pass around to them; and even the two fish they shared with everybody.	¹⁶Then he took the five loaves and two fish, looked up to the sky, gave a blessing, and broke them, and started handing them out to the disciples to pass around to the crowd.	numbered about five thousand.) ¹¹Jesus took the loaves, gave thanks, and passed them around to the people sitting there, along with the fish, and all of them had as much as they wanted.
²⁰And everybody had more than enough to eat.	⁴²Everybody had more than enough to eat.	¹⁷And everybody had more than enough to eat.	¹²And when they had eaten their fill, he says to his disciples, "Gather up the leftovers so that nothing goes to waste."
Then they picked up twelve baskets full of leftovers.	⁴³Then they picked up twelve baskets full of leftovers, including some fish.	Then the leftovers were collected, twelve baskets full.	¹³So they gathered them up and filled twelve baskets with scraps from the five barley loaves—from what was left over. ¹⁴When these folks saw the sign he had performed they were saying, "This has to be the Prophet who is to come into the world!" ¹⁵Jesus perceived that they were about to come and force him to be king, so he retreated once again to the mountain by himself.
²¹The number of people who had eaten came to about five thousand, not counting women and children.	⁴⁴And the number of men who had some bread came to five thousand.		

* Ⓓ Mt 15:32–39 / Mk 8:1–10 (#115, p. 95)

294. Jesus walks on the sea (Jn)

SEE #108, P. 89

Mt 14:22–27, 32–33	Mk 6:45–51	Lk	Jn 6:16–21
[22]And right away he made the disciples get in a boat and go ahead of him to the other side, while he dispersed the crowds. [23]After he had dispersed the crowds, he went up to the mountain privately to pray. He remained there alone well into the evening. [24]By this time the boat was already some distance from land and was being pounded by waves because the wind was against them. [25]About three o'clock in the morning he came toward them walking on the sea. [26]But when the disciples saw him walking on the sea, they were terrified. "It's a ghost," they said, and cried out in fear. [27]Right away Jesus spoke to them, saying, "Be brave; it's me! Don't be afraid." [32]And by the time they had climbed into the boat, the wind had died down. [33]Then those in the boat paid homage to him, saying, "You really are God's son."	[45]And right away he made his disciples embark in the boat and go ahead to the opposite shore toward Bethsaida, while he himself dispersed the crowd. [46]And once he got away from them, he went off to the mountain to pray. [47]When evening came, the boat was in the middle of the sea, and he was alone on the land. [48]When he saw they were having a rough time making headway, because the wind was against them, at about three o'clock in the morning he comes toward them walking on the sea and intending to go past them. [49]But when they saw him walking on the sea, they thought he was a ghost and they cried out, [50]because they all saw him and were terrified. But right away he spoke with them and says to them, "Take heart, it's me! Don't be afraid." [51]And he climbed into the boat with them, and the wind died down. By this time they were completely dumbfounded.		[16]As evening approached, his disciples went down to the sea. [17]They boarded a boat and were trying to cross the sea to Capernaum. It had already gotten dark, and Jesus still had not joined them. [18]A strong wind began to blow and the sea was getting rough. [19]When they had rowed about three or four miles, they catch sight of Jesus walking on the sea and coming toward the boat. They were frightened, [20]but he says to them, "Don't be afraid! It's me." [21]Then they would have taken him on board, but the boat instantly arrived at the shore they had been making for.

295. Looking for Jesus by Boat (Jn)

Mt	Mk	Lk	Jn 6:22–24
14:34–36	*6:53–56*		[22]The next day, the crowd, which was still on the other side of the sea, remembered that there had been only one boat there, and that Jesus had not gotten into that boat with the disciples, but that his disciples had set off alone. [23]Other boats came out from Tiberias, near the place where they had eaten bread. [24]So when the crowd saw that neither Jesus nor his disciples were there, they too got into boats and set out for Capernaum to look for Jesus.

296. Demanding a Sign (Jn)
SEE #116, P. 96

Mt 16:1	Mt 12:38	Mk 8:11	Lk 11:16	Jn 6:30
And the Pharisees and Sadducees came, and they put him to the test by asking him to show them a sign from heaven.	Then some of the scholars and Pharisees responded to him, "Teacher, we would like to see a sign from you."	The Pharisees came out and started to argue with him. To put him to the test, they demanded a sign from heaven.	Others were putting him to the test by demanding a sign from heaven.	They asked him, "What sign are you going to perform so we can see it and come to believe in you? What 'work' are you going to do?"

297. Isn't Jesus Joseph's son? (Jn)
SEE #95, P. 75

Mt 13:54b–56	Mk 6:2b–3	Lk 4:22	Jn 6:42
[54b]They were astounded and said so: "Where did this wisdom and these miracles come from?	[2b]Many who heard him were astounded and said so: "Where's he getting all this?" and "Where'd he get all this wisdom?" and "Where'd he get the power to perform such miracles?	And they all were responding favorably to him, and marveling at the pleasing speech that he delivered; and they were saying,	They were saying,
[55]This is the carpenter's son, isn't it? Isn't his mother called Mary?	[3]This is the carpenter, isn't it? Isn't he the son of Mary?	"Isn't this the son of Joseph?"	"Isn't this Jesus, son of Joseph? Don't we know both his father and his mother? How can he now say, 'I've come down from heaven'?"
And aren't his brothers James and Joseph and Simon and Judas? [56]And aren't all his sisters neighbors of ours? So where did he get all this?"	And aren't his brothers James, Joses, Judas, and Simon? And aren't his sisters our neighbors?"		

298. Peter proclaims Jesus the holy one of God (Jn)

SEE #119, P. 100

Mt	Mk	Lk	Jn 6:66–69	Th 1

			[66]Many of his disciples dropped out and would no longer travel around with him.
			    [67]Jesus then said to the Twelve, "Do you want to leave too?"
			    [68]Simon Peter replied to him, "Master, is there anyone else we can turn to? You have the words of unending life.*
			    [69]We have become believers and have realized that you are the holy one of God."
				And ⟨Jesus⟩ said,
				"Whoever discovers the interpretation of ⟨my⟩ sayings will not taste death."

16:15	8:27	9:20		

* Jn 8:51–52 (#302, p. 243)

299. Uneducated Jesus (Jn)

SEE #95, P. 75

Mt 13:54b–55	Mk 6:2b–3a	Lk 4:22	Jn 7:15
[54b]They were astounded and said so: "Where did this wisdom and these miracles come from?	[2b]Many who heard him were astounded and said so: "Where's he getting all this?" and "Where'd he get all this wisdom?" and "Where'd he get the power to perform such miracles?	And they all were responding favorably to him, and marveling at the pleasing speech that he delivered; and they were saying,	The Judeans were taken aback, saying,
[55]This is the carpenter's son, isn't it? Isn't his mother called Mary?	[3a]This is the carpenter, isn't it? Isn't he the son of Mary?	"Isn't this the son of Joseph?"	"This man is uneducated; how come he's so articulate?"

300. Seeking Jesus, But Not Finding Him (Jn)

Mt	Mk	Lk	Jn 7:33–34	Th 38:2
			[33]Then Jesus said, "I'll be with you a little longer; then I'll return to the one who sent me. [34]You'll look for me, but you won't find me; where I am you can't come."	There will be days when you'll seek me and you won't find me.

301. The Light of the World (Jn)

SEE #18, 470, PP. 21, 354

Mt 5:14	Mk	Lk	Jn 8:12	Jn 9:5
You are the light of the world.			I am the light of the world.	While I am in the world I am the light of the world.

302. Words of Immortality (Jn)

Mt	Mk	Lk	Jn 8:51–52*	Th 1
			[51]"Let me tell you this: whoever follows my teaching will never die. [52]To this the Judeans retorted, "Now we're certain you're possessed! ⟨Even⟩ Abraham died, and so did the prophets, and here you are claiming, 'Whoever follows my teaching will never taste death.'"	And ⟨Jesus⟩ said, "Whoever discovers the interpretation of ⟨my⟩ sayings will not taste death."

*Jn 6:68 (#298, p. 242)

303. Pharisees don't know Jesus' origins (Jn)
SEE #509, P. 386

Mt	Mk	Lk	Jn 9:28–29	EgerG 1:4
			[28]⟨The Pharisees⟩ hurled insults at ⟨the man born blind⟩: "You may be his disciple; we're disciples of Moses. [29]We know God spoke to Moses; we don't even know where this man came from."	We know God spoke to Moses. But you—we don't know [where you come from.]

304. The Good Shepherd (Jn)
SEE #141, 369, PP. 115, 302

Mt 11:27b	Mk	Lk 10:22b	Jn 10:14–15
No one knows the son except the Father, nor does anyone know the Father except the son— and anyone to whom the son wishes to reveal him.		No one knows who the son is except the Father, or who the Father is except the son— and anyone to whom the son wishes to reveal him.	[14]I am the good shepherd. I know my sheep and my sheep know me, [15]just as the Father knows me and I know the Father, and I give my life for my sheep.

305. Jesus escapes stoning (Jn)
SEE #510, P. 387

Mt	Mk	Lk 4:28–30	Jn 10:31, 39	EgerG 1:8–10
		[28]Everyone in the meeting place was filled with rage when they heard this. [29]They rose up, ran him out of town, and led him to the brow of the hill on which their town was built, intending to hurl him over the cliff. [30]But he slipped through their fingers and got away.	[31]Again the Judeans picked up stones to stone him. [39]Again they tried to arrest him, but he escaped.	[8][The rulers] laid their hands on him to arrest him and [turn him] over to the crowd. [9]But they couldn't arrest him because the time for him to be turned over hadn't yet arrived. [10]So the Master himself slipped through their hands and got away.

306. The authorities plot to kill Jesus (Jn)

SEE #234, P. 180

Mt	Mk	Lk	Jn 11:45–53
			[45]As a result, many of the Judeans who had come to Mary and observed what Jesus had done came to believe in him. [46]But some of them went to the Pharisees and reported what Jesus had done.
			[47]So the chief priests and Pharisees called the Council together and posed this question to them: "What are we going to do now that this man performs so many signs? [48]If we let him go on like this, everybody will come to believe in him. Then the Romans will come and destroy our ⟨holy⟩ place and our nation."
			[49]Then one of them, Caiaphas, that year's chief priest, addressed them as follows: "Don't you know anything? [50]Don't you realize that you're better off having one man die for the people than having the whole nation wiped out?"
			([51]He didn't say this on his own authority, but since he was that year's chief priest he could foresee that Jesus would die for the nation. [52]In fact, he would die not only for the nation, but to gather together all God's dispersed children and make them one people.)
26:1–5	14:1–2	22:1–2	[53]So from that day on they began plotting how to kill him.

307. Mary anoints Jesus' feet (Jn)

= #235, P. 180

Mt 26:6–13	Mk 14:3–9	Lk 7:36–39	Jn 12:1–8
[6]While Jesus was in Bethany at the house of Simon the leper,	[3]When he was in Bethany at the house of Simon the leper,	[36]One of the Pharisees invited him to dinner; he entered the Pharisee's house, and reclined ⟨for the meal⟩. [37]A local woman, who was a sinner, found out that he was having dinner at the Pharisee's house.	[1]Six days before Passover Jesus came to Bethany, where Lazarus lived, the one Jesus had raised from the dead. [2]There they gave a dinner for him; Martha did the serving, and Lazarus was one of those who ate with him.
[7]a woman who had an alabaster jar of very expensive aromatic ointment came up to him and poured it over his head while he was reclining ⟨at table⟩.	he was just reclining there, and a woman came in carrying an alabaster jar of aromatic ointment made from pure and expensive nard. She broke the jar and poured ⟨the ointment⟩ on his head.	She suddenly showed up with an alabaster jar of aromatic ointment, [38]and stood there behind him weeping at his feet. Her tears wet his feet, and she wiped them dry with her hair; she kissed his feet, and anointed them with the ointment.	[3]Mary brought in a pound of expensive aromatic ointment made from pure nard and anointed Jesus' feet and wiped them with her hair. And the house was filled with the ointment's fragrance.
[8]When they saw this, the disciples were annoyed, and said,	[4]Now some were annoyed ⟨and thought⟩ to themselves,	[39]The Pharisee who had invited him saw this and said to himself,	[4]Judas Iscariot, the disciple who was going to turn him in, says,

"What good is this waste?	"What good does it do to waste this ointment?	"If this man were a prophet, he would know who this is and what kind of woman is touching him, since she is a sinner."	
[9]She could have sold it for a good price and given ⟨the money⟩ to the poor."	[5]She could have sold the ointment for more than three hundred denarii and given ⟨the money⟩ to the poor." And they were angry with her.		[5]"Why wasn't this ointment sold? It would bring three hundred denarii, and the money could have been given to the poor." ([6]He didn't say this because he cared about the poor, but because he was a thief. He was in charge of the common purse and now and again would pilfer money put into it.)
[10]But Jesus knew what was going on and said to them, "Why are you giving this woman a hard time?	[6]Then Jesus said, "Let her alone! Why are you giving her a hard time?		[7]"Leave her alone," Jesus said. "Let her keep it for the day of my burial.
v. 12 After all, she has done a good deed for me. [11]Remember, the poor will always be around; but I won't always be around. [12]After all, by pouring this ointment on my body she has prepared me for burial. [13]Let me tell you, wherever this good news is announced in all the world, the story of what she's done will be told in her memory."	v. 8 She has done a good deed for me. [7]Remember, the poor will always be around, and whenever you want you can do good for them, but I won't always be around. [8]She did what she could; she has planned ahead by anointing my body for burial. [9]Let me tell you, wherever the good news is announced in all the world, the story of what she's done will be told in her memory."		[8]There will always be poor around, but I won't always be around."[a] v. 7b

[a] Jn 12:8 A few mss lack this verse.

308. Jesus rides into Jerusalem (Jn)

SEE #204, P. 155

Mt 21:8–9, 7, 4–5	Mk 11:8–10, 7	Lk 19:36–38, 35	Jn 12:12–15
			[12]The next day the huge crowd that had come for the festival heard that Jesus was coming into Jerusalem.
[8]The enormous crowd spread their cloaks on the road, and others cut branches from the trees and spread them on the road.	[8]And many people spread their cloaks on the road, while others cut leafy branches from the fields.	[36]And as he rode along, people would spread their cloaks on the road.	[13]They got palm fronds and went out to meet him.
[9]The crowds leading the way and those following kept shouting,	[9]Those leading the way and those following kept shouting,	[37]As he approached the slope of the Mount of Olives, the entire throng of his disciples began to cheer and shout praise to God for all the miracles they had seen. [38]They kept repeating,	They began to shout,
"Hosanna to the son of David! Blessed is the one who comes in the name of the Lord! Hosanna in the highest ⟨heaven⟩."	"Hosanna! Blessed is the one who comes in the name of the Lord! [10]Blessed is the coming kingdom of our father David! Hosanna in the highest ⟨heaven⟩!"	"Blessed is the king who comes in the name of the Lord! Peace in heaven and glory in the highest ⟨heaven⟩!"	"Hosanna! Blessed is the one who comes in the name of the Lord! ⟨Blessed is⟩ the King of Israel!"
[7]⟨They⟩ brought the donkey and colt and they placed their cloaks on them, and he sat on top of them. [4]This happened in order to fulfill the prediction spoken through the prophet: [5]"Tell the daughter of Zion, "Look, your king comes to you gently, mounted on a donkey and on a colt, the foal of a pack animal."	[7]So they bring the colt to Jesus, and they throw their cloaks over it; then he got on it.	[35]So they brought it to Jesus. They threw their cloaks on the colt and helped Jesus mount it.	[14]Then Jesus found a young donkey and rode on it, as scripture puts it: [15]"Fear not, daughter of Zion. Look, your king comes riding on a donkey's colt."

309. Jesus is glorified (Jn)

SEE #121, 243, PP. 102, 187

Mt 16:25; 10:39; 26:37–39	Mk 8:35; 14:33–36	Lk 9:24; 17:33; 22:41–42; 10:18	Jn 12:23–33
			[23]The time has come for the Human One to be glorified. [24]Let me tell you this: unless the kernel of wheat falls to the earth and dies, it remains a single seed, but if it dies, it produces a great harvest.
Mt 16:25 Remember, if you try to save your life you'll lose it, but if you lose your life for my sake, you'll find it.	**Mk 8:35** Remember, if you try to save your life, you'll lose it, but if you lose your life for the sake of the good news, you'll save it.	**Lk 9:24** Remember, if you try to save your life, you'll lose it, but if you lose your life for my sake, you'll save it.	[25]If you love your life you'll lose it, but if you hate your life in this world you'll preserve it for unending life.
Mt 10:39 By finding your life, you'll lose it, but by losing your life for my sake, you'll find it.		**Lk 17:33** Whoever tries to hang on to life will lose it, but whoever loses it will preserve it.	
			[26]Whoever serves me must follow me, for wherever I am, my servant must be there also. Whoever serves me, the Father will honor.
Mt 26:37–39 [37]And taking Peter and the two sons of Zebedee, he began to feel dejected and full of anguish. [38]He says to them, "I'm so sad I could die. You stay here with me and be alert!" [39]And he went a little farther, knelt with his face to the ground, and prayed,	**Mk 14:33–36** [33]And he takes Peter and James and John along with him, and he grew apprehensive and full of anguish. [34]He says to them, "I'm so sad I could die. You stay here and be alert." [35]And he would move on a little, lay facedown on the ground, and pray that he might avoid the crisis, if possible.	**Lk 22:41–42** [41]And he withdrew from them about a stone's throw away, got down on his knees, and began to pray,	
			[27]Now my life is in turmoil, but should I say, 'Father, rescue me from this moment'? No, it was to face this moment that I came.
"My Father, if it's possible, take this cup away from me. But it's your will that matters, not mine."	[36]And he was saying, "*Abba* (Father), all things are possible for you. Take this cup away from me. But it's your will that matters, not mine."	[42]"Father, if you so choose, take this cup away from me! Yet not my will, but yours, be done."	

Mt 16:25; 10:39; 26:37–39	Mk 8:35; 14:33–36	Lk 9:24; 17:33; 22:41–42; 10:18	Jn 12:23–33
17:5	*9:7*	*9:35*	[28]Father, glorify your name!" Then a voice spoke out of the sky, "I have glorified it and I will glorify even more."
			[29]The crowd there heard this, and some people remarked that it was thunder, others that a heavenly messenger had spoken to him.
		Lk 10:18 I was watching Satan fall like lightning from heaven.	[30]"That voice did not come for me but for you," Jesus answered. [31]"Now sentence is passed on this world; now the ruler of this world will be driven out. [32]And if I'm elevated from the earth, I'll take everyone with me." ([33]He said this to show what kind of death he was going to die.)

310. Isaiah saw Jesus' glory (Jn)

SEE #77, P. 62

Mt 13:11–15	Mk 4:11–12	Lk 8:10	Jn 12:37–41
			[37]Although he had performed so many signs before their eyes, they did not believe in him, [38]in order that the word the prophet Isaiah spoke would be fulfilled: "Lord, who has believed our message? To whom is God's might revealed?"
[11]You've been given the privilege of knowing the secrets of the empire of Heaven, but that privilege has not been granted to anyone else. [12]In fact, to those who have, more will be given, and then some; and from those who don't have, even what they do have will be taken away. [13]That is why I tell them parables, because "When they look they don't really see	[11]You have been given the secret of the empire of God; but to those outside everything is presented in parables,	[10a]You have been given the privilege of knowing the secrets of the empire of God; but the rest get only parables,	
	4:25	8:18	
and when they listen they don't really hear or understand." [14]Moreover, in them the prophecy of Isaiah is fulfilled, the one which says, "You listen closely, yet you won't ever understand, and you look intently but won't ever see. [15]For the mind of this people has grown dull, and their ears are hard of hearing, and they have shut their eyes, otherwise they might actually see with their eyes, and hear with their ears, and understand with their minds, and turn around and I would heal them."	[12]so that "They may look with eyes wide open but never quite see, and may listen with ears attuned but never quite understand,	[10b]so that "They may look but not see, listen but not understand."	[39]So they were unable to believe, for Isaiah also said, [40]"He has blinded their eyes, and closed their minds, to make sure they don't see with their eyes and understand with their minds, or else they would turn ⟨their lives⟩ around and I would heal them." [41]Isaiah said these things because he saw his glory and spoke about it.
	otherwise they might turn around and find forgiveness."		

311. Believing in Jesus and the One Who Sent Him (Jn)

SEE #103, 127, 313, PP. 84, 107, 251

Mt	Mk 9:37	Lk 9:48a	Jn 12:44–45	Jn 13:20
	Whoever welcomes a child like this in my name is welcoming me.	Whoever welcomes this child in my name is welcoming me.		Let me tell you this: if they receive anyone I send, they are receiving me;
			44Those who believe in me believe not only in me, but in the one who sent me.	
10:40	And whoever welcomes me is not so much welcoming me as the one who sent me.*	And whoever welcomes me is welcoming the one who sent me.*	45And those who see me see the one who sent me.	and if they receive me, they are receiving the one who sent me.

*Lk 10:16 (#103, p. 84)

312. The Father left everything up to Jesus (Jn)

SEE #141, P. 115

Mt 11:27a	Mk	Lk 10:22a	Jn 13:3*	Th 61:3
My Father has turned everything over to me.		My Father has turned everything over to me.	Jesus could tell that the Father had left everything up to him and that he had come from God and was going back to God.	I am the one who comes from the one who is unwavering. I have been given some of the things of my Father.

*Jn 3:35 (#284, p. 232)

313. Jesus sets an example (Jn)
SEE #99, P. 80

Mt 10:24	Mk	Lk 6:40	John 13:12–17
			[12]When he had washed their feet, he put his shirt back on and returned to his place at the meal. "Do you realize what I've done?" he asked. [13]"You call me Teacher and Master, and you're right: that's who I am. [14]So if I am your master and teacher and have washed your feet, you should wash each other's feet. [15]In other words, I've set you an example: you are to do as I've done to you. [16]Let me tell you this:
Students are not above their teachers, nor slaves above their masters.		Students are not above their teachers.	slaves are never better than their masters;* messengers are never superior to those who send them. [17]If you understand this, congratulations if you can do it.

* ⒟ Jn 15:20a (#319, p. 255)

314. You, Me, and the One Who Sent Me (Jn)
SEE #103, 127, 311, PP. 84, 107, 250

Mt 10:40	Mk 9:37b	Lk 10:16	Jn 13:20
The one who welcomes you is welcoming me, and the one who welcomes me is welcoming the one who sent me.*	Whoever welcomes me is not so much welcoming me as the one who sent me.*	Whoever hears you hears me, and whoever rejects you rejects me, and whoever rejects me rejects the one who sent me.	If they receive anyone I send, they are receiving me; and if they receive me, they are receiving the one who sent me. 15:23; 5:23

* Mt 18:5 / Lk 9:48 (#127, p. 107)

315. The Betrayer's Identity (Jn)

SEE #238, P. 182

Mt 26:21–25	Mk 14:18–21	Lk 22:21–23; 22:3–4	Jn 13:21–27
[21]And as they were eating, he said, "Let me tell you, one of you is going to turn me in."	[18]And as they reclined ⟨for dinner⟩ and were eating, Jesus said, "Let me tell you, one of you eating with me is going to turn me in!"	[21]"But look! Right here with me at this very table is the one who is going to turn me in. [22]The Human One goes to meet his destiny; and yet damn the one responsible for turning him in!"	[21]When he had said all this, Jesus became agitated. He declared, "Let me tell you this: one of you will turn me in."
v. 24	v. 21	[23]And they began to ask one another which of them could possibly attempt such a thing.	
[22]And they were very upset and each one said to him in turn, "I'm not the one, am I, Master?"	[19]They got very upset and said to him one after another, "I'm not the one, am I?"		[22]The disciples stole glances at each other, at a loss to understand who it was he was talking about. [23]One of them, the disciple Jesus loved, was reclining next to him. [24]So Simon Peter leans over to ask that disciple who it was Jesus was talking about. [25]He, in turn, leans back on Jesus' chest and asks him, "Master, who is it?"
[23]In response he said, "The one who dips his hand in the bowl with me—that's who's going to turn me in. [24]The Human One departs just as the scriptures predict, but damn the one responsible for turning the Human One in! That man would be better off if he'd never been born!"	[20]But he said to them, "It's one of the Twelve, the one who is dipping into the bowl with me. [21]The Human One departs just as the scriptures predict, but damn the one responsible for turning the Human One in! That man would be better off if he'd never been born!"	v. 22	[26]Jesus answers, "I am going to dip this piece of bread, and the one I give it to is the one."
[25]Judas, the one who was going to turn him in, responded, "You can't mean me, can you, Rabbi?"		[3]Then Satan took possession of Judas, the one called Iscariot, who was a member of the Twelve. [4]He went off to negotiate with the chief priests and ⟨temple⟩ police how to turn Jesus over to them.	So he dips the piece of bread and gives it to Judas, son of Simon Iscariot. [27]The moment ⟨he had given Judas⟩ the piece of bread, Satan took possession of him.
26:14–15	14:10		Then Jesus says to him, "Go ahead and do what you're going to do."

316. Peter's Denial Predicted (Jn)
SEE #241, P. 186

Mt 26:33–34	Mk 14:29–30	Lk 22:31–33	Jn 13:36–38
			[36]Simon Peter says to him, "Master, where are you going?" Jesus answered, "For now you can't follow me where I'm going; you'll follow later."
		[31]"Simon, Simon, look out: Satan is after all of you, to sift you like wheat. [32]But I have prayed for you that your trust won't give out. And once you've recovered, you are to shore up these brothers of yours."	
[33]In response Peter said to him, "Even if everyone else is shaken and falls away because of you, I never will." [34]Jesus said to him,	[29]Peter said to him, "Even if everyone else is shaken and falls away, I won't!" [30]And Jesus says to him,	[33]He said to him, "Master, I'm prepared to follow you not only to prison but all the way to death." [34]He said,	[37]Peter says to him, "Master, why can't I follow you now? I'd give my life for you." [38]Jesus responded, "You'd give your life for me? Let me tell you this:
"Let me tell you, tonight before the rooster crows you will disown me three times."	"Let me tell you, tonight before the rooster crows twice you will disown me three times."	"Let me tell you, Peter, the rooster will not crow tonight until you deny three times that you know me."	the rooster won't crow before you disown me three times."

317. Asking Using Jesus' Name (Jn)
SEE #209, 321, PP. 159, 256

Mt 21:22	Mk 11:24b	Lk	Jn 14:12–14
Everything you ask for in prayer you'll get if you trust.	Trust that you will receive everything you pray and ask for, and that's the way it will turn out.		[12]Let me tell you this: anyone who believes in me will perform the works I perform and will be able to perform even greater feats, because I'm on my way to the Father. [13]In addition, I'll do whatever you request using my name, so the Father can be glorified in the son. [14]If you request anything using my name, I'll do it.*

*Jn 15:7; 16:24 (#318, 321, pp. 254, 256)

318. Vine and Branches (Jn)

SEE #36, 209, PP. 31, 159

Mt 21:22; 7:7–8	Mk 11:24b	Lk 11:9–10	Jn 15:5–8
			[5]I am the vine, you are the branches. Those who stay attached to me—and I to them—produce a lot of fruit; without me you can't do anything. [6]Those who don't remain attached to me are thrown away like dead branches: they're collected, tossed into the fire, and burned. [7]If you stay attached to me and my words live in you,
Mt 21:22 Everything you ask for in prayer you'll get if you trust. **Mt 7:7–8** [7]Ask—it'll be given to you; seek—you'll find; knock—it'll be opened for you.† [8]Everyone who asks receives; everyone who seeks finds; and for the one who knocks it is opened.	Trust that you will receive everything you pray and ask for, and that's the way it will turn out.	[9]Ask—it'll be given to you; seek—you'll find; knock—it'll be opened for you.† [10]For everyone who asks receives; everyone who seeks finds; and for the one who knocks it is opened.	ask whatever you want and it will happen to you.*
			[8]My Father is glorified by the great quantity of fruit you produce in being my disciples.

* Jn 14:13–14; 16:24 (#317, 321, pp. 253, 256)
† Th 92:1; 94:1–2; 2:1 (#479, 481, 414, pp. 357, 358, 330)

319. Slaves are never better than their masters (Jn)

SEE # 99, 103, PP. 80, 84

Mt 10:24–25	Mk	Lk 6:40; 10:16	Jn 15:18–25
			[18]If the world hates you, don't forget that it hated me first. [19]If you were at home in the world, the world would befriend ⟨you as⟩ its own. But you are not at home in the world. On the contrary, I have chosen you out of the world; that's why the world hates you. [20]Recall what I told you:
[24]Students are not above their teachers, nor slaves above their masters.		**Lk 6:40** Students are not above their teachers.	
[25]It's enough for students to become like their teachers and slaves to be like their masters. If they have dubbed the master of the house 'Beelzebul,' aren't they even more likely to malign the members of his household?		But those who are fully taught will be like their teachers.	"slaves are never better than their masters."*
			If they persecuted me, they'll surely persecute you. If they follow my teaching, they'll also follow yours. [21]Yet they are going to do all these things to you because of me, since they don't know the one who sent me. [22]If I hadn't come and spoken to them, they wouldn't be guilty of sin. But as it is, they have no excuse for their sin.
		Lk 10:16 Whoever hears you hears me, and whoever rejects you rejects me, and whoever rejects me rejects the one who sent me.	[23]Those who hate me also hate my Father.†
			[24]If I hadn't performed feats among them such as no one else has ever performed, they wouldn't be guilty of sin. But as it is, they have witnessed ⟨these feats⟩ and come to hate both me and my Father. [25]This has happened so the saying in their Law would be fulfilled: "They hated me for no reason."

* Ⓓ Jn 13:16 (#313, p. 251)
† Jn 5:23 (#290, p. 236)

320. Former Secrets Now Revealed (Jn)

Mt	Mk	Lk	Jn 16:1–5	Th 92:2
			[1]I've told you these things to keep you from being misled. [2]They are going to throw you out of their congregations. But the time is coming when those who kill you will think they are offering devotion to God. [3]They are going to do these things because they never knew the Father or me. [4]Yet I have told you all this so, when the time comes, you'll recall that I told you about them. I didn't tell you these things at first because I was with you then. [5]Now I am on my way to the one who sent me, and not one of you asks me, "Where are you going?"	In the past I didn't tell you the things about which you asked me then. Now I'm willing to tell them, but you're not seeking them.

321. Asking the Father Using Jesus' Name (Jn)

SEE #36, 209, 317, PP. 31, 159, 253

Mt 21:22; 7:7–8	Mk 11:24b	Lk 11:9–10	Jn 16:23b–24
Mt 21:22 Everything you ask for in prayer you'll get if you trust. **Mt 7:7–8** [7]Ask—it'll be given to you; seek—you'll find; knock—it'll be opened for you.† [8]Everyone who asks receives; everyone who seeks finds; and for the one who knocks it is opened.	Trust that you will receive everything you pray and ask for, and that's the way it will turn out.	[9]Ask—it'll be given to you; seek—you'll find; knock—it'll be opened for you.† [10]For everyone who asks receives; everyone who seeks finds; and for the one who knocks it is opened.	[23b]Let me tell you this: if you ask the Father for anything using my name, he will grant it to you. [24]Up until now you haven't asked for anything using my name. Ask and you'll receive,* so your joy will be complete.

*Jn 14:13–14; 15:7 (#317, 318, pp. 253, 254)

† Th 92:1; 94:1–2; 2:1 (#479, 481, 414, pp. 357, 358, 330)

322. Jesus surrenders (Jn)
SEE #243, 244, PP. 187, 189

Mt 26:30, 36, 47, 51–52, 39b	Mk 14:26, 32, 43, 47, 36	Lk 22:39, 47, 49–51, 42	Jn 18:1–11
[30]And they sang a hymn and left for the Mount of Olives. [36]Then Jesus goes with them to a place called Gethsemane, and he says to the disciples, "Sit down here while I go over there and pray." [47]And while he was still speaking, suddenly Judas, one of the Twelve, arrived and with him a great crowd wielding swords and clubs, dispatched by the chief priests and elders of the people. [49]And right away he came up to Jesus and said, "Hello, Rabbi," and kissed him.	[26]And they sang a hymn and left for the Mount of Olives. [32]And they go to a place named Gethsemane, and he says to his disciples, "Sit down here while I pray." [43]And right away, while he was still speaking, Judas, one of the Twelve, shows up, and with him a crowd, dispatched by the chief priests and the scholars and the elders, wielding swords and clubs. [45]And right away he arrives, comes up to him, and says, "Rabbi," and kissed him.	[39]Then he left and walked, as usual, over to the Mount of Olives; and the disciples followed him. [47]Suddenly, while he was still speaking, a crowd appeared with the one called Judas, one of the Twelve, leading the way. He stepped up to Jesus to give him a kiss.	[1]When he had said all this, Jesus went out with his disciples across the Kidron valley. There was a garden there where he and his disciples went. [2]But because Jesus had often gone there with his disciples, Judas, who was about to turn him in, knew the place too. [3]So it wasn't long before Judas arrives, bringing with him the battalion ⟨of Roman soldiers⟩ and some of the police from the chief priests and the Pharisees, with their lanterns and torches and weapons. [4]Jesus, of course, knew just what would happen to him, so he went right up to them and says, "Who is it you're looking for?" [5]"Jesus the Nazarene," was their reply. "I am," says Jesus. (And all the while Judas, who was turning him in, was standing there with them.) [6]But as soon as he said, "I am," they all retreated and fell to the ground. [7]So Jesus asked them again, "Who is it you're looking for?" "Jesus the Nazarene," they said. [8]"I told you that I am," Jesus answered, "so if it's me you're looking for, let the others go." ([9]This was so the prediction he had made would be fulfilled: "I haven't lost one—not one of those you gave me.")

Mt 26:30, 36, 47, 51–52, 39b	Mk 14:26, 32, 43, 47, 36	Lk 22:39, 47, 49–51, 42	Jn 18:1–11
		49And when those around him realized what was coming next, they said, "Master, should we use our swords?"	
51All of a sudden one of those with Jesus lifted his hand, drew his sword, struck the chief priest's slave,	47One of those standing around drew his sword and swung at the chief priest's slave	50And one of them struck the chief priest's slave	10Simon Peter had brought along a sword, and now he drew it, slashed at the chief priest's slave, who was called Malchus,
and cut off his ear.	and cut off his ear.	and cut off his right ear.	and cut off his right ear.
52Then Jesus says to him, "Put your sword back where it belongs. For everyone who takes up the sword will be destroyed by the sword."		51But Jesus responded, "Stop! That's enough!"	11"Put the sword back in its scabbard," Jesus told Peter.
		And he touched his ear and healed him.	
39b"My Father, if it's possible, take this cup away from me. But it's your will that matters, not mine."	36"Abba (Father), all things are possible for you. Take this cup away from me. But it's your will that matters, not mine."	42"Father, if you so choose, take this cup away from me! Yet not my will, but yours, be done."a	"I have to drink from the cup my Father has given me, don't I?"

a Lk 22:42 Many mss add another two verses, traditionally numbered 22:43–44: "43An angel from heaven appeared to him and gave him strength. 44In his anxiety he prayed more fervently, and it so happened that his sweat fell to the ground like great drops of blood." (It is very doubtful that these verses were part of the original text.)

323. Jesus is arrested (Jn)

SEE #245, P. 191

Mt 26:57	Mk 14:53	Lk 22:54a	Jn 18:12–14
Those who had arrested Jesus brought him before Caiaphas the chief priest, where the scholars and elders had assembled.	And they brought Jesus before the chief priest, and all the chief priests and elders and scholars assemble.	They arrested him and marched him away to the house of the chief priest.	12Then the battalion and their captain, with the Judean police, arrested Jesus and bound him. 13They took him first to Annas. (Annas was the father-in-law of that year's chief priest, Caiaphas. 14Remember, it was Caiaphas who had given the Judeans this advice: You're better off having one man die for the people.)

324. Peter denies Jesus for the first time (Jn)

SEE #245, P. 191

Mt 26:58, 69–70	Mk 14:54a, 66–68, 54b	Lk 22:54b, 56–57, 55	Jn 18:15–18
[58]But Peter followed him at a distance	[54a]Peter followed him at a distance	[54b]Peter followed at a distance.	[15]Simon Peter and another disciple were trailing along behind Jesus. This other disciple, who was an acquaintance of the chief priest, went in with Jesus to the chief priest's courtyard. [16]Peter was standing outside the gate; so this other disciple, the acquaintance of the chief priest, went out, had a word with the woman who kept watch at the gate, and got Peter in.
as far as the courtyard of the chief priest. He went inside and sat with the attendants to see how things would turn out.	until he was inside the courtyard of the chief priest.		
[69]Meanwhile Peter was sitting outside in the courtyard, and one slave woman came up to him,	[66]And while Peter was below in the courtyard, one of the chief priest's slave women comes over, [67]and sees Peter warming himself; she looks at him closely and says,	[56]Then a slave woman noticed him sitting there in the glow of the fire. She stared at him, then spoke up,	[17]The slave woman who kept watch at the gate says to Peter,
and said, "You too were with Jesus the Galilean."	"You too were with that Nazarene, Jesus."	"This guy was with him too."	"You're not one of this man's disciples too, are you?"
[70]But he denied it in front of everyone, saying, "I don't know what you're talking about."	[68]But he denied it, saying, "I haven't the slightest idea what you're talking about." And he went outside into the forecourt.	[57]He denied it. "Lady," he said, "I don't know him."	"No, I'm not," he replies.
	[54b]and was sitting with the attendants and keeping warm by the fire.	[55]When they had started a fire in the middle of the courtyard and were sitting around it, Peter joined them.	[18]Meanwhile, since it was cold, the slaves and police had made a charcoal fire and were standing around it, trying to keep warm. Peter was standing there too, warming himself.

325. Jesus defends himself to the chief priest (Jn)

Mt	Mk	Lk	Jn 18:19–24
			[19]Now the chief priest interrogated Jesus about his disciples and about his teaching.
26:55	*14:49*	*22:53*	[20]"I have spoken openly to anyone and everyone," Jesus replied. "I've always taught in meeting places and in the temple area, in places where all Jewish people gather. I've said nothing in secret. [21]Why are you asking me? Ask those who heard what I said. You'll see that they know what I said."
			[22]As soon as he said this, one of the policemen on duty there slapped Jesus. "How dare you talk back to the chief priest!" he said.
			[23]"If I've said something wrong, show what's wrong with it," Jesus said in reply. "But if I'm right, why are you slapping me?"
26:57	14:53	22:54a	[24]At that Annas sent him, still bound, to the chief priest, Caiaphas.

326. Peter denies Jesus again (Jn)
= #246, P. 194

Mt 26:69–75	Mk 14:66–72	Lk 22:56–62	Jn 18:25–27
[69]Meanwhile Peter was sitting outside in the courtyard,	[66]And while Peter was below in the courtyard,		[25]Meanwhile, Simon Peter was still standing outside, keeping warm.
and one slave woman came up to him,	one of the chief priest's slave women comes over, [67]and sees Peter warming himself; she looks at him closely and says,	[56]Then a slave woman noticed him sitting there in the glow of the fire. She stared at him, then spoke up,	
and said, "You too were with Jesus the Galilean."	"You too were with that Nazarene, Jesus."	"This guy was with him too."	The others there said to him, "You're not one of his disciples too, are you?" He denied it.
[70]But he denied it in front of everyone, saying, "I don't know what you're talking about."	[68]But he denied it, saying, "I haven't the slightest idea what you're talking about." And he went outside into the forecourt.	[57]He denied it. "Lady," he said, "I don't know him."	"No, I'm not," he said.
[71]After Peter went out to the entrance, another slave woman saw him and says to those there,	[69]And when the slave woman saw him, she once again began to say to those standing nearby,	[58]A little later someone else noticed him and said,	[26]One of the chief priest's slaves, a relative of the one whose ear Peter had cut off, says, "I saw you in the garden with him, didn't I?"
"This guy was with that Nazarean, Jesus."	"This guy is one of them."	"You're one of them too."	
[72]And again he denied it with an oath: "I don't know the man!"	[70]But once again he denied it.	"Not me, mister," Peter replied.	[27]Once again Peter denied it.
[73]A little later those standing around came and said to Peter, "You really are one of them; even the way you talk gives you away!"	And a little later, those standing nearby were saying to Peter, "You really are one of them, since you also are a Galilean."	[59]About an hour went by and someone else insisted, "No question about it; this guy's also one of them; he's even a Galilean!"	
[74]Then he began to curse and swear: "I don't know the man!"	[71]But he began to curse and swear, "I don't know this man you're talking about!"	[60]But Peter said, "Mister, I don't know what you're talking about." And all of a sudden, while he was still speaking, a rooster crowed.	
And just then a rooster crowed.	[72]And just then a rooster crowed a second time,		At that very moment a rooster crowed.
		[61]And the Master turned and looked straight at Peter. And Peter remembered what the Master had told him:	
[75]And Peter remembered what Jesus had said: "Before the rooster crows you will disown me three times."	and Peter remembered what Jesus had told him: "Before a rooster crows twice you will disown me three times."	"Before the rooster crows tonight, you will disown me three times."	
And he went outside and wept bitterly.	And he broke down and started to cry.	[62]And he went outside and wept bitterly.	

327. Jesus before Pilate (Jn)

SEE #247, 249, PP. 195, 196

Mt 27:1–2, 11	Mk 15:1–2	Lk 23:1, 3	Jn 18:28–38a
¹When morning came, all the chief priests and elders of the people plotted against Jesus to put him to death. ²And they bound him and led him away and turned him over to Pilate the ⟨Roman⟩ governor.	¹And right away, at day-break, the chief priests, after consulting with the elders and scholars and the whole Council, bound Jesus and led him away and turned him over to Pilate.	¹At this point the whole assembly got up and took him before Pilate.	²⁸They then take Jesus from Caiaphas' place to the governor's residence. By now it was early morning. (They didn't actually go into the governor's residence, or else they would become unclean, and unable to eat the Passover meal.) ²⁹So Pilate came out and says to them, "What charge are you bringing against this man?"
		23:2	³⁰"If he hadn't committed a crime," they retorted, "we wouldn't have turned him over to you."
			³¹"Deal with him yourselves," Pilate said to them. "Judge him by your own law." "But it's illegal for us to execute anyone," the Judeans said to him. (³²They said this so Jesus' prediction of how he would die would be fulfilled.)
¹¹Jesus stood before the ⟨Roman⟩ governor, and the governor questioned him, "*You* are 'the King of the Judeans'?"	²And Pilate questioned him, "*You* are 'the King of the Judeans'?"	³Pilate questioned him, "*You* are 'the King of the Judeans'?"	³³Then Pilate went back into his residence. He summoned Jesus and asked him, "*You* are 'the King of the Judeans'?"
			³⁴"Is this what you think," Jesus answered, "or what other people have told you about me?"
			³⁵"Am I a Judean?!" countered Pilate. "It's your own people and the chief priests who have turned you over to me. What have you done?"
			³⁶To this Jesus responded, "My empire is not part of this world. If it were, my people would be fighting to keep me from being turned over to the Judeans. But the truth is that my empire does not belong here."

			³⁷"So you are a king!" said Pilate.
Jesus said, "If you say so."	And in response he says to him, "If you say so."	In response he said to him, "If you say so."	"You're the one saying I'm a king," responded Jesus. "This is what I was born for, and this is why I came into the world: to testify to the truth. Everyone who belongs to the truth listens to my voice." ^{38a}"What is the truth?" says Pilate.

328. Jesus or Barabbas? (Jn)

SEE #252, P. 198

Mt 27:15, 17, 16	Mk 15:6, 8, 7	Lk 23:4, 18–19	Jn 18:38b–40
		⁴And Pilate said to the chief priests and the crowds, "In my judgment there is no case against this man."	^{38b}When he had said this, he again went out to the Judeans. "In my judgment there is no case against him," he says to them.
¹⁵At each festival it was the custom for the governor to set one prisoner free for the crowd, whichever one they wanted. ¹⁷When the crowd had gathered, Pilate said to them, "Do you want me to set Jesus^a Barabbas free for you or Jesus who is known as 'the Anointed One'?"	⁶At each festival it was the custom for ⟨the Roman governor⟩ to set one prisoner free for them, whichever one they requested. ⁸And when the crowd arrived, they began to demand that he do what he usually did for them.		³⁹"But it's your privilege at Passover to have me free one prisoner for you. So, do you want me to free 'the King of the Judeans' for you?"
27:20–21	15:11	¹⁸But they all cried out in unison, "Do away with this man, and set Barabbas free." (¹⁹This man had been thrown into prison for murder and for an act of insurrection carried out in the city.)	⁴⁰At this they shouted back, "Not this guy—Barabbas!"
¹⁶⟨The Romans⟩ were then holding a notorious prisoner named Jesus^a Barabbas.	⁷And one called Barabbas was being held with the insurgents who had committed murder during the insurrection.		(Barabbas was an insurgent.)

^a Mt 27:16; 17 Many mss omit *Jesus*.

329. Soldiers humiliate Jesus (Jn)

SEE # 252, 253, PP. 198, 200

Mt 27:26–30	Mk 15:15–19	Lk
[26]Then he set Barabbas free for them, but had Jesus flogged, and then turned him over to be crucified. [27]Then the governor's soldiers took Jesus into the governor's residence and surrounded him with the whole cohort ⟨of Roman troops⟩. [28]They stripped him and dressed him in a crimson cloak, [29]and they wove a crown out of thorns and put it on his head. They placed a stick in his right hand, and bowing down before him, they made fun of him, saying, "Greetings, 'King of the Judeans'!" [30]And spitting on him, they took the stick and hit him on the head.	[15]And because Pilate was always looking to satisfy the crowd, he set Barabbas free for them, had Jesus flogged, and then turned him over to be crucified. [16]And the ⟨Roman⟩ soldiers led him away to the courtyard of the governor's residence, and they summoned the whole company ⟨of troops⟩. [17]And they dressed him in purple and crowned him with a garland woven of thorns. [18]And they began to salute him: "Greetings, 'King of the Judeans'!" [19]And they kept striking him on the head with a stick, and spitting on him; and they were getting down on their knees and bowing down to him.	

Jn 19:1–3	Pt 3:2–4
[1]Then Pilate had Jesus taken away and flogged.	
[2]And the soldiers wove a crown out of thorns and put it on his head; they also dressed him up in a purple robe.	[2]And they threw a purple robe around him and sat him upon the judgment seat and said, "Judge justly, king of Israel." [3]And one of them brought a crown of thorns and set it on the head of the Master.
[3]They began marching up to him and saying,	
"Greetings, 'King of the Judeans,'" as they slapped him in the face.	[4]And others standing about would spit in his eyes, and others slapped his face, while others poked him with a rod. Some kept flogging him as they said, "Let's pay proper respect to the son of God."

330. Pilate tries to free Jesus (Jn)

Mt	Mk	Lk	Jn 19:4–15
			[4]Pilate went outside once more. "See here," he says, "I'm bringing him out to make it clear to you that in my judgment there is no case against him."
			[5]Now Jesus came outside, still wearing the crown of thorns and the purple robe.
			Pilate says to them, "Look at the man!"
			[6]When the chief priests and the police saw him, they screamed, "Crucify! Crucify!"
			"Deal with him yourselves," Pilate tells them. "You crucify him. I've told you already: I don't find him guilty of any crime."
			[7]"We have our law," the Judeans answered, "and our law says that he must die because he has made himself out to be God's son."
			[8]When Pilate heard this kind of talk he was even more afraid. [9]He went back into his residence.
			"Where are you from?" he asks Jesus.
			But Jesus didn't answer him.
			[10]"You won't speak to me?" says Pilate. "Don't you get it? I have the power to free you, and I have the power to crucify you."
			[11]"You would have no power of any kind over me," said Jesus, "unless it was given to you from above. That is why the one who turned me in to you has committed the greater sin."
			[12]At this, Pilate began to look for a way to release him. But the Judeans screamed at him, "If you free this man, you're no Friend of Caesar! Every self-appointed king is in rebellion against Caesar."
			[13]Pilate heard all this, but still he brought Jesus out and sat him on the judge's seat in the place called Stone Pavement (*Gabbatha* in Hebrew). [14](It was now about twelve noon on the day of preparation for Passover.) He says to the Judeans, "Look, here's your king."
			[15]But they screamed, "Get him out of here! Crucify him!"
			"Am I supposed to crucify your king?" asks Pilate. The chief priests answered him, "The only king we have is Caesar!"

331. Jesus carries his cross (Jn)

SEE #254, P. 200

Mt 27:26c, 31b–32	Mk 15:15c, 20b–21	Lk 23:25b–26
26c⟨Pilate⟩ turned him over to be crucified.	15c⟨Pilate⟩ turned him over to be crucified.	25bJesus he handed over to their will.
31bAnd they led him out to crucify him.	20bAnd they lead him out to crucify him.	26And as they were marching him away,
32As they were going out, they came across a Cyrenian named Simon. This man they conscripted to carry his cross.	21And they conscript someone named Simon of Cyrene, who was coming in from the country, the father of Alexander and Rufus, to carry his cross.	they grabbed someone named Simon, a Cyrenian, as he was coming in from the country. They loaded the cross on him, to carry behind Jesus.

332. Jesus is crucified (Jn)

SEE #256, P. 202

Mt 27:33–35a, 38	Mk 15:22–24a, 27	Lk 23:33
33And when they reached the place known as Golgotha (which means "Place of the Skull"), 34they gave him a drink of wine mixed with gall, but once he tasted it, he didn't want to drink it. 35aAfter crucifying him . . . 38Then they crucified two insurgents with him, one on his right and one on his left.	22And they bring him to the place Golgotha (which means "Place of the Skull"). 23And they tried to give him wine mixed with myrrh, but he didn't take it. 24aAnd they crucify him . . . 27And with him they crucify two insurgents, one on his right and one on his left.a	And when they reached the place called "The Skull," they crucified him there along with the criminals, one on his right and the other on his left.

a Mk 15:27 Some mss add a verse here, traditionally numbered 15:28: "And the scripture that says, 'And he was considered one of the lawless' was fulfilled."

333. The Inscription on the Cross (Jn)

SEE #256, P. 202

Mt 27:37	**Mk 15:26**	**Lk 23:38**
And over his head they put an inscription that identified his crime: "This is Jesus, the King of the Judeans."	And the placard, on which the charge against him was inscribed, read, "The King of the Judeans."	There was also this placard over him: "This is the King of the Judeans."a

a Lk 23:38 Many mss add that the notice "was written in Greek, Latin, and Hebrew."

Jn 19:16–17a	Pt 2:5
[16]And so, in the end, Pilate turned him over to them to be crucified. So they took Jesus, [17a]who carried the cross by himself	And he turned him over to the people on the day before their festival, known as Unleavened Bread, began.

Jn 19:16b–18	Pt 4:1a
[16b]So they took Jesus, [17]who carried the cross by himself, out to the place called Skull (known in Hebrew as *Golgotha*). [18]There they crucified him, and with him two others—one on each side, with Jesus in the middle.	 And they brought two criminals and crucified the Master between them.

Jn 19:19	Pt 4:2
Pilate also had a notice written and posted it on the cross; it read: "Jesus the Nazorean, the King of the Judeans."	And when they set up the cross, they put an inscription on it, "This is the king of Israel."

334. Reactions to the Inscription (Jn)

Mt	Mk	Lk	Jn 19:20–22
			[20]Many of the Judeans read the notice, since Jesus was crucified near the city and it was written in Hebrew, Latin, and Greek. [21]The chief Judean priests tried protesting to Pilate: "Don't write, 'The King of the Judeans,' but instead, 'This man said, "I am King of the Judeans."'" [22]Pilate answered them, "What I have written stays written."

335. Gambling for Jesus' Clothes (Jn)

SEE #256, P. 202

Mt 27:35	Mk 15:24	Lk 23:34
After crucifying him, they divided up his clothes	And they crucify him, and they divide up his clothes,	They divided up his clothes
by casting lots.	casting lots to see who would get what.	after they cast lots ⟨for them⟩.

Jn 19:23–24	Pt 4:3
[23]When the soldiers had crucified Jesus, they took his clothes and divided them into four shares, one share for each soldier. But his shirt was woven continuously without seam. [24]So they said to each other, "Let's not tear it, but toss to see who gets it." This happened so that the scripture would be fulfilled that says, "They divided my garments among them, and for my clothes they cast lots." So that is what the soldiers did.	And they piled his clothes in front of him; then they divided them among themselves and gambled for them.

336. Jesus' Loved Ones at the Cross (Jn)
= #261, P. 209

Mt 27:55–56	Mk 15:40–41	Lk 23:49	Jn 19:25–27
[55]Many women were there observing from a distance—those who had followed Jesus from Galilee to minister to him, [56]among whom were Mary of Magdala, and Mary the mother of James and Joseph, and the mother of the sons of Zebedee.	[40]Now some women were observing from a distance, among whom were Mary of Magdala, and Mary the mother of James the younger and Joses, and Salome. [41]These women had regularly followed and assisted him when he was in Galilee, along with many other women who had come up to Jerusalem in his company.	And all his acquaintances, including the women who had followed him from Galilee, were standing off at a distance watching these events.	[25]Meanwhile, Jesus' mother, his mother's sister, Mary the wife of Klopas, and Mary of Magdala were standing near his cross. [26]When Jesus saw his mother, and the disciple he loved standing nearby, he says to his mother, "Lady, here is your son." [27]Then he says to the disciple, "Here is your mother." And from that moment the disciple made her part of his family.

337. Jesus dies (Jn)
SEE #259, P. 206

Mt 27:48–49, 46, 50	Mk 15:36, 34, 37	Lk 23:36, 46
[48]And right then one of them ran and took a sponge filled with sour wine and stuck it on a stick and offered him a drink. [49]But the rest were saying, "Wait! Let's see if Elijah comes to rescue him." [46]And about three o'clock in the afternoon Jesus shouted at the top of his voice, "*Eli, Eli, lema sabachthani*" (which means "My God, my God, why have you abandoned me?"). [50]Jesus again shouted at the top of his voice and surrendered the spirit.	[36]And someone ran and filled a sponge with sour wine, stuck it on a stick, and offered him a drink, saying, "Let's see if Elijah comes to rescue him!" [34]And at three o'clock in the afternoon Jesus shouted at the top of his voice, "*Eloi, Eloi, lema sabachthani*" (which means "My God, my God, why have you abandoned me?"). [37]But Jesus let out a great shout and breathed his last.	[36]The soldiers also made fun of him. They would come up and offer him sour wine. [46]Then Jesus shouted at the top of his voice, "Father, into your hands I entrust my spirit!" Having said this, he breathed his last.

*GHeb 1:7 After they had raised him on the cross, the Father took him up into heaven to himself. (#513, p. 391)

Jn 19:28–30	Pt 5:2, 5
[28]Then, since Jesus knew that everything was now completed, he says (in order to fulfill the scripture), "I'm thirsty."	
[29]A bowl of sour wine was sitting there, and so they filled a sponge with wine, stuck it on some hyssop, and held it to his mouth.	[2]And one of them said, "Give him vinegar mixed with something bitter to drink." And they mixed it and gave it to him to drink.
[30]When Jesus had taken some wine, he said, "Now it's complete."	[5]And the Master cried out, saying, "My power, ⟨my⟩ power, you have abandoned me."
Lowering his head, he handed over the spirit.	When he said this, he was taken up.*

338. Jesus' corpse is pierced (Jn)

SEE #499, P. 370

Mt	Mk	Lk	Jn 19:31–37	Pt 4:4–5
			³¹Since it was the day of preparation, the Judeans asked Pilate to have the legs of the three broken and the bodies taken away. Otherwise their bodies would remain on the cross during the Sabbath. (You see, that Sabbath was a high holy day.)	
		23:39–41		⁴But one of those criminals reproached them and said, "We're suffering for the evil that we've done, but this man, who has become a savior of humanity, what wrong has he done to you?" ⁵And they got angry at him and ordered that his legs not be broken so he would die in agony.
			³²So the soldiers came and broke the legs of the first man, and then of the other who had been crucified with him. ³³But when they came to Jesus, they could see that he was already dead, so they didn't break his legs. ³⁴Instead, one of the soldiers jabbed him in the side with his spear, and right away blood and water came pouring out. (³⁵The one who observed this has given this testimony and his testimony is true. He knows he is telling the truth, so you too will believe.) ³⁶This happened so the scripture that says, "No bone of his shall be broken," would be fulfilled, ³⁷as well as another scripture that says, "They shall look at the one they have pierced."	

339. Jesus is buried (Jn)

SEE #262, P. 210

Mt 27:57–60	Mk 15:42–46	Lk 23:50–53
[57]It was dark when a rich man from Arimathea, by the name of Joseph,	[42]And since it was the preparation day (the day before the Sabbath), and already getting dark, [43]Joseph of Arimathea, a respected Council member,	[50]There was a man named Joseph, a Council member, a decent and upright man, [51]who had not endorsed their decision or gone along with their action. He was from the town of Arimathea in Judea, and he lived in anticipation of the empire of God.
who himself was a follower of Jesus, showed up [58]and went to Pilate and requested the body of Jesus.	who himself was anticipating the empire of God, came forward and dared to go to Pilate to request the body of Jesus. [44]And Pilate was surprised that he had died so soon. He summoned the Roman officer and asked him whether he had been dead for long. [45]And when he had	[52]This man went to Pilate and requested the body of Jesus.
Then Pilate ordered it to be turned over to him. [59]And taking the body,	been briefed by the officer, he granted the body to Joseph. [46]And he bought a shroud and took him down	[53]Then he took it down
Joseph wrapped it in a clean linen shroud	and wrapped him in the shroud,	and wrapped it in a shroud,
[60]and put it in his new tomb, which had been cut in the rock. He rolled a huge stone across the opening of the tomb and left.	and placed him in a tomb that had been hewn out of rock, and rolled a stone up against the opening of the tomb.	and laid him in a tomb cut from the rock, where no one had ever been buried.

Jn 19:38–42	Pt 2:1–2; 6:3a, 4
	Pt 2:1–2
[38]After all this, Joseph of Arimathea	[1]Joseph, the friend of Pilate and the Master, stood there. When he realized that they were about to crucify him,
—a disciple of Jesus, but a secret one because he was afraid of the Judeans— asked Pilate's permission to take Jesus' body down.	he went to Pilate and asked for the Master's body for burial. [2]And Pilate sent to Herod and asked for his body.
	Pt 6:3a, 4
Pilate agreed,	[3a]Now the Judeans rejoiced and gave his body to Joseph so that he might bury it. [4]⟨Joseph⟩ took the Master,
so Joseph came and took his body down. [39]Nicodemus, the one who had first gone to him at night, came too, bringing a mixture of myrrh and aloes weighing about seventy-five pounds. [40]So they took Jesus' body, and wound it up in strips of burial cloth along with the spices, as the Jews customarily do to bury their dead. [41]Now there was a garden in the place where he had been crucified, and a new tomb in the garden where no one had ever been laid to rest. [42]Since this tomb was handy and because it was the Jewish day of preparation, it was here that they laid Jesus.	washed ⟨his body⟩ and wound a linen ⟨shroud⟩ around him,
	and brought him to his own tomb, called "Joseph's Garden."

340. Mary of Magdala discovers the empty tomb (Jn)

SEE #264, P. 214

Mt 28:1–2	Mk 16:1–2, 4	Lk 24:1–2, 9
[1]After the Sabbath, at first light on Sunday, Mary of Magdala and the other Mary came to inspect the tomb.	[1]And when the Sabbath was over, Mary of Magdala and Mary the mother of James and Salome bought spices so they could go and anoint him. [2]And very early on Sunday they got to the tomb just as the sun was coming up.	[1]On Sunday, at daybreak, ⟨the women⟩ made their way to the tomb, bringing the spices they had prepared.
[2]And just then there was a strong earthquake. You see, a messenger of the Lord had come down from the sky, arrived ⟨at the tomb⟩, rolled away the stone, and was sitting on it.	[4]Then they look up and discover that the stone has been rolled away.	[2]They found the stone rolled away from the tomb. [9]And returning from the tomb, they related everything to the Eleven and to everybody else.
28:8	16:8	

341. Peter and the other disciple see the tomb (Jn)

SEE #268, P. 219

Mt	Mk	Lk 24:12[a]	Jn 20:3–10
		But Peter got up and ran to the tomb.	[3]So Peter and the other disciple went out and they make their way to the tomb. [4]The two of them were running along together, but the other disciple ran faster than Peter and was the first to reach the tomb. [5]Stooping down, he could see the strips of burial cloth lying there; but he didn't go in. [6]Then Simon Peter comes along behind him and went in. He too sees the strips of burial cloth there, [7]and also the cloth they had used to cover his head, lying not with the strips of burial cloth but rolled up by itself. [8]Then the other disciple, who had been the first to reach the tomb, came in. He saw all this, and he believed. [9]But since neither of them yet understood the prophecy that he was destined to rise from the dead, [10]these disciples went back home.
		He peeked in and saw only the linen wrappings,	
		and returned home, marveling at what had happened.	

[a] Lk 24:12 A few mss omit this verse.

Jn 20:1–2	Pt 12:1a; 13:1a
[1]Early on Sunday, while it was still dark, Mary of Magdala	**Pt 12:1a** Early on the Lord's day, Mary of Magdala . . .
comes to the tomb and sees that the stone has been moved away. [2]So she runs and comes to Simon Peter and the other disciple, the one that Jesus loved, and tells them, "They've taken the Master from the tomb, and we don't know where they've put him."	**Pt 13:1a** And they went and found the tomb open.

342. Jesus appears to Mary of Magdala (Jn)
= #267, P. 218

Mt	Mk 16:9–11	Lk	Jn 20:11–18
	⁹Now after he arose at daybreak on Sunday, he appeared first to Mary of Magdala, from whom he had driven out seven demons. ¹⁰She went and told those who were close to him, who were mourning and weeping. ¹¹But when those folks heard that he was alive and had been seen by her, they did not believe it.		¹¹Mary, however, stood crying outside, and in her tears she stooped to look into the tomb, ¹²and she sees two heavenly messengers in white seated where Jesus' body had lain, one at the head and the other at the feet. ¹³"Lady, why are you crying?" they ask her. "They've taken my master away," she tells them, "and I don't know where they've put him." ¹⁴No sooner had she said this than she turned around and sees Jesus standing there—but she didn't realize that it was Jesus. ¹⁵"Lady," Jesus says to her, "why are you crying? Who is it you're looking for?" Thinking that he was the gardener, she says to him, "Please, mister, if you've moved him, tell me where you've put him so I can take him away." ¹⁶"Mary," says Jesus. She turns around and exclaims in Hebrew, "*Rabbuni!*" (which means "Teacher"). ¹⁷"Let go of me," Jesus tells her, "because I have not yet ascended to the Father. But go to my brothers and tell them this: 'I'm ascending to my Father and your Father—to my God and your God.'" ¹⁸Mary of Magdala goes and reports to the disciples, "I've seen the Master," and relates everything he had told her.

343. Jesus appears to the disciples (Jn)

SEE #271, P. 221

Mt	Mk	Lk 24:36–39	Jn 20:19–20
	16:14	[36]While they were talking about this, he himself appeared among them and says to them, "Peace be with you."[a] [37]But they were terrified and frightened, and figured that they were seeing a ghost. [38]And he said to them, "Why are you upset? Why do such thoughts run through your minds? [39]You can see from my hands and my feet that it's really me. Touch me and see—a ghost doesn't have flesh and bones as you can see that I have."[b]	[19]Now that Sunday evening, the disciples had locked the doors out of fear of the Judeans, but Jesus came and stood in front of them and he greets them: "Peace." [20]Then he showed them his hands and his side. The disciples were delighted to see the Master.

[a] Lk 24:36 A few mss omit *and says to them, "Peace be with you."*
[b] Lk 24:39 Many mss add a v. 40, "As he said this, he showed them his hands and his feet," taken from John 20:20.

344. Jesus sends his disciples (Jn)

SEE #119, 271, P. 100, 221

Mt 16:19	Mk	Lk	Jn 20:21–23
28:18–20 I will give you [Peter] the keys of the empire of Heaven, and whatever you uphold on earth will be upheld in heaven, and whatever you dismiss on earth will be dismissed in heaven.*			[21]Jesus greets them again: "Peace," he says. "Just as the Father sent me, so now I'm sending you." [22]And at this he breathed over them and says, "Here's some holy spirit. Take it. [23]If you cancel anyone's sins, they are cancelled; if you retain them, they are retained."

* Ⓓ Mt 18:18 (#132, p. 110)

345. Jesus appears to Thomas (Jn)

Mt	Mk	Lk	Jn 20:24–29
			[24]Now Thomas, the one known as "the Twin," one of the Twelve, hadn't been with them when Jesus showed up. [25]So the other disciples tried to tell him, "We've seen the Master." But he responded, "Unless I see the holes the nails made, and put my finger in them and my hand in his side, I'll never believe." [26]A week later the disciples were again indoors, and this time Thomas was with them. The doors were locked, but Jesus comes and stood in front of them, and said, "Peace." [27]Then he says to Thomas, "Put your finger here, and look at my hands; take your hand and put it in my side. Stop doubting and start believing." [28]Thomas responded, "My Master! My God!" [29]"Do you believe because you've seen me?" asks Jesus. "Congratulations to those who believe without seeing."

346. First Conclusion to John's Gospel (Jn)

Mt	Mk	Lk	Jn 20:30–31
			[30]Although Jesus performed many more signs for his disciples to see than could be written down in this book, [31]these are written down so you will come to believe that Jesus is the Anointed One, the son of God—and by believing this have life in his name.

347. Jesus appears by the Sea of Tiberias (Jn)

SEE #50, P. 40

Mt	Mk	Lk 5:1–11	Jn 21:1–14	Pt 14:2–3
13:1–3	*4:1–2*	[1]It came to pass, when the crowd pressed him to hear the word of God, that he was standing by Lake Gennesaret. [2]He noticed two boats moored there at the shore; the fishermen had left them and were washing their nets. [3]He got into one of the boats, the one belonging to Simon, and asked him to put out a little from the shore. Then he sat down and began to teach the crowds from the boat. [4]When he had finished speaking, he said to Simon, "Put out	[1]Some time after these events, Jesus again appeared to his disciples by the Sea of Tiberias. This is how he did it. [2]When Simon Peter and Thomas, the one known as "the Twin," were together, along with Nathanael from Cana, Galilee, the sons of Zebedee, and two other disciples, [3]Simon Peter says to them, "I'm going fishing." "We're coming with you," they reply. They went down and got into	[2]We, the twelve disciples of the Master, continued to weep and mourn, and each one, still grieving because of what had happened, left for his own home. [3]But I, Simon Peter, and Andrew, my brother, took our fishing nets and went away to the sea. And with us was Levi, the son of Alphaeus, whom the Master . . .[a]

into deep water and lower your nets for a catch."

⁵But Simon replied, "Master, we've been hard at it all night and haven't caught a thing. But if you insist, I'll lower the nets." ⁶So they did and netted such a huge number of fish that their nets began to tear apart. ⁷They signaled to their partners in the other boat to come and lend a hand. They came and loaded both boats until they nearly sank.

⁸At the sight of this, Simon Peter fell to his knees in front of Jesus and said, "Get away from me, Master; I'm a sinful man." ⁹(You see, he and his companions were stunned at the catch of fish they had taken, ¹⁰as were James and John, sons of Zebedee and partners of Simon.)

4:18–22 *1:16–20*

Jesus said to Simon, "Don't be afraid; from now on you'll be catching people." ¹¹They then brought their boats to shore, abandoned everything, and followed him.

the boat, but that night they didn't catch a thing.

⁴It was already getting light when Jesus appeared on the shore, but his disciples didn't recognize that it was Jesus.

⁵"You boys haven't caught any fish, have you?" Jesus asks them.

"No," they replied.

⁶He told them, "Cast your net on the right side of the boat and you'll have better luck."

So they cast the net, but then couldn't haul it in because of the huge number of fish. ⁷That disciple whom Jesus loved exclaims to Peter, "It's the Master!"

When Simon Peter heard, "It's the Master," he tied his cloak around himself, since he was stripped for work, and threw himself into the water. ⁸The rest of the disciples came by boat, dragging the net full of fish. (Actually, they were not far from land, only about a hundred yards.)

⁹When they got to shore, they see a charcoal fire burning, with fish cooking on it, and some bread. ¹⁰Jesus says to them, "Bring some of the fish you've just caught."

¹¹Then Simon Peter went aboard and ⟨helped⟩ haul in the net full of large fish ashore—one hundred fifty-three of them. Even though there were so many of them, the net still didn't tear.

¹²Jesus says to them, "Come on, eat."

None of the disciples dared ask, "Who are you?" They knew it was the Master. ¹³Jesus comes, takes the bread, and gives it to them, and passes the fish around as well.

¹⁴This was now the third time after he had been raised from the dead that Jesus appeared to his disciples.

ᵃPt 14:3 At this point in the ms the text breaks off abruptly.

348. Second Conclusion to John's Gospel (Jn)

Mt	Mk	Lk	Jn 21:15–25
			[15]When they had eaten, Jesus asks Simon Peter, "Simon, son of John, do you love me more than they do?" "Of course, Master; you know I love you," he replies. "Then feed my lambs," Jesus tells him. [16]Jesus asks him again, for the second time, "Simon, son of John, do you love me?" "Yes, Master; you know I love you," he replies. "Tend my sheep." [17]Jesus says to him a third time, "Simon, son of John, do you love me?" Peter was hurt that he had asked him for the third time, "Do you love me?" and he says to him, "Master, you know everything; you know I love you." Jesus says to him, "Feed my sheep. [18]Let me tell you this: when you were young you used to gather your cloak about you and go where you wanted to go. But when you've grown old, you'll stretch out your arms, and someone else will get you ready and take you where you don't want to go." ([19]He said this to indicate the kind of death by which Peter would glorify God.) And after saying this, he adds, "Keep following me." [20]Peter turns and sees the disciple Jesus loved following them, the one who had leaned back on Jesus' chest at supper and asked, "Master, who's going to turn you in?" [21]When Peter saw this disciple ⟨following⟩, he asks Jesus, "Master, what about this one?" [22]Jesus replies to him, "What's it to you if I want him to stay around till I come? You keep on following me." ([23]Because of this the rumor spread among the family of believers that this disciple wouldn't die. But Jesus had not said to him, "He won't die"; he said, "What's it to you if I want him to stay around till I come?") [24]This is the disciple who is testifying to all this and has written it down, and we know that his testimony is truthful. [25]Jesus of course did many other things. If they were all to be recorded in detail, I doubt that the entire world would hold the books that would have to be written.

The Q Gospel

―――――― ❧ ――――――

349. Introduction of John the Baptizer (Q)

SEE #3, P. 10

Mk	Mt 3:1, 5	Q 3:2–3[a]	Lk 3:2–3
1:5	[1]In due course John the Baptizer appears in the Judean desert [5]Then Jerusalem, and all Judea, and all the region around the Jordan streamed out to him, [6]and got baptized in the Jordan River by him, admitting their sins.	[2]John . . . [3]the whole region around the Jordan . . .	[2]while Annas and Caiaphas were chief priests, the word of God came to John, son of Zechariah, in the desert. [3]And he went into the whole region around the Jordan, calling for baptism and a change of heart that lead to forgiveness of sins.

[a] Q 3:2–3 These are the only words that can be reconstructed with any confidence.

350. The Preaching of John the Baptizer (Q)

SEE #4, P. 11

Mt 3:7–10	Q 3:7–9	Lk 3:7–9
[7]When he saw that many of the Pharisees and Sadducees were coming for baptism, John said to them, "You spawn of Satan! Who warned you to flee from the impending doom? [8]Well then, start producing fruit suitable for a change of heart, [9]and don't even think of saying to yourselves, "We have Abraham for our father." Let me tell you, God can raise up children for Abraham right out of these rocks! [10]Even now the axe is aimed at the root of the trees. So every tree not producing choice fruit gets cut down and tossed into the fire.	[7]John would say to the crowds that came out to get baptized, "You spawn of Satan! Who warned you to flee from the impending doom? [8]Well then, start producing fruit suitable for a change of heart, and don't even think of saying to yourselves, "We have Abraham for our father." Let me tell you, God can raise up children for Abraham right out of these rocks! [9]Even now the axe is aimed at the root of the trees. So every tree not producing choice fruit gets cut down and tossed into the fire.	[7]So John would say to the crowds that came out to get baptized by him, "You spawn of Satan! Who warned you to flee from the impending doom? [8]Well then, start producing fruits suitable for a change of heart, and don't even start saying to yourselves, "We have Abraham for our father." Let me tell you, God can raise up children for Abraham right out of these rocks! [9]Even now the axe is aimed at the root of the trees. So every tree not producing choice fruit gets cut down and tossed into the fire.

351. Someone More Powerful than John (Q)

SEE #5, P. 12

Mk	Mt 3:11–12	Q 3:16–17	Lk 3:16–17	Jn
1:7–8	[11]I baptize you with water for a change of heart, but someone more powerful than I will succeed me. I'm not fit to take off his sandals. He'll baptize you with holy spirit and fire. [12]His pitchfork is in his hand, and he'll make a clean sweep of his threshing floor, and gather the wheat into his granary, but the chaff he'll burn in a fire that can't be put out.	[16]I baptize you with water, but someone more powerful than I will succeed me. I'm not fit to take off his sandals. He'll baptize you with holy spirit and fire. [17]His pitchfork is in his hand, and he'll make a clean sweep of his threshing floor, and gather the wheat into his granary, but the chaff he'll burn in a fire that can't be put out.	[16]I baptize you with water; but someone more powerful than I is coming. I'm not fit to untie his sandal straps. He'll baptize you with holy spirit and fire. [17]His pitchfork is in his hand, to make a clean sweep of his threshing floor and to gather the wheat into his granary, but the chaff he'll burn in a fire that can't be put out.	1:26–27

352. Jesus is baptized (Q)

SEE #6, P. 13

Mk	Mt 3:16–17	Q 3:21–22[a]	Lk 3:21–22	Jn
1:9–11	[16]Right after Jesus had been baptized, he got up out of the water, and—amazingly—the skies opened up and he saw God's spirit coming down on him like a dove, perching on him, [17]and—listen!—there was a voice from the skies, which said, "This is my son, the one I love—I fully approve of him."	[21]Jesus . . . baptized, the sky opened up [22]and the spirit . . . on him . . . son . . .	[21]And it came to pass when all the people were baptized, and after Jesus had been baptized and while he was praying, that the sky opened up, [22]and the holy spirit came down on him in bodily form like a dove, and a voice came from the sky, "You are my son; today I have fathered you."[b]	*1:32*

[a] Q 3:21–22 These are the only words that can be reconstructed with any confidence.

[b] Lk 3:22 Most mss read "You are my son, the one I love—I fully approve of you."

353. Jesus is tempted (Q)*

SEE #8, P. 15

Mt 4:1–11	Q 4:1–4, 9–12, 5–8, 13	Lk 4:1–4, 9–12, 5–8, 13
[1]Then Jesus was guided into the desert by the spirit to be put to the test by the devil. [2]And after he had fasted forty days and forty nights, he was famished.	[1]Jesus was guided into the desert by the spirit [2]to be put to the test by the devil. He ate nothing for forty days and forty nights he was famished.	[1]Jesus departed from the Jordan full of holy spirit and was guided by the spirit into the desert, [2]where he was put to the test by the devil for forty days. He ate nothing that whole time; and when it was all over, he was famished.
[3]And the tester confronted him and said, "To prove you're God's son, order these stones to turn into bread."	[3]The devil said to him, "To prove you're God's son, order these stones to turn into bread."	[3]The devil said to him, "To prove you're God's son, order this stone to turn into bread."
[4]He responded, "It is written, 'Human beings shall not live on bread alone, but on every word that comes from God's mouth.'"	[4]Jesus responded, "It is written, 'Human beings shall not live on bread alone.'"	[4]Jesus responded to him, "It is written, 'Human beings shall not live on bread alone.'"
[5]Then the devil conducts him to the holy city, sets him on the high point of the temple, [6]and says to him, "To prove you're God's son, jump off; remember, it is written, 'To his heavenly messengers he will give orders about you,' and 'With their hands they will catch you, so you won't even stub your toe on a stone.'"	[9]Then the devil took him to Jerusalem, set him on the high point of the temple, and said to him, "To prove you're God's son, jump off; [10]remember, it is written, 'To his heavenly messengers he will give orders about you,' [11]and 'With their hands they will catch you, so you won't even stub your toe on a stone.'"	[9]Then he took him to Jerusalem, set him on the high point of the temple, and said to him, "To prove you're God's son, jump off from here; [10]remember, it is written, 'To his heavenly messengers he will give orders about you, to protect you,' [11]and 'With their hands they will catch you, so you won't even stub your toe on a stone.'"
[7]Jesus said to him, "Elsewhere it is written, 'You shall not put the Lord your God to the test.'"	[12]And in response Jesus said to him, "It is written, 'You shall not put the Lord your God to the test.'"	[12]And in response Jesus said to him, "It is said, 'You shall not put the Lord your God to the test.'"
[8]Again the devil takes him to a very high mountain and shows him all the empires of the world and their splendor, [9]and says to him, "I'll give you all these, if you will kneel down and pay homage to me."	[5]Then the devil takes him to a very high mountain and shows him all the empires of the world and their splendor, [6]and says to him, "I'll give you all these, [7]if you will kneel down and pay homage to me."	[5]Then he took Jesus up, and in an instant of time showed him all the empires of the civilized world. [6]The devil said to him, "I'll give you authority over all this and the glory that comes with it; it has been turned over to me, and I can give it to anyone I want. [7]So, if you will pay homage to me, it will all be yours."
[10]Finally Jesus says to him, "Get out of here, Satan! Remember, it is written, 'You shall pay homage to the Lord your God, and him alone shall you revere.'"	[8]Jesus responded, "It is written, 'You shall pay homage to the Lord your God, and him alone shall you revere.'"	[8]Jesus responded, "It is written, 'You shall pay homage to the Lord your God, and him alone shall you revere.'"
[11]Then the devil leaves him, and heavenly messengers arrive out of nowhere and look after him.	[13]And the devil left him.	[13]So when the devil had tried every kind of test, he let him alone, for the time being.

*Mk 1:12–13 (#8, p. 15)

354. Congratulations and Curses (Q)

SEE #44, P. 35

Mk	Mt 5:2–12	Q 6:20–26	Lk 6:20–26	Th
	[2]He then began to speak, and this is what he would teach them:	[20]Then he looked squarely at his disciples and said,	[20]Then he would look squarely at his disciples and say:	
	[3]Congratulations to the poor in spirit! The empire of Heaven belongs to them.	Congratulations, you poor! God's empire belongs to you.	Congratulations, you poor! God's empire belongs to you.	54
	[5]Congratulations to the gentle! They will inherit the earth.			
	[6]Congratulations to those who hunger and thirst for justice! They will have a feast.	[21]Congratulations, you hungry! You will have a feast.	[21]Congratulations, you hungry! You will have a feast.	69:2
	[4]Congratulations to those who grieve! They will be consoled.	Congratulations, you who grieve! You will be consoled.	Congratulations, you who weep now! You will laugh.	
	[7]Congratulations to the merciful! They will receive mercy.			
	[8]Congratulations to those whose motives are pure! They will see God.			
	[9]Congratulations to those who work for peace! They will be called God's children.			
	[10]Congratulations to those who have suffered persecution for the sake of justice! The empire of Heaven belongs to them.			
	[11]Congratulations to you when they denounce you and persecute you and spread malicious gossip[a] about you because of me. [12]Rejoice and be glad!	[22]Congratulations to you when they denounce you and persecute you and spread malicious gossip about you because of the Human One. [23]Rejoice and be glad!	[22]Congratulations to you when people hate you, and when they ostracize you and spread malicious gossip about you and scorn your name as evil, because of the Human One! [23]Rejoice on that day and jump for joy! Because look:	68
	Your reward is great in heaven. Remember, that is how they persecuted the prophets who preceded you.	Your reward is great in heaven. Remember, this is how they persecuted the prophets who preceded you. ?[24]?*Damn you rich!* *You already have your consolation.* ?[25]?*Damn you who are well-fed now!* *You will know hunger.* *Damn you who laugh now!*	your reward is great in heaven. Bear in mind that their ancestors treated the prophets the same way. [24]Damn you rich! You already have your consolation. [25]Damn you who are well-fed now! You will know hunger. Damn you who laugh now!	

Mk	Mt 5:2–12	Q 6:20–26	Lk 6:20–26	Th
		You will learn to weep and grieve. *[26?]Damn you when everybody speaks well of you! Bear in mind that their ancestors treated the phony prophets the same way.*[b]	You will learn to weep and grieve. [26]Damn you when everybody speaks well of you! Bear in mind that their ancestors treated the phony prophets the same way.	

[a] Mt 5:11 A few mss add "tell lies" to the triad of *denounce and persecute and spread malicious gossip.*

[b] Q 6:24–26 SV includes these verses in Q; IQP does not.

355. Love your enemies (Q)

SEE #45, P. 36

Mt 5:44–45, 39b–42	Q 6:27–28, 35, 29, [QMt 5:41, 6:30]	Lk 6:27b–28, 35, 29–30
[44]Love your enemies	[27]Love your enemies	[27b]Love your enemies, do good to those who hate you, [28]bless those who curse you, pray for your abusers.
and pray for your persecutors.	[28]and pray for your persecutors.	[35]But love your enemies, and do good, and lend, expecting nothing in return. Your reward will be great, and you'll be children of the Most High.
[45]You'll then become children of your Father in the heavens, for God makes the sun rise on both the bad and the good, and sends rain on both the just and the unjust.	[35]You'll then become children of your Father, for God makes the sun rise on both the bad and the good, and sends rain on both the just and the unjust.	As you know, the Most High is generous to the ungrateful and the evil.
[39b]When someone slaps you on the right cheek, turn the other as well.	[29]When someone slaps you on the cheek,[a] turn the other as well.	[29]When someone strikes you on the cheek, offer the other as well.
[40]If someone is determined to sue you for your shirt, let him have your coat along with it.	If someone is determined to sue you for your shirt, let him have your coat along with it.	If someone takes away your coat, don't prevent him from taking your shirt along with it.
[41]Further, when anyone conscripts you for one mile, go along an extra mile.	[QMt 5:41]*Further, when anyone conscripts you for one mile, go along an extra mile.*	
[42]Give to those who beg from you; and don't turn away those who want to borrow from you.	[30]Give to those who beg from you; and when someone borrows your things, don't ask for them back.	[30]Give to everyone who begs from you; and when someone takes your things, don't ask for them back.

[a] Q 6:29 *cheek*: It is possible that Q read "right cheek" as in Matt 5:39.

356. The Golden Rule (Q)

SEE #45, P. 36

Mk	Mt 7:12; 5:46–48	Q 6:31–32, 34, 36	Lk 6:31–36	Th
	Mt 7:12 Always treat people the way you want them to treat you. This sums up the Law and the Prophets. **Mt 5:46–48** [46]If you love those who love you, why should you be rewarded for that? Even the toll collectors do as much, don't they? [47]And if you greet only your friends, what have you done that is exceptional? Even the pagans[a] do as much, don't they?	[31]Treat people the way you want them to treat you. [32]If you love those who love you, why should you be rewarded for that? Even the toll collectors do as much, don't they? *[34]And if you lend to those from whom you hope to gain, why should you be rewarded for that?* Even the pagans do as much, don't they?	[31]Treat people the same way you want them to treat you. [32]If you love those who love you, what merit is there in that? After all, even sinners love those who love them. [33]And if you do good to those who do good to you, what merit is there in that? After all, even sinners do as much. [34]And if you lend to those from whom you hope to gain, what merit is there in that? Even sinners lend to sinners, in order to get as much in return. [35]But love your enemies, and do good, and lend, expecting nothing in return. Your reward will be great, and you'll be children of the Most High. As you know, the Most High is generous to the ungrateful and the evil.	95:1–2
	5:45	6:35		
	[48]To sum up, you shall be perfect, in the same way your heavenly Father is perfect.	[36]Be as compassionate as your Father is.	[36]Be as compassionate as your Father is.	

[a] Mt 5:47 Many mss read "toll collectors" instead of *pagans*.

357. On Passing Judgment (Q)

SEE #46, P. 37

Mk	Mt 7:1–2; 15:14; 10:24–25a	Q 6:37–40	Lk 6:37–40	other
	Mt 7:1–2 ¹Don't pass judgment, so you won't be judged. ²Don't forget, the judgment you hand out will be the judgment you get back.	³⁷Don't pass judgment, so you won't be judged. *Don't forget, the judgment you hand out will be the judgment you get back.*	³⁷Don't pass judgment, and you won't be judged;	
			don't condemn, and you won't be condemned; forgive, and you'll be forgiven. ³⁸Give, and it'll be given to you: they'll put in your lap a full measure, packed down, sifted, and over-flowing.	
4:24	And the standard you apply will be the standard applied to you.	³⁸And the standard you apply will be the standard applied to you.	For the standard you apply will be the standard applied to you. ³⁹And he posed a riddle for them:	
	Mt 15:14 They are blind guides of blind people! If one blind person guides another, both will end up in some ditch. **Mt 10:24–25a** ²⁴Students are not above their teachers, nor slaves above their masters. ²⁵ªIt's enough for students to become like their teachers and slaves to be like their masters.	³⁹Can one blind person guide another? Won't they both end up in some ditch? ⁴⁰Students are not above their teachers. It's enough for students to become like their teachers.	Can one blind person guide another? Won't they both end up in some ditch? ⁴⁰Students are not above their teachers. But those who are fully taught will be like their teachers.	Th 34 Jn 13:16, 15:20

358. Wood in the Eye (Q)

SEE #46, P. 37

Mk	Mt 7:3–5	Q 6:41–42	Lk 6:41–42	Th
	³Why do you notice the sliver in your friend's eye, but overlook the timber in your own? ⁴How can you say to your friend, "Let me get the sliver out of your eye," when there is that timber in your own? ⁵You phony, first take the timber out of your own eye and then you'll see well enough to remove the sliver from your friend's eye.	⁴¹Why do you notice the sliver in your friend's eye, but overlook the timber in your own? ⁴²How can you say to your friend, "Let me get the sliver out of your eye," when there is that timber in your own? You phony, first take the timber out of your own eye and then you'll see well enough to remove the sliver from your friend's eye.	⁴¹Why do you notice the sliver in your friend's eye, but overlook the timber in your own? ⁴²How can you say to your friend, "Friend, let me get the sliver in your eye," when you don't notice the timber in your own? You phony, first take the timber out of your own eye and then you'll see well enough to remove the sliver in your friend's eye.	26:1 26:2

359. By Their Fruits (Q)

SEE #47, P. 38

Mk	Mt 7:18; 12:33; 7:16; 12:35, 34	Q 6:43–45	Lk 6:43–45	Th
	Mt 7:18 A healthy tree cannot produce spoiled fruit, any more than a rotten tree can produce choice fruit. **Mt 12:33** If you make the tree choice, its fruit will be choice; if you make the tree rotten, its fruit will be rotten. After all, the tree is known by its fruit. **Mt 7:16** You'll know who they are by what they produce. Since when do people pick grapes from thorns or figs from thistles? **Mt 12:35, 34** ³⁵The good person produces good things out of a fund of good; and the evil person produces evil things out of a fund of evil. ³⁴You spawn of Satan, how can your speech be good when you are evil? As you know, the mouth gives voice to what the heart is full of.	⁴³A choice tree does not produce rotten fruit, any more than a rotten tree produces choice fruit; ⁴⁴for each tree is known by its fruit. Since when are figs picked from thorns, or grapes from thistles? ⁴⁵The good person produces good things out of a fund of good; and the evil person produces evil things out of a fund of evil. As you know, the mouth gives voice to what the heart is full of.	⁴³A choice tree does not produce rotten fruit, any more than a rotten tree produces choice fruit; ⁴⁴for each tree is known by its fruit. Figs are not gathered from thorns, nor are grapes picked from brambles. ⁴⁵The good person produces good from the fund of good in the heart, and the evil person produces evil from the evil within. As you know, the mouth gives voice to what the heart is full of.	 45:1 45:2–3

360. Foundations (Q)

SEE #48, 49, P. 39

Mt 7:21, 24–27	Q 6:46–49	Lk 6:46–49
[21]Not everyone who addresses me as "Master, master," will get into the empire of Heaven—only those who carry out the will of my Father in heaven. [24]Everyone who listens to these words of mine and acts on them will be like a prudent man who built a house on bedrock. [25]Later the rain fell, and the torrents came, and the winds blew and pounded that house, yet it did not collapse, since its foundation rested on bedrock. [26]Everyone who listens to these words of mine and doesn't act on them will be like a stupid man, who built a house on sand. [27]When the rain fell, and the torrents came, and the winds blew and pounded that house, it collapsed —it totally collapsed.	[46]Why do you call me "Master, master," and not do what I tell you? [47]Everyone who listens to my words and acts on them [48]is like a person who built a house on bedrock. Later the rain fell, and the floods came, and the winds blew and pounded that house, yet it did not collapse, since its foundation rested on bedrock. [49]Everyone who listens ⟨to my words⟩ and doesn't act ⟨on them⟩ is like a person who built a house on sand. When the rain fell, and the floods came, and the winds blew and pounded that house, it collapsed —it totally collapsed.	[46]Why do you call me "Master, master," and not do what I tell you? [47]Everyone who comes to me and pays attention to my words and acts on them—I'll show you what such a person is like: [48]That one is like a person building a house, who dug deep and laid the foundation on bedrock; when a flood came, the torrent slammed against that house, but could not shake it, because it was well built. [49]But the one who listens ⟨to my words⟩ and doesn't act ⟨on them⟩ is like a person who built a house on the ground without a foundation; when the torrent slammed against it, it immediately collapsed. And so the ruin of that house was total.

361. An official's boy is healed (Q)

SEE #52, P. 42

Mk	Mt 8:5–10	Q 7:1, 3, 6–9	Lk 7:1–9	Jn 4:46–53
	7:28	¹And so it happened that, when he had completed this discourse, he went into Capernaum.	¹After he had completed all he had to say to his audience, he went into Capernaum.	
	⁵When he had entered Capernaum,			
			²A Roman officer had a slave he was very fond of but who was sick and about to die. ³So when he heard about Jesus, the officer sent some elders of the Jewish community to him, and asked him to come and cure his slave. ⁴When they came to Jesus, they pleaded with him urgently, saying, "He deserves to have you do this for him ⁵because he loves our people, and even built a meeting place for us."	
	a Roman officer approached him and pleaded with him, ⁶"Sir, my servant boy was struck down with paralysis and is in terrible pain."	³A Roman officer approached him and pleaded with him, "My servant boy is sick."		
	⁷And he said to him, "I'll come and cure him."	And Jesus said to him, "I'll come and cure him."	⁶So Jesus went with them. When he got close to the house, the officer dispatched friends to say to him, "Don't trouble yourself, sir, for	
	⁸And the officer replied, "Sir,	⁶And the officer replied, "Sir,	I don't deserve to have you in my house; ⁷that's why I didn't presume to come to you in person.	
	I don't deserve to have you in my house,	I don't deserve to have you in my house,		
	but only say the word and my boy will be cured. ⁹After all, I myself am under orders, and I have soldiers under me. I order one to go, and he goes; I order another to come, and he comes; and I order my slave to do something, and he does it."	⁷but only say the word and my boy will be cured. ⁸After all, I myself am under orders, and I have soldiers under me. I order one to go, and he goes; I order another to come, and he comes; and I order my slave to do something, and he does it."	Just say the word, and let my boy be cured. ⁸After all, I myself am under orders and I have soldiers under me. I order one to go, and he goes; I order another to come, and he comes; and I order my slave to do something, and he does it."	
	¹⁰As Jesus listened he was amazed and said to those who followed,	⁹As Jesus listened he was amazed and said to those who followed,	⁹As Jesus listened to this he was amazed at him. He turned and said to the crowd that followed,	
	"Let me tell you, I have not found such trust in a single Israelite."	"I'm telling you, not even in Israel have I found such trust."	"I'm telling you, not even in Israel have I found such trust."	

362. Messengers from John the Baptizer (Q)

SEE #54, P. 44

Mt 11:2–6	Q 7:18–19, 22–23	Lk 7:18–23
[2]While John was in prison he heard about what the Anointed One had been doing and he sent his disciples [3]to ask, "Are you the one who is to come, or do we have to wait for another?"	[18]When John heard about all these things, he sent his disciples [19]to ask him, "Are you the one who is to come, or do we have to wait for another?"	[18]John's disciples reported all these things to him. [19]John summoned a couple of his disciples and sent them to the Master to ask, "Are you the one who is to come, or do we have to wait for someone else?" [20]And when the men came to Jesus, they said, "John the Baptizer sent us to you to ask: 'Are you the one who is to come, or do we have to wait for someone else?'" [21]Jesus had just cured many of their diseases and plagues and evil spirits, and restored sight to many who were blind.
[4]And so Jesus answered them, "Go report to John what you have heard and seen: [5]the blind see again and the lame walk; lepers are cleansed and the deaf hear; the dead are raised, and the poor have the good news preached to them. [6]Congratulations to those who don't take offense at me."	[22]And so he answered them, "Go report to John what you have heard and seen: the blind see again and the lame walk; lepers are cleansed and the deaf hear; the dead are raised, and the poor have the good news preached to them. [23]Congratulations to those who don't take offense at me."	[22]And so he answered them, "Go report to John what you have seen and heard: the blind see again, the lame walk, lepers are cleansed, the deaf hear, the dead are raised, and the poor have the good news preached to them. [23]Congratulations to those who don't take offense at me."

363. More than a Prophet (Q)

SEE #55, P. 45

Mk	Mt 11:7–11	Q 7:24–30	Lk 7:24–30	Th
	[7]After ⟨John's disciples⟩ had departed, Jesus began to talk to the crowds about John. "What did you go out to the desert to gawk at? A reed shaking in the wind? [8]What did you really go out to see? A man dressed in fancy clothes? But wait! Those who wear fancy clothes are found in royal houses.	[24]After they had left, Jesus began to talk to the crowds about John. "What did you go out to the desert to gawk at? A reed shaking in the wind? [25]What did you really go out to see? A man dressed in fancy clothes? But wait! Those who dress fashionably are found in royal houses.	[24]After John's messengers had left, Jesus began to talk to the crowds about John. "What did you go out to the desert to gawk at? A reed shaking in the wind? [25]What did you really go out to see? A man dressed in fancy clothes? But wait! Those who dress fashionably and live in luxury are found in palaces.	78:1–3
	[9]Come on, what did you go out to see? A prophet? Yes, that's what you went out to see, and even more than a prophet. [10]This is the one about whom it was written: 'Here is my messenger, whom I send on ahead of you to prepare your way before you.' [11]Let me tell you, among those born of women no one has arisen who is greater than John the Baptizer; yet the least ⟨important⟩ in the empire of Heaven is greater than he is."	[26]Come on, what did you go out to see? A prophet? Yes, that's what you went out to see, and even more than a prophet. [27]This is the one about whom it was written: 'Here is my messenger, whom I send on ahead of you to prepare your way before you.' [28]I'm telling you, among those born of women no one has arisen who is greater than John; yet the least ⟨important⟩ in the empire of God is greater than he is." (*[29]After all, John came to you . . . toll collectors and . . .*[a] *but the Pharisees and the legal experts* didn't believe him.)	[26]Come on, what did you go out to see? A prophet? Yes, that's what you went out to see, and even more than a prophet. [27]This is the one about whom it was written: 'Here is my messenger, whom I send on ahead of you to prepare your way before you.' [28]I'm telling you, among those born of women none is greater than John; yet the least ⟨important⟩ in the empire of God is greater than he is." ([29]All the people, even the toll collectors, who were listening and had been baptized by John, vindicated God's plan; [30]but the Pharisees and the legal experts, who had not been baptized by him, subverted God's plan for themselves.)	46:1–2

[a] Q 7:29 The words describing what the toll collectors did cannot be reconstructed, but probably had the sense of "responded positively."

364. Like Children in the Marketplace (Q)

SEE #56, P. 46

Mt 11:16–19	Q 7:31–35	Lk 7:31–35
[16]What does this generation remind me of? It is like children sitting in marketplaces who call out to others, "[17]We played the flute for you, but you wouldn't dance; we sang a dirge but you wouldn't mourn." [18]Just remember, John appeared on the scene neither eating nor drinking, and they say, "He's possessed." [19]The Human One appeared on the scene both eating and drinking, and they say, "There's a glutton and a drunk, a crony of toll collectors and sinners!" Indeed, Wisdom is vindicated by her deeds.	[31]What does this generation remind me of? What is it like? [32]It is like children sitting in marketplaces who call out to others, "We played the flute for you, but you wouldn't dance; we sang a dirge, but you wouldn't weep." [33]Just remember, John appeared on the scene, eating no bread and drinking no wine, and you say, "He's possessed." [34]The Human One appeared on the scene both eating and drinking, and you say, "There's a glutton and a drunk, a crony of toll collectors and sinners!" [35]Indeed, Wisdom is vindicated by her children.	[31]What do the people of this generation remind me of? What are they like? [32]They are like children sitting in the marketplace and calling out to one another, "We played the flute for you, but you wouldn't dance; we sang a dirge, but you wouldn't weep." [33]Just remember, John the Baptizer appeared on the scene, eating no bread and drinking no wine, and you say, "He's possessed." [34]The Human One appeared on the scene both eating and drinking, and you say, "There's a glutton and a drunk, a crony of toll collectors and sinners!" [35]Indeed, Wisdom is vindicated by all her children.

365. Demands of Discipleship (Q)

SEE #137, P. 112

Mk	Mt 8:19–22	Q 9:57–62	Lk 9:57–62	Th
	[19]And one scholar came forward and said to him, "Teacher, I'll follow you wherever you go." [20]And Jesus says to him, "Foxes have dens, and birds of the sky have nests, but the Human One has nowhere to rest his head."	[57]Someone said to him, "I'll follow you wherever you go." [58]And Jesus said to him, "Foxes have dens, and birds of the sky have nests, but the Human One has nowhere to rest his head."	[57]As they were going along the road, someone said to him, "I'll follow you wherever you go." [58]And Jesus said to him, "Foxes have dens, and birds of the sky have nests, but the Human One has nowhere to rest his head." [59]To another he said, "Follow me."	86:1–2
	[21]Another of his disciples said to him, "Master, first let me go and bury my father." [22]But Jesus says to him, "Follow me, and leave it to the dead to bury their own dead."	[59]Another said to him, "Master, first let me go and bury my father." [60]But he said to him, "Follow me, and leave it to the dead to bury their own dead."	But he said, "First, let me go and bury my father." [60]Jesus said to him, "Leave it to the dead to bury their own dead; but you, go out and announce the empire of God."	
		[61]Another said, "I'll follow you, sir; but let me first say good-bye to my people at home." [62]Jesus said to him, "No one who puts his hand to the plow and looks back is qualified for the empire of God."[a]	[61]Another said, "I'll follow you, sir; but let me first say good-bye to my people at home." [62]Jesus said to him, "No one who puts his hand to the plow and looks back is qualified for the empire of God."	

[a] Q 9:61–62 SV includes these verses in Q; IQP does not.

366. The Mission of the Seventy-Two (Q)

SEE #138, P. 113

Mk	Mt 9:37–38; 10:16a, 9–10a, 11–13, 10b, 7–8a, 14–15	Q 10:2–12	Lk 10:2–12	Th
	Mt 9:37–38 [37]Then he said to his disciples, "The crop is good, but there are few to harvest it. [38]So beg the harvest boss to dispatch workers to the fields. **Mt 10:16a** Look, I'm sending you out like sheep into a pack of wolves.	[2]He would say to his disciples, "The crop is good, but there are few to harvest it. So beg the harvest boss to dispatch workers to the fields. [3]Get going; look, I'm sending you out like sheep into a pack of wolves.	[2]He would say to them, "The crop is good, but there are few to harvest it. So beg the harvest boss to dispatch workers to the fields. [3]Get going; look, I'm sending you out like lambs into a pack of wolves.	73

Mk	Mt 9:37–38; 10:16a, 9–10a, 11–13, 10b, 7–8a, 14–15	Q 10:2–12	Lk 10:2–12	Th
6:8–9	**Mt 10:9–10a** ⁹Don't get gold or silver or copper coins for spending money, ¹⁰don't take a knapsack for the road, or two shirts, or sandals, or a staff.	⁴Carry no purse, no knapsack, no sandals, no staff. Don't greet anyone on the road.	⁴Carry no purse, no knapsack, no sandals. Don't greet anyone on the road.	
6:10	**Mt 10:11–13** ¹¹Whichever town or village you enter, find out who is deserving; stay there until you leave. ¹²When you enter a house, greet it. ¹³And if the house is deserving, give it your peace blessing, but if it is unworthy, withdraw your peace blessing.	⁵Whenever you enter a house, first say, 'Peace to this house.' ⁶If peaceful people live there, your peace will rest on them. But if not, withdraw your peace blessing. ⁷*Stay at that one house, eating and drinking whatever they provide,* for workers deserve their wages. *Do not move from house to house.* ⁸Whenever you enter a town and they welcome you, eat whatever they offer you.	⁵Whenever you enter a house, first say, 'Peace to this house.' ⁶If peaceful people live there, your peace will rest on them. But if not, it will return to you. ⁷Stay at that one house, eating and drinking whatever they provide, for workers deserve their wages. Do not move from house to house. ⁸Whenever you enter a town and they welcome you, eat whatever they offer you.	
6:11	**Mt 10:10b** For "the worker deserves to be fed"			
	Mt 10:7–8a ⁷Go and announce: 'The empire of Heaven has arrived.' ⁸ᵃHeal the sick, raise the dead, cleanse the lepers, drive out demons.	⁹Cure the sick there and tell them, 'For you, God's empire has arrived.'	⁹Cure the sick there and tell them, 'For you, God's empire has arrived.'	14:4
	Mt 10:14–15 ¹⁴And if anyone will not welcome you, or listen to your words, as you are going out of that house or town shake the dust off your feet.	¹⁰But whenever you enter a town and they don't welcome you, as you are going out of that town, ¹¹shake the dust off your feet.	¹⁰But whenever you enter a town and they don't welcome you, go out into its streets and say, ¹¹'Even the dust of your town that sticks to our feet, we wipe off against you. But know this: the empire of God is arriving.'	
	10:7 ¹⁵Let me tell you, the land of Sodom and Gomorrah will be better off on judgment day than that town.	¹²I'm telling you, on that day Sodom will be better off than that town.	¹²I'm telling you, on that day Sodom will be better off than that town.	

367. Damn you, Chorazin and Bethsaida (Q)
SEE #139, P. 114

Mt 11:21–24	Q 10:13–15, ^{QMt}11:23–24	Lk 10:13–15
[21]Damn you, Chorazin! Damn you, Bethsaida! If the miracles done in you had been done in Tyre and Sidon, they would have ⟨sat⟩ in sackcloth and ashes and changed their ways long ago. [22]So I'm telling you, Tyre and Sidon will be better off on judgment day than you. [23]And you, Capernaum, you don't think you'll be exalted to heaven, do you? No; you'll go to hell. Because if the miracles done within your boundaries had been done in Sodom, Sodom would still be around. [24]So I'm telling you, the land of Sodom will be better off on judgment day than you.	[13]Damn you, Chorazin! Damn you, Bethsaida! If the miracles done in you had been done in Tyre and Sidon, they would have ⟨sat⟩ in sackcloth and ashes and changed their ways long ago. [14]But Tyre and Sidon will be better off at the judgment than you. [15]And you, Capernaum, you don't think you'll be exalted to heaven, do you? No; you'll go to hell. QMt 11:23 *Because if the miracles done within your boundaries had been done in Sodom, Sodom would still be around.* QMt 11:24 *I'm telling you, the land of Sodom will be better off on judgment day than you.*[a]	[13]Damn you, Chorazin! Damn you, Bethsaida! If the miracles done in you had been done in Tyre and Sidon, they would have sat in sackcloth and ashes and changed their ways long ago. [14]But Tyre and Sidon will be better off at the judgment than you. [15]And you, Capernaum, you don't think you'll be exalted to heaven, do you? No; you'll go to hell.

[a] QMt 11:23–24 SV includes these verses in Q; IQP does not.

368. You, Me, and the One Who Sent Me (Q)
SEE #103, P. 84

Mk	Mt 10:40	Q 10:16	Lk 10:16	Jn
9:37b	The one who welcomes you is welcoming me, and the one who welcomes me is welcoming the one who sent me.	The one who welcomes you is welcoming me, and the one who welcomes me is welcoming the one who sent me.	Whoever hears you hears me, and whoever rejects you rejects me, and whoever rejects me rejects the one who sent me.	13:20

369. Son and Father (Q)

SEE #141, P. 115

Mk	Mt 11:25–27	Q 10:21–22	Lk 10:21–22	other
	[25]At that point, Jesus responded, "I praise you, Father, master of earth and sky, because you have hidden these things from the wise and the learned but revealed them to the unsophisticated; [26]yes indeed, Father, because that is the way you want it. [27]My Father has turned everything over to me. No one knows the son except the Father, nor does anyone know the Father except the son —and anyone to whom the son wishes to reveal him."	[21]At that point he said, "I praise you, Father, master of earth and sky, because you have hidden these things from the wise and the learned but revealed them to the unsophisticated; yes indeed, Father, because that is the way you want it. [22]My Father has turned everything over to me. No one knows the son except the Father, nor does anyone know the Father except the son —and anyone to whom the son wishes to reveal him."	[21]At that moment Jesus was overjoyed by the holy spirit and said, "I praise you, Father, master of earth and sky, because you have hidden these things from the wise and the learned but revealed them to the unsophisticated; yes indeed, Father, because that's the way you want it. [22]My Father has turned everything over to me. No one knows who the son is except the Father, or who the Father is except the son —and anyone to whom the son wishes to reveal him."	Jn 3:35 Jn 13:3 Th 61:3b Jn 10:15a

370. Privileged Eyes (Q)

SEE #143, P. 116

Mk	Mt 13:16–17	Q 10:23–24	Lk 10:23b–24	Th
	[16]How privileged are your eyes because they see, and your ears because they hear. [17]Let me tell you, many prophets and just persons longed to see what you see and never saw it, and to hear what you hear and never heard it.	[23]How privileged are the eyes that see what you see! [24]I'm telling you, many prophets and kings wanted to see what you see and never saw it, and to hear what you hear and never heard it.	[23b]How privileged are the eyes that see what you see! [24]I'm telling you, many prophets and kings wanted to see what you see and never saw it, and to hear what you hear and never heard it.	38:1–2

371. The Lord's Prayer (Q)

SEE #28, P. 27

Mt 6:9–13	Q 11:2–4	Lk 11:2–4
[9]You should pray like this: Our Father in the heavens, your name be revered. [10]Your empire be established, your will be done on earth as it is in heaven. [11]Provide us with the bread we need for the day.* [12]Forgive our debts to the extent that we have forgiven[a] those in debt to us. [13]And don't make us face the test, but rescue us from the evil one.[b]	[2]When you pray, you should say: Father, your name be revered. Your empire be established. [3]Provide us with the bread we need for the day.* [4]Forgive our sins, since we too forgive everyone in debt to us. And don't make us face the test.	[2]When you pray, you should say: Father, your name be revered. Your empire be established. [3]Provide us with the bread we need day by day.* [4]Forgive our sins, since we too forgive everyone in debt to us. And don't make us face the test.

---

* GNaz 3 Provide us with the bread we need for tomorrow. (#518, p. 394)

[a] Mt 6:12 Many mss read "we forgive" instead of *we have forgiven*.

[b] Mt 6:13 At the end of the verse, many mss insert "for yours is the kingdom, the power, and the glory. Amen."

372. Ask, Seek, Knock (Q)

SEE #36, P. 31

Mk	Mt 7:7–11	Q 11:9–13	Lk 11:9–13	Th
	[7]Ask—it'll be given to you; seek—you'll find; knock—it'll be opened for you.* [8]For everyone who asks receives; everyone who seeks finds; and for the one who knocks it is opened. [9]Who among you would hand a son a stone when he's asking for bread? [10]Again, who would hand him a snake when he's asking for fish? Of course no one would! [11]So if you, worthless as you are, know how to give your children good gifts, isn't it much more likely that your Father in the heavens will give good things to those who ask him?	[9]And I'm telling you: ask—it'll be given to you; seek—you'll find; knock—it'll be opened for you.* [10]For everyone who asks receives; everyone who seeks finds; and for the one who knocks it is opened. [11]Who among you would hand a son a stone when he's asking for bread? [12]Again, who would hand him a snake when he's asking for fish? [13]So if you, worthless as you are, know how to give your children good gifts, isn't it much more likely that your Father in the heavens will give good things to those who ask him?	[9]And I'm telling you: ask—it'll be given to you; seek—you'll find; knock—it'll be opened for you.* [10]For everyone who asks receives; everyone who seeks finds; and for the one who knocks it is opened. [11]Which of you fathers would hand his son a snake[a] instead of a fish when he's asking for fish? [12]Or a scorpion when he's asking for an egg? [13]So if you, worthless as you are, know how to give your children good gifts, isn't it much more likely that the heavenly Father will give holy spirit to those who ask him?	92:1 2:1 94:1–2

---

* Jn 15:5–8; 16:23–24 (#318, 321, pp. 254, 256)

[a] Lk 11:11 Some mss insert "stone, if he asks for bread, or give him a" before *snake*.

373. The Beelzebul Controversy (Q)

SEE #69, 71, 72, PP. 56, 57

Mk	Mt 12:22–30	Q 11:14–15, 17–23	Lk 11:14–23	Th
3:22–27	[22]Then they brought to him a blind and mute person who was demon possessed, and he cured him so the mute could both speak and to see. [23]And the entire crowd was beside itself and was saying, "This man can't be the son of David, can he?"	[14]Jesus was driving out a demon that was mute, and when the demon had departed the mute man spoke. And the crowds were amazed.	[14]Jesus was driving out a demon that was mute, and when the demon had departed the mute man spoke. And the crowds were amazed.	
	[24]But when the Pharisees heard of it, they said, "This guy drives out demons only with the power of Beelzebul, the head demon."	[15]But some of them said, "He drives out demons with the power of Beelzebul, the head demon."	[15]But some of them said, "He drives out demons with the power of Beelzebul, the head demon." [16]Others were putting him to the test by demanding a sign from heaven.	
	[25]But he knew how they thought, and said to them, "Every empire divided against itself is devastated, and no town or household divided against itself can survive. [26]So if Satan drives out Satan, he is divided against himself. In that case, how can his empire survive? [27]Suppose I do drive out demons with the power of Beelzebul, then with whose power do your own people drive ⟨them⟩ out? That's why they will be your judges. [28]But if I drive out demons with the spirit of God, then the empire of God has come for you. [29]Or how can anyone enter a strong man's house and plunder his belongings, unless he first ties him up? Only then does he plunder his house. [30]Those who aren't with me are against me, and those who don't gather with me scatter.	[17]But he knew what they were thinking, and said to them, "Every empire divided against itself is devastated, and no household divided against itself can survive. [18]If Satan is divided against himself, how will his empire survive? [19]Suppose I do drive out demons with the power of Beelzebul, then with whose power do your own people drive ⟨them⟩ out? That's why they will be your judges. [20]But if I drive out demons with the finger of God, then the empire of God has come for you. [21]. . .[a] [22]. . .[a] [23]Those who aren't with me are against me, and those who don't gather with me scatter.	[17]But he knew what they were thinking, and said to them, "Every empire divided against itself is devastated, and a house divided against a house falls. [18]If Satan is divided against himself—since you claim I drive out demons with Beelzebul's power— how will his empire survive? [19]Suppose I do drive out demons with the power of Beelzebul, then with whose power do your own people drive ⟨them⟩ out? That's why they will be your judges. [20]But if I drive out demons with the finger of God, then the empire of God has come for you. [21]When a strong man is fully armed and guards his courtyard, his possessions are safe. [22]But when a stronger man attacks and overpowers him, he takes away the weapons on which he was relying and divides up his loot. [23]Those who aren't with me are against me, and those who don't gather with me scatter.	35:1–2

[a] Q 11:21–22 Q probably had some text here, but it cannot be reconstructed with any confidence. The sense of this passage was probably something like: "A strong man's home cannot be looted. But if a stronger man overpowers him, he does get looted."

374. One demon brings back seven more (Q)

SEE #148, P. 118

Mt 12:43–45	Q 11:24–26	Lk 11:24–26
[43]When an unclean spirit leaves a person, it wanders through waterless places in search of a place to rest. When it doesn't find one, [44]it then says, "I will return to the home I left." It then returns, and finds the place empty, swept, and put in order. [45]Next, it goes out and brings back with it seven other spirits more vile than itself, who enter and settle in there. So that person ends up worse off than when he or she started. That's how it will be for this evil generation.	[24]When an unclean spirit leaves a person, it wanders through waterless places in search of a place to rest. When it doesn't find one, it says, "I will go back to the home I left." [25]It then returns, and finds the place swept and put in order. [26]Next, it goes out and brings back seven other spirits more vile than itself, who enter and settle in there. So that person ends up worse off than when he or she started.	[24]When an unclean spirit leaves a person, it wanders through waterless places in search of a place to rest. When it doesn't find one, it says, "I will go back to the home I left." [25]It then returns, and finds the place swept and put in order. [26]Next, it goes out and brings back seven other spirits more vile than itself, who enter and settle in there. So that person ends up worse off than when he or she started.

375. The Sign of Jonah (Q)

SEE #150, P. 119

Mk	Mt 12:38–40, 42, 41	Q 11:16, 29–32	Lk 11:16, 29–32	Jn
8:11	[38]Then some of the scholars and Pharisees responded to him, "Teacher, we would like to see a sign from you."	[16]Some were demanding a sign from him.	[16]Others were putting him to the test by demanding a sign from heaven. [29]As more and more people were crowding around him,	6:30
8:12	[39]In response he said to them, "An evil and adulterous generation demands a sign, and no sign will be given it—except the sign of Jonah the prophet! [40]You see, just as Jonah was in the belly of a sea monster for three days and three nights, so the Human One will be in the heart of the earth for three days and three nights. [42]On judgment day, the queen of the south will be brought back to life along with this generation, and she will condemn it, because she came from the ends of the earth to listen to Solomon's wisdom. Yet take note: what is right here is greater than Solomon. [41]On judgment day, the citizens of Nineveh will come back to life along with this generation and condemn it, because they had a change of heart in response to Jonah's message. Yet take note: what is right here is greater than Jonah."	[29]But he said, "This generation is an evil generation. It demands a sign, but it will be given no sign—except the sign of Jonah! [30]You see, just as Jonah became a sign for the Ninevites, so the Human One will be a sign for this generation. [31]On judgment day, the queen of the south will be brought back to life along with members of this generation, and she will condemn them, because she came from the ends of the earth to listen to Solomon's wisdom. Yet take note: what is right here is greater than Solomon. [32]On judgment day, the citizens of Nineveh will come back to life along with this generation and condemn it, because they had a change of heart in response to Jonah's message. Yet take note: what is right here is greater than Jonah."	he began to say, "This generation is an evil generation. It demands a sign, but it will be given no sign—except the sign of Jonah! [30]You see, just as Jonah became a sign for the Ninevites, so the Human One will be a sign for this generation. [31]On judgment day, the queen of the south will be brought back to life along with members of this generation, and she will condemn them, because she came from the ends of the earth to listen to Solomon's wisdom. Yet take note: what is right here is greater than Solomon. [32]On judgment day, the citizens of Nineveh will come back to life along with this generation and condemn it, because they had a change of heart in response to Jonah's message. Yet take note: what is right here is greater than Jonah."	

376. Lamps go on lampstands (Q)

SEE #151, P. 120

Mk	Mt 5:15	Q 11:33	Lk 11:33*	Th
4:21	People do not light a lamp and put it under a bushel basket, but instead on a lampstand, where it sheds light for everyone in the house.	No one lights a lamp and then puts it in a cellar, but instead on a lampstand so that those who come in can see the light.	No one lights a lamp and then puts it in a cellar or under a bushel basket,[a] but instead on a lampstand so that those who come in can see the light.	33:2–3

* ⓓ Lk 8:16 (#79, p. 64)

[a] Lk 11:33 A few mss omit *or under a bushel basket.*

377. The eye is the body's lamp (Q)

SEE #152, P. 120

Mk	Mt 6:22–23	Q 11:34–35	Lk 11:34–35	Th
	[22]The eye is the body's lamp. It follows that if your eye is clear, your whole body will be flooded with light. [23]If your eye is clouded, your whole body will be shrouded in darkness. If, then, the light within you is darkness, how dark that can be!	[34]The eye is the body's lamp. If your eye is clear, your whole body will be flooded with light. If your eye is clouded, your whole body is shrouded in darkness. [35]If, then, the light within you is darkness, how dark that can be!	[34]Your eye is the body's lamp. When your eye is clear, your whole body is flooded with light. When your eye is clouded, your body is shrouded in darkness. [35]Take care, then, that the light within you is not darkness.	24:3 61:5

378. Damn you, Pharisees! (Q)

SEE #153, P. 121

Mk	Mt 23: 23, 25, 26, 6, 27	Q 11:42, 39b, 41, 43–44	Lk 11:42, 39–41, 43–44	Th
	23You scholars and Pharisees, you impostors! Damn you! You pay tithes on mint and dill and cumin too, but ignore the really important matters of the Law, such as justice and mercy and trust. It's these you should have practiced without ignoring the others. 25You scholars and Pharisees, you impostors! Damn you! You wash the outside of cups and plates, but inside they are full of greed and self-indulgence.	42Damn you, Pharisees! You pay tithes on mint and dill and cumin too, but ignore justice and mercy and trust. It's these you should have practiced without ignoring the others. 39bDamn you, Pharisees! You wash the outside of cups and plates, but inside they are full of greed and self-indulgence.	42Damn you, Pharisees! You pay tithes on mint and rue and every herb, but neglect justice and the love of God. It's these you should have practiced without neglecting the others. 39But the Master said to him, "You Pharisees clean the outside of cups and dishes, but inside you are full of greed and evil. 40You fools! Did not the one who made the outside also make the inside? 41Still, donate what is inside to charity, and then you'll see how everything comes clean for you.	89:1–2
12:38–39	26You blind Pharisee, first clean the inside of the cup and then the outside will be clean too. 6They love the best couches at banquets and the prominent seats in synagogues 7and respectful greetings in marketplaces and having everyone call them 'Rabbi.' 27You scholars and Pharisees, you impostors! Damn you! You're like whitewashed tombs: on the outside they look beautiful, but inside they are full of dead bones and every kind of decay.	41Clean the inside of the cup and the outside will be clean too. 43Damn you, Pharisees! You love the best couches at banquets and the prominent seats in synagogues and respectful greetings in marketplaces. 44Damn you, Pharisees! You're like unmarked graves that people walk on without realizing it.	43Damn you, Pharisees! You love the prominent seat in synagogues and respectful greetings in marketplaces. 44Damn you! You're like unmarked graves that people walk on without realizing it.	

379. Damn you, legal experts! (Q)
SEE #153, P. 121

Mk	Mt 23:4, 13	Q 11:46, 52	Lk 11:46, 52	Th
	[4]They invent heavy burdens and lay them on folks' shoulders, but they themselves won't lift a finger to move them. [13]You scholars and Pharisees, you impostors! Damn you! You slam the door of the empire of Heaven in people's faces. You yourselves don't go in, and you block the way of those trying to go in.	[46]Damn you legal experts too! You load people down with crushing burdens, but you yourselves don't lift a finger to help carry them. [52]Damn you legal experts! You slam the door of the empire of God in people's faces. You yourselves don't go in, and you block the way of those trying to go in.	[46]Damn you legal experts too! You load people down with crushing burdens, but you yourselves don't lift a finger to help carry them. [52]You legal experts, damn you! You've taken away the key of knowledge. You yourselves haven't gone in and you have blocked the way of those trying to go in.	39:1–2

380. Answering for the Blood of the Prophets (Q)
SEE #153, P. 121

Mt 23:29–36	Q 11:47–51	Lk 11:47–51
[29]You scholars and Pharisees, you impostors! Damn you! You build the tombs of the prophets and decorate the graves of the just [30]and claim, "If we had lived in the days of our ancestors, we wouldn't have joined them in spilling the prophets' blood." [31]So, you witness against yourselves: you are descendants of those who murdered the prophets, [32]and you're the spitting image of your ancestors. [33]You serpents! You spawn of Satan! How are you going to escape Gehenna's judgment? [34]Look, that is why I send you prophets and sages and scholars. Some you're going to kill and crucify, and some you're going to flog in your synagogues and hound from town to town. [35]And so all the innocent blood that has ever been shed on the earth will be on you, from the blood of innocent Abel to the blood of Zechariah, son of Baruch, whom you murdered between the temple and the altar. [36]Let me tell you, all these things are going to rain down on this generation.	[47]Damn you! You build the tombs of the prophets whom your ancestors murdered. [48]So, you witness against yourselves: you are descendants of your ancestors. [49]That's why Wisdom has said, "I will send them prophets and sages, and some of them they are always going to kill and persecute." [50]So, this generation will have to answer for the blood of all the prophets that has been shed since the world was founded, [51]from the blood of Abel to the blood of Zechariah, who perished between the altar and the sanctuary. Yes, I'm telling you, this generation will have to answer for it.	[47]Damn you! You build monuments to the prophets whom your ancestors murdered. [48]You are therefore witnesses to and approve of the deeds of your ancestors: they killed ⟨the prophets⟩ and you build ⟨monuments⟩ to them. [49]That's why the Wisdom of God has said, "I will send them prophets and apostles, and some of them they are always going to kill and persecute." [50]So, this generation will have to answer for the blood of all the prophets that has been shed since the world was founded, [51]from the blood of Abel to the blood of Zechariah, who perished between the altar and the sanctuary. Yes, I'm telling you, this generation will have to answer for it.

381. Cover ups will be exposed (Q)

SEE #100, P. 82

Mk	Mt 10:26b–27	Q 12:2–3	Lk 12:2–3	Th
4:22	[26b]There is nothing covered up that won't be exposed, or hidden that won't be made known. [27]What I say to you in the dark, say in the light, and what you hear whispered in your ear, announce from the rooftops.	[2]There is nothing covered up that won't be exposed, or hidden that won't be made known. [3]What I say to you in the dark, say in the light, and what you hear whispered in your ear, announce from the rooftops.	[2]There is nothing covered up that won't be exposed, or hidden that won't be made known. [3]And so whatever you've said in the dark will be heard in the light, and what you've whispered behind closed doors will be announced from the rooftops.	5:2 6:5–6 33:1

382. What do sparrows cost? (Q)

SEE #155 P. 123

Mt 10:28–31	Q 12:4–7	Lk 12:4–7
[28]And don't fear those who kill the body but cannot kill the soul; instead, you ought to fear the one who can destroy both the soul and the body in Gehenna. [29]What do two sparrows cost? A couple of bucks? Yet not one of them will fall to the ground without your Father's consent. [30]As for you, even the hairs on your head have all been counted. [31]So, don't be so timid; you're worth more than a flock of sparrows.	[4]And don't fear those who kill the body but cannot kill the soul; [5]instead, fear the one who can destroy both the soul and the body in Gehenna. [6]What do five sparrows cost? Five bucks? Yet not one of them will fall to the ground without your Father's consent. [7]As for you, even the hairs on your head have all been counted. So, don't be so timid; you're worth more than a flock of sparrows.	[4]I'm telling you, my friends, don't fear those who kill the body, and after that can do no more. [5]I'll show you whom you ought to fear: fear the one who can kill and then has authority to cast into Gehenna. Believe me, that's the one you should fear! [6]What do five sparrows cost? Five bucks? Yet not one of them is overlooked by God. [7]In fact, even the hairs of your head have all been counted. Don't be so timid; you're worth more than a flock of sparrows.

383. Witnessing in Public (Q)
SEE #156, 157, PP. 123, 124

Mk	Mt 10:32-33; 12:32; 10:19-20	Q 12:8-12	Lk 12:8-12	Th
	Mt 10:32-33 ³²Everyone who acknowledges me in public, I too will acknowledge before my Father in the heavens. ³³But the one who disowns me in public, I too will disown in front of my Father in the heavens.	⁸Everyone who acknowledges me in public, the Human One will acknowledge in front of God's messengers. ⁹But whoever disowns me in public will be disowned in front of God's messengers.	⁸Everyone who acknowledges me in public, the Human One will acknowledge in front of God's messengers. ⁹But whoever disowns me in public will be disowned in front of God's messengers.	
3:28–29	**Mt 12:32** And the one who speaks a word against the Human One will be forgiven; but the one who speaks a word against the holy spirit won't be forgiven, neither in this age nor in the age to come.	¹⁰And the one who speaks a word against the Human One will be forgiven; but the one who speaks a word against the holy spirit won't be forgiven.	¹⁰And everyone who utters a word against the Human One will be forgiven; but whoever blasphemes against the holy spirit won't be forgiven.	44:1–3
13:9 13:11	**Mt 10:19-20** ¹⁹And when they lock you up, don't worry about how you should speak or what you should say. It will occur to you at that moment what to say. ²⁰For it's not you who are speaking but your Father's spirit speaking through you.	¹¹And when they make you appear in front of synagogues, don't worry about how or what you should say. ¹²The holy spirit will teach you at that moment what you ought to say.	¹¹And when they make you appear in front of synagogues and haul you up before rulers and authorities, don't worry about how or in what way you should defend yourself or what you should say. ¹²The holy spirit will teach you at that very moment what you ought to say.	

384. Don't fret about life (Q)

SEE #33, P. 29

Mk	Mt 6:25-34	Q 12:22-31	Lk 12:22-31	Th
	[25]That's why I'm telling you: don't fret about your life, what you're going to eat and drink— or about your body, what you're going to wear. There's more to living than food and clothing, isn't there? [26]Take a look at the birds of the sky: they don't plant or harvest or gather into barns. Yet your heavenly Father feeds them. You're worth more than they, aren't you? [27]Can any of you add one hour to life by fretting about it?	[22]That's why I'm telling you: don't fret about your life, what you're going to eat — or about your body, what you're going to wear. [23]There's more to living than food and clothing, isn't there? [24]Think about the crows: they don't plant or harvest or gather into barns. Yet God feeds them. You're worth more than the birds, aren't you? [25]Can any of you add one hour to life by fretting about it?	[22]That's why I'm telling you: don't fret about life, what you're going to eat— or about your body, what you're going to wear. [23]Remember, there's more to living than food and clothing. [24]Think about the crows: they don't plant or harvest, they don't have storerooms or barns. Yet God feeds them. You're worth a lot more than the birds! [25]Can any of you add an hour to life by fretting about it? [26]So if you can't do a little thing like that, why worry about the rest?	36
	[28]Why worry about clothes? Notice how the wild lilies grow: they don't toil and they never spin. [29]But let me tell you, even Solomon at the height of his glory was never decked out like one of them. [30]If God dresses up the grass in the field, which is here today and is thrown into an oven tomorrow, won't ⟨God take care of⟩ you even more, you with your meager trust? [31]So don't fret. Don't say, "What are we going to eat?" or "What are we going to drink?" or "What are we going to wear?" [32]These are all things pagans seek. After all, your heavenly Father is aware that you need them all. [33]Seek God's empire and his justice first, and all these things will come to you as a bonus. [34]So don't fret about tomorrow. Let tomorrow fret about itself. The troubles that the day brings are enough.	[26]Why worry about clothes? [27]Notice how the wild lilies grow: they don't toil and they never spin. But let me tell you, even Solomon at the height of his glory was never decked out like one of them. [28]If God dresses up the grass in the field, which is here today and is thrown into an oven tomorrow, won't ⟨God take care of⟩ you even more, you with your meager trust? [29]So don't fret. Don't say, "What are we going to eat?" or "What are we going to drink?" or "What are we going to wear?" [30]These are all things pagans seek. After all, your heavenly Father is aware that you need them all. [31]Seek God's empire and all these things will come to you as a bonus.	[26]Why worry about the rest? [27]Think about how the lilies grow: they don't toil and they never spin. But let me tell you, even Solomon at the height of his glory was never decked out like one of them. [28]If God dresses up the grass in the field, which is here today and is tossed into the oven tomorrow, how much more will ⟨God take care of⟩ you, you with your meager trust. [29]And don't be constantly on the lookout for what you're going to eat and what you're going to drink. Don't give it a thought. [30]These are all things the world's pagans seek, and your Father is aware that you need them. [31]Instead, seek his empire and these things will come to you as a bonus.	

385. Treasure in Heaven (Q)
SEE #30, P. 28

Mk	Mt 6:19-21	Q 12:33-34	Lk 12:33-34	Th
	¹⁹Don't pile up possessions here on earth, where moths and insects eat away and where burglars break in and steal.	*³³Don't pile up possessions here on earth, where moths and insects eat away and where burglars break in and steal.*		76:3
	²⁰Instead, gather your nest egg in heaven, where neither moths nor insects eat away and where no burglars break in or steal. ²¹As you know, what you treasure is your heart's true measure.	Instead, gather your nest egg in heaven, where neither moths nor insects eat away and where no burglars break in or steal. ³⁴As you know, what you treasure is your heart's true measure.	³³Sell your belongings, and donate to charity; make yourselves purses that don't wear out, with inexhaustible wealth in heaven, where no burglar can get to it and no moth can destroy it. ³⁴As you know, what you treasure is your heart's true measure.	

386. Anticipating the Burglar (Q)
SEE #160, P. 125

Mk	Mt 24:43-44	Q 12:39-40	Lk 12:39-40	Th
	⁴³Mark this well: if the homeowner had known when the burglar was coming, he would have been on guard and not have allowed anyone to break into his house. ⁴⁴Therefore, you too should be prepared. Remember, the Human One is coming when you least expect it.	³⁹Mark this well: if the homeowner had known what time the burglar was coming, he would not have let anyone break into his house. ⁴⁰You too should be prepared. Remember, the Human One is coming when you least expect it.	³⁹Mark this well: if the homeowner had known what time the burglar was coming,[a] he would not have let anyone break into his house. ⁴⁰You too should be prepared. Remember, the Human One is coming when you least expect it.	21:5 *103*

[a] Lk 12:39 Many mss insert "he would have watched and" after *coming*.

387. The Trustworthy Slave and the Dismembered Slave (Q)
SEE #161, P. 126

Mk	Mt 24:45-51	Q 12:42-46	Lk 12:42-46	Th
13:35	[45]Who then is the trustworthy and prudent slave to whom the master assigns responsibility for his household, to provide them with food at the right time? [46]Congratulations to the slave who's on the job when his master arrives. [47]Let me tell you, he'll put him in charge of all his property. [48]But suppose that worthless slave says to himself, "My master is taking his time," [49]and begins to beat his fellow slaves, and starts eating and drinking with drunks, [50]that slave's master will show up on the day he least expects and at an hour he doesn't suspect. [51]He'll cut him to pieces and assign him a fate among the impostors, where they'll weep and grind their teeth.	[42]Who then is the trustworthy and prudent slave to whom the master assigns responsibility for his household, to provide them with food at the right time? [43]Congratulations to the slave who's on the job when his master arrives. [44]Let me tell you, he'll put him in charge of all his property. [45]But suppose that slave says to himself, "My master is taking his time," and begins to beat his fellow slaves, and starts eating and drinking with drunks, [46]that slave's master will show up on the day he least expects and at an hour he doesn't suspect. He'll cut him to pieces and assign him a fate among the disloyal.	[42]Who then is the trustworthy and prudent manager to whom the master assigns responsibility for his household staff, to dole out their food allowance at the right time? [43]Congratulations to the slave who's on the job when his master arrives. [44]I'm telling you the truth: he'll put him in charge of all his property. [45]But suppose that slave says to himself, "My master is taking his time getting here," and begins to beat the servants and the maids, and to eat and drink and get drunk, [46]that slave's master will show up on the day he least expects and at an hour he doesn't suspect. He'll cut him to pieces and assign him a fate among the disloyal.	

388. Jesus brings fire and conflict (Q)
SEE #162, P. 127

Mk	Mt 10:34-36	Q 12:49, 51, 53	Lk 12:49-53	Th
13:12		*[49]I came to set the earth on fire, and how I wish it were already ablaze!*	[49]I came to set the earth on fire, and how I wish it were already ablaze! [50]I have a baptism to be baptized with, and what pressure I'm under until it's over!	10 *82:1-2*
	[34]Don't get the idea that I came to bring peace on earth. I didn't come to bring peace, but a sword!	[51]Do you think I came here to bring peace on earth? I didn't come to bring peace, but a sword!	[51]Do you think I came here to bring peace on earth? No, I'm telling you, on the contrary: conflict. [52]As a result, from now on in any given house there will be five in conflict, three against two and two against three. [53]Father will be pitted against son and son against father, mother against daughter and daughter against mother, mother-in-law against daughter-in-law	16:1-3
	[35]After all, I've come to pit a man against his father, a daughter against her mother, and a daughter-in-law against her mother-in-law. [36]Your enemies live under your own roof.	[53]After all, I've come to pit a man against his father, a daughter against her mother, and a daughter-in-law against her mother-in-law.	and daughter-in-law against mother-in-law.	

389. Reading the Face of the Sky (Q)
SEE #163, P. 127

Mk	Mt 16:2-3	Q 12:54-56	Lk 12:54-56	Th
	[2]In response he said to them, "When it's evening, you say, 'It'll be fair weather because the sky looks red.' [3]Early in the morning you say, 'The day will bring winter weather because the sky looks red and dark.'	[54]He said to them, "When it's evening, you say, 'It'll be fair weather because the sky looks red.' [55]Early in the morning you say, 'The day will bring winter weather because the sky looks red and dark.'	[54]He would also say to the crowds, "When you see a cloud rising in the west, right away you say that it's going to rain; and so it does. [55]And when the wind blows from the south, you say we're in for scorching heat; and we are. [56]You phonies!	
	You know how to interpret the face of the sky, but you can't ⟨do that for⟩ the signs of the times.	[56]You know how to interpret the face of the sky, but you can't ⟨do that for⟩ the present time.	You know the lay of the land and can read the face of the sky, so why don't you know how to read the present time?	91:2

390. Settle out of court (Q)
SEE #164, P. 128

Mt 5:25-26	Q 12:58-59	Lk 12:58-59
[25]You should settle quickly with your accuser while you are both on the way ⟨to court⟩, or else your accuser will turn you over to the judge, and the judge to the bailiff, and you are thrown in jail.	[58]When you're on your way ⟨to court⟩ with your accuser, do your best to settle with him on the way, or else your accuser will turn you over to the judge, and the judge to the bailiff, and the bailiff will throw you in jail.	[58]When you're about to appear with your accuser before the magistrate, do your best to settle with him on the way, or else he might drag you up before the judge, and the judge turn you over to the jailer, and the jailer throw you in prison.
[26]Let me tell you, you'll never get out of there until you've paid the last dime.	[59]I'm telling you, you'll never get out of there until you've paid the last dime.	[59]I'm telling you, you'll never get out of there until you've paid every last cent.

391. The Parable of the Mustard (Q)
SEE #83, P. 66

Mk	Mt 13:31b-32	Q 13:18-19	Lk 13:18-19	Th
4:30–32	[31b]The empire of Heaven is like a mustard seed that a man took and sowed in his field. [32]Though it is the smallest of all seeds, when it grows up, it is the largest of garden plants, and becomes a tree, so that the birds of the sky come and roost in its branches.	[18]What is the empire of God like? What does it remind me of? [19]It's like a mustard seed that a man took and tossed into his garden. It grew and became a tree, and the birds of the sky roosted in its branches.	[18]What is the empire of God like? What does it remind me of? [19]It's like a mustard seed that a man took and tossed into his garden. It grew and became a tree, and the birds of the sky roosted in its branches.	20:1–4

392. The Parable of the Leaven (Q)
SEE #84, P. 67

Mk	Mt 13:33	Q 13:20-21	Lk 13:20-21	Th
	He told them another parable: "The empire of Heaven is like leaven that a woman took and concealed in fifty pounds of flour until it was all leavened."	[20]And again: "What does the empire of God remind me of? [21]It's like leaven that a woman took and concealed in fifty pounds of flour until it was all leavened."	[20]And again he said: "What does the empire of God remind me of? [21]It's like leaven that a woman took and concealed in fifty pounds of flour until it was all leavened."	96:1–2

393. The Narrow Door (Q)
SEE #168, P. 129

Mt 7:13–14; 25:10b–12; 7:22–23	Q 13:24–27	Lk 13:24–27
Mt 7:13–14 [13]Get in through the narrow gate. Wide and smooth is the road that leads to destruction. Many are taking that route. [14]Narrow and rough is the road that leads to life. Only a few discover it. **Mt 25:10b–12** [10b]The bridegroom arrived and those who had come prepared accompanied him to the wedding; then the door was closed. [11]The other maidens finally come and say, "Master, master, open the door for us." [12]He responded, "Let me tell you, I don't recognize you." **Mt 7:22–23** [22]On that day many will say to me, "Master, master, didn't we use your name when we prophesied? Didn't we use your name when we exorcised demons? Didn't we use your name when we performed all those miracles?" [23]Then I will tell them honestly, "I never knew you; get away from me, you subverters of the Law!"	[24]Get in through the narrow door; many will try to get in, but only a few get through it. [25]Once the master of the house gets up and bars the door, you'll be left standing outside and knocking at the door: "Master, open up for us." But he'll answer you, "I don't know you." [26]Then you'll start saying, "We ate and drank with you, and you taught in our streets." [27]But he'll reply, "I don't know you; get away from me, you subverters of the Law!"	[24]Struggle to get in through the narrow door; I'm telling you, many will try to get in, but won't be able. [25]Once the master of the house gets up and bars the door, you'll be left standing outside and knocking at the door: "Master, open up for us." But he'll answer you, "I don't know where you come from." [26]Then you'll start saying, "We ate and drank with you, and you taught in our streets." [27]But he'll reply, "I don't know where you come from; get away from me, all you evildoers!"

394. Thrown out of the Patriarchs' Banquet (Q)

SEE #169, 170, P. 130

Mk	Mt 8:11–12; 20:16	Q 13:29, 28, 30	Lk 13:28–30	Th
	Mt 8:11–12 11Many will come from east and west and dine with Abraham and Isaac and Jacob in the empire of Heaven, 12but those who think the empire of Heaven belongs to them will be thrown out into the utter darkness.	29Many will come from east and west and dine 28with Abraham and Isaac and Jacob in the empire of God, but you'll be thrown out into the utter darkness.	28There'll be weeping and grinding of teeth out there when you see Abraham and Isaac and Jacob and all the prophets in the empire of God and yourselves thrown out. 29And people will come from east and west, from north and south, and dine in the empire of God.	
10:31	There'll be weeping and grinding of teeth out there. **Mt 20:16** The last will be first and the first last.	There'll be weeping and grinding of teeth out there. 30The last will be first and the first last.	30And remember, those who will be first are last, and those who will be last are first.	4:2

395. Jerusalem, Murderer of Prophets (Q)

SEE #220, P. 171

Mt 23:37–39	Q 13:34–35	Lk 13:34–35
37Jerusalem, Jerusalem, you murder the prophets and stone those sent to you! How often I wanted to gather your children as a hen gathers her chicks under her wings, but you wouldn't let me. 38Can't you see, your house is being abandoned as a ruin? 39I'm telling you, you certainly won't see me again until you say, "Blessed is the one who comes in the name of the Lord."	34Jerusalem, Jerusalem, you murder the prophets and stone those sent to you! How often I wanted to gather your children as a hen gathers her chicks under her wings, but you wouldn't let me. 35Can't you see, your house is being abandoned? I'm telling you, you certainly won't see me until the time comes when you say, "Blessed is the one who comes in the name of the Lord."	34Jerusalem, Jerusalem, you murder the prophets and stone those sent to you! How often I wanted to gather your children as a hen ⟨gathers⟩ her own chicks under her wings, but you wouldn't let me. 35Can't you see, your house is being abandoned? I'm telling you, you certainly won't see me until the time comes when you say, "Blessed is the one who comes in the name of the Lord."

396. Promotion and Demotion (Q)

SEE #173, P. 131

Mt 23:12	Q 14:11	Lk 14:11*
Those who promote themselves will be demoted and those who demote themselves will be promoted.	Those who promote themselves will be demoted, and those who demote themselves will be promoted.	Those who promote themselves will be demoted, and those who demote themselves will be promoted.

* Ⓓ Lk 18:14b (#192, p. 144)

397. The Parable of the Dinner Guests Who Had Excuses (Q)

SEE #175, P. 132

Mk	Mt 22:2–14	Q 14:16–18, 21, 23	Lk 14:16–24	Th
	[2]The empire of Heaven is like a king who gave a wedding celebration for his son. [3]Then he sent his slaves to summon those who had been invited to the wedding, but they declined to attend.	[16]Someone was giving a big dinner and invited many guests. [17]At the dinner hour the host sent his slave to tell the guests, "Come, it's ready now."	[16]Someone was giving a big dinner and invited many guests. [17]At the dinner hour the host sent his slave to tell the guests, "Come, it's ready now."	64:1–11
		[18]⟨One excused himself because of his⟩ farm . . . ?19? . . .ᵃ ?20? . . .ᵃ [21]So the slave ⟨came back and reported⟩ these ⟨excuses⟩ to his master.	[18]But one by one they all began to make excuses. The first said to him, "I just bought a farm and I have to go and inspect it; please excuse me." [19]And another said, "I just bought five pairs of oxen and I'm on my way to check them out; please excuse me." [20]And another said, "I just got married and so I cannot attend." [21]So the slave came back and reported these ⟨excuses⟩ to his master.	
	[4]He sent additional slaves with the instructions: "Tell those invited, 'Look, the feast is ready, the oxen and fat calves have been slaughtered, and everything is set. Come to the wedding.'" [5]But they couldn't be bothered and went off, one to his own farm, one to his business, [6]while the rest seized his slaves, attacked and killed them.			
	[7]Now the king was outraged and sent his armies to destroy those murderers and burn their city. [8]Then he tells his slaves, "The wedding celebration is ready, but those we've invited didn't deserve it.	Then the master of the house was outraged and instructed his slave,	Then the master of the house was outraged and instructed his slave, "Quick! Go out into the streets and alleys of the town, and usher in the poor, and crippled, the blind, and the lame." [22]And the slave said, "Master, your orders have been carried out, and there's still room." [23]And the master said to the slave, "Then go out into the roads and the country lanes, and force people to come in so my house will be filled. [24]For I'm telling you, not one of those who were invited will taste my dinner."	
	[9]So go to the city gates and invite anybody you find to the wedding."	[23]"Go out into the streets and invite anybody you find so my house will be filled."		

Mk	Mt 22:2–14	Q 14:16–18, 21, 23	Lk 14:16–24	Th
	[10]Those slaves then went out into the streets and collected everybody they could find, the good and bad alike. And the wedding hall was full of guests. [11]The king came in to see the guests for himself and noticed this one man without proper attire. [12]And he says to him, "Look pal, how'd you get in here without dressing for the occasion?" And he was speechless. [13]Then the king ordered his waiters, "Bind him hand and foot and throw him out into the utter darkness. They'll weep and grind their teeth out there. [14]After all, many are called but few are chosen."			

[a] Q 14:19–20 Q must have had some text here, but it cannot be reconstructed. The sense of the missing verses apparently was something like: "Another excused himself because of his business. A third excused himself . . ."

398. The Price of Discipleship (Q)
SEE # 176, P. 134

Mk	Mt 10:37–38	Q 14:26–27	Lk 14:26–27	Th
	[37]If you love your father and mother more than me, you're not worthy of me, and if you love your son or daughter more than me, you're not worthy of me. [38]Unless you take your cross and come along with me, you're not worthy of me.*	[26]Unless you hate your father and mother, you cannot be my disciple; and unless you hate your son and daughter, you cannot be my disciple. [27]Unless you carry your cross and follow after me, you cannot be my disciple.*	[26]If any of you comes to me and does not hate your own father and mother and wife and children and brothers and sisters— yes, even your own life— you cannot be my disciple. [27]Unless you carry your own cross and come along with me, you cannot be my disciple.*	101:1 55:1 55:2

* Mt 16:24 / Mk 8:34 / Lk 9:23 (#121, p. 102)

399. Finding and Losing Your Life (Q)*
SEE #102, P. 83

Mk	Mt 10:39	Q 17:33	Lk 17:33	Jn
	By finding your life, you'll lose it, but by losing your life for my sake, you'll find it.	By finding your life, you'll lose it, but by losing your life for my sake, you'll find it.	Whoever tries to hang on to life will lose it, but whoever loses it will preserve it.	12:25

* Mt 16:25 / Mk 8:35 / Lk 9:24 (#121, p. 102)

400. Useless Salt (Q)
SEE #18, P. 21

Mk	Mt 5:13	Q 14:34–35	Lk 14:34–35a	Th
9:50	You are the salt of the earth. But if salt loses its zing, how will it be made salty? It's then good for nothing, except to be thrown out and stomped on.	34Salt is good, but if it loses its zing, how will it be renewed? 35It's no good for either earth or manure. It just gets thrown away.	34Salt is good, but if it loses its zing, how will it be renewed? 35aIt's no good for either earth or manure. It just gets thrown away.	

401. God or Mammon (Q)
SEE #181, P. 137

Mk	Mt 6:24	Q 16:13	Lk 16:13	Th
	No one can be a slave to two masters. That slave will either hate one and love the other, or be devoted to one and disdain the other. You can't be enslaved to both God and Mammon.	No one can be a slave to two masters. That slave will either hate one and love the other, or be devoted to one and disdain the other. You can't be enslaved to both God and Mammon.	No servant can be a slave to two masters. That slave will either hate one and love the other, or be devoted to one and disdain the other. You can't be enslaved to both God and mammon.	47:2

402. Violence and God's Empire (Q)
SEE #183, P. 138

Mt 11:12–13; 5:18	Q 16:16–17	Lk 16:16–17
Mt 11:12–13 12From the time of John the Baptizer until now the empire of Heaven has been breaking in violently, and violent men are trying to seize it. 13You see, the Prophets and the Law predicted everything up to John's time. **Mt 5:18** Let me tell you, before earth and sky pass away, not one iota, not one serif, will disappear from the Law, until it all happens.	16The Law and the Prophets were until John; since then the empire of God has been breaking in violently, and violent men are trying to seize it. 17But it's easier for earth and sky to pass away than for one iota or one serif of the Law to drop out.	16Right up to John's time you have the Law and the Prophets; since then the empire of God has been proclaimed as good news and everyone is breaking into it violently. 17But it's easier for earth and sky to pass away than for one serif of the Law to drop out.

403. On Divorce and Adultery (Q)

SEE #22, 525, PP. 23, 398

Mk	Mt 19:9*	Q 16:18	Lk 16:18	Th
10:11–12	Whoever divorces his wife, except for immorality, and marries another commits adultery.	Everyone who divorces his wife and marries another commits adultery; and the one who marries a divorced woman commits adultery.	Everyone who divorces his wife and marries another commits adultery; and the one who marries a woman divorced from her husband commits adultery.	

* Ⓓ Mt 5:32 (#22, p. 23)

404. Don't exploit the little ones (Q)

SEE #131, P. 109

Mk	Mt 18:7, 6	Q 17:1–2	Lk 17:1–2	Th
9:42	[7]Damn the world for the snares it sets! It's inevitable that traps will be set; but still, damn those who set them! [6]Any of you who entraps and exploits one of these little ones who trusts me would be better off having a millstone hung around your neck and being drowned in the deepest part of the sea!	[1]It's inevitable that traps will be set; but still, damn those who set them! [2]You'd be better off if you had a millstone tied around your neck and were dumped into the sea than to entrap and exploit one of these little ones.	[1]There's no way that traps won't be set; but still, damn those who set them! [2]You'd be better off if you had a millstone tied around your neck and were dumped into the sea than to entrap and exploit one of these little ones.	

405. The Parable of the Lost-and-Found Sheep (Q)

SEE #177, P. 135

Mk	Mt 18:12b–14	Q 15:4–5, 7	Lk 15:4–7	Th
	[12b]If someone has a hundred sheep and one of them wanders off, won't he leave the ninety-nine in the hills and go look for the one that wandered off? [13]And if he should find it,	[4]Is there any one of you who owns a hundred sheep and one of them gets lost, who wouldn't leave the ninety-nine in the hills and go look for the one that got lost? [5]And if he should find it,	[4]Is there any one of you who owns a hundred sheep and one of them gets lost, who wouldn't leave the ninety-nine in the wild and go after the one that got lost until he finds it? [5]And when he finds it, he is happy and hoists it onto his shoulders. [6]Once he gets home, he invites his friends and his neighbors over, and says to them, "Celebrate with me, because I've found my lost sheep."	107:1–3
	let me tell you, he'll rejoice over it more than over the ninety-nine that didn't wander off. [14]And so it is the intention of your Father in heaven that not one of these little ones be lost.	[7]I'm telling you, he'll rejoice over it more than over the ninety-nine that didn't wander off.	[7]I'm telling you, it'll be just like that in heaven: there'll be more celebrating over one sinner who has a change of heart than over ninety-nine virtuous people who have no need to change their hearts.	

406. The Parable of the Lost-and-Found Coin (Q)

SEE #178, P. 135

Mt	Q 15:8–10	Lk 15:8–10
	[8]*Or is there any woman with ten drachmas, who if she loses one, wouldn't light a lamp and sweep the house and search high and low until she finds it?* [9]*When she finds it, she invites her friends and neighbors over and says,* "Celebrate with me, because I've found the drachma I lost." [10]*I'm telling you, it's just like that among God's messengers: they celebrate when one sinner has a change of heart.*	[8]Or again, is there any woman with ten drachmas, who if she loses one, wouldn't light a lamp and sweep the house and search high and low until she finds it? [9]When she finds it, she invites her friends and neighbors over and says, "Celebrate with me, because I've found the drachma I lost." [10]I'm telling you, it's just like that among God's messengers: they celebrate when one sinner has a change of heart.

407. Serial Forgiving (Q)
SEE #134, 185, PP. 111, 140

Mt 18:15, 21–22	Q 17:3–4	Lk 17:3–4
[15]If some companion does wrong, go have it out between the two of you privately. If that person listens to you, you have won your companion over. [21]Then Peter came up and asked him, "Master, how many times can a companion wrong me and still expect my forgiveness? As many as seven times?" [22]Jesus replies to him, "My advice to you is not seven times, but seventy-seven times."	[3]If your companion wrongs you, scold that person; if there is a change of heart, forgive the person. [4]If someone wrongs you seven times a day, you must forgive that person seven times.	[3]So be on your guard. If your companion does wrong, scold that person; if there is a change of heart, forgive the person. [4]If someone wrongs you seven times a day, and seven times turns around and says to you, "I'm sorry," you must forgive that person.

408. How to Move Trees (Q)
SEE #186, P. 140

Mk	Mt 21:21	Q 17:6	Lk 17:6	Th
11:23	If you have trust and do not doubt, not only can you do this to a fig tree but you can even say to this mountain, "Up with you and into the sea," and that's what will happen.	If you had trust no bigger than a mustard seed, you could tell this mulberry tree, "Uproot yourself and plant yourself in the sea," and it would obey you.	If you had trust no bigger than a mustard seed, you could tell this mulberry tree, "Uproot yourself and plant yourself in the sea," and it would obey you.	48 106:2

409. Empire of God Among You (Q)
SEE #189, P. 141

Mk	Mt	Q 17:20–21	Lk 17:20–21	Th
		[20]When asked when the empire of God would come, he answered them, "You won't be able to observe the coming of the empire of God. [21]People won't be able to say, 'Look, here it is!' or 'Over there!' On the contrary, the empire of God is among you."	[20]When asked by the Pharisees when the empire of God would come, he answered them, "You won't be able to observe the coming of the empire of God. [21]People won't be able to say, 'Look, here it is!' or 'Over there!' On the contrary, the empire of God is among you."	113:1–4 3:1–3

410. The Day of the Human One (Q)

SEE #190, P. 142

Mk	Mt 24:26–28, 37–39, 17–18, 40–41	Q 17:23–24, 37, 26–30, 34–35	Lk 17:22–37	Th
			²²And he said to the disciples, "There'll come a time when you will yearn to see one of the days of the Human One, and you won't see it. ²³And they'll be telling you, 'Look, there it is!' or 'Look, here it is!'	
	²⁶If they should say to you, "Look, he's in the desert," don't go out there; or "Look, he's in one of the inner rooms," don't count on it. ²⁷For just as lightning comes out of the east and is visible all the way to the west, that's what the coming of the Human One will be like. ²⁸For wherever there's a corpse, that's where vultures gather.	²³If they should say to you, "Look, he's in the desert," don't go out there; or, "Look, he's in one of the inner rooms," don't pursue it. ²⁴For just as lightning comes out of the east and is visible all the way to the west, that's what the Human One will be like in his day. ³⁷For wherever there's a corpse, that's where vultures gather.	Don't rush off; don't pursue it. ²⁴For just as lightning flashes and lights up the sky from one end to the other, that's what the Human One will be like in his day. *v. 37*	
			²⁵But first he is destined to endure much and be rejected by this present generation.	
	³⁷The Human One's coming will be just like the days of Noah. ³⁸That's how people behaved then before the flood came: they ate and drank, married and were given in marriage, until the day Noah boarded the ark, ³⁹and they were oblivious until the flood came and swept them all away.	²⁶And just as it was in the days of Noah, that's how it will be in the day of the Human One. ²⁷That's how people behaved then: they ate and drank, married and were given in marriage, until the day Noah boarded the ark, and the flood came and swept them all away.	²⁶And just as it was in the days of Noah, that's how it will be in the days of the Human One. ²⁷They ate, drank, got married, and were given in marriage, until the day Noah boarded the ark. Then the flood came and destroyed them all.	
		⸢²⁸⸣*That's also the way it was in the days of Lot. Everyone ate, drank, bought, sold, planted, and built.* ⸢²⁹⸣*But on the day Lot left Sodom, fire and sulfur rained down from the sky and destroyed them all.*[a]	²⁸That's also the way it was in the days of Lot. Everyone ate, drank, bought, sold, planted, and built. ²⁹But on the day Lot left Sodom, fire and sulfur rained down from the sky and destroyed them all.	
	That's how it will be when the Human One comes.	³⁰It will be like that on the day the Human One is revealed.	³⁰It will be like that on the day the Human One is revealed. ³¹On that day, if any are on the roof and their things are in the house, they had better not go down to fetch them. The same goes for those in the field: they had better not turn back for anything left behind. ³²Remember Lot's wife. ³³Whoever tries to	
	¹⁷No one on the roof should go downstairs to retrieve anything; ¹⁸and no one in the field should turn back to get a coat.			

Mk	Mt 24:26–28, 37–39, 17–18, 40–41	Q 17:23–24, 37, 26–30, 34–35	Lk 17:22–37	Th
			hang on to life will lose it, but whoever loses it will preserve it.	
	[40]Then there will be two men in the field; one will be taken and one will be left. [41]Two women will be grinding at the mill; one will be taken and one left.	[34]I'm telling you, there will be two men in the field; one will be taken and one will be left. [35]Two women will be grinding at the mill; one will be taken and one left.	[34]I'm telling you, on that night there will be two on one couch; one will be taken and the other left. [35]There will be two women grinding together; one will be taken and the other left."[b] [37]Then they asked him, "Taken where, Master?" And he said to them, "Vultures collect wherever there's a carcass."	61:1
	v. 28	v. 37		

[a] Q 17:28–29 SV includes these verses in Q; IQP does not.

[b] Lk 17:35 Some mss add another verse, traditionally numbered 17:36: "Two will be in the fields; one will be taken, the other left."

411. The Parable of the Ruthless Master (Q)

SEE #203, P. 154

Mt 25:14–30	Q 19:12–13, 15–24, 26	Lk 19:12–27
[14]You know, it's like a man going on a trip who called his slaves and turned his property over to them. [15]To the first he gave five talents' worth of silver, to the second two talents' worth, and to the third one talent's worth, to each in proportion to his ability. Then he left.	[12]A man was going on a trip. [13]He called ten of his slaves, gave them ten minas, and told them, "Do business with this while I'm away."	[12]A nobleman went off to a distant land intending to acquire a kingship for himself and then return. [13]Calling ten of his slaves, he gave them ten minas and told them, "Do business with this while I'm away." [14]His fellow citizens, however, hated him and sent a delegation right on his heels, with the petition: "We don't want this man to rule us."
[16]The one who had received five talents' worth of silver went right out and put the money to work; he doubled his investment. [17]The second also doubled his money. [18]But the third, who had received the smallest amount, went out, dug a hole, and hid his master's silver. [19]After a long absence, the master of those slaves returned to settle accounts with them. [20]The first, who had received five talents' worth of silver, came and produced an additional five, with this report: "Master, you handed me five talents of silver; as you can see, I've made you five more." [21]His master commended him: "Well done, you competent and trustworthy slave.	[15]After a long absence, the master of those slaves returned to settle accounts with them. [16]The first came in and reported, "Master, your mina has increased ten times over." [17]He said to him, "Well done, you competent slave!	[15]And it came to pass that he got the kingship and returned. He had those slaves summoned to whom he had given the money, in order to find out what profit they had made. [16]The first came in and reported, "Master, your mina has increased ten times over." [17]He said to him, "Well done, you competent slave!

You've been trustworthy in a little, so I'll put you in charge of a lot.
Come celebrate with your master."

²²The one with two talents of silver also came and reported,
"Master, you handed me two talents of silver; as you can see, I've made you two more."

²³His master commended him:
"Well done, you competent and trustworthy slave. You've been trustworthy in a little, so I'll put you in charge of a lot. Come celebrate with your master."

²⁴The one who had received one talent's worth of silver also came and reported, "Master, I know that you're a ruthless man, reaping where you didn't sow and gathering where you didn't scatter.

²⁵Since I was afraid, I went out and buried your money in the ground. Look, here it is!"

²⁶But his master replied to him, "You incompetent and timid slave!

So you knew that I reap where I didn't sow and gather where I didn't scatter, did you? ²⁷Then you should have taken my money to the bankers. Then when I returned I would have recovered what's mine, plus interest.

²⁸So take the talent away from this guy and give it to the one who has ten.

²⁹In fact, to everyone who has, more will be given and then some;
and from those who don't have, even what they do have will be taken away.*

³⁰And throw this worthless slave out into the utter darkness, where they'll weep and grind their teeth."

You've been trustworthy in a little so I'll put you in charge of a lot."

¹⁸The second came in and reported,

"Master, your mina has increased five times over."

¹⁹And he said to him,
"Well done, you competent and trustworthy slave. You've been trustworthy in a little so I'll put you in charge of a lot."

²⁰Then the other ⟨slave⟩ came in and

said, "Master, ²¹I know that you're a ruthless man, reaping where you didn't sow and gathering where you didn't scatter.

Since I was afraid, I went out and buried your money in the ground. Look, here it is!"

²²He said to him,
"You incompetent slave!

So you knew that I reap where I didn't sow and gather where I didn't scatter, did you? ²³Then you should have taken my money to the bankers. Then when I returned I would have recovered what's mine, plus interest.

²⁴So take the mina away
and give it to the one who has ten."

²⁶In fact, to everyone who has, more will be given;
and from those who don't have, even what they do have will be taken away.*

Because you've been trustworthy in this small matter, you are to be in charge of ten towns."

¹⁸The second came in and reported,

"Master, your mina has increased five times over."

¹⁹And he said to him,

"And you are to be in charge of five towns."

²⁰Then the other ⟨slave⟩ came in and

said, "Master, here is your money. I kept it tucked away safe in a handkerchief. ²¹You see, I was afraid of you, because you're a demanding man: you withdraw what you didn't deposit and reap what you didn't sow."

²²He said to him,
"You incompetent slave!
Your own words convict you.
So you knew I was a demanding man, did you? That I withdraw what I didn't deposit and reap what I didn't sow? ²³So why didn't you put my money in the bank? Then I could have collected it with interest when I got back."

²⁴Then he said to his attendants,
"Take the mina away from this guy and give it to the one who has ten."

²⁵"But master," they said to him, "he already has ten minas."

²⁶He replied, "I'm telling you,
to everyone who has, more
will be given;
and from those who don't have, even what they do have will be taken away.*

²⁷But now, about those enemies of mine, the ones who didn't want me to rule them: bring them here and slaughter them in front of me."

---

* ⓓ Mt 13:12 / Mk 4:25 / Lk 8:18 / Th 41:1–2 (#80, p. 65)

412. Judging the Twelve Tribes (Q)
SEE #240, P. 185

Mt 19:28	Q 22:28, 30	Lk 22:28–30
You who have followed me, when the Human One is seated on his throne of glory in the renewal ⟨of creation⟩, you also will be seated on twelve thrones and sit in judgment on the twelve tribes of Israel.	[28]You who have followed me [30]will be seated on thrones and sit in judgment on the twelve tribes of Israel.	[28]You are the ones who have stuck by me in my ordeals. [29]And I confer on you the right to rule, just as surely as my Father conferred that right on me, [30]so you may eat and drink at my table in my empire, and be seated on thrones and sit in judgment on the twelve tribes of Israel.

The Gospel of Thomas

413. Words of Immortality (Th)

Mk	Mt	Lk	Th Prologue & Saying 1	Jn 8:51, 52b	Jn 6:68
			These are the secret sayings that the living Jesus spoke and Didymos Judas Thomas recorded. ¹And he said, "Whoever discovers the interpretation of these sayings will not taste death."	⁵¹Let me tell you this: whoever follows my teaching will never die. ⁵²ᵇWhoever follows my teaching will never taste death.	Simon Peter replied to him, "Master, is there anyone else we can turn to? You have the words of unending life."

414. Seeking and Finding (a) (Th)
SEE #36, 479, 481, PP. 31, 357, 358

Mt 7:7–8	Mk	Lk 11:9–10
⁷Ask—it'll be given to you; seek—you'll find; knock—it'll be opened for you.* ⁸For everyone who asks receives; everyone who seeks finds; and for the one who knocks it is opened.		⁹Ask—it'll be given to you; seek—you'll find; knock—it'll be opened for you.* ¹⁰For everyone who asks receives; everyone who seeks finds; and for the one who knocks it is opened.

* Jn 15:5–8; 16:23–24 (#318, 321, pp. 254, 256)

415. Empire of God Inside You and Outside You (Th)
SEE #189, 494, PP. 141, 363

Mt	Mk	Lk 17:20–21	Th 3:1–3	Th 113:1–4
		²⁰When asked by the Pharisees when the empire of God would come, he answered them, "You won't be able to observe the coming of the empire of God. ²¹People won't be able to say, 'Look, here it is!' or 'Over there!'* On the contrary, the empire of God is among you."	¹If your leaders say to you, 'Look, the ⟨Father's⟩ empire is in the sky,' then the birds of the sky will precede you. ²If they say to you, 'It's in the sea,' then the fish will precede you. ³Rather, the ⟨Father's⟩ empire is inside you and outside you.	¹His disciples said to him, "When will the ⟨Father's⟩ empire come?" ²"It won't come by watching for it. ³It won't be said, 'Look, here!' or 'Look, there!'* ⁴Rather, the Father's empire is spread out upon the earth, and people don't see it."

* Mt 24:23 / Mk 13:21 (#226, p. 175)

Th 2:1–4	Th 92:1; 94:1–2	GHeb 6b
[1]Those who seek should not stop seeking until they find.*	**Th 92:1** Seek and you will find.* **Th 94:1–2** [1]The one who seeks will find,* [2]and for [one who knocks] it will be opened.	Those who seek should not stop until they find;
[2]When they find, they will be disturbed. [3]When they are disturbed, they will marvel [4]and will rule the universe.		when they find, they will marvel. When they marvel, they will rule, and when they rule, they will rest.

416. The first will be last (Th)

SEE #170, P. 130

Mt 19:30; 20:16	Mk 10:31	Lk 13:30	Th 4:1–3
Mt 19:30 Many of the first will be last, and many of the last will be first. **Mt 20:16** The last will be first and the first last.	Many of the first will be last, and many of the last will be first.	Those who will be first are last, and those who will be last are first.	[1]The person old in days won't hesitate to ask a little child seven days old about the place of life, and that person will live. [2]For many of the first will be last, [3]and will become a single one.

417. Hidden and Revealed (a) (Th)
SEE #79, 418, PP. 64, 332

Mt 10:26b	Mk 4:22	Lk 8:17; 12:2
There is nothing covered up that won't be exposed, or hidden that won't be made known.	There is nothing hidden except to be brought to light, nor anything kept secret that won't be exposed.	**Lk 8:17** There is nothing hidden that won't be brought to light, nor kept secret that won't be made known and exposed. **Lk 12:2** There is nothing covered up that won't be exposed, or hidden that won't be made known.

418. Hidden and Revealed (b) (Th)
SEE #79, 417, PP. 64, 332

Mt 10:26b	Mk 4:22	Lk 8:17; 12:2
There is nothing covered up that won't be exposed, or hidden that won't be made known.	There is nothing hidden except to be brought to light, nor anything kept secret that won't be exposed.	**Lk 8:17** There is nothing hidden that won't be brought to light, nor kept secret that won't be made known and exposed. **Lk 12:2** There is nothing covered up that won't be exposed, or hidden that won't be made known.

Th 5:1–2	**Th 6:5–6**
[1]Know what's in front of your face, and what's hidden from you will be disclosed to you. [2]After all, there's nothing hidden that won't be revealed.	[5]After all, there's nothing hidden that won't be revealed, [6]and there's nothing covered up that will remain undisclosed.

Th 6:2–6	**Th 5:2**
[2]Don't lie, [3]and don't do what you hate, [4]because all things are disclosed before heaven. [5]After all, there's nothing hidden that won't be revealed, [6]and there's nothing covered up that will remain undisclosed.	After all, there's nothing hidden that won't be revealed.

419. The Parable of the Wise Fisherman (Th)
= #89, P. 68

Mt 13:47–50	Mk	Lk	Th 8:1–4
[47]The empire of Heaven is like a net that is cast into the sea and catches all kinds of fish. [48]When the net is full, they haul it ashore. Then they sit down and collect the good fish into baskets, but the worthless fish they throw away.			[1]The human being is like a wise fisherman who cast his net into the sea and drew it up from the sea full of little fish. [2]Among them the wise fisherman discovered a fine large fish. [3]He threw all the little fish back into the sea, and easily chose the large fish. [4]Whoever has ears to hear should listen.*
[49]This is how the present age will end. God's messengers will go out and separate the evil from the just [50]and throw the evil into the fiery furnace. People in that place will weep and grind their teeth.		.	

* Mt 11:15; 13:9; 13:43b; Mk 4:9; 4:23; Lk 8:8b; 14:35b; Th 21:10; 24:2; 63:4; 65:8; 96:3

420. The Parable of the Sower (Th)
SEE #76, P. 61

Mt 13:3b–8	Mk 4:3–8	Lk 8:5–8a	Th 9:1–5
[3b]This sower went out to sow. [4]While he was sowing, some seed fell along the path, and the birds came and devoured it. [5]Other seed fell on rocky ground where there wasn't much soil, and it came up right away because the soil had no depth. [6]When the sun came up it was scorched, and because it had no roots it withered. [7]Still other seed fell among thorns, and the thorns came up and choked them. [8]Other seed fell on good soil and started producing fruit: one part had a yield of one hundred, another a yield of sixty, and a third a yield of thirty.	[3]This sower went out to sow. [4]While he was sowing, some seed fell along the path, and the birds came and devoured it. [5]Other seed fell on rocky ground where there wasn't much soil, and it came up right away because the soil had no depth. [6]But when the sun came up it was scorched, and because it had no root it withered. [7]Still other seed fell among thorns, and the thorns came up and choked it, so that it produced no fruit. [8]Finally, some seed fell on good soil and started producing fruit. The seed sprouted and grew: one part had a yield of thirty, another part sixty, and a third part one hundred.	[5]A sower went out to sow his seed; and while he was sowing, some seed fell along the path, and was trampled under foot, and the birds of the sky devoured it. [6]Other seed fell on the rock; when it grew, it withered because it lacked moisture. [7]Still other seed fell among thorns; the thorns grew with it and choked it. [8a]Other seed fell on fertile soil; and when it matured, it produced fruit a hundredfold.	[1]Look, the sower went out, took a handful ⟨of seeds⟩, and scattered ⟨them⟩. [2]Some fell on the road, and the birds came and gathered them. [3]Others fell on rock, and they didn't take root in the soil and didn't produce heads of grain. [4]Others fell on thorns, and they choked the seeds and worms ate them. [5]And others fell on good soil, and it produced a good crop: it yielded sixty per measure and one hundred twenty per measure.

421. Jesus casts fire (Th)
SEE #162, P. 127

Mt	Mk	Lk 12:49	Th 10	Th 82:1–2; 16:1–2
		I came to set the earth on fire, and how I wish it were already ablaze!	I have cast fire upon the world, and look, I'm guarding it until it blazes.	**Th 82:1–2** ¹Whoever is near me is near the fire, ²and whoever is far from me is far from the ⟨Father's⟩ empire. **Th 16:1–2** ¹Perhaps people think that I've come to cast peace upon the world. ²They don't know that I've come to sow conflict upon the earth: fire, sword, war.

422. Heaven will pass away (Th)
SEE #19, 402, PP. 22, 321

Mt 5:18	Mk	Lk 16:17	Th 11:1
Let me tell you, before earth and sky pass away, not one iota, not one serif, will disappear from the Law, until it all happens.	*13:31*	It's easier for earth and sky to pass away than for one serif of the Law to drop out.	This heaven will pass away and the one above it will pass away.

423. What am I like? (Th)
SEE #119, P. 100

Mt 16:15–16	Mk 8:29	Lk 9:20	Th 13:1–4
¹⁵He says to them, "What about you, who do you say I am?" ¹⁶And Simon Peter responded, "You are the Anointed One, the son of the living God!"*	But he kept pressing them, "What about you, who do you say I am?" Peter responds to him, "You are the Anointed One!"*	Then he said to them, "What about you, who do you say I am?" And Peter responded, "God's Anointed One!"*	¹Jesus said to his disciples, "Compare me to something and tell me what I'm like." ²Simon Peter said to him, "You are like a just angel." ³Matthew said to him, "You are like a wise philosopher." ⁴Thomas said to him, "Teacher, my mouth is utterly unable to say what you're like."

*Jn 1:40–41 (#281, p. 230)

424. Avoid pious deeds (Th)

Mt 6:16, 5, 2	Mk	Lk	Th 14:1–3
[16]When you fast, don't make a spectacle of your remorse as the phonies do. As you know, they make their faces unrecognizable so their fasting may be publicly recognized. Let me tell you, they've already received their reward. [5]When you pray, don't act like phonies. They love to stand up and pray in synagogues and on street corners, so they can show off in public. Let me tell you, they've already received their reward. [2]When you give to charity, don't bother to toot your own horn as some phonies do in synagogues and on the street. They are seeking human recognition. Let me tell you, they've already received their reward.			[1]If you fast, you'll bring sin upon yourselves, [2]and if you pray, you'll be condemned, [3]and if you give to charity, you'll harm your spirits.

425. Sharing Food and Healing (Th)

SEE #138, P. 113

Mt 10:7–8a	Mk	Lk 10:8–9	Th 14:4
[7]Go and announce: "The empire of Heaven has arrived." [8a]Heal the sick, raise the dead, cleanse the lepers, drive out demons.		[8]Whenever you enter a town and they welcome you, eat whatever they offer you. [9]Cure the sick there and tell them, "For you, the empire of God has arrived."	When you go into any region and walk about in the countryside, when people take you in, eat what they serve you and care for the sick among them.

426. What Defiles You (Th)

SEE #111, P. 92

Mt 15:11	Mk 7:15	Lk	Th 14:5
What goes into your mouth doesn't defile you; what comes out of your mouth does.	What goes into you can't defile you; what comes out of you can.		What goes into your mouth won't defile you; what comes out of your mouth will.

427. Jesus brings family conflict (Th)

SEE #162, P. 127

Mt 10:34–35	Mk	Lk 12:51–53	Th 16:1–4	Th 10
[34]Don't get the idea that I came to bring peace on earth. I didn't come to bring peace, but a sword!		[51]Do you think I came here to bring peace on earth? No, I'm telling you, on the contrary: conflict.	[1]Perhaps people think that I've come to cast peace upon the world. [2]They don't know that I've come to sow conflict upon the earth: fire, sword, war.	I have cast fire upon the world, and look, I'm guarding it until it blazes.*
	13:12	[52]As a result, from now on in any given house there will be five in conflict, three against two and two against three. [53]Father will be pitted against son and son against father, mother against daughter and daughter against mother, mother-in-law against daughter-in-law and daughter-in-law against mother-in-law.	[3]For there'll be five in a house: there'll be three against two and two against three, father against son and son against father,	
[35]After all, I've come to pit a man against his father, a daughter against her mother, and a daughter-in-law against her mother-in-law.			[4]and they will stand alone.	

*Lk 12:49; Th 82:1 (#162, 474, pp. 127, 356)

428. What No Eye Has Seen (Th)

Mt	Mk	Lk	Th 17	1 Cor 2:9
			I will give you what no eye has seen, what no ear has heard, what no hand has touched, what has not arisen in the human heart.	The scripture says, "No eye has ever seen, no ear has ever heard, or has the human mind ever imagined what God has prepared for those who love him."

429. The Parable of the Mustard (Th)
= #83, P. 66

Mt 13:31–32	Mk 4:30–32	Lk 13:18–19	Th 20:1–4
[31]He put another parable before them with these words: The empire of Heaven is like a mustard seed that a man took and sowed in his field. [32]Though it is the smallest of all seeds, when it grows up, it is the largest of garden plants, and becomes a tree, so that the birds of the sky come and roost in its branches.	[30]And he was saying: To what should we compare the empire of God, or what parable should we use for it? [31]Think about the mustard seed: when it is sown on the ground, though it is the smallest of all the seeds on the earth, [32]—yet when it is sown, it comes up, and becomes the biggest of all garden plants, and produces branches, so that the birds of the sky can nest in its shade. 4:33–34 #85, p. 67	[18]Then he was saying, What is the empire of God like? What does it remind me of? [19]It's like a mustard seed that a man took and tossed into his garden. It grew and became a tree, and the birds of the sky roosted in its branches.	[1]The disciples said to Jesus, "Tell us what Heaven's empire is like." [2]He said to them, It's like a mustard seed. [3]⟨It's⟩ the smallest of all seeds, [4]but when it falls on prepared soil, it produces a large branch and becomes a shelter for birds of the sky.

430. Anticipating the Thief (Th)
SEE #160, P. 125

Mt 24:43	Mk	Lk 12:39	Th 21:5–7	Th 103
Mark this well: if the homeowner had known when the burglar was coming, he would have been on guard and not have allowed anyone to break into his house. *24:44*		Mark this well: if the homeowner had known what time the burglar was coming,[a] he would not have let anyone break into his house. *12:40*	[5]For this reason I say, if the owners of a house know that a thief is coming, they will be on guard before the thief arrives, and won't let the thief break into their house and steal their possessions. [6]As for you, then, be on guard against the world. [7]Prepare yourselves with great strength, so the robbers can't find a way to get to you, for the privation you expect will come.	Congratulations to the one who knows where the brigands are going to attack. [He] can take action, mobilize his kingdom, and be prepared before the brigands invade.

[a]Lk 12:39 Many mss insert "he would have watched and" after *coming*.

431. Understanding and Harvesting (Th)
SEE #81, P. 65

Mt	Mk 4:29	Lk	Th 21:8–10
	But when the grain ripens, right away he sends for the sickle, because it's harvest time.		[8]Let there be among you a person who understands. [9]When the crop ripened, he came quickly carrying a sickle and harvested it. [10]Whoever has ears to hear should listen.*

*Mt 11:15; 13:9; 13:43b; Mk 4:9; 4:23; Lk 8:8b; 14:35b; Th 8:4; 24:2; 63:4; 65:8; 96:3

432. Babies and the Father's Empire (Th)
SEE #195, P. 146

Mt 19:13–14	Mk 10:13–14	Lk 18:15–16	Th 22:1–2
[13]Then children were brought to him so he could lay his hands on them and pray, but the disciples scolded them. [14]Now Jesus said, "Let the children alone. Don't try to stop them from coming up to me. After all, the empire of Heaven belongs to people like these."*	[13]And they would bring children to him so he could bless them with his hands, but the disciples scolded them. [14]Then Jesus grew indignant when he saw this and said to them, "Let the children come up to me; don't try to stop them. After all, the empire of God belongs to people like these."*	[15]They would even bring him their babies so he could bless them with his hands. But when the disciples noticed it, they scolded them. [16]Jesus called for the babies and said, "Let the children come up to me, and don't try to stop them. After all, the empire of God belongs to people like these."*	[1]Jesus saw some babies nursing. [2]He said to his disciples, "These nursing babies are like those who enter the ⟨Father's⟩ empire."

*Mt 18:3 (#127, p. 107)

433. A Person of Light (Th)
SEE #152, P. 120

Mt 6:22–23a	Mk	Lk 11:34	Th 24:1–3
[22]The eye is the body's lamp. It follows that if your eye is clear, your whole body will be flooded with light. [23a]If your eye is clouded, your whole body will be shrouded in darkness.		Your eye is the body's lamp. When your eye is clear, your whole body is flooded with light. When your eye is clouded, your body is shrouded in darkness.	[1]His disciples said, "Show us the place where you are, for we must seek it." [2]He said to them, "Whoever has ears to hear should listen.* [3]There is light within a person of light, and it shines on the whole world. If it does not shine, it is dark."†

*Mt 11:15; 13:9; 13:43b; Mk 4:9; 4:23; Lk 8:8b; 14:35b; Th 8:4; 21:10; 63:4; 65:8; 96:3
† Th 61:5 (#457, p. 348)

434. Love your friends (Th)

SEE #215, P. 166

Mt 22:37–39	Mk 12:30–31	Lk 10:27	Th 25:1–2
[37]You shall love the Lord your God with all your heart and all your soul and all your mind. [38]This commandment is first and foremost. [39]And the second is like it: You shall love your neighbor as yourself.	[30]You shall love the Lord your God with all your heart and all your soul and all your mind and all your strength. [31]The second is this: You shall love your neighbor as yourself.	You shall love the Lord your God with all your heart and all your soul and all your strength and all your mind; and your neighbor as yourself.	[1]Love your friends like your own soul, [2]protect them like the pupil of your eye.

435. Removing Wood from the Eye (Th)

SEE #46, 358, PP. 37, 293

Mt 7:3–5	Mk	Lk 6:41–42	Th 26:1–2
[3]Why do you notice the sliver in your friend's eye, but overlook the timber in your own? [4]How can you say to your friend, "Let me get the sliver out of your eye," when there is that timber in your own? [5]You phony, first take the timber out of your own eye and then you'll see well enough to remove the sliver from your friend's eye.		[41]Why do you notice the sliver in your friend's eye, but overlook the timber in your own? [42]How can you say to your friend, "Friend, let me get the sliver in your eye," when you don't notice the timber in your own? You phony, first take the timber out of your own eye and then you'll see well enough to remove the sliver in your friend's eye.	[1]You see the sliver in your friend's eye, but you don't see the timber in your own eye. [2]When you take the timber out of your own eye, then you'll see well enough to remove the sliver from your friend's eye.

436. Assurance of Abiding Presence (Th)

SEE #133, P. 110

Mt 18:20	Mk	Lk	Th 30:1–2[a]
Wherever two or three are gathered together in my name, I will be there among them.			[1]Where there are three deities, they are divine. [2]Where there are two or one, I am with that one.

[a] Th 30:2 The Coptic version of this saying is deficient, based perhaps on a scribal error. The Greek version is closer to the original: "Where there are [three, they are without] God, and where there is only [one,] I say, I am with that one."

437. The Rejected Prophet (Th)

SEE #95, P. 75

Mt 13:57b	Mk 6:4	Lk 4:24	Th 31:1–2	Jn 4:44b
No prophet is disrespected, except on his home turf and at home.	No prophet is disrespected, except on his home turf and among his relatives and at home.	No prophet is welcome on his home turf.	[1]No prophet is welcome in his home town; [2]doctors don't cure those who know them.	A prophet gets no respect on his own turf.

438. A City on a Hill (Th)

SEE #18, P. 21

Mt 5:14b	Mk	Lk	Th 32
A city sitting on top of a mountain can't be concealed.			A city fortified and built on a high hill cannot fall, nor can it be hidden.

439. Rooftop Proclamation (Th)

SEE #100, P. 82

Mt 10:27	Mk	Lk 12:3	Th 33:1
What I say to you in the dark, say in the light, and what you hear whispered in your ear, announce from the rooftops.		And so whatever you've said in the dark will be heard in the light, and what you've whispered behind closed doors will be announced from the rooftops.	What you will hear in your ear,[a] proclaim from your rooftops.

[a] Th 33:1 Between *ear* and *proclaim* the Coptic has "in the other ear." This is very likely a scribal error (dittography, the inadvertent repetition of a phrase). It is therefore omitted from the translation.

440. Lamps go on lampstands (Th)

SEE #79, P. 64

Mt 5:15	Mk 4:21	Lk 8:16	Lk 11:33	Th 33:2–3
Nor do people light a lamp and put it under a bushel basket, but instead on a lampstand, where it sheds light for everyone in the house.	Since when is the lamp brought in to be put under the bushel basket or under the bed? It's put on the lampstand, isn't it?	No one lights a lamp and covers it with a pot or puts it under a bed; instead, one puts it on a lampstand, so that those who come in can see the light.	No one lights a lamp and then puts it in a cellar or under a bushel basket, but instead on a lampstand so that those who come in can see the light.	[2]No one lights a lamp and puts it under a basket, nor does one put it in a hidden place. [3]Rather, one puts it on a lampstand so that all who come and go will see its light.

441. The Blind Leading the Blind (Th)
SEE #46, 357, PP. 37, 292

Mt 15:14b	Mk	Lk 6:39b	Th 34
If one blind person guides another, both will end up in some ditch.		Can one blind person guide another? Won't they both end up in some ditch?	If a blind person leads a blind person, both of them will fall into a hole.

442. Looting a Strong Man's House (Th)
SEE #72, P. 57

Mt 12:29	Mk 3:27	Lk 11:21–22	Th 35:1–2
Or how can anyone enter a strong man's house and plunder his belongings, unless he first ties him up? Only then does he plunder his house.	No one can enter a strong man's house to plunder his belongings unless he first ties him up. Only then does he plunder his house.	[21]When a strong man is fully armed and guards his courtyard, his possessions are safe. [22]But when a stronger man attacks and overpowers him, he takes away the weapons on which he was relying and divides up his loot.	[1]You can't enter a strong man's house and take it by force without tying his hands. [2]Then you can loot his house.

443. Don't fret about clothing (Th)
SEE #33, 384, PP. 29, 312

Mt 6:25b	Mk	Lk 12:22b	Th 36[a]
Don't fret about your life, what you're going to eat and drink —or about your body, what you're going to wear.		Don't fret about life, what you're going to eat —or about your body, what you're going to wear.	Don't fret, from morning to evening and from evening to morning, about what you're going to wear.

[a] Th 36 The Greek version of this saying is longer. After the second *morning* it adds: "[about] your [food], what [you're going to] eat, or about [your clothing]. . . ." At the end of the saying it adds: [2]"[You're much] better than the lilies, which don't card and never [spin]. [3]As for you, when you have no garment, what [are you going to put] on? [4]Who could add to your life span? That same one will give you your garment."

444. Seeking Jesus, but Not Finding Him (Th)
SEE #143, 300, PP. 116, 242

Mt	Mk	Lk	Th 38:1–2	Jn 7:34
16:17		10:24	[1]You've often wanted to hear these sayings that I am speaking to you, and you have no one else from whom to hear them. [2]There will be days when you'll seek me and you won't find me.	You'll look for me, but you won't find me; where I am you can't come.

445. Hiding the Keys of Knowledge (Th)

= #487; SEE #153, 379, PP. 361, 121, 309

Mt 23:13	Mk	Lk 11:52	Th 39:1–2	Th 102
You scholars and Pharisees, you impostors! Damn you! You slam the door of the empire of Heaven in people's faces. You yourselves don't go in, and you block the way of those trying to go in.		You legal experts, damn you! You've taken away the key of knowledge. You yourselves haven't gone in and you have blocked the way of those trying to go in.	[1]The Pharisees and the scholars have taken the keys of knowledge and hidden them. [2]They have not entered, nor have they allowed those who want to enter to do so.	Damn the Pharisees! They are like a dog sleeping in the cattle's feeding trough: the dog neither eats nor [lets] the cattle eat.

446. Snakes and Pigeons (Th)

SEE #99, P. 80

Mt 10:16	Mk	Lk	Th 39:3
You must be as sly as snakes and as simple as pigeons.			As for you, be as sly as snakes and as simple as pigeons.

447. The haves get more (Th)

SEE #80, P. 65

Mt 13:12; 25:29	Mk 4:25	Lk 8:18b; 19:26	Th 41:1–2
Mt 13:12 In fact, to those who have, more will be given, and then some; and from those who don't have, even what they do have will be taken away. **Mt 25:29** In fact, to everyone who has, more will be given and then some; and from those who don't have, even what they do have will be taken away.	In fact, to those who have, more will be given, and from those who don't have, even what they do have will be taken away.	**Lk 8:18b** In fact, to those who have, more will be given, and from those who don't have, even what they seem to have will be taken away. **Lk 19:26** I'm telling you, to everyone who has, more will be given; and from those who don't have, even what they do have will be taken away.	[1]Those who have something in hand will be given more, [2]and those who have nothing will be deprived of even the little they have.

448. Blaspheming the Holy Spirit (Th)

SEE #73, 383, PP. 58, 311

Mt 12:31–32	Mk 3:28–29	Lk 12:10	Th 44:1–3
[31]Every offense and blasphemy will be forgiven humankind, but the blasphemy of the spirit won't be forgiven. [32]And the one who speaks a word against the Human One will be forgiven; but the one who speaks a word against the holy spirit won't be forgiven, neither in this age nor in the age to come.	[28]All offenses and whatever blasphemies humankind might blaspheme will be forgiven them. [29]But whoever blasphemes against the holy spirit is never forgiven, but is guilty of an eternal sin.	And everyone who utters a word against the Human One will be forgiven; but whoever blasphemes against the holy spirit won't be forgiven.	[1]Whoever blasphemes against the Father will be forgiven, [2]and whoever blasphemes against the son will be forgiven, [3]but whoever blasphemes against the holy spirit will not be forgiven, either on earth or in heaven.

449. Good produces good (Th)

SEE #74, 359, PP. 59, 293

Mt 7:16; 12:35, 34b	Mk	Lk 6:44–45	Th 45:1–3
Mt 7:16 You'll know who they are by what they produce. Since when do people pick grapes from thorns or figs from thistles? **Mt 12:35, 34b** [35]The good person produces good things out of a fund of good; and the evil person produces evil things out of a fund of evil. [34b]As you know, the mouth gives voice to what the heart is full of.		[44]Each tree is known by its fruit. Figs are not gathered from thorns, nor are grapes picked from brambles. [45]The good person produces good from the fund of good in the heart, and the evil person produces evil from the evil within. As you know, the mouth gives voice to what the heart is full of.	[1]Grapes are not harvested from thorn trees, nor are figs gathered from thistles, for they yield no fruit. [2]Good persons produce good from what they've stored up; [3]bad persons produce evil from the wickedness they've stored up in their hearts, and say evil things. For from the overflow of the heart comes evil.

450. Greater than John the Baptizer (Th)
SEE #55, 195, 363, PP. 45, 146, 297

Mt 11:11a; 18:3; 11:11b	Mk 10:15	Lk 7:28a; 18:17; 7:28b	Th 46:1–2
Mt 11:11a Among those born of women no one has arisen who is greater than John the Baptizer; **Mt 18:3** If you don't turn yourself around and become like children, you'll never enter the empire of Heaven. **Mt 11:11b** yet the least ⟨important⟩ in the empire of Heaven is greater than he is.	Whoever doesn't welcome the empire of God the way a child would, will never set foot in ⟨his empire⟩.	**Lk 7:28a** Among those born of women none is greater than John; **Lk 18:17** Whoever doesn't welcome the empire of God the way a child would, will never enter it. **Lk 7:28b** yet the least ⟨important⟩ in the empire of God is greater than he is.	[1]From Adam to John the Baptizer, among those born of women, no one is so much greater than John the Baptizer, so his eyes should not be downcast. [2]But I have said that whoever among you becomes a child will recognize the ⟨Father's⟩ empire and will become greater than John.

451. Two Masters (Th)
SEE #32, 401, PP. 28, 321

Mt 6:24	Mk	Lk 16:13	Th 47:1–2
No one can be a slave to two masters. That slave will either hate one and love the other, or be devoted to one and disdain the other. You can't be enslaved to both God and Mammon.		No servant can be a slave to two masters. That slave will either hate one and love the other, or be devoted to one and disdain the other. You can't be enslaved to both God and mammon.	[1]No one can mount two horses or bend two bows. [2]And a slave cannot serve two masters, otherwise that slave will honor the one and offend the other.

452. New Wine and New Garments (Th)

SEE #61, P. 50

Mt 9:17, 16	Mk 2:22, 21	Lk 5:39, 37–38, 36b	Th 47:3–5
		³⁹Besides, nobody wants new wine after drinking aged wine. As they say, "Aged wine is just fine!"	³Nobody drinks aged wine and immediately wants to drink new wine.
¹⁷Nor do they pour new wine into old wineskins, otherwise the wineskins burst, the wine gushes out, and the wineskins are destroyed.	²²And nobody pours new wine into old wineskins, otherwise the wine will burst the wineskins, and destroy both the wine and the wineskins.	³⁷And nobody pours new wine into old wineskins, otherwise the new wine will burst the wineskins, it will gush out, and the wineskins will be destroyed.	⁴New wine is not poured into old wineskins, or they might break, and aged wine is not poured into a new wineskin, or it might spoil.
Instead, they put new wine in new wineskins and both are preserved. ¹⁶Nobody patches an old garment with a piece of unshrunken cloth, since the patch pulls away from the garment and creates a worse tear.	²¹Nobody sews a piece of unshrunk cloth on an old garment, otherwise the new, unshrunk patch pulls away from the old and creates a worse tear.	³⁸Instead, new wine must be put into new wineskins. ³⁶ᵇNobody tears a piece from a new garment and puts it on an old one, since the new one will tear and the piece from the new will not match the old.	⁵An old patch is not sewn onto a new garment, since it would create a tear.

453. How to Move a Mountain (Th)

= #490; SEE #209, PP. 362, 159

Mt 21:21b	Mk 11:23	Lk	Th 48	Th 106:1–2
Let me tell you, if you have trust and do not doubt, not only can you do this to a fig tree but you can even say to this mountain, "Up with you and into the sea!" and that's what will happen.*	Let me tell you, those who say to this mountain, "Up with you and into the sea!" and do not waver in their conviction, but trust that what they say will happen, that's the way it will be.		If two make peace with each other in a single house, they will say to the mountain, "Move from here!" and it will move.	¹When you make the two into one, you will become children of Adam, ²and when you say, "Mountain, move from here!" it will move.

* Ⓓ Mt 17:20 / Lk 17:6 (#186, p. 140)

454. Congratulations to the Poor (Th)

SEE #17, 354, PP. 20, 289

Mt 5:3	Mk	Lk 6:20b	Th 54
Congratulations to the poor in spirit! The empire of Heaven belongs to them.		Congratulations, you poor! the empire of God belongs to you.	Congratulations to the poor, for the empire of Heaven belongs to you.

455. Hating Father and Mother (a) (Th)
SEE #176, 486, PP. 134, 360

Mt 10:37–38		Lk 14:26–27	Th 55:1–2	Th 101:1
[37]If you love your father and mother more than me, you're not worthy of me, and if you love your son or daughter more than me, you're not worthy of me.		[26]If any of you comes to me and does not hate your own father and mother and wife and children and brothers and sisters—yes, even your own life—you cannot be my disciple.	[1]Whoever does not hate father and mother cannot be my disciple, [2]and whoever does not hate brothers and sisters,	Whoever does not hate [father] and mother as I do cannot be my [disciple].
[38]Unless you take your cross and come along with me, you're not worthy of me.*		[27]Unless you carry your own cross and come along with me, you cannot be my disciple.*	and carry the cross as I do, will not be worthy of me.*	

* Mt 16:24 / Mk 8:34 / Lk 9:23 (#121, p. 102)

456. The Parable of the Weeds and the Wheat (Th)
= #82, P. 66

Mt 13:24b–30	Mk	Lk	Th 57:1–4
[24b]The empire of Heaven is like someone who sowed good seed in his field. [25]And while everyone was asleep, his enemy came and scattered weed seed around in his wheat and stole away. [26]And when the crop sprouted and produced grain, then the weeds also appeared. [27]The owner's slaves came and asked him, "Master, didn't you sow good seed in your field? Then why are there weeds everywhere?" [28]He replied to them, "Some enemy has done this." The slaves said to him, "So do you want us to go and pull the weeds?" [29]He replied, "No, otherwise you'll uproot the wheat at the same time as you pull the weeds. [30]Let them grow up together until the harvest, and at harvest time I'll say to the harvesters, 'Gather the weeds first and bind them in bundles for burning, but gather the wheat into my granary.'"			[1]The Father's empire is like someone who had [good] seed. [2]His enemy came during the night and sowed weeds among the good seed. [3]The man did not let the ⟨workers⟩ pull up the weeds, but said to them, "Don't, or else you might go to pull up the weeds and pull up the wheat along with them." [4]For on the day of the harvest the weeds will be conspicuous, and will be pulled up and burned.

457. Unwavering Discipleship (Th)

SEE #152, 141, 190, PP. 120, 115, 142

Mt 24:40–41; 11:27a; 6:23b	Mk	Lk 17:34–35; 10:22a; 11:35–36	Th 61:1–5
Mt 24:40–41 40Then two men will be in the field; one will be taken and one will be left. 41Two women will be grinding at the mill; one will be taken and one left.		**Lk 17:34–35** 34On that night there will be two on one couch; one will be taken and the other left. 35There will be two women grinding together; one will be taken and the other left.[a]	1Jesus said, "Two will recline on a couch; one will die, one will live."
			2Salome said, "Who are you, mister? You have climbed onto my couch and eaten from my table as a stranger."
Mt 11:27a My Father has turned everything over to me.*		**Lk 10:22a** My Father has turned everything over to me.*	3Jesus said to her, "I am the one who comes from the one who is unwavering. I have been given some of the things of my Father."
Mt 6:23b If, then, the light within you is darkness, how dark that can be!		**Lk 11:35–36** 35Take care, then, that the light within you is not darkness. 36So if your whole body is flooded with light, and no corner of it is darkness, it will be completely illuminated as when a lamp's rays engulf you.	4"I am your disciple." 5"For this reason I say, if anyone becomes unwavering, they will be filled with light, but if anyone becomes divided, they will be filled with darkness."

* Jn 3:35; 13:3 (#284, 312, pp. 232, 250)

---

[a] Lk 17:35 Some mss add another verse, traditionally numbered 17:36: "Two will be in the fields; one will be taken, the other left."

458. Left Hand in the Dark (Th)
SEE #26, P. 26

Mt 6:3–4	Mk	Lk	Th 62:1–2
³When you give to charity, don't let your left hand in on what your right hand is up to, ⁴so your acts of charity will stay secret. And your Father, who sees what happens in secret, will reward you.			¹I disclose my mysteries to those [who are worthy] of [my] mysteries. ²Don't let your left hand know what your right hand is doing.

459. The Parable of the Rich Fool (Th)
SEE #158, P. 124

Mt	Mk	Lk 12:16b–21	Th 63:1–4
		¹⁶ᵇThere was a rich man whose fields produced a bumper crop. ¹⁷"What do I do now?" he asked himself, "since I don't have any place to store my crops. ¹⁸I know!" he said, "I'll tear down my barns and build larger ones so I can store all my grain and my goods. ¹⁹Then I'll say to myself, 'You have plenty put away for years to come. Take it easy; eat, drink, and enjoy yourself.'" ²⁰But God said to him, "You fool! This very night your life will be demanded back from you. All this stuff you've collected—whose will it be now?" ²¹That's the way it is with those who save up for themselves, but aren't rich where God is concerned.	¹There was a rich man who had a great deal of money. ²He said, "I shall invest my money so that I may sow, reap, plant, and fill my storehouses with produce, that I may lack nothing." ³These were the things he was thinking in his heart, but that very night he died. ⁴Whoever has ears to hear should listen.*

*Mt 11:15; 13:9; 13:43b; Mk 4:9; 4:23; Lk 8:8b; 14:35b; Th 8:4; 21:10; 24:2; 65:8; 96:3

460. The Parable of the Dinner Guests Who Had Excuses (Th)

SEE #175, P. 132

Mt 22:2–3	Mk	Lk 14:16–21a, 23	Th 64:1–12
[2]The empire of Heaven is like a king who gave a wedding celebration for his son. [3]Then he sent his slaves to summon those who had been invited to the wedding, but they declined to attend.		[16]Someone was giving a big dinner and invited many guests. [17]At the dinner hour the host sent his slave to tell the guests, "Come, it's ready now." [18]But one by one they all began to make excuses. The first said to him, "I just bought a farm and I have to go and inspect it; please excuse me." [19]And another said, "I just bought five pairs of oxen and I'm on my way to check them out; please excuse me." [20]And another said, "I just got married and so I cannot attend." [21a]So the slave came back and reported these ⟨excuses⟩ to his master. [23]And the master said to the slave, "Then go out into the roads and the country lanes, and force people to come in so my house will be filled. [24]For I'm telling you, not one of those who were invited will taste my dinner."	[1]A man was receiving guests. When he had prepared the dinner, he sent his slave to invite the guests. [2]The slave went to the first and said, "My master invites you." [3]He replied, "Some merchants owe me money; they're coming to me tonight. I have to go and give them instructions. Please excuse me from dinner." [4]The slave went to another and said, "My master has invited you." [5]He said to him, "I've bought a house and I've been called away for a day. I won't have any time." [6]He went to another and said, "My master invites you." [7]He said to him, "My friend is to be married and I have to arrange the banquet. I won't be able to come. Please excuse me from dinner." [8]He went to another and said, "My master invites you." [9]He said to him, "I've bought an estate and I'm going to collect the rent. I won't be able to come. Please excuse me." [10]The slave returned and said to his master, "Those whom you invited to dinner have asked to be excused." [11]The master said to his slave, "Go out on the roads and bring back whomever you find to have dinner." [12]Buyers and merchants [will] not enter the places of my Father.

461. The Parable of the Tenants (Th)

SEE #212, P. 162

Mt 21:33b–46	Mk 12:1b–12	Lk 20:9b–19	Th 65:1–8
33bThere once was a landlord who planted a vineyard, put a hedge around it, dug a winepress in it, built a tower, leased it out to some farmers, and went abroad.	1bA man planted a vineyard, put a hedge around it, dug a winepress, built a tower, leased it out to some farmers, and went abroad.	9bA man planted a vineyard, leased it out to some farmers, and went abroad for an extended time.	1A [greedy]a man owned a vineyard and rented it to some farmers, so they could work it and he could collect its crop from them.
34Now when harvest time arrived, he sent his slaves to the farmers to collect his crop.	2In due time he sent a slave to the farmers to collect his share of the vineyard's crop from them.	10In due course he sent a slave to the farmers, so they could pay him his share of the vineyard's crop.	2He sent his slave so the farmers would give him the vineyard's crop.
35And the farmers grabbed his slaves, and one they beat and another they killed, and another they stoned.	3But they grabbed him, beat him, and sent him away empty-handed.	But the farmers beat him and sent him away empty-handed.	3They grabbed him, beat him, and almost killed him, and the slave returned and told his master. 4His master said, "Perhaps he didn't know them."b
36Again he sent other slaves, more than the first group, and they did the same thing to them.	4And again he sent another slave to them, but they attacked him and abused him. 5Then he sent another, and this one they killed; many others followed, some of whom they beat, others of whom they killed.	11He repeated his action by sending another slave; but they beat him up too, and humiliated him, and sent him away empty-handed. 12And he sent yet a third slave; but they injured him and threw him out. 13Then the owner of the vineyard asked himself, "What should I do now? I'll send my son, the one I love. They'll probably show him some respect."	5He sent another slave, and the farmers beat that one as well.
37Then finally he sent his son to them, with the thought, "They'll show my son some respect." 38But when the farmers recognized the son they said to one another, "This guy's the heir! Come on, let's kill him and we'll have his inheritance!" 39And they grabbed him, dragged him outside the vineyard, and killed him.	6Finally he sent his son, whom he loved. He said to himself, "They will show this son of mine some respect." 7But those farmers said to one another, "This guy's the heir! Come on, let's kill him and the inheritance will be ours!" 8So they grabbed him, and killed him, and threw him outside the vineyard.	14But when the farmers recognized him, they talked it over, and concluded, "This guy's the heir. Let's kill him so the inheritance will be ours." 15So they dragged him outside the vineyard and killed him.	6Then the master sent his son and said, "Perhaps they'll show my son some respect." 7Because the farmers knew that he was the heir to the vineyard, they grabbed him and killed him. 8Whoever has ears to hear should listen.*
40When the owner of the vineyard comes, what will he do to those farmers then? 41They say to him,	9What will the owner of the vineyard do? He will come in person, and	So what will the owner of the vineyard do to them? 16He will come in person,	

Mt 21:33b–46	Mk 12:1b–12	Lk 20:9b–19	Th 65:1–8
"He'll massacre those scum and lease the vineyard out to other farmers who will deliver their produce to him at the proper time."	massacre those farmers, and give the vineyard to others.	massacre those farmers, and give the vineyard to others.	

* Mt 11:15; 13:9; 13:43b; Mk 4:9; 4:23; Lk 8:8b; 14:35b; Th 8:4; 21:10; 24:2; 63:4; 96:3

----

a Th 65:1 A lacuna in the papyrus makes the Coptic here uncertain; the hole can be filled in to read either "good man" or "greedy man."

462. The Rejected Keystone (Th)
SEE #212, P. 162

Mt 21:42	Mk 12:10–11	Lk 20:17	Th 66
It seems you haven't read in scripture: "A stone that the builders threw away has ended up as the keystone. It was the Lord's doing, something we find amazing."	10It seems you haven't read in scripture: "A stone that the builders threw away has ended up as the keystone. 11It was the Lord's doing, something we find amazing."	What can this scripture possibly mean: "A stone that the builders threw away has ended up as the keystone"?	Show me the stone that the builders rejected: that is the keystone.

463. Congratulations to the Persecuted (Th)
SEE #17, 354, PP. 20, 289

Mt 5:11	Mk	Lk 6:22	Th 68:1–2
Congratulations to you when they denounce you and persecute you and spread malicious gossip[a] about you because of me.		Congratulations to you when people hate you, and when they ostracize you and spread malicious gossip about you and scorn your name as evil, because of the Human One!	1Congratulations to you when you are hated and persecuted; 2and no place will be found, wherever you've been persecuted.

a Mt 5:11 A few mss add "and tell lies" to the triad of *denounce and persecute and spread malicious gossip*.

464. Congratulations to the Persecuted and the Hungry (Th)
SEE #17, 354, PP. 20, 289

Mt 5:10, 6	Mk	Lk 6:21a	Th 69:1–2
10Congratulations to those who have suffered persecution for the sake of justice! The empire of Heaven belongs to them. 6Congratulations to those who hunger and thirst for justice! They will have a feast.		Congratulations, you hungry! You will have a feast.	1Congratulations to those who've been persecuted in their hearts: they are the ones who have truly come to know the Father. 2Congratulations to those who go hungry, so the stomach of the needy may be filled.

465. I will destroy this house (Th)
SEE #283, P. 232

Mt 26:59–61	Mk 14:57–58	Lk	**Th 71**	Jn 2:18–19
⁵⁹The chief priests and the whole Council were looking for false testimony against Jesus so they might issue a death sentence; ⁶⁰but they couldn't find many perjurers to come forward. Finally, two men came forward ⁶¹and said, "This man said, 'I can destroy the temple of God and rebuild it within three days.'"	⁵⁷And some people stood up and testified falsely against him, ⁵⁸"We have heard him saying, 'I'll destroy this temple made with hands and in three days I'll build another, not made with hands!'"		I will destroy [this] house, and no one will be able to build it [. . .].	¹⁸To this the Judeans responded, "What sign can you show us to justify doing all this?" ¹⁹Jesus replied, "Destroy this temple and I'll raise it in three days."

466. Jesus refuses to be a divider (Th)
SEE #158, P. 124

Mt	Mk	**Lk 12:13–14**	**Th 72:1–3**
		¹³Someone in the crowd said to him, "Teacher, tell my brother to divide the inheritance with me." ¹⁴But Jesus said to him, "Mister, who appointed me your judge or arbiter?"	¹A [person said] to him, "Tell my brothers to divide my father's possessions with me." ²He said to the person, "Mister, who made me a divider?" ³He turned to his disciples and said to them, "I'm not a divider, am I?"

467. Huge Crop, Few Workers (Th)
SEE #138, 365, PP. 113, 299

Mt 9:37b–38	Mk	**Lk 10:2**	**Th 73**
³⁷ᵇThe crop is good, but there are few to harvest it.* ³⁸So beg the harvest boss to dispatch workers to the fields.		The crop is good, but there are few to harvest it.* So beg the harvest boss to dispatch workers to the fields.	The crop is huge, but the workers are few,* so beg the boss to dispatch workers to the fields.

* Jn 4:35–36 (#286, p. 233)

468. The solitary will enter the wedding hall (Th)

SEE #168, 393, PP. 129, 317

Mt 7:13–14	Mk	Lk 13:24	Th 75
[13]Get in through the narrow gate. Wide and smooth is the road that leads to destruction. Many are taking that route. [14]Narrow and rough is the road that leads to life. Only a few discover it.		Struggle to get in through the narrow door; I'm telling you, many will try to get in, but won't be able.	There are many standing at the door, but those who are solitary will enter the wedding hall.

469. The Parable of the Pearl (Th)

SEE #88, 30, 385, PP. 68, 28, 313

Mt 13:45–46; 6:20	Mk	Lk 12:33	Th 76:1–3
Mt 13:45–46 [45]Again, the empire of Heaven is like some merchant looking for beautiful pearls. [46]When he finds one priceless pearl, he sells everything he owns and buys it. **Mt 6:20** Gather your nest egg in heaven, where neither moths nor insects eat away and where no burglars break in or steal.	 *10:21*	 Sell your belongings, and donate to charity; make yourselves purses that don't wear out, with inexhaustible wealth in heaven,* where no burglar can get to it and no moth can destroy it.	[1]The Father's empire is like a merchant who had a supply of merchandise and then found a pearl. [2]That merchant was prudent; he sold the merchandise and bought the single pearl for himself. [3]Seek his treasure that is unfailing and enduring, where no moth comes to eat and no worm destroys.

* Mt 19:21 / Mk 10:21/ Lk 18:22 (#196, p. 147)

470. I am the Light (Th)

SEE #301, P. 242

Mt	Mk	Lk	Th 77:1–3	Jn 8:12	Jn 9:5
5:14			[1]I am the light that is over all things. I am all: from me all came forth, and to me all attained. [2]Split a piece of wood; I'm there. [3]Lift up the stone and you'll find me there.[a]	I am the light of the world.	So long as I am in the world, I am the light of the world.

[a] Th 77:2–3 The Greek version of this saying is preceded by the words: [Jesus says], "Where there are [three, they are without] God, and where there is only [one], I say, I am with that one." In the Coptic version these words are found in Thom 30:1–2.

471. Why have you come out? (Th)
SEE #55, 363, PP. 45, 297

Mt 11:7–9	Mk	Lk 7:24–26	Th 78:1–3
[7]After ⟨John's disciples⟩ had departed, Jesus began to talk to the crowds about John. "What did you go out to the desert to gawk at? A reed shaking in the wind? [8]What did you really go out to see? A man dressed in fancy clothes? But wait! Those who wear fancy clothes are found in royal houses. [9]Come on, what did you go out to see? A prophet? Yes, that's what you went out to see, and even more than a prophet.	1:2	[24]After John's messengers had left, Jesus began to talk to the crowds about John. "What did you go out to the desert to gawk at? A reed shaking in the wind? [25]What did you really go out to see? A man dressed in fancy clothes? But wait! Those who dress fashionably and live in luxury are found in palaces. [26]Come on, what did you go out to see? A prophet? Yes, that's what you went out to see, and even more than a prophet.	[1]Why have you come out to the countryside? To see a reed shaken by the wind? [2]And to see a person dressed in soft clothes, [like your] rulers and your powerful ones? [3]They are dressed in soft clothes and they cannot understand truth.

472. Congratulations to the Womb that Carried Jesus (Th)
SEE #149, 255, PP. 119, 200

Mt	Mk	Lk 11:27–28; 23:28–29	Th 79:1–3
		Lk 11:27–28 [27]And it came to pass, as he was making these remarks, that a woman from the crowd raised her voice and said to him, "Congratulations to the womb that carried you and the breasts that nursed you!" [28]"Rather," he replied, "congratulations to those who hear the word of God and keep it."* **Lk 23:28–29** [28]Jesus turned to them and said, "Daughters of Jerusalem, do not weep for me. Weep instead for yourselves and for your children. [29]Look, the time is coming when they will say, 'Congratulations to those who are infertile, to the wombs that never gave birth, and to the breasts that never nursed!'"	[1]A woman in the crowd said to him, "Congratulations to the womb that carried you and the breasts that fed you." [2]He said to [her], "Congratulations to those who've heard the word of the Father and have truly kept it." [3]There will be days when you will say, "Congratulations to the womb that has not conceived and the breasts that have not given milk."

*Lk 8:21 (#75, p. 60)

473. How the Wealthy Should Rule (Th)
= #493, P. 363

Mt	Mk	Lk	Th 81:1–2	Th 110
			[1]Whoever has become wealthy should rule, [2]and whoever has power should renounce ⟨it⟩.	Whoever has found the world, and has become wealthy, should renounce the world.

474. Jesus is like fire (Th)

SEE #162, P. 127

Mt	Mk	Lk 12:49*	Th 82:1–2	Th 10*
		I came to set the earth on fire, and how I wish it were already ablaze!	[1]Whoever is near me is near the fire, [2]and whoever is far from me is far from the ⟨Father's⟩ empire.	I have cast fire upon the world, and look, I'm guarding it until it blazes.

* Th 16:2 (#427, p. 337)

475. Foxes and Birds (Th)

SEE #137, 365, PP. 112, 299

Mt 8:20	Mk	Lk 9:58	Th 86:1–2
Foxes have dens, and birds of the sky have nests, but the Human One has nowhere to rest his head.		Foxes have dens, and birds of the sky have nests, but the Human One has nowhere to rest his head.	[1][Foxes have] their dens and birds have their nests, [2]but the human being has no place to lie down and rest.

476. Inside and Outside (Th)

SEE #153, 378, PP. 121, 308

Mt 23:25–26	Mk	Lk 11:39–41	Th 89:1–2
[25]You scholars and Pharisees, you impostors! Damn you! You wash the outside of cups and plates, but inside they are full of greed and self-indulgence. [26]You blind Pharisee, first clean the inside of the cup and then the outside will be clean too.		[39]You Pharisees clean the outside of cups and dishes, but inside you are full of greed and evil. [40]You fools! Did not the one who made the outside also make the inside? [41]Still, donate what is inside to charity, and then you'll see how everything comes clean for you.	[1]Why do you wash the outside of the cup? [2]Don't you understand that the one who made the inside is also the one who made the outside?

477. The Comfortable Yoke (Th)

= #142, P. 116

Mt 11:28–30	Mk	Lk	Th 90:1–2
[28]All you who toil and are overloaded come to me, and I will refresh you. [29]Take my yoke upon you and learn from me, because I am gentle and modest and your lives will find rest. [30]For my yoke is comfortable and my load is light.			[1]Come to me, for my yoke is comfortable and my authority is gentle, [2]and you will find rest for yourselves.

478. Examining the Face of the Sky (Th)
SEE #163, 389, PP. 127, 315

Mt 16:3b	Mk	Lk 12:56	Th 91:1–2
[3b]You know how to interpret the face of the sky, but you can't ⟨do that for⟩ the signs of the times.		[56]You phonies! You know the lay of the land and can read the face of the sky, so why don't you know how to read the present time?	[1]They said to him, "Tell us who you are so that we can believe in you." [2]He said to them, "You examine the face of heaven and earth, but you have not come to know the one who is in your presence, and you don't know how to examine the present moment."

479. Seeking and Finding (b) (Th)
SEE #36, 320, 372, 414, 481, PP. 31, 256, 303, 330, 358

Mt 7:7–8	Mk	Lk 11:9–10	Th 92:1–2	other
[7]Ask—it'll be given to you; seek—you'll find; knock—it'll be opened for you.* [8]For everyone who asks receives; everyone who seeks finds; and for the one who knocks it is opened.		[9]Ask—it'll be given to you; seek—you'll find; knock—it'll be opened for you.* [10]For everyone who asks receives; everyone who seeks finds; and for the one who knocks it is opened.	[1]Seek and you will find.* [2]In the past, however, I didn't tell you the things about which you asked me then. Now I'm willing to tell them, but you're not seeking them.	**Th 2:1** Those who seek should not stop seeking until they find.† **Th 94:1–2** [1]The one who seeks will find,* [2]and for [one who knocks] it will be opened. **Jn 16:4b–5** [4b]I didn't tell you these things at first because I was with you then. [5]Now I am on my way to the one who sent me, and not one of you asks me, "Where are you going?"

*Jn 15:5–8; 16:23–24 (#318, 321, pp. 254, 256)
† GHeb 6b (#517, p. 392)

480. Profaning the Holy (Th)
= #35, P. 30

Mt 7:6	Mk	Lk	Th 93:1–2
Don't offer to dogs what is sacred, and don't throw your pearls to pigs, or they'll trample them underfoot and turn and tear you to shreds.			[1]Don't give what is sacred to dogs, or else they might throw them on the manure pile. [2]Don't throw pearls [to] pigs, or they might . . . it [. . .].ᵃ

ᵃ Th 93:2 The text is deficient here. Among proposals for its restoration are the following: "bring it [to naught]" and "grind it [to bits]."

481. Seeking and Finding (c) (Th)

SEE #36, 372, 414, 479 PP. 31, 303, 330, 357

Mt 7:7–8	Mk	Lk 11:9–10	Th 94:1–2	Th 92:1; 2:1
[7]Ask—it'll be given to you; seek—you'll find; knock—it'll be opened for you.* [8]For everyone who asks receives; everyone who seeks finds; and for the one who knocks it is opened.		[9]Ask—it'll be given to you; seek—you'll find; knock—it'll be opened for you.* [10]For everyone who asks receives; everyone who seeks finds; and for the one who knocks it is opened.	[1]The one who seeks will find,* [2]and for [one who knocks] it will be opened.	**Th 92:1** Seek and you will find.* **Th 2:1** Those who seek should not stop seeking until they find.†

*Jn 15:5–8; 16:23–24 (#318, 392, pp. 254, 317)
† GHeb 6b (#517, p. 392)

482. Don't charge interest (Th)

SEE #24, 355, PP. 24, 290

Mt 5:42	Mk	Lk 6:30	Th 95:1–2
Give to those who beg from you; and don't turn away those who want to borrow from you.		Give to everyone who begs from you; and when someone takes your things, don't ask for them back.	[1]If you have money, don't lend it at interest. [2]Instead, give [it] to someone from whom you won't get it back.

483. The Parable of the Leaven (Th)

SEE #84, 392, PP. 67, 317

Mt 13:33b	Mk	Lk 13:20–21	Th 96:1–3
The empire of Heaven is like leaven that a woman took and concealed in fifty pounds of flour until it was all leavened.		[20]What does the empire of God remind me of? [21]It's like leaven that a woman took and concealed in fifty pounds of flour until it was all leavened.	[1]The Father's empire is like [a] woman [2]who took a little leaven, [hid] it in dough, and made it into large loaves of bread. [3]Whoever has ears to hear should listen.*

*Mt 11:15; 13:9; 13:43b; Mk 4:9; 4:23; Lk 8:8b; 14:35b; Th 8:4; 21:10; 24:2; 63:4; 65:8

484. Jesus' True Family (Th)

= #75, P. 60

Mt 12:46–50	Mk 3:31–35	Lk 8:19–21	Th 99:1–3
[46]While he was still speaking to the crowds, his mother and brothers showed up outside; they had come to speak to him. [47]Someone said to him, "Look, your mother and your brothers are outside and they want to speak to you."[a]	[31]Then his mother and his brothers arrive. While still outside, they send in and ask for him. [32]A crowd was sitting around him, and they say to him, "Look, your mother and your brothers are outside looking for you."	[19]Then his mother and his brothers came to see him, but they could not reach him because of the crowd. [20]When he was told, "Your mother and your brothers are outside and want to see you,"	[1]The disciples said to him, "Your brothers and your mother are standing outside."
[48]In response he said to the one speaking to him, "Who is my mother and who are my brothers?"	[33]In response he says to them, "Who are my mother and brothers?"		
[49]And he pointed to his disciples and said,	[34]And looking right at those seated around him in a circle, he says,	[21]he replied to them,	[2]He said to them,
"Here are my mother and my brothers. [50]For whoever does the will of my Father in heaven, that's my brother and sister and mother."*	"Here are my mother and my brothers. [35]Whoever does God's will, that's my brother and sister and mother."*	"My mother and my brothers are those who listen to God's message and do it."*	"Those here who do what my Father wants are my brothers and my mother.
			[3]They're the ones who will enter my Father's empire."

* GHeb 4a My mother, the holy spirit, took me by one of my hairs and brought me to
Tabor, the great mountain. (#516, p. 392)

---

[a] Mt 12:47 Many mss lack v. 47.

485. God and Caesar (Th)

SEE #213, P. 164

Mt 22:15–22	Mk 12:14b–17a	Lk 20:22–25	Th 100:1–4
[17b]"Is it permissible to pay the poll tax to Caesar or not?"	[14b]"Is it permissible to pay the poll tax to Caesar or not? Should we pay or should we not pay?"	[22]"Is it permissible for us to pay taxes to Caesar or not?"	[1]They showed Jesus a gold coin and said to him, "Caesar's people demand taxes from us."
[18]Jesus knew how devious they were, and said, "Why do you provoke me, you phonies? [19]Show me the money used to pay the poll tax." And they handed him a denarius.	[15]But he saw through their trap, and said to them, "Why do you provoke me like this? Let me have a look at a denarius." [16]They handed him one,	[23]But he saw through their duplicity, and said to them, [24]"Show me a denarius."	
[20]And he says to them, "Whose image is this? Whose name is on it?" [21]They say to him, "Caesar's." Then he says to them, "Pay to Caesar what belongs to Caesar, and to God what belongs to God!"	and he says to them, "Whose image is this? Whose name is on it?" They replied, "Caesar's." [17a]Jesus said to them, "Pay to Caesar what belongs to Caesar, and to God what belongs to God."	Whose image and inscription is on it?" They said, "Caesar's." [25]So he said to them, "Then pay to Caesar what belongs to Caesar, and to God what belongs to God!"	[2]He said to them, "Give Caesar what belongs to Caesar, [3]give God what belongs to God, [4]and give me what is mine."

486. Hating Father and Mother (b) (Th)

SEE #176, 398, 455, PP. 134, 320, 347

Mt 10:37–38	Mk	Lk 14:26–27	Th 101:1–3	Th 55:1–2
[37]If you love your father and mother more than me, you're not worthy of me, and if you love your son or daughter more than me, you're not worthy of me.		[26]If any of you comes to me and does not hate your own father and mother and wife and children and brothers and sisters—yes, even your own life—you cannot be my disciple.	[1]Whoever does not hate [father] and mother as I do cannot be my [disciple], [2]and whoever does [not] love [father and] mother as I do cannot be my [disciple]. [3]For my mother [. . .],[a] but my true [mother] gave me life.	[1]Whoever does not hate father and mother cannot be my disciple, [2]and whoever does not hate brothers and sisters,
[38]Unless you take your cross and come along with me, you're not worthy of me.*		[27]Unless you carry your own cross and come along with me, you cannot be my disciple.*		and carry the cross as I do, will not be worthy of me.*

* Mt 16:24 / Mk 8:34 / Lk 9:23 (#121, p. 102)

---

[a] Th 101:3 The lacuna cannot be filled in with certainty. One proposal: "For my mother [gave me falsehood]."

487. A Dog in the Feeding Trough (Th)
= #445; SEE #153, 379, PP. 343, 121, 309

Mt 23:13	Mk	Lk 11:52	**Th 102**	Th 39:1–2
You scholars and Pharisees, you impostors! Damn you! You slam the door of the empire of Heaven in people's faces. You yourselves don't go in, and you block the way of those trying to go in.		You legal experts, damn you! You've taken away the key of knowledge. You yourselves haven't gone in and you have blocked the way of those trying to go in.	Damn the Pharisees! They are like a dog sleeping in the cattle's feeding trough: the dog neither eats nor [lets] the cattle eat.	[1]The Pharisees and the scholars have taken the keys of knowledge and hidden them. [2]They have not entered, nor have they allowed those who want to enter to do so.

488. Anticipating the Brigands (Th)
SEE #160, 386, 430, PP. 125, 313, 338

Mt 24:43	Mk	Lk 12:39	**Th 103**	**Th 21:5**
Mark this well: if the homeowner had known when the burglar was coming, he would have been on guard and not have allowed anyone to break into his house.		Mark this well: if the homeowner had known what time the burglar was coming,[a] he would not have let anyone break into his house.	Congratulations to the one who knows where the brigands are going to attack. [He] can take action, mobilize his kingdom, and be prepared before the brigands invade.	For this reason I say, if the owners of a house know that a thief is coming, they will be on guard before the thief arrives, and won't let the thief break into their house and steal their possessions.

[a] Lk 12:39 Many mss insert "he would have watched and" after *coming*.

489. When the Groom Leaves (Th)
SEE #61, P. 50

Mt 9:15b	Mk 2:20	Lk 5:35	**Th 104:1–3**
			[1]They said to Jesus, "Come on, let's pray today, and let's fast." [2]Jesus said, "What sin have I committed, or how have I been undone?
But the days will come when the groom is taken away from them, and then they will fast.	But the days will come when the groom is taken away from them, and then they will fast, on that day.	But the days will come when the groom is taken away from them, and then they will fast, in those days.	[3]When the groom leaves the wedding hall, then let people fast and pray."

490. How to Move a Mountain (Th)

= #453; SEE #209, PP. 346, 159

Mt 21:21b	Mk 11:23	Lk	Th 106:1–2	Th 48
Let me tell you, if you have trust and do not doubt, not only can you do this to a fig tree but you can even say to this mountain, "Up with you and into the sea!" and that's what will happen.*	Let me tell you, those who say to this mountain, "Up with you and into the sea!" and do not waver in their conviction, but trust that what they say will happen, that's the way it will be.		¹When you make the two into one, you will become children of Adam, ²and when you say, "Mountain, move from here!" it will move.	If two make peace with each other in a single house, they will say to the mountain, "Move from here!" and it will move.

* ① Mt 17:20 / Lk 17:6 (#186, p. 140)

491. The Parable of the Lost-and-Found Sheep (Th)

SEE #177, 405, PP. 135, 323

Mt 18:12–14	Mk	Lk 15:4–7	Th 107:1–3
¹²What do you think about this? If someone has a hundred sheep and one of them wanders off, won't he leave the ninety-nine in the hills and go look for the one that wandered off? ¹³And if he should find it, let me tell you, he'll rejoice over it more than over the ninety-nine that didn't wander off. ¹⁴And so it is the intention of your Father in heaven that not one of these little ones be lost.		⁴Is there any one of you who owns a hundred sheep and one of them gets lost, who wouldn't leave the ninety-nine in the wild and go after the one that got lost until he finds it? ⁵And when he finds it, he is happy and hoists it onto his shoulders. ⁶Once he gets home, he invites his friends and his neighbors over, and says to them, "Celebrate with me, because I've found my lost sheep." ⁷I'm telling you, it'll be just like that in heaven: there'll be more celebrating over one sinner who has a change of heart than over ninety-nine virtuous people who have no need to change their hearts.	¹The ⟨Father's⟩ empire is like a shepherd who had a hundred sheep. ²One of them, the largest, went astray. He left the ninety-nine and looked for the one until he found it. ³After he had struggled, he said to the sheep, "I love you more than the ninety-nine."

492. The Parable of the Treasure (Th)
= #87, P. 68

Mt 13:44	Mk	Lk	Th 109:1–3
The empire of Heaven is like treasure hidden in a field. When someone finds it, that person covers it up again, and out of sheer joy goes and sells every last possession and buys that field.			[1]The ⟨Father's⟩ empire is like a man who had a treasure in his field but didn't know it. [2]And [when] he died he left it to his [son]. The son [did] not know ⟨about it either⟩. He took over the field and sold it. [3]The buyer went plowing, [discovered] the treasure, and began to lend money at interest to whomever he wished.

493. The wealthy should renounce the world (Th)
= #473, P. 355

Mt	Mk	Lk	Th 110	Th 81:1–2
			Whoever has found the world, and has become wealthy, should renounce the world.	[1]Whoever has become wealthy should rule, [2]and whoever has power should renounce ⟨it⟩.

494. Empire of God Spread Out on the Earth (Th)
= #189, #415, PP. 141, 330

Mt	Mk	Lk 17:20–21	Th 113:1–4	Th 3:1–3
		[20]When asked by the Pharisees when the empire of God would come, he answered them, "You won't be able to observe the coming of the empire of God. [21]People won't be able to say, 'Look, here it is!' or 'Over there!'* On the contrary, the empire of God is among you."	[1]His disciples said to him, "When will the ⟨Father's⟩ empire come?" [2]"It won't come by watching for it. [3]It won't be said, 'Look, here!' or 'Look, there!'* [4]Rather, the Father's empire is spread out upon the earth, and people don't see it."	[1]If your leaders say to you, 'Look, the ⟨Father's⟩ empire is in the sky,' then the birds of the sky will precede you. [2]If they say to you, 'It's in the sea,' then the fish will precede you. [3]Rather, the ⟨Father's⟩ empire is inside you and outside you.

*Mt 24:23 / Mk 13:21 (#226, p. 175)

The Gospel of Peter

495. Joseph asks Pilate for the Master's body (Pt)

SEE #262, P. 210

Mt 27:57–58	Mk 15:43–45, 42	Lk 23:50–52, 54
[57]It was dark when a rich man from Arimathea, by the name of Joseph, who himself was a follower of Jesus, showed up	[43]Joseph of Arimathea, a respected Council member, who himself was anticipating the empire of God,	[50]There was a man named Joseph, a Council member, a decent and upright man, [51]who had not endorsed their decision or gone along with their action. He was from the town of Arimathea in Judea, and he lived in anticipation of the empire of God.
[58]and went to Pilate and requested the body of Jesus.	came forward and dared to go to Pilate to request the body of Jesus. [44]And Pilate was surprised that he had died so soon. He summoned the Roman officer and asked him whether he had been dead for long. [45]And when he had been briefed by the officer, he granted the body to Joseph.	[52]This man went to Pilate and requested the body of Jesus.
Then Pilate ordered it to be turned over to him.		
	[42]And since it was the preparation day (the day before the Sabbath), and already getting dark,	[54]It was the day of preparation, and the Sabbath was about to begin.

496. Jesus is turned over to the people (Pt)

SEE #252, 331, PP. 198, 268

Mt 27:26	Mk 15:15	Lk 23:24–25
Then he set Barabbas free for them, but had Jesus flogged,	And because Pilate was always looking to satisfy the crowd, he set Barabbas free for them, had Jesus flogged,	[24]Pilate ruled that their demand should be carried out. [25]He set free the man they had asked for, who had been thrown into prison for insurrection and murder;
and then turned him over to be crucified.	and then turned him over to be crucified.	but he turned over Jesus to their will.

Jn 19:38	Pt 2:1–4
[38]After all this, Joseph of Arimathea—a disciple of Jesus, but a secret one because he was afraid of the Judeans—	[1]Joseph, the friend of Pilate and the Master, stood there.
asked Pilate's permission to take Jesus' body down.	When he realized that they were about to crucify him, he went to Pilate and asked for the Master's body for burial.
Pilate agreed,	
	[2]And Pilate sent to Herod and asked for his body [3]And Herod replied, "Brother Pilate, even if no one had asked for him, we would have buried him, since the Sabbath is drawing near. [4]For it is written in the Law, 'The sun must not set upon one who has been executed.'"

Jn 19:16	Pt 2:5
And so, in the end, Pilate turned him over to them to be crucified.	And he turned him over to the people on the day before their festival, known as Unleavened Bread, began.

497. The Humiliating Ordeal (Pt)

SEE #253, 329, PP. 200, 264

Mt 27:27–30	Mk 15:16–19	Lk	Jn 19:2–3	Pt 3:1–4
[27]Then the governor's soldiers took Jesus into the governor's residence and surrounded him with the whole cohort ⟨of Roman troops⟩.	[16]And the ⟨Roman⟩ soldiers led him away to the courtyard of the governor's residence, and they summoned the whole company ⟨of troops⟩.			They took the Master and kept pushing him along as they ran;
[28]They stripped him and dressed him in a crimson cloak,	[17]And they dressed him in purple			and they were saying, "Let's drag the son of God along, since we have him in our power." [2]And they threw a purple robe around him and sat him upon the judgment seat and said, "Judge justly, king of Israel." [3]And one of them brought a crown of thorns and set it on the head of the Master. [4]And others standing about would spit in his eyes, and others slapped his face, while others poked him with a rod. Some kept flogging him as they said,
[29]and they wove a crown out of thorns and put it on his head.	and crowned him with a garland woven of thorns.		[2]And the soldiers wove a crown out of thorns and put it on his head; they also dressed him up in a purple robe.	
They placed a stick in his right hand, and bowing down before him, they made fun of him, saying, "Greetings, 'King of the Judeans'!" [30]And spitting on him, they took the stick and hit him on the head.	[18]And they began to salute him: "Greetings, 'King of the Judeans'!" [19]And they kept striking him on the head with a stick, and spitting on him; and they were getting down on their knees and bowing down to him.		[3]They began marching up to him and saying, "Greetings, 'King of the Judeans,'" as they slapped him in the face.	"Let's pay proper respect to the son of God."

498. Jesus is crucified (Pt)

SEE #256, P. 202

Mt 27:38, 37, 35	Mk 15:24a, 26, 24b	Lk 23:33, 38, 34
[38]Then they crucified two insurgents with him, one on his right and one on his left.	[24a]And they crucify him,	[33]They crucified him there along with the criminals, one on his right and the other on his left.
[37]And over his head they put an inscription that identified his crime: "This is Jesus, the King of the Judeans."	[26]And the placard, on which the charge against him was inscribed, read, "The King of the Judeans."	[38]There was also this placard over him: "This is the King of the Judeans."[a]
[35]After crucifying him, they divided up his clothes by casting lots.	[24b]and they divide up his clothes, casting lots to see who would get what.	[34]They divided up his clothes after they cast lots ⟨for them⟩.[b]

[a] Lk 23:38 Many mss add that the notice "was written in Greek, Latin, and Hebrew."

[b] Lk 23:34 Many mss add "And Jesus said, 'Father, forgive them because they don't know what they're doing'" at the beginning of the verse.

499. A criminal defends Jesus (Pt)

SEE #258, P. 205

Mt 27:44	Mk 15:32b	Lk 23:39–43
In the same way, the insurgents who were crucified with him were also insulting him.	Even those being crucified along with him were insulting him.	[39]One of the criminals hanging there kept taunting him: "Aren't you supposed to be the Anointed One? Save yourself and us!" [40]But the other ⟨criminal⟩ rebuked the first: "Don't you even fear God, since you're under the same sentence? [41]We are getting justice, since we are getting what we deserve. But this man has done nothing wrong." [42]And he implored, "Jesus, remember me when you come into your empire."[a] [43]And Jesus said to him, "Let me tell you, today you'll be with me in Paradise."

[a] Lk 23:42 Many mss read "with" instead of *into*.

Jn 19:18–19, 23–24a	Pt 4:1–3
[18]There they crucified him, and with him two others—one on each side, with Jesus in the middle.	[1]And they brought two criminals and crucified the Master between them. But he himself remained silent, as if in no pain.
[19]Pilate also had a notice written and posted it on the cross; it read:	[2]And when they set up the cross, they put an inscription on it,
"Jesus the Nazorean, the King of the Judeans." [23]When the soldiers had crucified Jesus, they took his clothes and divided them into four shares, one share for each soldier. But his shirt was woven continuously without seam. [24a]So they said to each other, "Let's not tear it, but toss to see who gets it."	"This is the king of Israel." [3]And they piled his clothes in front of him; then they divided them among themselves and gambled for them.

Jn 19:32–33	Pt 4:4–5
	[4]But one of those criminals reproached them and said, "We're suffering for the evil that we've done, but this man, who has become a savior of humanity, what wrong has he done to you?"
[32]So the soldiers came and broke the legs of the first man, and then of the other who had been crucified with him. [33]But when they came to Jesus, they could see that he was already dead, so they didn't break his legs.	[5]And they got angry at him and ordered that his legs not be broken so he would die in agony.

500. Jesus is taken up (Pt)

SEE # 259, P. 206

Mt 27:45, 34, 46, 50	Mk 15:33, 23, 34, 37	Lk 23:44–45a, 46
[45]Beginning at noon darkness blanketed the entire land until mid-afternoon.	[33]And when noon came, darkness blanketed the whole land until mid-afternoon.	[44]It was already about noon, and darkness blanketed the whole land until mid-afternoon, [45a]during an eclipse of the sun.
[34]they gave him a drink of wine mixed with gall, but once he tasted it, he didn't want to drink it.	[23]And they tried to give him wine mixed with myrrh, but he didn't take it.	
[46]And about three o'clock in the afternoon Jesus shouted at the top of his voice, "*Eli, Eli, lema sabachthani*" (which means "My God, my God, why have you abandoned me?") [50]Jesus again shouted at the top of his voice and surrendered the spirit.	[34]And at three o'clock in the afternoon Jesus shouted at the top of his voice, "*Eloi, Eloi, lema sabachthani*" (which means "My God, my God, why have you abandoned me?"). [37]But Jesus let out a great shout and breathed his last.	[46]Then Jesus shouted at the top of his voice, "Father, into your hands I entrust my spirit!" Having said this, he breathed his last.

*GHeb 1:7 After they had raised him on the cross, the Father took him up into heaven to himself. (#513, p. 391)

†Mk 16:9 / Lk 24:51 / Acts 1:9 (#527, p. 401)

Jn 19:28–30	Pt 5:1–5
	¹It was midday and darkness covered the whole of Judea.
	They were confused and anxious for fear that the sun had set while he was still alive. ⟨For⟩ it is written, "The sun must not set upon one who has been executed."
²⁸Then, since Jesus knew that everything was now completed, he says (in order to fulfill the scripture), "I'm thirsty." ²⁹A bowl of sour wine was sitting there, and so they filled a sponge with wine, stuck it on some hyssop, and held it to his mouth. ³⁰When Jesus had taken some wine,	²And one of them said, "Give him vinegar mixed with something bitter to drink." And they mixed it and gave it to him to drink.
he said, "Now it's complete."	³And they fulfilled all things and brought to completion the sins on their head. ⁴Now many went around with lamps, and, thinking that it was night, they lay down.
	⁵And the Master cried out, saying, "My power, ⟨my⟩ power, you have abandoned me."
Lowering his head, he handed over the spirit.	When he said this, he was taken up.* †

501. Omens at the Death of Jesus (Pt)
SEE #260, P. 208

Mt 27:51–53	Mk 15:38	Lk 23:45b	Pt 5:6–6:2
⁵¹And suddenly the curtain of the temple was torn in two from top to bottom,	And the curtain of the temple was torn in two from top to bottom!	The curtain of the temple was torn down the middle.	⁵:⁶And at that moment, the curtain of the Jerusalem temple was torn in two.
and the earth quaked,			⁶:¹And then they pulled the nails from the Master's hands and set him on the ground. And the whole earth shook and there was great fear. ⁶:²Then the sun came out and it turned out to be three o'clock in the afternoon.
vv. 45–46	vv. 33–34		
rocks were split apart, ⁵²and tombs were opened and many bodies of sleeping saints came back to life. ⁵³And they came out of the tombs after his resurrection and went into the holy city, where they appeared to many.			

502. Jesus is buried (Pt)
SEE #262, P. 210

Mt 27:58b–61	Mk 15:45b–47	Lk 23:53, 55
⁵⁸ᵇThen Pilate ordered ⟨the body⟩ to be turned over to ⟨Joseph⟩. ⁵⁹And taking the body,	⁴⁵ᵇ⟨Pilate⟩ granted the body to Joseph. ⁴⁶And he bought a shroud and took him down	⁵³Then he took ⟨the body⟩ down
Joseph wrapped it in a clean linen shroud	and wrapped him in the shroud,	and wrapped it in a shroud,
⁶⁰and put it in his new tomb, which had been cut in the rock.	and placed him in a tomb that had been hewn out of rock,	and laid him in a tomb cut from the rock, where no one had ever been buried.
He rolled a huge stone across the opening of the tomb and left. ⁶¹But Mary of Magdala and the other Mary stayed there, sitting across from the tomb.	and rolled a stone up against the opening of the tomb. ⁴⁷And Mary of Magdala and Mary the mother of Joses noted where he had been laid to rest.	⁵⁵The women who had come with him from Galilee followed. They kept an eye on the tomb, to see how his body was laid to rest.

Jn 19:38b–42	Pt 6:3–4
v. 38a 38b so Joseph came and took his body down. 39 Nicodemus, the one who had first gone to him at night, came too, bringing a mixture of myrrh and aloes weighing about seventy-five pounds. 40 So they took Jesus' body, and wound it up in strips of burial cloth along with the spices, as the Jews customarily do to bury their dead. 41 Now there was a garden in the place where he had been crucified, and a new tomb in the garden where no one had ever been laid to rest. 42 Since this tomb was handy and because it was the Jewish day of preparation, it was here that they laid Jesus.	3 Now the Judeans rejoiced and gave his body to Joseph so that he might bury it. 4 ⟨Joseph⟩ took the Master, washed ⟨his body⟩ and wound a linen ⟨shroud⟩ around him, and brought him to his own tomb, called "Joseph's Garden."

503. Guards are posted at Jesus' tomb (Pt)
SEE #263, P. 213

Mt 27:54, 62b–66	Mk 15:39	Lk 23:48, 47	Pt 8:1–6
			¹When the scholars and the Pharisees and the priests had gathered together, and when they heard that all the people were moaning
		⁴⁸And when the throng of people that had gathered for this spectacle observed what had transpired, they all returned home beating their chests.	and beating their chests, and saying
⁵⁴The Roman officer and those with him keeping watch over Jesus witnessed the sign and what had happened, and were terrified, and said,	When the Roman officer in charge saw that he had died like this, he said,	⁴⁷Now when the Roman officer saw what happened, he praised God and said,	
"This man really was God's son."	"This man really was God's son!"	"This man really was innocent!"	"If his death has produced these overwhelming signs, he must have been completely innocent!"
⁶²ᵇThe chief priests and the Pharisees met with Pilate. ⁶³"Your Excellency, we remember what that deceiver said while he was still alive: 'After three days I'm going to be raised up.' ⁶⁴So order the tomb sealed for three days so his disciples won't come and steal his body and tell everyone, 'He has been raised from the dead.' If that were to happen, the last deception will be worse than the first."			²They became frightened and went to Pilate and begged him, ³"Give us soldiers so that ⟨we⟩ can guard his tomb for three [days], in case his disciples come and steal his body and the people assume that he is risen from the dead and do us harm."
⁶⁵Pilate replied to them, "You have guards; go and secure it as you think best." ⁶⁶They went and secured the tomb by sealing ⟨it with a⟩ stone and posting a guard.			
			⁴So Pilate gave them the officer Petronius with soldiers to guard the tomb. And elders and scholars went with them to the tomb. ⁵And all who were there ⟨with⟩ the officer and the soldiers helped roll a large stone against the entrance to the tomb. ⁶And they put seven seals on it. Then they pitched a tent there and kept watch.

504. Guards and Two Young Men (Pt)

SEE #264, P. 214

Mt 28:2–4	Mk 16:2, 4–5	Lk 24:2, 4
	²And very early on Sunday they got to the tomb just as the sun was coming up.	
²And just then there was a strong earthquake. You see, a messenger of the Lord had come down from the sky, arrived ⟨at the tomb⟩, rolled away the stone, and was sitting on it. ³The messenger gave off a dazzling light and wore clothes as white as snow. ⁴Now those who kept watch were quaking with fear and looked like corpses themselves.		
	⁴Then they look up and discover that the stone has been rolled away. (You see, the stone was very large.)	²They found the stone rolled away from the tomb.
	⁵And when they went into the tomb, they saw a young man sitting on the right, wearing a white robe, and they grew apprehensive.	⁴And it came to pass, while they were still uncertain about what to do, that two men in dazzling clothes suddenly appeared and stood beside them.

Jn 20:1	Pt 9:1–4
Early on Sunday, while it was still dark, Mary of Magdala comes to the tomb	[1]Early, at first light on the Sabbath, a crowd came from Jerusalem and the surrounding countryside to see the sealed tomb. [2]But during the night before the Lord's day dawned, while the soldiers were on guard, in pairs during each watch, a loud noise came from the sky, [3]and they saw the skies open up and two men come down from there in a burst of light and approach the tomb.
	[4]The stone that had been pushed against the entrance began to roll by itself and moved away to one side;
and sees that the stone has been moved away.	
	then the tomb opened up and both young men went inside.

505. The Official Cover Up (Pt)
SEE # 252, P. 198

Mt 27:24	Mk	Lk	Pt 11:3–7
			³When those in the officer's unit saw this, they rushed out into the night to Pilate, leaving the tomb that they were supposed to be guarding. And as they were recounting everything they had seen, they became deeply disturbed and cried, "He really was God's son!"
27:54 Now when Pilate could see that he was getting nowhere, but that a riot was starting instead, he took water and washed his hands in full view of the crowd and said, "I'm not responsible for this man's blood. That's your business!"	*15:39*	*23:47*	⁴Pilate responded by saying, "I am clean of the blood of the son of God; this was all your doing." ⁵Then they all crowded around ⟨Pilate⟩ and began to beg and urge him to order the officer and his soldiers to tell no one what they had seen. ⁶"You see," they said, "it's better for us to be guilty of the greatest sin before God than to fall into the hands of the Judean people and be stoned." ⁷Pilate then ordered the officer and the soldiers to say nothing.
28:11–15			

506. Approaching the Tomb (Pt)
SEE #264, P. 214

Mt 28:1	Mk 16:1, 3, 4b	Lk 24:1
After the Sabbath, at first light on Sunday, Mary of Magdala and the other Mary came to inspect the tomb.	¹And when the Sabbath was over, Mary of Magdala and Mary the mother of James and Salome bought spices so they could go and anoint him. ²And very early on Sunday they got to the tomb just as the sun was coming up.	On Sunday, at daybreak, they made their way to the tomb, bringing the spices they had prepared.
	³And they had been asking themselves, "Who will help us roll the stone away from the opening of the tomb?"	
	⁴ᵇ(You see, the stone was very large.)	

Jn 20:1	Pt 12:1–5
Early on Sunday, while it was still dark, Mary of Magdala comes to the tomb.	[1]Early on the Lord's day, Mary of Magdala, a disciple of the Master, was fearful on account of the Judeans and, since they were inflamed with rage, she did not do at the Master's tomb what women usually do for their loved ones who die. [2]Nevertheless, she took her friends with her and went to the tomb where he had been laid. [3]And they were afraid that the Judeans might see them and were saying, "Although on the day he was crucified we could not weep and beat our breasts, we should now perform these rites at his tomb. [4]But who will roll away the stone for us, the one placed at the entrance of the tomb, so that we can enter and sit beside him and do what ought to be done?" [5](Remember, it was a huge stone.) "We fear that someone might see us. And if we are unable ⟨to roll the stone away⟩ we should, at least, place at the entrance the memorial we brought for him, and we should weep and beat our breasts until we go home."

507. Questions at the Empty tomb (Pt)

SEE #265, P. 216

Mt 28:2b, 5–8	Mk 16:4–8	Lk 24:2–9
2bYou see, a messenger of the Lord had come down from the sky, arrived ⟨at the tomb⟩, rolled away the stone, and was sitting on it.	4Then they look up and discover that the stone has been rolled away. (You see, the stone was very large.)	2They found the stone rolled away from the tomb.
	5And when they went into the tomb,	3but when they went inside they did not find the body of the Master Jesus. 4And it came to pass, while they were still uncertain about what to do, that two men in dazzling clothes suddenly appeared and stood beside them. 5They were terrified and knelt with their faces to the ground. The men said to them,
	they saw a young man sitting on the right, wearing a white robe, and they grew apprehensive.	
5In response the messenger said to the women, "Don't be afraid! I know you are looking for Jesus who was crucified.	6He says to them, "Don't be alarmed. You are looking for Jesus the Nazarene who was crucified. He was raised,	"Why are you looking for the living among the dead?
6He is not here. You see, he was raised, just as he said. Come here; look at the spot where he was lying.	he is not here. Look at the spot where they put him.	6He is not here—he was raised.a
		Remember what he told you while he was still in Galilee: 7'the Human One is destined to be turned over to sinners, to be crucified, and on the third day to rise.'" 8Then they recalled what he had said.
7Go quickly and tell his disciples that he has been raised from the dead. Don't forget, he is going ahead of you to Galilee. There you will see him. That's what I came to tell you." 8And they hurried away from the tomb, afraid and filled with joy,	7But go and tell his disciples, including 'Rock,' 'He is going ahead of you to Galilee. There you will see him, just as he told you.'" 8And once they got outside, they ran away from the tomb, because great fear and excitement got the better of them. And they didn't breathe a word of it to anyone: talk about terrified . . .b	9And returning from the tomb,
and ran to tell his disciples.		they related everything to the Eleven and to everybody else.*

* Jn 20:2 ⟨Mary of Magdala⟩ runs and comes to Simon Peter and the other disciple, the one that Jesus loved, and tells them, "They've taken the Master from the tomb, and we don't know where they've put him." (#340 p. 278)

a Lk 24:6 A few mss omit *He is not here—he was raised.*

b Mk 16:8 The best ancient mss conclude the Gospel of Mark with this verse. Other mss supply lengthier narrative endings. See "Mark's Longer Ending" and "Mark's Shorter Ending." (#272, 273, pp. 222, 223)

Jn 20:1, 11–13	Pt 13:1–3
[1]Mary of Magdala comes to the tomb and sees that the stone has been moved away.* [11]Mary, however, stood crying outside, and in her tears she stooped to look into the tomb,	[1]And they went and found the tomb open. They went up to ⟨the tomb⟩, stooped down,
[12]and she sees two heavenly messengers in white seated where Jesus' body had lain, one at the head and the other at the feet.	and saw a young man sitting there ⟨in⟩ the middle of the tomb; he was handsome and wore a splendid robe.
[13]"Lady, why are you crying?" they ask her.	He said to them, [2]"Why have you come? Who are you looking for? Surely not the one who was crucified? He is risen and gone. If you don't believe it, stoop down and take a look at the place where he lay—he's not there. You see, he is risen and has gone back to the place he was sent from."
"They've taken my master away," she tells them, "and I don't know where they've put him."	
	[3]Then the women fled in fear.

508. Some disciples prepare to fish (Pt)

SEE #50, 270, PP. 40, 220

Mt	Mk	Lk	Jn	Pt 14:1–3
				¹Now it was the last day of Unleavened Bread, and many began to return to their homes because the festival was over. ²But we, the twelve disciples of the Master, continued to weep and mourn, and each one, still grieving because of what had happened, left for his own home.
	16:12	24:13		
			21:1–11	³But I, Simon Peter, and Andrew, my brother, took our fishing nets and went away to the sea. And with us was Levi, the son of Alphaeus, whom the Master . . .ᵃ

ᵃ Pt 14:3 The text breaks off abruptly. The ms has ornamentation immediately following these words, which suggests that it was copied from an already fragmented text.

The Other Gospels
and Early Christian Writings

The Egerton Gospel

509. The Scriptures, Moses, and Jesus (EgerG)

SEE #292, P. 237

Mt	Mk	Lk	Jn 5:39, 45; 9:29; 5:46	EgerG 1:1–6
				[1][. . .] to the legal experts [. . .] everyone who acts unjustly [. . .] and not me [. . .] he does, how does he? [2]Turning to the rulers of the people, ⟨Jesus⟩ made this statement:
			Jn 5:39, 45 [39]You pore over the scriptures, because you imagine that in them there's unending life to be had. They do indeed give evidence on my behalf. [45]Don't suppose that I'll be your accuser before the Father. You have an accuser, and it's Moses—the one you were relying on.	"Pore over the scriptures. You imagine that in them there's life to be had. They do indeed give evidence on my behalf. [3]Don't suppose that I've come to be your accuser before my Father. The one accusing you is Moses, the one you were relying on."
			Jn 9:29 We know God spoke to Moses; we don't even know where this man came from."	[4]They say, "We know God spoke to Moses. But you— we don't know [where you come from."][a] [5]Jesus replied: "Now you stand accused for not trusting those who are [commended by ⟨Moses⟩.]
			Jn 5:46 But if you really believed Moses, you'd believe me; after all, I'm the one he wrote about.	[6]If you had believed Moses, you would've believed me; after all, he [wrote][b] about me to your ancestors."

[a] EgerG 1:4 *[where you come from]:* The Greek letters are completely lost, so the restoration is based on the parallel to John 9:29.

[b] EgerG1:6 *[wrote]* is a restoration based on the parallel to John 5:46; "spoke" is another possible restoration.

510. Jesus escapes arrest (EgerG)

SEE #305, P. 243

Mt	Mk	Lk 4:28–30	Jn 7:30	Jn 8:20b; 10:39	EgerG 1:7–10
					[. . .⁷. . .] stones to-gether [. . .] him [. . .] ⁸[The rulers] laid their hands on him to arrest him and [turn him] over[a] to the crowd. ⁹But they couldn't arrest him because the time for him to be turned over hadn't yet arrived.
			They would have arrested him then and there, but no one laid a hand on him, because his time had not yet come.	**Jn 8:20b** No one arrested him because his time had not yet come.	
		²⁸Everyone in the meeting place was filled with rage when they heard this. ²⁹They rose up, ran him out of town, and led him to the brow of the hill on which their town was built, intending to hurl him over the cliff. ³⁰But he slipped through their fingers and got away.		**Jn 10:39** Again they tried to arrest him, but he escaped.	¹⁰So the Master himself slipped through their hands and got away.

[a] 1:8 *[turn him] over:* The number of missing letters is uncertain and another suggested restoration is "throw him to."

511. A leper is healed (EgerG)
= #51, P. 41

Mt 8:1–4	Mk 1:40–45	Lk 5:12–16	EgerG 2:1–4
[1]When he came down from the mountain, huge crowds followed him. [2]Just then a leper appeared, bowed down to him, and said,	[40]Then a leper comes up to him, pleads with him, falls down on his knees, and says to him,	[12]And it came to pass, while he was in one of the towns, that there was this man covered with leprosy. Seeing Jesus, he knelt with his face to the ground and begged him,	[1]Just then a leper comes up to him and says, "Teacher Jesus, in wandering around with lepers and eating with them in the inn, I became a leper myself. [2]If you want to, I'll be made clean."
"Master, if you want to, you can make me clean."	"If you want to, you can make me clean." [41]Although Jesus was indignant,[a]	"Master, if you want to, you can make me clean."	
[3]And he stretched out his hand, touched him, and says,	he stretched out his hand, touched him, and says to him,	[13]Jesus stretched out his hand, touched him, saying,	[3]The Master said to him,
"Okay—you're clean!" And right away his leprosy was cleansed.	"Okay—you're clean!" [42]And right away the leprosy disappeared, and he was made clean. [43]And Jesus snapped at him, and right away threw him out [44]with this warning:	"Okay—you're clean!" And right away the leprosy disappeared.	"Okay—you're clean!" And right away his leprosy disappeared from him.
[4]Then Jesus warns him, "Don't tell anyone, but go, have a priest examine you. Then offer the gift that Moses commanded, as evidence ⟨of your cure⟩."	"Don't tell anyone anything, but go, have a priest examine you. Then offer for your cleansing what Moses commanded, as evidence ⟨of your cure⟩."	[14]He ordered him to tell no one. "But go, have a priest examine you. Then make an offering, as Moses commanded, for your cleansing, as evidence ⟨of your cure⟩."	[4]Jesus says to him, "Go and have the priests examine ⟨your skin⟩. Then offer for your purification what Moses commanded —and no more sinning."
	[45]But after he left, he started telling everyone and spreading the story, so that Jesus could no longer enter a town openly, but had to stay out in isolated places. Yet they continued to come to him from everywhere.	[15]Yet the story about him spread around all the more. Great crowds would gather to hear him and to be healed of their diseases. [16]But he would withdraw to isolated places and pray.	

[a] Mk 1:41 Most mss read "And Jesus was moved" in place of *Although Jesus was indignant.*

512. The Question of Paying Rulers (EgerG)

SEE #213, 110, PP. 164, 90

Mt 22:15–18a; 7:21; 15:7–9; 22:18b–21	Mk 12:13–15a; 7:6–7; 12:15b–17a	Lk 20:20–23a; 6:46; 20:23b–25	EgerG 3:1–6

Mt 22:15–18a
[15]Then the Pharisees went and conferred on how to trap him with a riddle.
 	
[16]And they send their disciples to him along with the Herodians to say,
 	
"Teacher, we know that you are honest and that you teach God's way forthrightly, and that you are impartial, because you pay no attention to appearances.
[17]So tell us what you think: is it permissible to pay the poll tax to Caesar or not?"
 	
[18a]Jesus knew how devious they were.
Mt 7:21
Not everyone who addresses me as 'Master, master,' will get into the empire of Heaven—only those who carry out the will of my Father in heaven.
Mt 15:7–9
[7]How accurately Isaiah prophesied about you phonies when he said,
"[8]This people honors me with their lips, but their heart stays far away from me. [9]Their worship of me is empty, because they insist on teachings that are human regulations."
Mt 22:18b–21*
[18b]He said,
"Why do you provoke me, you phonies?
[19]Show me the money used to pay the poll tax."
  And they handed him a denarius. [20]And he says to them,
	Mk 12:13–15a
	[13]And they send some of the Pharisees and the Herodians to him to trap him with a riddle.
	
	[14]They come and say to him, "Teacher, we know that you are honest and impartial, because you pay no attention to appearances, but instead you teach God's way forthrightly.
	
	Is it permissible to pay the poll tax to Caesar or not? Should we pay or should we not pay?"
	[15a]But he saw through their trap.
	
	Mk 7:6–7
	[6]How accurately Isaiah foretold you phonies when he wrote,
	"This people honors me with their lips, but their heart stays far away from me. [7]Their worship of me is empty, because they insist on teachings that are human regulations."
	Mk 12:15b–17a*
	[15b]He said to them, "Why do you provoke me like this? Let me have a look at a denarius."
	  [16]They handed him one, and he says to them,
		Lk 20:20–23a
		[20]So they kept him under surveillance, and sent spies, who feigned sincerity, so they could twist something he said and turn him over to the authority and jurisdiction of the governor.
		[21]They asked him, "Teacher, we know that what you speak and teach is correct, that you show no favoritism, but instead teach God's way forthrightly.
		[22]Is it permissible for us to pay taxes to Caesar or not?"
		
		[23a]But he saw through their duplicity.
		
		Lk 6:46
		Why do you call me "Master, master," and not do what I tell you?
		
		Lk 20:23b–25*
		[23b]He said to them,
		
		[24]"Show me a denarius.
			[1]They come to him and interrogate him as a way of putting him to the test.
			
			[2]They ask, "Teacher, Jesus, we know that you are [from God],[a] since the things you do put you above all the prophets.
			
			[3]Tell us, then, is it permissible to pay to rulers what is due them? Should we pay them or not?"
			
			[4]Jesus knew what they were up to, and became indignant.
			
			[5]Then he said to them, "Why do you pay me lip service as a teacher but not [do][b] what I say?
			
			[6]How accurately Isaiah prophesied about you when he said,
			"This people honors me with their lips, but their heart stays far away from me. Their worship of me is empty, [because they insist on teachings that are human] regulations."

Mt 22:15–18a; 7:21; 15:7–9; 22:18b–21	Mk 12:13–15a; 7:6–7; 12:15b–17a	Lk 20:20–23a; 6:46; 20:23b–25	EgerG 3:1–6
"Whose image is this? Whose name is on it?" [21]They say to him, "Caesar's." Then he says to them, "Pay to Caesar what belongs to Caesar, and to God what belongs to God."	"Whose image is this? Whose name is on it?" They replied, "Caesar's." [17]Jesus said to them, "Pay to Caesar what belongs to Caesar, and to God what belongs to God."	Whose image and inscription is on it?" They said, "Caesar's." [25]So he said to them, "Then pay to Caesar what belongs to Caesar, and to God what belongs to God."	

*Th 100:1–4 (#485, p. 360)

———

[a] EgerG 3:2　*[from God]:* The letters are completely lost, so the restoration is based on the loose parallel to John 3:2.

[b] EgerG 3:5　*[do]:* Another possible restoration is "hear."

The Gospel of the Hebrews

513. The Father takes Jesus up (GHeb)

SEE #259, 500, PP. 206, 372

Mt	Mk	Lk	Pt 5:5*	GHeb 1:7*
			And the Master cried out, saying, "My power, ⟨my⟩ power, you have abandoned me." When he said this, he was taken up.	After they had raised him on the cross, the Father took him up into heaven to himself.

*Mk 16:19 / Lk 24:51 / Acts 1:9 (#527, p. 401)

514. Does Jesus need baptism? (GHeb)

SEE #6, P. 13

Mt 3:13–15	Mk	Lk	GHeb 2:1–2
[13]Then Jesus comes from Galilee to John at the Jordan to get baptized by him. [14]And John tried to stop him with these words: "I'm the one who needs to get baptized by you, yet you come to me?" [15]In response, Jesus said to him, "Let it go for now. This is the right thing for us to do." Then John gave into to him.	1:9	3:21	[1]The mother of the Master and his brothers said to him, "John the Baptizer baptized for the forgiveness of sins. Let's go and get baptized by him." [2]But he said to them, "How have I sinned? So why should I go and get baptized by him? Only if I don't what I'm talking about."

515. The Fountain of the Spirit (GHeb)
SEE #6, P. 13

Mt 3:16–17	Mk 1:10–11	Lk 3:21–22
[16]Right after Jesus had been baptized, he got up out of the water, and—amazingly—the skies opened up and he saw God's spirit coming down on him like a dove, perching on him, [17]and—listen!—there was a voice from the skies, which said, "This is my son, the one I love—I fully approve of him."*	[10]And right away as he got up out of the water, he saw the skies torn open and the spirit coming down toward him like a dove. [11]There was also a voice from the skies: "You are my son, the one I love—I fully approve of you."*	[21]And it came to pass when all the people were baptized, and after Jesus had been baptized and while he was praying, that the sky opened up, [22]and the holy spirit came down on him in bodily form like a dove, and a voice came from the sky, "You are my son; today I have fathered you."[a]*

* ⓓ Mt 17:5 / Mk 9:7 / Lk 9:35 (#122, p. 103)

[a] Lk 3:22 Most mss read "You are my son, the one I love—I fully approve of you" (as in Mark 1:11).

516. Taken by the Hair (GHeb)
SEE #8, P. 15

Mt 4:8	Mk	Lk	GHeb 4a
The devil takes him to a very high mountain and shows him all the empires of the world and their splendor.*			Just now my mother, the holy spirit, took me by one of my hairs and brought me to Tabor, the great mountain.

* Lk 4:5 (#8, p. 15)

517. Seeking and Finding (GHeb)
= #414, P. 330

Mt 7:7–8	Mk	Lk 11:9–10
[7]Ask—it'll be given to you; seek—you'll find; knock—it'll be opened for you.* [8]For everyone who asks receives; everyone who seeks finds; and for the one who knocks it is opened.		[9]Ask—it'll be given to you; seek—you'll find; knock—it'll be opened for you.* [10]For everyone who asks receives; everyone who seeks finds; and for the one who knocks it is opened.

* Jn 15:5–8; 16:23–24 (#318, 321, pp. 254, 256)

Jn 1:32	GHeb 3:2–4
John continued his testimony: "I have seen the spirit coming down like a dove out of the sky, and it hovered over him."	[2]And it happened that when the Master came up out of the water, the whole fountain of the holy spirit came down on him and rested on him. [3]It said to him, "My son, I was waiting for you in all the prophets, waiting for you to come so I could rest in you. [4]For you are my rest; you are my first-begotten son who rules forever."

Th 2:1–4	Th 92:1; 94:1–2	GHeb 6b
[1]Those who seek should not stop seeking until they find.*	**Th 92:1** Seek and you will find.* **Th 94:1–2** [1]The one who seeks will find,* [2]and for [one who knocks] it will be opened.	Those who seek should not stop until they find;
[2]When they find, they will be disturbed. [3]When they are disturbed, they will marvel [4]and will rule the universe.		when they find, they will marvel. When they marvel, they will rule, and when they rule, they will rest.

The Gospel of the Nazoreans

518. Bread for Tomorrow (GNaz)
SEE #28, P. 27

Mt 6:9–13	Mk	Lk 11:2–4	GNaz 3
[9]You should pray like this: Our Father in the heavens, your name be revered. [10]Your empire be established, your will be done on earth as it is in heaven. [11]Provide us with the bread we need for the day. [12]Forgive our debts to the extent that we have forgiven[a] those in debt to us. [13]And don't make us face the test, but rescue us from the evil one.[b]		[2]When you pray, you should say: Father, your name be revered. Your empire be established. [3]Provide us with the bread we need day by day. [4]Forgive our sins, since we too forgive everyone in debt to us. And don't make us face the test.	Provide us today with the bread we need for tomorrow.

[a] Mt 6:12 Many mss read "we forgive" instead of *we have forgiven*.

[b] Mt 6:13 At the end of the verse, many mss insert "for yours is the kingdom, the power, and the glory. Amen."

519. Serial Forgiving (GNaz)
= #134, 407, PP. 111, 324

Mt 18:21–22	Mk	Lk 17:4	GNaz 5:1
		If someone wrongs you seven times a day, and seven times turns around and says to you, "I'm sorry," you must forgive that person.	If your brother or sister has wronged you verbally and made amends, welcome him or her seven times a day.
[21]Then Peter came up and asked him, "Master, how many times can a companion wrong me and still expect my forgiveness? As many as seven times?" [22]Jesus replies to him, "My advice to you is not seven times, but seventy-seven times.			His disciple Simon said to him, "Seven times a day?" The Master answered him, "That's right; in fact, up to seventy times seven times."

520. The Second Rich Man (GNaz)
= #196, P. 147

Mt 19:16–22	Mk 10:17–22	Lk 18:18–23	GNaz 6:1–4
[16]And just then someone came and asked him, "Teacher, what good do I have to do to have eternal life?"	[17]As he was traveling along the way, someone ran up, knelt before him, and started questioning him, "Good teacher, what do I have to do to inherit eternal life?"	[18]Someone from the ruling class asked him, "Good teacher, what do I have to do to inherit eternal life?"	[1]The second rich man said to him, "Teacher, what good do I have to do to live?"
[17]He said to him, "Why ask me about the good? There is only One who is good. If you want to enter life, observe the commandments."	[18]Jesus said to him, "Why do you call me good? No one is good except God alone. [19]You know the commandments:	[19]Jesus said to him, "Why do you call me good? No one is good except God alone. [20]You know the commandments:	[2]He said to him, "Mister, follow the Law and the Prophets."
[18]He says to him, "Which ones?" Jesus replied, "'You shall not murder, you shall not commit adultery, you shall not steal, you shall not give false testimony, [19]you shall honor your father and mother, and you shall love your neighbor as yourself.'"	'You shall not murder, you shall not commit adultery, you shall not steal, you shall not give false testimony, you shall not defraud, and you shall honor your father and mother.'"	'You shall not commit adultery, you shall not murder, you shall not steal, you shall not give false testimony, and you shall honor your father and mother.'"	
[20]The young man says to him, "I have observed all these; what am I missing?"	[20]He said to him, "Teacher, I have observed all these things since I was a child."	[21]And he said, "I have observed all these since I was a child."	He answered, "I've done that."
[21]Jesus said to him, "If you want to be perfect, make your move, sell your belongings, and give ⟨the money⟩ to the poor and you will have treasure in heaven. And then come on, follow me!"	[21]Jesus looked at him and loved him and said to him, "You are missing one thing: make your move, sell whatever you have, and give ⟨the money⟩ to the poor, and you will have treasure in heaven. And then come on, follow me!"	[22]When Jesus heard this, he said to him, "You are still short one thing. Sell everything you have and distribute ⟨the money⟩ among the poor, and you will have treasure in heaven. And then come on, follow me!"	He said to him, "Go sell everything you own and give it away to the poor and then come on, follow me."
[22]When the young man heard this advice, he went away dejected since he had a fortune.	[22]But stunned by this advice, he went away dejected, since he had a fortune.	[23]But when he heard this, he became very sad, for he was extremely rich.	[3]But the rich man didn't want to hear this and began to scratch his head. And the Master said to him, "How can you say that you follow the Law and the Prophets? In the Law it says: 'Love your neighbor as yourself.' [4]Look around you: many of your brothers and sisters, sons and daughters of Abraham, are living in filth and dying of hunger. Your house is full of good things and not a thing of yours manages to get out to them."
22:39	12:31	10:27b

16:19–31 | |

521. A Camel and the Eye of a Needle (GNaz)
SEE #197, P. 148

Mt 19:24	Mk 10:25	Lk 18:25	GNaz 6:5b
It's easier for a camel to squeeze through the eye of a needle than for the wealthy to get into the empire of God.	It's easier for a camel to squeeze through the eye of a needle than for the wealthy to get into the empire of God.	It's easier for a camel to squeeze through the eye of a needle than for the wealthy to get into the empire of God.	It's easier for a camel to squeeze through the eye of a needle than for the wealthy to get into the empire of Heaven.

Gospel Oxyrhynchus 1224

522. In Sinners' Company (GOxy 1224)
SEE #60, 177, PP. 49, 135

Mt 9:11–13	Mk 2:16–17	Lk 5:30–32	GOxy 1224 5:1–2
[11]And whenever the Pharisees saw this, they would question his disciples, "Why does your teacher eat with toll collectors and sinners?" [12]When Jesus overheard, he said, "Since when do the able-bodied need a doctor? It's the sick who do. [13]Go and learn what this means, 'It's mercy I desire instead of sacrifice.' After all, I did not come to enlist the upright but sinners!"	[16]And whenever the Pharisees' scholars saw him eating with sinners and toll collectors, they would question his disciples, "What's he doing eating with toll collectors and sinners?" [17]When Jesus overhears, he says to them, "Since when do the able-bodied need a doctor? It's the sick who do. I did not come to enlist the upright but sinners!"	[30]The Pharisees and their scholars would complain to his disciples, "Why do you people eat and drink with toll collectors and sinners?" [31]In response Jesus said to them: "Since when do the healthy need a doctor? It's the sick who do. [32]I have not come to enlist the upright to change their hearts, but sinners."	[1]When the scholars an[d Pharise]es and priests observ[ed hi]m, they were indignant [because he reclined ⟨at table⟩ in the com]pany of sin[ners].* [2]But Jesus overheard [them and said,] "Those who are he[althy don't need a doctor."]

*Lk 15:1 (#177, p. 135)

523. Pray for Enemies (GOxy 1224)
SEE #25, 129, 355, PP. 25, 108, 290

Mt 5:44	Mk 9:40	Lk 6:27–28; 9:50b	GOxy 1224 6:1–2
Love your enemies and pray for your persecutors.	For whoever is not against us is on our side.*	**Lk 6:27–28** [27]Love your enemies, do good to those who hate you, [28]bless those who curse you, pray for your abusers. **Lk 9:50b** Whoever is not against you is on your side.*	P[r]ay for your [ene]mies. For whoever is not [against y]ou is on your side. * [2][Whoever today i]s at a distance, tomorrow will [b]e [near you] and in [. . .] of the advers[ary].

*Mt 12:30 / Lk 11:23 (#72, p. 57)

1 Corinthians

524. What God Has Prepared (1 Cor)
= #428, P. 337

Mt	Mk	Lk	Th 17	1 Cor 2:9
			I will give you what no eye has seen, what no ear has heard, what no hand has touched, what has not arisen in the human heart.	The scripture says, "No eye has ever seen, no ear has ever heard, or has the human mind ever imagined what God has prepared for those who love him."

525. Advice On Divorce (1 Cor)
SEE #22, P. 23

Mt 5:32	Mt 19:9	Mk 10:12, 11
		12and if she divorces her husband and marries another, she commits adultery.
Anyone who divorces his wife (except in the case of immorality) forces her into adultery; and whoever marries a divorced woman commits adultery.	Whoever divorces his wife, except for immorality, and marries another commits adultery.	11Whoever divorces his wife and marries another commits adultery against her;

Lk 16:18	1 Cor 7:10–11
	[10]To the married my instruction (not mine, but the lord's) is that a wife should not divorce her husband—[11]but if she is already divorced, she should remain unmarried or be reconciled with her husband—and
[18]Everyone who divorces his wife	that a husband should not leave his wife.
and marries another commits adultery;	
and the one who marries a woman divorced from her husband commits adultery.	

526. Jesus' Body and Blood (1 Cor)
SEE #239, P. 184

Mt 26:26–28	Mk 14:22–24	Lk 22:19–20	1 Cor 11:23–25
[26]As they were eating, Jesus took a loaf, gave a blessing, and broke it into pieces. And he offered it to the disciples, and said, "Take some and eat; this is my body."	[22]And as they were eating, he took a loaf, gave a blessing, broke it into pieces, and offered it to them. And he said, "Take some; this is my body!"	[19]And he took a loaf, gave thanks, broke it into pieces, offered it to them, and said, "This is my body, which is offered for you. Do this as my memorial."[a]	[23]I received from the lord the same thing I passed on to you, that on the night when he was handed over, the lord Jesus took bread [24]and after he gave thanks he broke it and said, "This is my body broken for you. Do this to remember me."
[27]He also took a cup and gave thanks and offered it to them, saying, "Drink from it, all of you, [28]for this is my blood of the covenant, which has been poured out for many for the forgiveness of sins.	[23]He also took a cup, gave thanks, and offered it to them, and they all drank from it. [24]And he said to them, "This is my blood of the covenant, which has been poured out for many.	[20]And, in the same manner, he took the cup after dinner and said, "This cup is the new covenant in my blood, which is poured out for you.	[25]And in the same way he took the wine cup after the meal and said, "This cup is the new covenant ratified by my blood. Whenever you drink this, do it to remember me."

[a] Lk 22:19–20 A few mss omit *which is offered for you* and all of v. 20.

Acts of the Apostles

527. Jesus is carried into the sky (Acts)
SEE #275, 500, PP. 223, 372

Mt	Mk 16:19	Lk 24:50–51	Pt 5:5	Acts 1:3, 9
			And the Master cried out, saying, "My power, ⟨my⟩ power, you have abandoned me."	
		[50]Then he led them out as far as Bethany, and lifting up his hands he blessed them. [51]And while he was blessing them, it came to pass that he departed from them, and was carried up into the sky.[a]		[3]After his suffering he presented himself to them in many ways that proved he was alive, appearing to them over a forty-day period and speaking about the empire of God. . . . [9]As they were watching he was lifted up and a cloud carried him up until they could no longer see him.
	The Lord Jesus, after he said these things, was taken up into the sky and sat down at the right hand of God.		When he said this, he was taken up.*	

* GHeb 1:7 (#513, p. 391)

___
[a] Lk 24:51 Some mss omit *and was carried up into the sky.*

Indices

The Gospel of Matthew

The Gospel of Mark

The Gospel of Luke

The Gospel of John

The Q Gospel

The Gospel of Thomas

The Gospel of Peter

The Egerton Gospel

The Gospel of the Hebrews

The Gospel of the Nazoreans

～

Gospel Oxyrhynchus 1224

～

1 Corinthians

～

Acts of the Apostles

～

About the Authors

Arthur J. Dewey is Professor of Theology at Xavier University, Cincinnati, Ohio. A co-author of *The Authentic Letters of Paul* (2010), he is a regular presenter on the Saturday Morning Edition on the Public Radio Station WVXU in Cincinnati.

Robert J. Miller is Professor of Religious Studies at Juniata College in Pennsylvania. He is the editor of *The Complete Gospels* (4th ed. 2010), and author of *The Jesus Seminar and Its Critics* (1999) and *Born Divine* (2003).